W9-BGA-598

*Hippocrene Language and Travel Guide to*

# UKRAINE

**Linda Hodges**

**George Chumak**

*Fourth Edition*

## HIPPOCRENE BOOKS
*New York*

## Acknowledgments

A book undergoing periodical revisions is much indebted to past contributors. The authors are thankful to those who helped in the past—too numerous to list here—whose knowledge shared has made the book possible. Three past contributors continued to share their substantial professional knowledge of tourism in Ukraine for this fourth edition. Special thanks go to Tanya Borovik in Odesa, Alexander Denisenko in Lviv, and Vladislav Kiriya in Kharkiv for their valuable time and information.

Thanks to Oksana Hlyva for her always willing and reliable help. Miscellaneous insight and information came from these frequent travelers or native Ukrainians: Galina Butkovska, Oksana Dzyuban, Orysia Tracz, Ihor Slabicky, Andrij Hornjatkevyc, Morgan Williams, John Masura, Mariya Shymchyshyn, Roman Pechyzhak, Tony and Ulyana Spencer, Vyacheslav Rubel, Vladyslav Lovrov, Phil Baker, Eugene Snezhkin, Oksana Bas, Elizabeth Mayfield, Dick and Donna Gladon, Roger Nowadzky, and Ron Freund.

Peace Corps volunteers provided a wealth of information. We are grateful to Gary Anderson, Gerald Braniff, Sandy Girard, Jeffrey Hansen, Mindy Puga, Rosa Werthwein, Alex Petrovic, Norri Symonds, Chris Cavanagh, Chen Chang, Greg Higgins, Scott Lasher, Nathan Bucholz, Tom O'Keefe, Moji Nabavian, Larry Wishnick, and Victor Karamushka.

Our greatest thanks go to husband and friend Laurent Hodges for his help with photography, editing, typesetting, and miscellaneous technical support. His patient dependability was always a comfort.

Text copyright 1994-2004 by Linda Hodges and George Chumak.
*Fourth edition, 2004*

All rights reserved.

For information, address:
HIPPOCRENE BOOKS, INC.
171 Madison Avenue
New York, NY 10016

*Library of Congress Cataloging-in-Publication Data is available.*
ISBN 0-7818-1063-9

Jacket design by Ronnie McBride.
*Cover photo:* The newly rebuilt Dormition Cathedral in Kyiv.

Printed in the United States of America.

# Preface to the Fourth Edition

This book fills a need for the traveler who regards Ukraine as a destination in itself, not a stopping point on a larger itinerary. It's for the traveler who appreciates the distinctiveness of the Ukrainian people and who wants to speak to them in their native tongue, learn more about their culture, and view the historical sights from a Ukrainian perspective.

Ukraine has been a buried nation for much of its history. Now with unrestricted travel, a simplified visa process, efficient customs, and new or upgraded tourist facilities, the opportunity exists to experience a rich, traditional culture in a modern setting. One of the best pieces of advice we've heard from an enthusiastic visitor to Ukraine is "Go now before it's spoiled." Many of the yet-to-be-discovered, unspoiled places are discussed in the travel section, while the tourist cities are covered in depth. To enrich the travel experience, the book discusses highlights of Ukrainian history and culture. It also answers the most asked questions of those planning a trip to Ukraine.

The phrases are designed to cover the most typical situations a newcomer to Ukraine might encounter. They are expressed in up-to-date, idiomatic Ukrainian that should be understood by Ukrainian speakers anywhere in Ukraine. For those with no background in Slavic languages or in the Cyrillic alphabet, the guide to pronunciation will take the mystery out of this highly phonetic language. For those who understand spoken Ukrainian but can't read it, the inclusion of the Cyrillic phrases with their phonetic rendition will improve their literacy.

Readers should be aware that they may encounter variations from the language presented in this book. In many parts of Ukraine the Russian language is spoken more commonly in public than Ukrainian, or a mingling of the two languages may be heard. For those who feel that the Russian language will be more useful than Ukrainian, there are plenty of Russian phrase books on the market. However, Ukrainian is vital to those planning to converse in western Ukraine, and familiarity with Ukrainian is useful throughout the country (with the possible exception of the autonomous republic of Crimea) in order to read public signs and the names of businesses. And, attempting to speak the official language will indicate to many Ukrainians a respect for their country.

Ukraine has experienced fundamental and radical changes on all levels and in all spheres of life. It has emerged from 300 years of colonialism and 70 years of totalitarianism to independence. Building and rebuilding the country resulted in tremendous changes in the city centers, tourist destinations, hotels, restaurants, and businesses, and in delivery of tourist services. The changes have been sudden, often unexpected, and sometimes only temporary. More than a dozen years following independence, much of the growing pain has subsided. Changes affecting tourism are happening at a slower rate. Not only is tourism more predictable and dependable, it's been vastly improved, and almost always is a very positive experience.

In a growing free market economy, however, changes are always occurring. Accuracy has been our constant goal, but not something we can absolutely guarantee. Some details are bound to be outdated by the time the reader reaches Ukraine, and we invite you to write to the address below with any corrections.

Ukraine is a country of infinite variation. Each region has a distinct history, with cities and towns within regions subject to different influences. Also to be reckoned with is the legendary Ukrainian trait of individualism – the story goes that a committee of five Ukrainians will come up with six different plans. Add to that the blind-man-and-the-elephant phenomenon – the tendency of travelers to make generalizations and form opinions from limited experience, some giving positive interpretations, others making negative judgments – and we can't guarantee that your experiences in Ukraine will match our characterizations.

We hope, however, that you share our great enthusiasm for Ukraine. Without it, this book couldn't have been possible, wouldn't be fun, and certainly wouldn't have reached a fourth edition.

Linda Hodges and George Chumak
Ames, Iowa
L.Hodges@prodigy.net
http://AmesIowa.US

# Contents

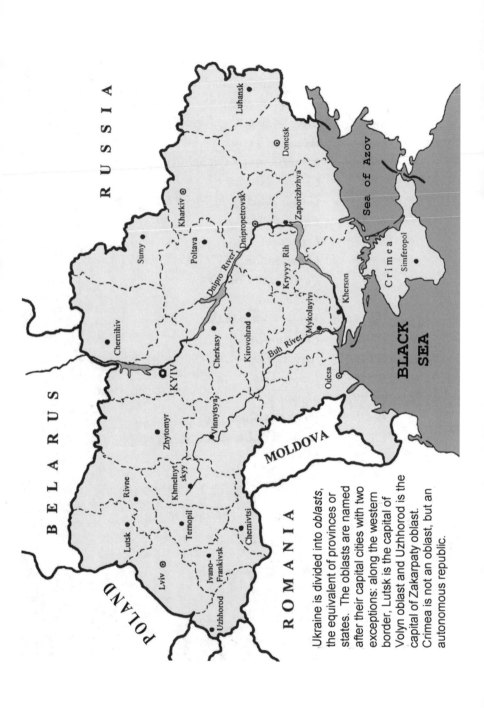

Ukraine is divided into *oblasts*, the equivalent of provinces or states. The oblasts are named after their capital cities with two exceptions: along the western border, Lutsk is the capital of Volyn oblast and Uzhhorod is the capital of Zakarpaty oblast. Crimea is not an oblast, but an autonomous republic.

# CHAPTER 1.
# DEVELOPING A UKRAINIAN PERSPECTIVE

*Ukrayina* means borderland. As a frontier land bridging the East and West, Ukraine was vulnerable to invaders from all sides. Among the many early peoples who roamed across the steppes and navigated the Dnipro River and Black Sea were Scythians, Greeks, Goths, Huns, and Khazars. After the establishment of the modern state, Ukraine was threatened by the ambitions of the Grand Duchy of Lithuania, the Ottoman Empire, the Polish Lithuanian Commonwealth, the Tatar Khanate, and Muscovy. For centuries various parts were under the Russian Empire, Poland, or Austria. The many foreign powers that occupied and ruled Ukraine enriched the country, but also brought exploitation and devastation.

The adage that history is written by the winners is well understood by those with roots in Ukraine. Without a Ukrainian state, Ukrainian history was handed down as a footnote, considered no more than a provincial expression of dominant powers. By an extension of a stunted, simplistic logic, without a Ukrainian state, Ukrainian identity did not exist. There ceased to be, for most of the world, not only a country with its own history, but a separate and distinct people who shared a unique language and a rich cultural heritage. With the possible exception of the batik Easter eggs, nearly every aspect of Ukrainian history and culture had been attributed to other groups. The mislabeling of things Ukrainian was carried to its logical absurdity in library card catalogs, encyclopedias, and history books. For example, college-level history of civilization textbooks discussed the Kyivan-Rus legacy without once mentioning Ukraine.

With the sudden breakup of the former Soviet Union in 1991, the Soviet Socialist Republic of Ukraine achieved a centuries-old desire for freedom without bloodshed. Much of the world was surprised by the new country, which asked to be called Україна (oo-krah-YEE-nah), or in translation, simply "Ukraine," rather than "*the* Ukraine," which implies that it's part of a larger country and signifies subordination.

## Some Basic Facts

With 233,100 square miles (603,700 sq. km.), Ukraine is the largest country completely in Europe. In size it's slightly bigger than France and slightly smaller than the state of Texas. To the north is Belarus; Russia is to the northeast and east; Moldova and Romania and Hungary are to the south and southwest; Slovakia and Poland border on the west and northwest. The southern border is on the Black Sea and Sea of Azov.

Ukraine is a relatively modern country with a highly educated population that is two-thirds urban. Even so, traditional family values prevail, including a strong work ethic. Since gaining independence, Ukraine's population has been declining as well as changing its ethnic orientation. In a 10-year period, the population dropped several million to 48,416,000 and identified itself as 77.8 percent Ukrainian and 17.3 percent Russian, a 26 percent drop in those who considered themselves Russian. Nationalities that have increased since independence include Georgians, Tatars, Azerbaijanis, and Romanians, while there's been a large out-migration of Jews, Belarusians, Poles, and Moldovans. Minority populations tend to be concentrated around the borders.

The country consists primarily of fertile steppe with a forest-steppe area across the north and low-lying mountains along the western border. The Dnipro River flows down through the center, separating the country into east and west regions and has played an active role in the country's development from prehistoric through modern times. Ukraine's rich soil and moderate climate make it ideally suited to agriculture. Its huge coal reserves and deposits of iron and manganese ore have led to heavy industrial development, especially in the eastern part of the country.

## Historical Highlights

Kyiv Rus, the historical antecedent of Ukraine, was established by Vikings and peopled by various Slavic tribes. Kyiv was the center of this powerful princely state that stretched from the Baltic to the Black Sea and dominated eastern Europe from the 10th through the 13th centuries. It was a center of trade, Slavic culture, and Byzantine Christianity. Internal dissent, however, weakened the state and it collapsed after Mongol invasions in the mid-13th century.

Kozak Period: *Kozak* (Козак), often spelled Cossack in English, comes from a Turkish word meaning free man. The term was originally applied to refugees from serfdom and slavery who fled to the borderland that was Ukraine between the 15th and 18th centuries. The term was later applied to Ukrainians who went to the steppes to practice various trades and engage in hunting, fishing, beekeeping, and the collection of salt. The Kozaks set up democratic military communities and elected their leaders, who were called hetmans. From their island stronghold on the Dnipro, the Kozaks launched attacks against the Turks and Tatars and struggled against the Polish and Russians. Their establishment of an autonomous Ukrainian state is a high point of Ukrainian history.

During the mid-17th century, Poland controlled most of Right Bank Ukraine (the lands west of the Dnipro) while Muscovy controlled most of the Left Bank. Ukrainian culture enjoyed a great revival during this period of ambiguous political status. Religious and educational activity flourished and there was a high rate of literacy.

By the late 18th century, however, 85 percent of Ukrainian land had fallen under Russian control, and Ukraine's window to the west was closed. It was a time of colonialism and Russification during which Ukrainian culture and language was suppressed.

The 20th century was a time of great turmoil and suffering in Ukraine. After the Bolshevik Revolution of 1917, Ukraine was engulfed in a chaotic civil war in which many different factions and foreign powers fought for control. On January 22, 1918, the Ukrainian Central Rada formally proclaimed Ukraine's independence and the next year joined with the Western Ukrainian People's Republic as a united, independent country. Soon, however, the western Ukrainians were defeated by Polish expansionists and Soviet troops seized Kyiv, incorporating much of Ukraine into the Soviet Union. The Ukrainian intelligentsia was forced to either move or perish. In 1932–1933 some 4 to 10 million peasants (according to differing estimates) were starved to death in a deliberately engineered famine designed to force them onto collective farms. It was a number of years following independence before the *Holodomor* ("terror and death by famine") was officially recognized and commemorated. During the Second World War, Ukraine bore the brunt of the Nazi drive to Stalingrad and the Red Army counteroffensive. Another 7.5 million people were lost, including almost 4 million civilians killed and 2.2 million taken to Germany as laborers. Cities, towns, and thousands of villages were devastated.

Ukraine was not able to hold on to independence during its struggles for national liberation in the early twentieth century. In the second half of the century Ukraine's dissident movement thrived, but as a buried nation, the world paid little attention. With the collapse of the Soviet

Union, the Ukrainian Parliament proclaimed independence on August 24, 1991. On December 1, some 90 percent of the Ukrainian electorate endorsed independence and chose Leonid Kravchuk as Ukraine's first democratically elected president. A further show of democracy was the defeat of Kravchuk by Leonid Kuchma in a close election with high voter turnout in 1995. Kuchma won reelection in 1999, but his lack of reforms resulted in widespread disapproval.

### Heroes, Poets, and Patriots

In forging a new national identity, Ukraine has looked to its past, turning to its most durable symbols as a rallying point for patriotism. There's something appealing about a nation whose greatest hero is a poet and painter. Taras Hryhorovych Shevchenko (Тарас Григорович Шевченко), was born on March 9, 1814 to a serf family in Moryntsi, a village that today is in the Cherkasy region. Orphaned as a teen, Shevchenko accompanied his master on his travels, serving as a houseboy. Noticing his artistic talent, Shevchenko's master apprenticed him to a painter in St. Petersburg. In 1838 Shevchenko's Russian artist colleagues bought him from his master and set him free.

Shevchenko enrolled in the St. Petersburg Academy of Art where he had many contacts with Ukrainian and Russian artists and writers. His first collection of Ukrainian poetry, *Kobzar* (The Bard), published in 1840, was hailed as work of genius by Ukrainian and Russian critics alike. Drawing upon Ukrainian history and folklore, Shevchenko wrote in the Romantic style prevalent in his day. Soon his poems evolved from nostalgia for Kozak life to an indictment of rulers who abuse their power and then to sympathy for oppressed people everywhere.

As a painter, Shevchenko was skilled in portraiture, landscape, and architectural monuments, but his most noteworthy paintings are scenes of country life and historical events that are sympathetic to Ukraine and critical of its oppressors. For example, Shevchenko's tragic story of Kateryna, a Ukrainian girl who was seduced, impregnated, and abandoned by a Russian soldier, expressed in ballad and later in a painting, are allegorical references to the fate of Ukraine under the Russian tsars who introduced serfdom.

Shevchenko's reputation as a leading Ukrainian poet and artist was already established when he came to Kyiv in 1846. There he joined the first modern Ukrainian political organization, the Brotherhood of Sts. Cyril and Methodius. In 1847 the brotherhood members were arrested. Shevchenko was the most severely punished when authorities discovered his unpublished collection of poetry satirizing the oppression of Ukraine by Russia. He was sentenced to ten years' military service in a labor battalion in Siberia. Although Tsar Nicholas I stipulated that Shevchenko was to be "under the strictest supervision, forbidden to write and sketch," he managed during part of his term to write and paint clandestinely. After his release, Shevchenko was a broken man. He was not allowed to live in Ukraine, but permitted to visit. However, during one visit, he was re-arrested and banished to St. Petersburg, where he remained under police surveillance until his death in 1861. His gravesite, monument, and museum in Kaniv (in the Cherkasy *oblast*) are popular tourist destinations.

Even without his poetry, Shevchenko would be renowned for his art. His existing works number 835 paintings and engravings, with several hundred lost. His writings have had a greater significance, however, not only for their literary merit but also for the role they played in the development of the Ukrainian language. Shevchenko blended several Ukrainian dialects with elements of Church Slavonic, thus expanding the range, flexibility and resources of the Ukrainian language.

Elevating Ukrainian to a literary prose was equivalent to a literary declaration of Ukrainian independence, according to Orest Subtelny in *Ukraine: A History*. Shevchenko showed that Ukrainians didn't need to depend on the Russian language as a means of higher discourse because their own language was equally rich and expressive.

As a critic of tsarist autocracy and a champion of the universal struggle for justice, Shevchenko was exalted throughout the Soviet Union. His works were circulated and his memory honored in every republic. There's even a monument to him in Moscow. But to Ukrainians, Shevchenko has a special meaning. To them, he represents the right to *be* Ukrainian. Ukrainians understood that when Shevchenko referred to "Muscovy," he wasn't referring to a particular government, but to the Russian nation's subjugation of Ukraine. Ukrainians even knew which words in the official publications of his works the authorities had changed in order to conceal his nationalistic expression.

Following independence, many more monuments were erected in Shevchenko's honor in Ukraine, often replacing statutes of Lenin that were torn down. The depiction of Shevchenko as an old man is misleading, since he died when he was only 47, and made his impact when he was much younger.

Two Kozak hetmans are important in Ukrainian history. Both were great leaders and statesmen and fought to free Ukraine from foreign domination. Bohdan Khmelnytsky (1595–1657) headed the national uprising in 1648 that liberated a large part of Ukrainian territory from Poland. Khmelnytsky was recognized at home and abroad as the leader of a sovereign state. Under continual threat from Poland, in 1654 he entered a military pact with Muscovy for protection against the Polish. Ukrainians consider this a fatal turning point in their history. Moscow turned a military and political alliance into an act of Russian annexation of Ukraine, gradually subjugating Ukraine and instituting serfdom.

Today Ukraine looks to Ivan Mazepa (1639 –1709) as a more appropriate hero. Mazepa wanted to unite all Ukrainian territories into a unitary state modeled after existing European states with features of the traditional Kozak structure. At first Mazepa was allied with Tsar Peter I against foreign powers, but when he realized Russia intended to abolish the Kozak order and end Ukrainian autonomy, he sided with Charles XII of Sweden against Peter. After a disastrous defeat at the Battle of Poltava in 1709, Kyiv lost much of its autonomy and Kozak rule came to an end.

### National Emblem and Anthem

**Trident.** The trident (тризуб, *tryzub*), the official coat of arms of Ukraine, consists of a gold trident against an azure background. Archeological findings of the trident date back to the 1st century CE when it was apparently a mark of authority and a symbol of one or several of the various early tribes which inhabited Ukrainian territory and later became part of the Ukrainian people.

As a state emblem, the trident dates back to the ninth century, when the Rurik dynasty adopted it as their coat of arms. Prince Volodymyr the Great inherited the symbol. The design was engraved on gold and silver coins called *hryvni*, as well as imprinted on official seals, the portals of old Ukrainian cathedrals, palaces, and tombs of nobility.

Some historians interpret the trident design as an abbreviation of a compounded Old Slavonic word, " Володимирстов" (*Volodymyrstov*), which means "Volodymyr on the throne." Or perhaps the design is an amalgam of the letters Я, В, and О, from the names of the prominent Kyivan rulers Emperor Yaroslav the Wise, Prince Volodymyr, and Queen Olha. Others suggest the symbol comes from a stylistic rendition of the Cyrillic letters В, О, Л, and Я, which spell the word    *volya*, meaning "freedom." Or even more simply, the design may derive from the initial character "В" from Воля, written forwards and back.

For continuity with the past, Ukrainians adopted the trident as the official state symbol when they declared independence in 1917. Obviously, as a symbol of the struggle for Ukrainian sovereignty, the trident was forbidden under Soviet rule for being "nationalistic." Not surprisingly, it was reprised as the national emblem when Ukraine finally achieved independence in 1991.

**Flag.** Many different flags have flown over Ukraine through the centuries; some represented foreign ruling powers, others were the choice of Ukrainian ruling groups, such as the flags of the Kozak period. Independent Ukraine's official flag is a rectangle composed of two stripes, one blue and one yellow. It was designed by Ukrainian leaders under the Austro-Hungarian Empire and first flown on June 2, 1848 by the Ukrainian delegation to a pan-Slavic congress in Prague. It was used during the struggle for independence in 1917-1920.

The color on top varied, and some of the earlier flags included a coat of arms such as a lion or trident. On January 28, 1992, the Presidium of the Supreme Council of Ukraine adopted an unadorned blue-on-top and yellow-on-bottom version as the official national flag. Why blue and yellow are the Ukrainian colors is not clear. The popular interpretation is that blue represents the sky and the yellow is for golden wheat or sunflowers, while others say that the colors represent fire and water. The shades of blue and yellow are exactly the same as those used in the Swedish flag, but the link between the two is not exactly known.

**National Anthem.** In 1992 the Ukrainian Parliament chose as the national anthem music composed in 1863 by Mykhailo Verbytsky, a western Ukrainian composer and Catholic priest. Verbytsky wrote the score originally as a song and later as an orchestral composition for a patriotic poem written in 1862 by Pavlo Chubynsky, a prominent ethnographer in the Kyiv region. In the poem, Ще не вмерла Україна (*Shche ne vmerla Ukrayina*), which means "Ukraine is not yet dead," Chubynsky expressed the mixture of hope and desperation felt by Ukrainians over their continuous struggle to rule their own land. Widely sung around the country as the "Hymn to Ukraine," both the melody and lyrics were similar to Polish and Serbian anthems. In 1917 it was the anthem of the short-lived Ukrainian National Republic, but it was replaced during the Soviet era.

Over time, there have been various changes and additions to Chubynsky's original words, resulting in several slightly different versions of the Hymn to Ukraine. Following independence in 1991, many

Ukrainians were dissatisfied with the pessimistic tone, so the government made the Verbytsky score official, but hesitated to approve Chubynsky's lyrics. A commission sponsored several contests for new lyrics, but none were approved. Agreement finally came in 2003, when Parliament passed and the President signed an act recognizing a slight change to the usually-sung lyrics. Only the first stanza and the refrain (which is sung twice in succession) were approved for the official version.

### Державний Гімн України

Ще не вмерла України, і слава, і воля,
Ще нам, Браття молодії, усміхнеться доля.
Згинуть наші воріженьки, як роса на сонці,
Запануєм і ми, браття, у своїй сторонці.

Душу й тіло ми положим за нашу свободу
І покажем, що ми, браття, козацького роду.

### National Anthem of Ukraine

Ukraine's glory hasn't perished, nor her glory, nor freedom.
Upon us, fellow compatriots, fate shall smile once more.
Our enemies will vanish, like dew in the morning sun,
And we too shall rule, brothers, in a free land of our own.

We'll lay down our souls and bodies to attain our freedom,
And we'll show that we, brothers, are of the Kozak nation.

– translation by Ihor W. Slabicky

### To Learn More about Ukraine

We recommend the following sources whose help in compiling this guide we gratefully acknowledge:

*Encyclopedia of Ukraine*, 5 volumes, University of Toronto Press, 1984, 1993. This is the largest, most comprehensive and authoritative English-language source on everything Ukrainian ever published, the product of 20 years of research by writers, scientists, and scholars from around the world. Entries are organized alphabetically, written in-depth, and illustrated with photos and maps. The encyclopedia is gradually being made available online at the website www.encyclopediaofukraine.com.

*Ukraine: A History*, Orest Subtelny, University of Toronto Press, third edition 2000, is a highly readable in-depth examination of Ukrainian history from Kyivan Rus through modern times. *Choice*, a journal of reviews for North American college libraries selected it as an Outstanding Academic Book and *World Affairs Report* named it "the best history of Ukraine in English."

*Jewish Roots in Ukraine and Moldova: Pages from the Past and Archival Inventories*, Miriam Weiner, Routes to Roots Foundation, Inc. and YIVO Institute for Jewish Research, 1999, is an exhaustive inventory of Jewish documents in every archive in Ukraine. Supplemented by more than 1,000 graphics, most in color, pertaining to Jewish settlement in Ukraine, the book is designed to help Jews trace their ancestry. It's becoming rare, but may still be available for US$60 in Borders book store. A portion of its content is online at www.rtrfoundation.org.

*The Ukrainian Weekly*, published by the Ukrainian National Association, Inc., was founded in 1933 to serve a new generation of Ukrainian-Americans who did not always read Ukrainian. In-depth coverage of current events in Ukraine is supplemented with features on the arts, education, religion, and tourism in Ukraine. Yearly subscription is US$55 (US$45 for UNA members). Contact the *Ukrainian Weekly*, 2200 Route 10, P.O. Box 280, Parsippany, New Jersey 07054. Web site: www.ukrweekly.com.

*The Kyiv Post* is an English-language weekly with coverage of local and national news, restaurant and shopping reviews, and listings of cultural events. Ads give a glimpse of what's hot in Kyiv. Available free or at minimal price at kiosks, hotels, and businesses around Kyiv, an international subscription costs US$195 yearly including delivery. For US$225 the subscription includes four issues of the very informative *Kyiv Business Directory*. The quarterly *Business Directory* alone is US$50 yearly, mailed to the U.S. Online excerpts of the newspaper are found at www.kyivpost.com, with a full-access online subscription available for US$49 yearly. Write to kyivpost-subscribe@kievpost.com.

*The Ukrainian Observer* is a leading English language magazine in Ukraine with features on politics, business, and culture, and interviews with business and entertainment leaders. The writing and cartoons are lively. The monthly print version outside of Ukraine is US$64 yearly, including mailing costs. An Internet version is updated Monday through Friday.

Some areas are free; full access is US$47 yearly. See www.ukraine-observer.com /observer.html.

***Yevshan Ukrainian Catalog*** is a fine source of Ukrainian music and culture from Yevshan Corporation, Box 325, Beaconsfield, Quebec, Canada, H9W 5T8. Phone: 1-800-265-9858. The catalog offers a large selection of Ukrainian music on compact discs and cassettes; travel and historical videos; arts and crafts items; and books on history and culture, cookbooks, and children's books. Its web site is www.yevshan.com.

The ***Ukrainian Language, Culture and Travel Home Page*** is a large, nicely organized Web site with general background information on Ukraine, its culture, recipes, travel information, and links to cities throughout Ukraine. Chapter-by-chapter updates to this book will be placed on this site. Go to pages.prodigy.net/l.hodges/ukraine.htm or link to it from www.AmesIowa.US.

***The Ukraine Report***, an Internet news report from Ukraine, is published by Art Ukraine Information Service and distributed free of charge several times a week by www.ArtUkraine.com. Contact morgan@patriot.net.

***The Sky Unwashed***, by Irene Zabytko, Algonquin, 2000, is a critically acclaimed novel about the effects of the Chornobyl nuclear disaster on residents of the nearby town, as told by a grandmother. Wonderful background on Ukrainian culture and society.

***Return to Ukraine***, Ania Savage, Texas A&M University Press, 2000, is a masterfully written memoir of an American journalist tracing her family's roots in Ukraine shortly after independence. A good read, although some of the characterizations are now outdated.

***Borderland: A Journey through the History of Ukraine***, Anna Reid, Westview Press, 1999. The author focuses on the major eras of Ukrainian history as she examines the country's struggle to rebuild a national identity.

Look for books, CDs, cassettes, and videos in gift shops, bookstores, and community centers in the Ukrainian neighborhoods of larger cities.

# CHAPTER 2.
# PLANNING YOUR TRIP TO UKRAINE

More than 6 million foreign travelers visit Ukraine each year. Many are tourists, but others come on academic and cultural exchanges, for business, for charitable works, to visit relatives, to find wives, and to adopt children.

Those who discover Ukraine for the first time are impressed by the beauty of the cities and countryside, the richness of the culture, and especially by the warmth and hospitality of the Ukrainian people.

Independence, however, has resulted in tremendous growing pains. At first, run-away inflation put the necessities of life out of reach of most people, unemployment skyrocketed, and poverty became widespread. Inflation has stabilized, but economic reforms are slow in coming, and many live in poverty. A deteriorating infrastructure, erratic supplies of electricity, water, and heat throughout the country, and the unavailability of advanced medical care have also made life difficult for Ukrainians.

The reward for doing one's job does not always support a family in Ukraine, so when an affluent Westerner comes, some enterprising Ukrainians may not distinguish "free enterprise" from "highway robbery." A generation that feels robbed of what was theirs now feels that it's their turn to take their due.

You might see evidence of corruption. Bribes were a common way of conducting business under the Soviet system, and many public officials are holdovers from the former government. You may be expected to line the pocket of the customs official in order to cross the border hassle-free, but such incidents are becoming rarer. If you drive a car, you may have an encounter with the ubiquitous traffic police and fined for a minor infraction. Although crime has risen, crimes against foreigners are infrequent and are likely to be those of opportunity, such as pick-pocketing or purse-snatching. With normal precautions you should be safe, day or night. By and large, Ukraine remains a nation of civilized, law-abiding people who are polite to strangers and extremely hospitable to foreign visitors.

The good news is that the economy has been showing steady growth for several years, and the tourist infrastructure is improving by leaps and bounds. New hotels, restaurants, and shopping opportunities are abundant, while improved public transportation and renovated tourist attractions make Ukraine a very desirable destination.

Chances are that during your visit to Ukraine you'll have an official host – either a friend, a relative, or a business contact – who's more than willing to help you with sightseeing and transportation, making it unnecessary to go through institutional channels. If you need a car with a driver, you can arrange this through a travel service, but that may not be necessary because your Ukrainian host will have a relative or friend with a car who'll be glad to serve as your driver.

Don't hesitate to visit Ukraine. Those who go rarely regret it. But don't take anything for granted, and don't count on anything working the way it works in the West or even the way it used to work in Ukraine. Be like the Ukrainians – adaptable, resourceful, flexible, and unafraid to face the unknown with confidence and hope.

## Visa Application Process

Ukraine requires a visa from foreign visitors from almost all but its neighboring countries. In the U.S., visas are issued at the consular office of the Embassy of Ukraine in Washington, D.C. and at consular posts in New York, Chicago, and San Francisco. You may apply for a visa at the most convenient consulate location, but it's preferable to apply at the one in the jurisdiction you reside, especially if applying by mail.

Each consulate has a detailed phone recording of its business hours and the visa regulations and procedures. Generally, consulates are open for business on weekday mornings but several are closed on Wednesdays. They're also closed on legal Ukrainian and American holidays. You may obtain an application form directly from a consular office or use an application printed from a consulate Web site.

It's best to apply for your visa about four weeks before your scheduled departure, which allows time to resubmit a faulty application. Consulates advise applicants not to apply more than three months in advance of their expected travel date or before their airline tickets are purchased.

While the information required is uncomplicated, and filling out the form takes about ten minutes, you may not feel confident that you're doing it correctly. Ukrainian consulates rarely deny American visa applicants, and if your application form is incorrect or is missing important information, it'll be returned unprocessed with your payment for you to reapply.

Submit the completed form along with a money order covering your application fee; a passport that will be valid at least one month beyond your stay; a passport-sized photograph; plus any necessary support papers from Ukraine, such as a confirmation of tourist accommodations. If applying by mail, include a self-addressed, prepaid Express Mail return envelope and send your application by FedEx or Express Mail to one of the following:

Embassy of Ukraine Consular Division,
3350 M Street NW, Washington, D.C. 20007
Phone (202) 333-0606; 333-7507, 333-7508; Fax (202) 333-7510
Web site: www.ukremb.com/consular.html
The Embassy serves visa applicants from Alabama, Alaska, Arkansas, Delaware, District of Columbia, Florida, Georgia, Kentucky, Louisiana, Maryland, Mississippi, Missouri, North Carolina, Ohio, Oklahoma, South Carolina, Tennessee, Texas, Virginia, and West Virginia.

Consulate General of Ukraine in New York
240 East 49th Street, New York, NY 10017
Phone (212) 371-5690; Fax (212)371-5547
Web site: www.ukrconsul.org
For applicants in Connecticut, Maine, Massachusetts, New Hampshire, New Jersey, New York, Pennsylvania, Rhode Island, Vermont.

Consulate General of Ukraine in Chicago
10 East Huron Street, Chicago, Illinois 60611
Phone(312)642-4388;Fax (312) 642-4385
Web site: www.urkchicago.com
For applicants in Illinois, Indiana, Iowa, Kansas, Michigan, Minnesota, Nebraska, North Dakota, South Dakota, Wisconsin.

Consulate General of Ukraine in San Francisco
530 Bush Street, Suite 402; San Francisco, California 94108
Phone (415) 398-0240; Fax (415) 398-5039
Web site: www.UkraineSF.com
For applicants in Arizona, California, Colorado, Hawaii, Idaho, Montana, Nevada, New Mexico, Oregon, Utah, Washington, and Wyoming.

In Canada, apply to the Embassy of Ukraine, Consular Division, 331 Metcalfe Street, Ottawa, Ontario, K2P 1S3. Phone (613) 230-8015; Fax (613) 230-2655; Web site: www.infoukes.com/ukemb/consular.shtml.

**Visa Categories.** Be sure to specify on the application form the visa type you want, that is, your primary purpose for going to Ukraine. Apply for a private visa if your purpose is to visit friends or relatives. Letters of invitation are no longer necessary for citizens of the U.S., Canada, Japan or the European Union. Letters of invitation are also no longer required for certain other travel purposes, such as business, cultural, and sport exchanges; you need only to provide your itinerary and the name and address of your host on your visa application form. A tourist visa requires a hotel confirmation showing that you've booked accommodations or a letter of invitation from a licensed travel agency.

Foreign missionaries need a letter of invitation from a Ukrainian religious organization accompanied by a confirmation from an official of the national, regional, or local religious committee. Humanitarian aid workers need a letter of support from the state, regional, or a local humanitarian aid committee. The letters must bear the signature and seal of the inviting business or organization. Legible fax versions are accepted but scanned e-mail copies are not.

Private visas on U.S. passports are valid for three months, while business and tourist visas are valid for six months. If you expect to leave and re-enter Ukraine during your trip, apply for a double-entry visa. For frequent business travel to Ukraine, apply for a multiple entry business visa, which is valid for a one to five-year period.

Travelers on private or business visas no longer need to register with local law enforcement authorities after they arrive in Ukraine. They need to go to the VVIR office (Visa Permits and Passport Department, under the Ministry of Internal Affairs) only to request a visa extension, and should be prepared to support their request with documentation. The central VVIR office is at 34 Taras Shevchenko Boulevard in Kyiv. In Lviv the office is at 3 Voronoho Street, and in smaller cities the office is typically in militia stations.

**Visa Fees** are subject to frequent change and usually reflect what a Ukrainian citizen has to pay for an American visa at the U.S. Consulate in Kyiv. Be sure to check the Ukrainian consulate Web sites for the latest information. Currently, there's a US$100 application fee for all visas, which is not refundable in case the visa is denied. There's no extra fee for processing a single-entry visa; for a double-entry visa, add a US$10 processing fee; and for a multiple entry visa add US$65 to the nonrefundable application fee. Pay by a postal money order. Credit cards, cash and personal checks are not accepted.

The visa takes approximately 9 to 10 business days to process, depending on the consulate and the time of year you apply. The time frame is quite reliable, but applications submitted during the peak demand period in spring or summer may take several days longer to process. Rush processing takes three business days and costs twice as much as standard processing. There is no longer an option for one-day processing.

**Visas at the Border.** U.S. citizens are allowed to obtain transit visas at the border, allowing them to pass through Ukraine to another country, provided they provide proof – for example, air or railway tickets – that their immediate destination is another country. Five days are allowed for the transit.

If you're traveling abroad and decide to add Ukraine to your itinerary, you can get a short-term visa if you arrive at the international airport at Odesa or Simferopol or the Odesa seaport. These are inexpensive and are valid for only eight days, but may be extended by going to the proper local law enforcement authorities. For other border entry points, you'll need to apply in advance at the nearest Ukrainian consulate. The Ukrainian consulate in Moscow is at 18 Leontyevsky Lane; in Krakow at 41 Krakowska Street; in Warsaw at 7 Aleja Szucha; in Budapest at 8 Nogradi Street; in Prague at 29 Ch. de Gaulle Street; in Bratislava at 35 Radvanska Street; and in Vienna at 23 Naaffgasse. The same requirements pertain in these consulates as if you were applying for a Ukrainian visa at home. However, obtaining the visa before leaving home is easier and you'll avoid spending valuable business or vacation time waiting in bureaucratic lines.

In the case of an emergency, such as the death of a family member in Ukraine, a visa is no longer issued at the border. The applicant needs to contact a Ukrainian consulate by phone or fax with evidence – a telegram, for example – of the situation. To reach an officer on duty in the evenings and weekends, call the Ukrainian Embassy in Washington. The visa is granted immediately at the same cost as a standard visa.

**U.S. Fiancée Visa.** A recent phenomenon is the exodus from Ukraine of women of marriageable age. Driven by desperate economic conditions and lured by the promise of a better life, they register with international dating services, and their photos and personal data show up on many Web sites. While the U.S. Consulate does not grant tourist visas to unmarried women, it does have a fiancée visa category. This plan allows a Ukrainian woman to visit the U.S. for a 90-day period, during which she must marry her American suitor or return to Ukraine.

Applying for the K-1 fiancée visa is a complicated process, involving a great deal of red tape, all to prove that the couple is in love and really planning to marry. The man must first receive the petition forms from the U.S. Immigration and Naturalization Service, then make a trip to Ukraine to help his fiancée fill out her part of the forms. The couple needs to document that they are personally acquainted. By having themselves photographed in front of the large, digital clock-calendar at the Kyiv or Odesa train stations, for example, they can prove that their meeting took place within the previous two years. Photos of them in front of other city landmarks as well as with her family may be helpful, along with airplane ticket stubs, hotel bills, or other receipts to confirm the date of the trip.

The man then returns home and mails the completed petition forms, including an affidavit of support, birth certificates, divorce decrees, visa-appropriate photos, and other documentation to his regional INS office. Upon approval, the INS forwards the paperwork to the U.S. Embassy in Kyiv. The Ukrainian woman undergoes a medical exam, gets her documents in order, and makes an appointment with the consular department of the Embassy. An interviewer questions her on her relationship with the American, and it helps to have her fiancé at her side during the interview. The visa is awarded following that interview and she is then allowed to leave.

## Travel Services

During the Soviet period, travel in Ukraine was restricted to officially designated "open" cities and to groups under the supervision of the state tourism agency, Intourist. Groups that visited tended to consist of idealists who wanted to thaw the Cold War by making friends with Soviet people or Ukrainian-Americans, who viewed Ukraine as a captive nation and were highly suspicious of what they would find. For them the big attraction was the opportunity to visit family members from whom they had long been separated or relatives they had never met.

Their relatives came from towns and villages to meet with them either in the Intourist hotels, or more commonly, outdoors, in nearby parks where their conversations could not be recorded. Ukrainians, clutching photos of their relatives, didn't dare approach a foreigner unless they were absolutely certain of his or her identity. After the joyous reunion, many Americans disregarded the warnings of the travel agencies to stay in the official open cities and managed to find their way out to their relatives' villages to enjoy a few stolen hours in the home of their loved ones.

During the Cold War, a number of American and Canadian travel agencies served the Ukrainian diaspora. Working with Intourist, they provided escorted package tours to Ukraine. Today, of course, these agencies have much greater access to Ukraine and can offer group or customized tours to off-the-beaten-track destinations. They can book airline tickets and arrange for lodging and services in Ukraine.

**Travel Agencies in Ukraine.** In the past, North American agencies serving the Ukrainian diaspora had to depend on Intourist. The sole travel service in Ukraine, Intourist's large, professional staff had complete control over all aspects of foreign tourism, from operating hotels, motels, camping grounds, and buses, to arranging all tours and entertainment. Its customary emphasis on group travel, lack of flexibility, and unresponsiveness to individual wants and needs were legendary.

With the break-up of the Soviet Union, Ukraine inherited the former Intourist hotels, properties, and service bureaus on its territory. Most of the facilities have been privatized. There are now some 4,000 licensed tourist organizations in Ukraine. It's been more difficult for smaller businesses without their own buses, restaurants, or hotels to make a living; nevertheless many have succeeded by emphasizing customer service, a relatively new concept in Ukraine.

The government is setting standards and establishing certification for travel services and facilities. It also promotes Ukraine's attractions through trade shows and advertising, since it's become apparent that tourism is one of the most rapidly growing sectors of the economy. The realization that the profit from one foreign tourist in Ukraine for one day equals the income from exporting nine tons of coal or two tons of premium wheat has changed the ingrained negative attitude toward the service professions.

Travel services in Ukraine aren't able to reserve transatlantic airline tickets for you from overseas, but they can take care of all your specific travel and tourism needs in Ukraine, from visa support to arranging lodging, transportation, and providing guided tours. Make pre-trip arrangements by writing, phoning, faxing, or e-mailing:

*Alaris, Ltd.*, P.O. Box 10450, Kyiv-2, (23 vul. Maryna Raskova, #1117), Kyiv 02002, Ukraine, phone or fax (380)44-517-43-94; e-mail tour@ info.kiev.ua. Alaris specializes in excursions to historical and archeological sites, folk culture programs, and trips to beach and ski resorts.

*Algol Travel, Ltd.*,16a vul.Melnyka, Lviv 79044, Ukraine, phone or fax: (380) 322-97-41-21; e-mail algol@mail.lviv.ua. Algol Travel Agency offers group and individual tours across Lviv, Ternopil, and Ivano- Frankivsk regions. It arranges stays in health spas in Truskavets; visits to cultural events and programs in Verkhovyna, Yaremche, and Slavske; skiing and snowboarding in the Carpathians; summer holidays on the Crimean peninsula; and hunting and other sports.

*Lybid-Kyiv Tourist Agency*, 1 Peremohy Square, Kyiv 01135, Ukraine, phone and fax (380) 442-36-42-42; e-mail tour@lybid-kiev.com.ua. Lybid-Kyiv offers discount accommodations in the Hotel Lybid, in which it's based. This full-service agency can provide transportation, airport pick-up, interpreters, and arrange special excursions to cultural and recreation sites.

*Navkolo Svitu* (Around the World), vul. Saksahaskoho 5/2, Lviv 79005, Ukraine, phone (380)322-74-21-35; fax (380)322-97-18-69; e-mail navksvit@lviv.farlep.ua. Navkolo Svitu serves group or individual travelers to Lviv and western Ukraine. The agency offers a variety of package tours for diverse interests and needs, such as a *pysanka*-writing course or a birdwatching expedition.

*New Logic*, 6–a Mikhaylivska Street, Kyiv 01001, Ukraine, phone and fax (380) 444-62-04-62; e-mail info@newlogic.Kiev.ua. New Logic has been offering a full range of incoming tourist services since1994. Among its excursions throughout the country are a tour of Chornobyl, as well as art and culinary tours. It also arranges conferences and seminars.

*Save Travel*, 29 Dmytrivska Street, 3rd floor, Kyiv 01045, Ukraine, phone (380) 44-251-21-63; fax (380) 44 251-21-64; e-mail info@apt.kiev.ua. Save Travel specializes in providing cars with drivers and apartments in the center of Kyiv on a daily basis. It also can book hotels throughout Ukraine.

***Travel Ukraine Agency, Pvt.*** 38/9 Drahomanova Street, Lviv 79005, Ukraine, phone (380) 322 98-66-25; fax (503) 217-84-06; e-mail tuag@is.lviv.ua. TUA customizes travel for individuals and business groups and offers package tours across the country. It sets up visits to ancestral towns and works with certified genealogists from the U.S. and Israel to conduct genealogical research in Ukraine and neighboring countries.

***Ukraine-Rus',*** 63 Melnikova Street, office 310, Kyiv 04050, Ukraine, e-mail agency@ukr-rus.kiev.ua; phone and fax (380)442 13-05-12, 13-23-74. Operating since 1992, Ukraine-Rus' specializes in cultural heritage and business tours throughout Ukraine for individuals or groups. Its theme tours cover Ukrainian history, culture, traditions, and nature.

***UKRUS***, P.O. Box 10450 (29/1 Ivanova Street) Kharkiv 61002, Ukraine, phone (380) 57 700-67-30; phone and fax (380) 572 17-95-54; e-mail agency@ukrus.kharkov.ua. A full service agency, UKRUS also can provide translations and language lessons in Ukrainian or Russian, archival genealogical research or searches for lost living relatives, and cultural excursions. A Canadian partner is Chumak Travel Agency, phone (905) 804-8826 or e-mail ukrainetour@ukrainetour.com.

***Unipress BTD***, 5 Tiraspolska Street, Odesa 65045, Ukraine, phone (380) 482 21-05-16; fax (380) 482 21-06-21; e-mail travel@travel-2-ukraine.com. Unipress' energetic and creative staff can arrange all types of touring and recreation in the colorful Odesa region from sightseeing to a yacht with crew, as well as customized individual and group travel and specialized experiences such as Christmas parties in major cities.

For a link to these agencies' informative Web sites as well as a listing of **Western travel agencies** that specialize in Ukraine, see Web site http:pages.prodigy.net/l.hodges/travel.htm.

**Genealogy.** Interested in tracing your Ukrainian roots? A surprising number of records have survived in archives, though they are in poor condition and disorganized. Ukrainian officials welcome those tracing their roots, but prefer that trained archivists examine the documents. You can hire a qualified researcher to document your family history and locate and photograph living relatives and landmarks. On-site research can be expensive, however, and you should check prices of individual services.

Here are a few genealogy services that operate in Ukraine:

***Family Research Foundation*** is a nonprofit organization that helps Jews and ethnic Ukrainians find their roots. It provides free information for those initiating a search and sponsors an annual tour in which participants visit individual towns to search for family history. Contact Irene Bright, P.O. Box 24, Plainview, New York 11803-0024. Phone (516) 349-0425; e-mail Heritage@optonline.net.

***Can Steppe Connections***, 292 Seven Oaks Avenue, Winnipeg, Manitoba, Canada R2V0L1; phone (204)334-1425; e-mail lyanchyn@autobahn.mb.ca.

***East Europe Connection***, 1711 Corwin Drive, Silver Spring, Maryland 20901; e-mail Lkrupnak@erols.com.

***Routes to Roots Foundation, Inc.***, 136 Sandpiper Key, Secaucus, New Jersey 07094-2210; phone (201)866-4075; e-mail mweiner@routestoroots.com. Routes to Roots surveys, inventories, and documents archives in Ukraine for the preservation, study, and promotion of Jewish genealogical material.

***Travel Ukraine Agency*** (see page 19).

## Flights to Ukraine

A Ukrainian private airline company, Aerosvit, provides several weekly non-stop flights on a Boeing 767-300 ER to Kyiv from New York JFK Airport or from Toronto International Airport, connecting with Delta Airline flights from many American airports. (Aerosvit replaces Uzbekistan Airways which replaced the debt-ridden state airline Air Ukraine in providing a transatlantic flight to Ukraine.) The planes offer business or economy class and connect to several cities in Western Ukraine from Borispil Airport in Kyiv. Check Aerosvit's informative Web site, which promises a "European level of service and Ukrainian hospitality," for schedules and to book flights www.aerosvit.com. In New York, Aerosvit is located at 420 Lexington Avenue, Suite 2930, phone (888) 661-1620. Aerosvit's Toronto office is at 101 Bloor Street West, Suite 302, phone (416) 961-5948.

A few American airlines have European partners that fly into Ukraine. United Airlines, for example, coordiantes flights with Lufthansa for connections from Frankfurt to Kyiv; Northwest Airlines links with KLM to fly from Amsterdam to Kyiv; and Delta is a partner with Austrian Air, with a layover in Vienna. Trips using these European partners meet a U.S. government requirement for those participating in programs sponsored by government funds to fly only on U.S. carriers.

Many North American cities are gateways for European airline flights to countries with air connections to Ukraine: Atlanta, Boston, Chicago, Dallas/Fort Worth, Detroit, Edmonton, Los Angeles, Ottawa, Miami, Minneapolis, Montreal, Newark, New York (JFK), Pittsburgh, San Francisco, Toronto, Vancouver, and Washington, D.C. European airlines that fly from these cities to Kyiv include Alitalia, Air France, Balkan Airlines, British Airways, Czech Air, Finnair, KLM, Lot Polish Airlines, Lufthansa, Malev Hungarian, and Swissair. The layover in their home cities may be as brief as several hours or as long as overnight.

Besides entering through Kyiv, it's possible to fly directly into Lviv, Dnipropetrovsk, Kharkiv, Odesa or Simferopol. Lviv is serviced by Lot Polish Airlines, which runs daily flights from Warsaw, and by Ukraine International Airline (UIA) flights from Frankfurt and Vienna. Austrian Airlines flies from Vienna to Odesa daily, and UIA flies from Frankfurt to Simferopol, Dnipropetrovsk, and Kharkiv.

**Baggage Allowance.** Transatlantic flights departing from the U.S. usually allow two pieces of checked luggage per person, so long as each piece weighs no more than 70 pounds and the length plus width plus depth of each does not exceed 62 inches. There's an extra charge for additional luggage (US$90 to US$130 per bag depending on airline), so unless you're carrying irreplaceable gifts, it may be worthwhile to ship your extra baggage over in advance. Carry-on luggage must fit into the overhead compartment or underneath the seat directly in front. In coach class, the dimensions shouldn't exceed a total of 45 linear inches (9 by 14 by 22-inches) and 22 pounds. You may also carry a personal item onboard, such as a briefcase, purse, or laptop computer. Check with your individual carrier for variations.

### Packing the Right Stuff

Keeping within the two suitcase limit, you can fit everything you need for a two-week to month-long trip into a single 26-inch-long suitcase, leaving the other suitcase for gifts.

**Clothing.** While you can generally get by without a lot of clothes, what you need depends on your itinerary. If you're just sightseeing and visiting friends or relatives, casual clothing will be acceptable. However, when Ukrainians go out for a special event, they dress up. Blue jeans and "California casual" are not suitable for a night on the town. Ties for men and dresses for women are preferable, and business attire is suitable for daytime meetings, conferences, or for when you're an invited guest. Plan your wardrobe with layering in mind, in order to be prepared for weather changes.

Be sure to take a nylon raincoat, folding umbrella, and rain galoshes or shoes that won't be ruined when wet. Well-padded athletic walking shoes or at least comfortable low-heeled shoes are a must for cobblestone streets, uneven pavement, and dirt paths in rural areas.

**Personal Items.** While shops stock a good selection of toiletries and cosmetics, most of the brands are not what you're used to. Some items, such as Band-Aids, are simply not Ukrainian. Bring along all personal supplies required for your health, hygiene, and grooming: soap, moist towelettes, shampoo, deodorant, toothpaste, sunscreen lotion, sunglasses, razor and blades, tissues, feminine hygiene products, and contraceptives. Some necessities, such as toilet paper, are not of the quality Westerners are used to, and the supply in public restrooms – those in museums or theaters, for example – is likely to be exhausted.

**Health Needs.** Pack antidiarrheal medication and a good antacid. Alka-Seltzer, Pepto-Bismol, and aspirin or non-aspirin pain reliever may also come in handy. Pack an insect repellent containing DEET and an antibiotic ointment. Take along a spare pair of eyeglasses or contact lenses and a copy of your prescription. Contact lenses are difficult to obtain except in the largest cities.

A small first-aid kit containing adhesive bandages, antiseptic cream, and a thermometer is also a good idea. Include a medical identification card that lists your blood type, your social security number, your allergies or chronic health problems, and your medical insurance information. Be sure to carry an adequate supply of all medication and prescription drugs that you regularly take, packed in their original containers, in your carry-on case. It's also wise to carry a copy of the prescription and a note from your doctor listing the generic name of the drug in Latin.

**Snacks.** Peanut butter in plastic jars, tuna fish in small tins or pouches, dried fruits, granola bars, and soup mixes will provide a few calories, if you've missed a meal. Instant coffee or a small plastic coffee caddy that allows boiling water to flow through a filtered coffee basket, powdered milk or coffee creamer, cocoa mix and tea bags will take care of your hot drink requirements.

**Other Useful Items.**
- For snacking on the road or in your hotel room: a Swiss Army knife that includes a bottle opener and knife; plastic forks and spoons; a tea infuser that boils water; a heatproof unbreakable cup.
- A small flashlight. Brownouts sometimes occur in Ukraine.
- A washcloth. These are not widely used in Europe, including Ukraine.
- A nylon sport bag or day pack is useful for day excursions.
- Plastic Ziploc bags have dozens of uses.
- A universal sink stopper is handy when washing out your clothes in the evening.
- A money belt that can be worn under your clothes. Ukraine is largely a cash economy and you'll need to carry paper money.
- Notepads for memos and recording impressions.
- Business cards. Include name and address in both English and Ukrainian or Russian to give to new acquaintances.
- Ukraine is a craft collector's paradise. If shopping is a priority, pack a large nylon shopping bag, bubble wrap, and strapping tape.

**Camera Choices.** A <u>Polaroid camera</u> provides on-the-spot photos for those you meet in chance encounters or with whom you don't care to correspond when you return home. Polaroids are no longer bulky and don't require batteries, but you'll need to carry film with you since it's expensive and not widely available. A <u>digital</u> <u>camera</u> generally is small and lightweight, and allows an instant check on whether you captured the image you wanted. Be sure you take enough memory cards and batteries to cover your entire trip, unless your camera uses AA batteries, which are widely available in Ukraine. Simple, lightweight <u>disposable</u> <u>cameras</u> that shoot only one roll of film per camera may work for those who don't consider photos a priority. The most versatile camera is the "point-and-shoot," or <u>fully automatic</u> <u>camera</u>. Simpler ones have a single focal length, usually 35 mm. Pack more film than you think you'll need and an extra battery for your camera.

If you wish to avoid exposing your film to excessive X-rays at airports, there are lead-lined film pouches on the market that protect the film, particularly if you use high-speed films or pass through many airports on your trip. Avoid packing film in checked baggage because new screening machines may damage it. This is not a problem with digital cameras.

**For a Successful Power Trip.** The alternating current in Ukraine differs from that in the U.S. in two ways: it is 220 volts instead of 110 volts and has a frequency of 50 hertz instead of 60 hertz.

If you carry small American electrical appliances, such as an electric razor, travel iron, portable hair dryer, or battery charger, you'll need a converter to reduce the voltage from 220 to 110, or your appliance will burn and blow out. Converters are available for US$20 to US$30 and come in several sizes, some intended for low-wattage devices like electric razors and others for high-wattage devices like hair dryers.

In addition to the converter, you'll need an inexpensive adapter plug, a simple device that allows you to plug the converter into a Ukrainian electrical outlet. The adapter needed for Ukraine as well as other countries that were formerly part of the U.S.S.R. is the same as that used in most of Europe, including Austria, France, Germany, Italy, Poland, Scandinavia, and Spain, but it is different from that used in Great Britain. The correct kind has two round posts about an inch apart. Austin House and Royal Traveler by Samsonite both market a converter-with-adapters kit good for various countries. Look for these in electrical-supply stores or travel shops. An extension cord for the adapter may come in handy.

Your power conversion problems may not yet be solved, however. Converters cannot be used with appliances that are left on for long periods of time or that require a current with a frequency of 60 hertz instead of the 50 hertz standard in Ukraine, for example, some televisions, VCRs, movie cameras and projectors, and computers. For these, you may need to obtain a bulkier transformer rather than a converter. If you want to use a computer, make sure it will work at 50 hertz; newer computers (including laptops) usually have an AC adapter that will sense the electric voltage and frequency and work properly, so only an adapter plug is necessary. Portable radios, cassette and CD players, TVs, and many cameras run on battery power, but you need to bring enough batteries (or buy them in Ukraine) or plan to use a battery charger with your converter and adapter.

**Gifts.** In planning gifts consider the differences in lifestyle. Ukrainians have gotten along very well without disposable diapers, paper plates, adhesive bandages, convenience foods, and a legion of other consumer goods that Westerners consider essentials of modern life.

It may be preferable to accompany your hosts on a shopping trip in Ukraine and let them choose for themselves. Very likely they've kept up with current fashions and have seen the latest trends and styles from all over Europe in their open markets. Careful and frugal shoppers by necessity, they won't buy anything they can get along without or that isn't "just right."

If you want to give something from home, choose practical items that are trendy or the latest fashion, for example, T-shirts with a logo that means something to you; sportswear with your (or your recipient's) favorite team insignia; colorful and lightweight fleece jackets; scarves; socks and athletic shoes.

Practical items that are sure to please: hand and face cream, cosmetics, luxury soaps, hair-color products, vitamins and supplements, aspirin, first-aid items, sunscreen lotion, shopping bags, nylon duffle bags, back packs, raincoats, folding umbrellas, fabric, scissors, needles, thread, buttons, zippers. Fabric suitable for embroidering and embroidery floss. Seeds of open-pollinated varieties of common vegetables.

For children: clothing, children's vitamins and aspirin, classic toys such as Barbie dolls and accessories, Lego sets, coloring books and crayons, classic English-language story-books or alphabet books, sports equipment, and any popular fad toys.

Edibles: Modern supermarkets in Ukraine sell both Ukrainian and international products, but you're unlikely to find peanut butter or any coffee other than instant Nescafé. Give your favorite brand of instant coffee or a French press coffee maker with your favorite ground coffee. American brands of loose tea, herbal tea, hard candies, candy bars, snack food, canned meat or fish, or jam will also be welcome.

Technical items: solar-powered flashlights, calculators, radios, cassette players, tapes, CD players, and compact discs. Rechargeable batteries make a good gift, even though batteries are no longer hard to find. The recipient will need a battery charger, but 220-volt chargers for NiMH batteries are available in Ukraine. If you're planning to give a VCR, note that the video format in Ukraine is a double format (both PAL and SECAM) and that triple-format (PAL, SECAM, and NTSC, the American system) VCRs are available throughout the country. Remember that Ukrainian customs requires you to declare gifts valued more than US$300 and collects duty for electronic gifts.

Blank cassettes make good gifts because they can be recorded using Ukrainian equipment, but prerecorded American cassettes won't play on Ukrainian VCRs (unless they are triple-format); conversely if you buy cassettes recorded in Ukraine, they won't play on American VCRs.

Souvenirs: Finally, don't forget to pack a few mementos of your home city and state. Your hosts will welcome postcards, your state map and flag, label pins, insignia T-shirts, and picture books about your region's cities, natural wonders, and wildlife.

## Going Healthy, Staying Healthy

**General Precautions.** You don't need a vaccination to receive a Ukrainian visa, but you should be sure that your immunizations are up to date. If it's been ten years since you've gotten a tetanus/diphtheria booster, it's time for another. An influenza vaccine is recommended during the increased risk period from November through March for travelers over 65 and those with a compromised immune system. Pneumococcal vaccine is also recommended for at-risk travelers. Measles vaccine is strongly recommended for Americans born in 1957 or later (1970 or later for Canadians) who have had no previous contact with measles or the vaccine.

If you're concerned about a particular medical condition that could make travel difficult or risky, consult a travel physician for the inoculations and preventative medicine you need to carry.

**Specific Health Concerns for Ukraine.** Because the Ukrainian government is attempting to check black-market activity, medicines and medical supplies are monitored. Only diabetics are allowed to carry hypodermic needles, and they may have to show proof of their condition, such as a prescription for the needles and their insulin. Those discovered with antiretrovirals will be denied entry at customs.

Medical care is not up to par with that in Western countries. Advanced technology is lacking and there are shortages of medications. Because of decrepit water treatment facilities, Ukraine's water supply is contaminated with sewage and chemicals from factory wastes. Although outbreaks of food poisoning and water-borne disease are a moderate risk throughout the country, travelers are advised to drink only bottled water or water that's been boiled for ten minutes. Tap water can be purified by filtering it though an "absolute 1-micron or less" filter (available in camping and outdoor supply stores) and adding iodine tablets to the filtered water. Iodine tablets are safe for short-term use except for those with a thyroid condition or who are pregnant. It should be noted that drinking even purified water can result in mild stomach or intestinal upsets for those not accustomed to the local microbes. Other common sense preventative measures from the Center for Disease Control are to wash your hands often with soap and water, and eat only thoroughly cooked food and peeled raw produce: "boil it, cook it, peel it, or forget it."

HIV is a major health problem in Ukraine, with some infections resulting from contaminated donor blood supply. According to the U.S. Department of State, Ukraine requires anyone planning to stay longer than three months to be tested for HIV. Ukrainian health authorities will accept results of tests performed in other countries. Contact a Ukrainian consulate for details if you're planning a long-term visit.

Immunization for hepatitis A is recommended for all travelers to Ukraine. Hepatitis B immunization is recommended for those staying over three months or for anyone who might be exposed to blood or other body fluids, such as health-care workers or those receiving medical care. The typhoid vaccine is recommended for those with adventurous dietary habits, who travel off the usual tourist route, or who plan a prolonged stay. The risk of rabies occurs in most parts of the country, and vaccination is recommended for those who might be exposed to wild or domestic animals through work or recreation, especially adventure explorers who will be more than 24 hours' away from a reliable source of post-exposure rabies vaccine. Other precautions specific for Ukraine concern insects. There is a risk of tick-borne encephalitis between April and October throughout the country. Cutaneous and visceral leishmaniasis transmitted by sand flies may be a hazard in beach areas.

Plan to see your physician a month or two before your departure. Some immunizations require time to become effective, while others may result in a sore arm that can make it difficult to carry your luggage. It's advisable to ask your health-care provider for a prescription for a broad-spectrum antibiotic, such as Cipro. Consider self-treatment with loperamide and/or a quinolone antibiotic. In Kyiv there are good U.S.-dental centers that take credit cards, but for wider travel in Ukraine, have your dental care up to date before leaving home.

The incidence of infectious disease and other health hazards is changing rapidly. For the most up-to-date advisory and vaccination recommendations for traveling to Ukraine, check with the Center for Disease Control and Prevention. You may dial the CDC's 24-hour International Traveler's Information Line at 1-877-394-8747 to have the information faxed to you or you can access the information on the oganization's Web site at www.cdc.gov/travel. For general safety precautions about travel in Ukraine, check also with the 24-hour Citizens Emergency Center at the State Department (202-647-5225), or see the Web site at travel.state.gov.

Chornobyl, which is 100 km (60 miles) north of Kyiv, was the site of the infamous nuclear power plant accident in April 1986. Health experts agree that there is no danger whatsoever from the Chornobyl fallout to those visiting Kyiv for a short time. The food supply has been tested for radiation and thus far no elevated levels have been detected. However, the effects on the health of long-term visitors is yet unknown, and there is some concern for the residual effects from the radioactivity in the soil and in locally grown food.

**Travel Insurance.** If you have health concerns, check with your insurance agent to see whether your policy covers medical help abroad. Many policies provide the same medical coverage overseas as they do at home. Check also if they have emergency phone numbers in Ukraine. For many health emergencies, the more useful insurance covers expenses incurred in leaving Ukraine for treatment elsewhere. If your policy doesn't provide for medical evacuation, consider one that does. The Ukrainian National Association (1-800-253-9862, ext. 3013), a Ukrainian-American fraternal organization, offers several short-term insurance package options, including medical evacuation. You needn't be a member of UNA to take out a short-term travel policy.

# CHAPTER 3.
# THE UKRAINIAN LANGUAGE

*Ukrainian Proverb*: **Мова — це душа народу.**
MO-vah — tseh doo-SHAH nah-RO-doo
*Language is the soul of a nation.*

Language has been and is a complex issue in Ukraine, tied up with politics, patriotism, and prejudices. Ukraine is bilingual, with half the population speaking Ukrainian and half speaking Russian. The difference is largely along an east-west division, with Ukrainian spoken in Western Ukraine and Russian predominating in the east and south.

With independence, Ukrainian became the official state language. The government conducts business in Ukrainian, public signs are in Ukrainian, and much of public education switched from Russian to Ukrainian. However, the Russian language dominates the business world, popular culture, and the airwaves. In 2004 a controversial government regulation putting all television and radio broadcasts in Ukrainian was so impractical that it was considered a provocation designed to fuel Ukrainian-Russian hostilities.

Many Russian speakers feel that replacing the language they grew up with is unfair. Some regard those who advocate a much greater use of Ukrainian as rabid, right-wing nationalists, out of step with reality. Those who want a greater restoration of Ukrainian cite the centuries of repression under occupying powers, during which Ukrainian was considered culturally inferior and forbidden in print. Some see the Russian language as an instrument of Russia's continued economic and cultural imperialism.

The issue is further clouded by the blurring of the distinction between the two languages following the introduction of Ukrainian in public places. A hybrid language, *Surzhyk*, is on the rise, particularly among young Ukrainians in most eastern regions of the country exposed for the first time to the Ukrainian language. Most Ukrainians – regardless of their native tongue – lament the contamination of these two separate languages.

Even though language can be a flash point for deep political fears, in public there's been real accommodation for the sake of peaceful co-existence. You might observe, for example, Ukrainian spoken to a souvenir vendor or cabdriver who responds in Russian.

## Some Features of the Ukrainian Language

Ukrainian is the second most commonly spoken Slavic language. It's usually classified as an East Slavic language, together with Belarusian and Russian, but because of Ukraine's central location among the Slavic nations, the Ukrainian language is also historically connected to the West Slavic and the South Slavic languages.

Ukrainian has been a distinct recognizable language since the middle of the eleventh century, when the Slavic languages began to diverge. Russian, for example, assimilated many words of Scandinavian and Tatar origin, while Ukrainian remained truer to its Old Slavic roots. Though political conditions encouraged the growth of regional dialects, with the assimilation of Russian words in the east and Polish words in the west, there nevertheless exists today a standard Ukrainian language that is taught in school, used in literature, and understood by all Ukrainians.

The Ukrainian language is written in an adaptation of Cyrillic, an old Slavonic alphabet named after St. Cyril, the ninth-century Christian missionary to the Slavs. In the 860s, Cyril and his brother St. Methodius translated the Holy Scriptures into the language later known as Old Church Slavonic. In order to do this, they devised an alphabet based on Greek characters with adaptations from Hebrew. Various versions of that alphabet are used today by Russians, Belarusians, Bulgarians, Serbs, and Macedonians, as well as by Ukrainians.

A few letters of the Ukrainian alphabet, such as K, M, T, A, E, and O, correspond to certain English letters, in both appearance and sound. The Ukrainian vowels, however, have only a single sound and lack the range of their English counterparts. Many Ukrainian letters have equivalent sounds in English but look quite different: Б is B, Г is H, П is P, Ц is TS, and Ч is CH, to name a few. Perhaps most confusing for those unfamiliar with the Cyrillic alphabet are letters that look Roman but represent quite different sounds in Cyrillic. For example, B is V, C is S, P is R, and H is N.

The Ukrainian alphabet has 32 letters with sound values. Special note should be made of the difference between the Г (H) and Ґ (G). Following independence, linguists in Ukraine reintroduced the letter Ґ, which the Soviet government had dropped in order to make the Ukrainian language conform more closely to Russian. Relatively few Ukrainian words contain the Ґ, and they're primarily of foreign origin, an example being ґетто, ghetto. During the period in which the Ґ was banned, the letter Г (H), did a double duty as replacement for G. Because Ukrainians know which words are pronounced with a soft "H" sound and which take the hard "G" sound, some feel that the reintroduction of the infrequently used character Ґ originated from political overreaction, the linguistic equivalent of changing the names of streets that had been perfectly innocuous. Perhaps the linguists will decide that Ukrainian can get along perfectly well without the Ґ character, and it will die a natural death. In the meantime, we're including iit in the alphabet. While it doesn't occur frequently, and is not widely found in printed materials in Ukraine, it's especially useful to a non-native speaker who can't distinguish the H from the G sound in Ukrainian words. In this book, there are only a few words using the Ґ. The most common is the word for guide, ґід, which you should pronounce *geed* rather than *heed*.

Mastering the alphabet may be the most difficult part of learning to read Ukrainian because the pronunciation is simple and clear. *The Ukrainian alphabet is absolutely phonetic: each letter has a single pronunciation in every usage.* A stress put on a vowel does not change its pronunciation.

We need mention only a few other points about the Ukrainian language: There is no pattern to accentuation; stress may fall on any syllable in a given word. However, Ukrainian tends to have only one stress per word. Ukrainian sentence construction is more flexible than English. The Ukrainian language is highly inflectional; endings of nouns, pronouns, and adjectives change according to gender and case.

### Transliteration: Expressing Ukrainian Cyrillic in the Roman Alphabet

If Ukrainian is a phonetic language, why are so many Ukrainian names unpronounceable when they're written in English? Why do they have so many "j's" and "w's" when the Cyrillic alphabet doesn't include these letters? Actually, it's more precise to say that Ukrainian names are sometimes indecipherable, rather than unpronounceable, when they're written in English because they have been transcribed with a transliteration scheme that is not user-friendly to English speakers.

Those not familiar with the Ukrainian language are often stumped by the various systems that linguists have devised to replace Cyrillic letters with their Roman equivalents. The Ukrainian character  й, for example, sounds like the "y" that ends the words "boy" or starts the word "yet," but various transliteration systems express it with a "y," an "i," or a "j." Accordingly, the name Андрій (Andrew) may be transliterated as Andrey, Andri, Andriy, Andrii, Andry, and the mysteriously confusing Andrij.

To a native English speaker, "Andrij" is a mystery, but to a German or Scandinavian or Pole who pronounce *ja* as "ya" and *je* as "yeh," it makes a lot of sense. Similarly, the surname Вовк is pronounced "vovk" in any country in the world, even where it's spelled "Wowk."

In short, transliteration systems for Ukrainian reflect the sound values of particular Roman alphabet languages, and don't necessarily coincide with those given them in English. There is no universally accepted transliteration system from Ukrainian Cyrillic to Roman script, but with greater contact between Ukraine and English-speaking countries, it's practical to choose a scheme to which native English speakers can easily relate.

The United States Board on Geographic Names (USBGN) in its work transcribing Ukrainian place names, devised an English-friendly method that we chose for this guidebook. A new English transliteration system for the Ukrainian Cyrillic alphabet was issued in 1996 by the Legal Terminology Commission of the Ukrainian Language Institute of the National Academy of Sciences of Ukraine. Their system is very similar to the USBGN system, but a little more complicated. For purposes of simplicity, we continue to use the more practical USBGN. When you come across names in Ukrainian Cyrillic that you want to jot down in English, simply replace the Cyrillic letter with the corresponding Roman one according to the chart on the next page.

A shortcoming of the USBGN system is its heavy reliance on the letter "y." Y is used for the transliteration of several Ukrainian letters into English: both и and й are rendered as *y*; є is *ye*, ї is *yi*, ю is *yu*, and я is *ya*. Thus a proper name that ends with the adjectival -ий, such as Морський Вокзал (Sea Passenger Terminal) becomes *Morskyy Vokzal*. By this system, the name of Ukraine's capital, Київ, would be rendered *Kyyiv*. (The traditional English spelling, "Kiev," is a transliteration of the Russian name of the city.) While some map makers use the double *y*, this transliteration has not been well-received by many, especially by native Ukrainians. For simplicity, the spelling is usually shortened to *"Kyiv."*

## U.S. Board on Geographic Names Transliteration System

| *Ukrainian Letter* | | *English Equivalent* | |
|---|---|---|---|
| А | а | A | a |
| Б | б | B | b |
| В | в | V | v |
| Г | г | H | h |
| Ґ | ґ | G | g |
| Д | д | D | d |
| Е | е | E | e |
| Є | є | YE | ye |
| Ж | ж | ZH | zh |
| З | з | Z | z |
| И | и | Y | y |
| І | і | I | i |
| Ї | ї | YI | yi |
| Й | й | Y | y |
| К | к | K | k |
| Л | л | L | l |
| М | м | M | m |
| Н | н | N | n |
| О | о | O | o |
| П | п | P | p |
| Р | р | R | r |
| С | с | S | s |
| Т | т | T | t |
| У | у | U | u |
| Ф | ф | F | f |
| Х | х | KH | kh |
| Ц | ц | TS | ts |
| Ч | ч | CH | ch |
| Ш | ш | SH | sh |
| Щ | щ | SHCH | shch |
| Ь | ь | [soft sign, not transliterated] | |
| Ю | ю | YU | yu |
| Я | я | YA | ya |

## Phonetic Guide

For the Ukrainian phrases in this book, we use a phonetic transcription designed to render an even closer approximation of their sound values than could be done with a transliteration. A phonetic scheme facilitates Ukrainian pronunciation for English-speakers with no background in Slavic languages who cannot intuitively pick up the nuances of Ukrainian sounds and inflections. Among the advantages of using a phonetic scheme is that it indicates the stressed syllables. Thus a phonetic system would express the above examples like this: Київ as KIH-yeev, Хрещатик as Khreh-SHCHAH-tihk and Марія as mah-REE-yah.

The phonetic scheme we've devised for the *Hippocrene Language and Travel Guide to Ukraine* is designed to approximate literary language that is standard throughout Ukraine. It will be understood everywhere despite foreign influences on dialect in certain regions.

Read the phonetic transcriptions as if they were standard English, putting extra emphasis on the letters that are capitalized. While stress may fall on any syllable, Ukrainian tends to have only one stressed syllable in each word, regardless of the length of the word.

### *Consonants*

| Ukrainian Letter | Transcription and Approximate Pronunciation | | Example |
|---|---|---|---|
| Б б | b | like b in *b*at | без (behz) |
| В в | v | like v in *v*alve | він (veen) |
| Г г | h | like h in *h*at | гарно (HAR-no) |
| Ґ ґ | g | like g in *g*ot | ґанок (GAH-nok) |
| Д д | d͟ | like d in *d*og | дім (deem) |
| Ж ж | z͡h | like ge in gara*ge* or s in plea*s*ure | жінка (Z͡HEEN-kah) |
| З з | z | like z in *z*oo | зуб (zoob) |
| Й й | y̆ | like y in *y*olk | його (YO-ho) |
| К к | k | like k in *k*it | кітка (KEET-kah) |
| Л л | l | like l in *l*ab | літо (LEE-to) |
| М м | m | like m in *m*ore | мама (MAH-mah) |
| Н н | n | like n in *n*o | ніс (nees) |
| П п | p | like p in *p*oor | під (peed) |
| Р р | r | like r in erro*r* | рада (RAH-dah) |
| С с | s | like s in *s*it | сад (sahd) |

| Т т | t | like t in *t*oe | там (tahm) |
| Ф ф | f | like f in *f*it | фірма (feer-mah) |
| Х х | kh | like ch in Scottish lo*ch* | хліб (khleeb) |
| Ц ц | ts | like ts in ba*ts* | церква (TSERK-vah) |
| Ч ч | ch | like ch in *ch*ip | час (chahs) |
| Ш ш | sh | like sh in *sh*ot | школа (SHKOH-lah) |
| Щ щ | shch | like sh ch in fre*sh ch*eese | ще (shcheh) |

## *Vowels*

| А а | ah | like a in f*a*ther | там (tahm) |
| Е е | eh | like e in l*e*t | не (neh) |
| Є є | yeh | like ye in *ye*s | знає (ZNAH-yeh) |
| И и | ih | like i in *i*t or y in m*y*th | мити (MIH-tih) |
| І і | ee | like ee in m*ee*t | пісні (PEES-nee) |
| Ї ї | yee | like yie sound in *yie*ld | їм (yeem) |
| О о | o | like o in *o*ff, d*o*t | дорого (do-RO-ho) |
| У у | oo | like oo in b*oo*t | тут (toot) |
| Ю ю | yu | like the word *you* | любов (lyu-BOV) |
| Я я | ya | like ya in *ya*cht | моя (mo-YA) |

## *Other Symbols*

**The Apostrophe.** ь is the soft sign that sometimes follows the consonants д, з, л, н, с, т, and ц, and designates that they are softened (palatalized).

' is the apostrophe that sometimes occurs between the consonants б, в, м, п, ф and the vowels я, ю, є, ї. This character denotes a distinct, separate articulation of the consonant and vowel.

In our phonetic scheme we use an apostrophe ' to represent both of these Ukrainian symbols. In both instances, the apostrophe serves to add emphasis to the letters it separates.

For example, when скільки is transcribed as SKEEL'-kih, the apostrophe represents the soft sign ь and signals a soft pronunciation of the preceding consonant, the l. And when ім'я is transcribed as eem'YA, the apostrophe denotes an articulation of the *m* and *ya* sounds represented by the м and я.

**Diacritical Marks.** In addition to the apostrophe, we use two diacritical marks to help clarify the pronunciation:

1. The ligature over the $\widehat{zh}$ that represents the blended consonant sounds of ж distinguishes it from the two distinct and separate sounds required by the z and h when they occur in a word with a consecutive з and г. Thus in жінка, $\widehat{Z}$HEEN-kah, the zh representing the ж are blended to sound like the *ge* ending of the word garage, while in згинути, zhih-NOO-tih, the z and the h representing the з and г are pronounced separately as in the phrase "jazz heaven."

While other characters of the Ukrainian alphabet represent a blending of two or more Roman characters, their pronunciation is obvious from context and they don't require a linking sign: x = kh, ш = sh, щ = shch, ц = ts, ч = ch.

2. A wedge is used over the transcription of the letter й (ў) to distinguish it from the "y" sound of certain vowels:

добрий   DO-brihў

**The Letter "H."** The frequent use of the letter "h" in our transcription serves a number of purposes:

"H" is the Ukrainian letter "Г."

An "h" after a vowel (ah, eh, ih, yeh) forces the vowel to remain a short vowel. Thus невже is pronounced nehv-$\widehat{Z}$HEH and not neev-$\widehat{Z}$HEE and боєць is bo-YEHTS' not bo-YEETS. Note that the Ukrainian "o" is always a short vowel, but we do not use "oh" because that may suggest a long o.

When the Ukrainian г follows a short vowel, the transcription will include a double "h," which may or may not be separated by a dash, depending on the syllable break:

багато        bah-HAH-to
but  багно   bahh-no

### Just Enough Grammar

Ukrainian grammar follows the Slavic language pattern. Here is a brief summary of the nuts and bolts of the language. Pronunciation is not given for the Ukrainian sentences in order not to detract from the explanation.

## Nouns

Ukrainian nouns have three genders: masculine, feminine, and neuter, abbreviated as "*m.*" and "*f.*" and "*n.*" It's necessary to know the gender of a noun in order to know which ending it should receive, to modify it with an adjective, or to form its plural. Ukrainian does not have a definite article (*the*) or indefinite articles (*a, an*) that indicate the gender of a noun; the gender is usually revealed by its ending.

Masculine nouns end with a consonant:

брат, brother      лікар, doctor      чай, tea

Feminine nouns usually end with -a or -я:

вода, water      кухня, kitchen      надія, hope

Neuter nouns usually end with -o, -я, or -e:

село, village      ім'я, name      море, sea

Nouns that end in -ь can be either masculine or feminine, but in most instances are masculine.

учитель (m.), teacher      сіль (f.), salt

There are exceptions:

Some masculine nouns end with -a or -o: тато, dad
Some feminine nouns end in a consonant: ніч, night

**Plurals.** Although there are exceptions, masculine and feminine nouns usually end in -и or -i in the plural:

газети, newspapers      вулиці, streets
столи, tables      хлопці, boys.

Neuter nouns usually end in -a or -я in the plural:

міста, cities      поля, fields.

Some nouns change their internal spelling in the plural, so that they may be difficult to recognize:

ніч, ночі — night, nights
річ, речі — thing, things
день, дні — day, days.

**Declensions.** Nouns change their endings according to their function in a sentence. In Ukrainian these functions are grouped into different categories called cases. There are six different cases in Ukrainian that are used for all nouns.

**The nominative case (N)** refers to the subject of the sentence. In Ukrainian dictionaries, nouns are always given in the nominative case. They refer to an object's existence.

Це наш *готель* (N). This is our hotel.

Де *пошта* (N)? Where is the post office?

**The genitive case (G)** indicates ownership or possession. It answers the questions whose or which and can usually be translated into English using the word "of" or the apostrophe plus an "s" ('s).

машина *чоловіка* (G) — the car of the man, the man's car

The genitive case is also used in expressing the direct object of a negative sentence:

Я не маю *виделки* (G). I don't have a fork.

Another use of the genitive case is to indicate an indefinite quantity of something:

Я купила *хліба* (G). I bought some bread.

**The accusative case (A)** denotes the direct object of a verb.

Я бачу *річку* (A). I see the river.

Він знає точний *час* (A). He knows the correct time.

**The dative case (D)** is used to designate a person or thing to whom or to which something is done or given.

Дай це *своїй мамі* (D). Give this to your mom.

Я (*тобі*, *s*.) (*вам*, *pl*.) (D) допоможу. I'll help you.

**The locative case (L)** indicates the location or place of action. It answers the question "where?" The locative is always used with a preposition and is sometimes called the prepositional case. The most common prepositions used in locative case constructions are в (у) which means "in" or "at" and на which means "on," "at," and "in."

Він чекає *в готелі* (L). He's waiting at the hotel.

Вона лежить *на пляжі* (L). She's lying on the beach.

**The instrumental case (I)** answers the questions "by whom?" or "by what means?" In Ukrainian the preposition is not expressed:

Я пишу *олівцем* (I). I'm writing with a pencil.

Я поїду *автобусом* (I). I'll be going by bus.

The instrumental case is also used to denote a temporary or new condition or used with the verbs to be or to become:

Він був *студентом* (I). He was a student.
Вона хоче стати *лікарем* (I). She wants to become a doctor.

## Prepositions

Prepositions determine the case of nouns. Some prepositions are followed by more than one case, depending on their use in the sentence. For example, *в* (to) and *на* (on, at) are used with the accusative case when motion is involved, and with the locative to indicate simple position.

Іди в ту кімнату (A). Go into that room.
Він в музеї (L). He's at the museum.
Мій паспорт на столі (L). My passport is on the table.

Here are some of the most common prepositions, the cases they take, and their phonetic pronunciation:

| | | |
|---|---|---|
| across | напроти (G) | nah-PRO-tih |
| against | проти (G) | PRO-tih |
| around | навколо (G) | nahv-KO-lo |
| at | на (L) | nah |
| behind | за (A, I) | zah |
| between | між (I) | meezh |
| from | від, з, із (G) | veed, z, eez |
| in | в *or* у (A, L) | v *or* oo |
| in front of | перед (I) | peh-REHD |
| near | біля, коло (G) | BEE-lya, KO-lo |
| on | на (A, L) | nah |
| over | над (I) | nahd |
| to, as far as | до (G) | do |
| to | на, за (A) | nah, zah |
| under | під (A, I) | peed |
| with | з, зі, (I) | z, zee |

## Adjectives

In Ukrainian, adjectives change their endings to agree with the gender, number, and case of the noun they modify. Adjectives have masculine, feminine, and neuter forms. The plural form is the same for all genders:

| | | |
|---|---|---|
| a good boy | добрий хлопець | (masculine singular) |
| a good girl | добра дівчина | (feminine singular) |
| a good question | добре питання | (neuter singular) |
| good boys | добрі хлопці | (masculine plural) |
| good girls | добрі дівчата | (feminine plural) |
| good questions | добрі питання | (neuter plural) |

Like nouns, adjectives are declined according to their use in a sentence. The table below shows the declension of nouns and adjectives using the phrases *hot tea, cold cereal,* and *tasty cookie*:

| | Masculine *hot tea* | Feminine *cold cereal* | Neuter *tasty cookie* |
|---|---|---|---|
| **singular** | | | |
| N. | гарячий чай | холодна каша | смачне печиво |
| G. | гарячого чаю | холодної каші | смачного печива |
| D. | гарячому чаю | холодній каші | смачному печиву |
| A. | гарячий чай | холодну кашу | смачне печиво |
| L. | в гарячому чаї | в холодній каші | в смачному печиві |
| I. | гарячим чаєм | холодною кашою | смачним печивом |
| **plural** | | | |
| N. | гарячі чаї | холодні каші | смачні печива |
| G. | гарячих чаїв | холодних каш | смачних печив |
| D. | гарячим чаям | холодним кашам | смачним печивам |
| A. | гарячі чаї | холодні каші | смачні печива |
| L. | в гарячих чаях | в холодних кашах | на смачних печивах |
| I. | гарячими чаями | холодними кашами | смачними печивами |

## Pronouns

Personal pronouns also change depending on their use in the sentence.

|  | *I* | *you (s.)* | *he, it* | *she* | *we* | *you* | *they* |
|------|------|------|------|------|------|------|------|
| N. | я | ти | він, воно | вона | ми | ви | вони |
| G. | мене | тебе | його | її | нас | вас | їх |
| D. | мені | тобі | йому | їй | нам | вам | їм |
| A. | мене | тебе | його | її | нас | їх | їх |
| L. | на мені | на тобі | на ньому | на ній | на нас | на вас | на них |
| I. | мною | тобою | ним | нею | нами | вами | ними |

There are two ways to express the pronoun *you* in Ukrainian. *Ти* (*tih*), the familiar form, is used when addressing a close friend, a relative, or a child. *Ви* (*vih*) is for speaking to someone with whom you are not on close terms, someone in authority, and always to someone you've just met. Ви is also the plural form, used when addressing more than one person, regardless of how close you are to them. Phrases in this guide that include both forms of the pronoun "you" give the familiar, singular form first, followed by the polite or plural form.

**Possessive pronouns** are declined like adjectives, agreeing with the noun in number and gender. *Його* (his and its), *її* (her), and *їх* (their) are not declined. *Твій* (your, *s.*) and *свій* (one's own) are declined exactly like *мій* (my):

|  | masculine | feminine | neuter | plural |
|------|------|------|------|------|
| N. | мій | моя | моє | мої |
| G. | мого | моєї | мого | моїх |
| D. | моєму | моїй | моєму | моїм |
| A. | мій, мого | мою | моє | мої, моїх |
| L. | на моєму | на моїй | на моєму | на моїх |
| I. | моїм | моєю | моїм | моїми |

Наш (our) is declined like ваш (your, *pl.*):

|  | | | | |
|------|------|------|------|------|
| N. | ваш | ваша | ваше | ваші |
| G. | вашого | вашої | вашого | ваших |
| D. | вашому | вашій | вашому | вашим |
| A. | ваш | вашу | ваших | ваші |
| L. | на вашому | на вашій | на вашому | на ваших |
| I. | вашим | вашою | вашим | вашими |

**Declining Proper Names.** The names of persons and places change their spelling according to the way they are used in a sentence. It may be difficult to recognize the various forms of a name that changes internally. Here, for example, are the different spellings for the city Lviv in its case inflections:

| | |
|---|---|
| Nominative | Це **Львів**. **Львів** – прекрасне місто. |
| | This is Lviv. Lviv is a beautiful city. |
| | tseh l'veev. l'veev yeh preh-KRAHS-neh |
| | MEES-to |
| Genitive | Мій двоюрідний брат зі **Львова**. |
| | My cousin is from Lviv. |
| | meeў dvo-YU-reed-nihў braht zee L'VO-vah |
| | Він має карту **Львова**. |
| | He has a map of Lviv. |
| | veen MAH-yeh KAHR-too L'VO-vah |
| Dative | **Львову** майже 800 років. |
| | Lviv is almost 800 years old. |
| | (Literally, "To Lviv are almost 800 years.") |
| | L'VO-voo MAHЎ-zheh vee-seem-SOT RO-keev |
| Accusative | Я дуже люблю **Львів**. |
| | I like Lviv very much. |
| | ya DOO-zheh LYU-blyu l'veev |
| Instrumental | Я пишаюсь **Львовом**. |
| | I'm proud of Lviv. |
| | ya pih-SHAH-yus' L'VO-vom |
| Locative | У **Львові** багато чудових вулиць. |
| | In Lviv there are many beautiful streets. |
| | oo L'VO-vee bah-HAH-to choo-DO-vikh VOO-lihts' |

## Verbs

The infinitive form of Ukrainian verbs ends in - *ти*. Verbs are conjugated, that is, their endings change according to the gender and number of the subject of the sentence. There are three tenses: present, past, and future. Here are some common verbs conjugated in the present tense:

| Person | мати<br>(to have) | хотіти<br>(to want) | робити<br>(to do, to make) |
|---|---|---|---|
| я | маю (I have) | хочу | роблю |
| ти | маєш (you have, *s.*) | хочеш | робиш |
| він, вона, воно | має (he, she, it has) | хоче | робить |
| ми | маємо (we have, *pl.*) | хочемо | робимо |
| ви | маєте (you have) | хочете | робите |
| вони | мають (they have) | хочуть | роблять |

**"To be."** The present tense of the verb to be (бути) is **є** for all persons, singular and plural. It's usually not expressed in Ukrainian.

> Я [є] голодний (голодна, *f.*)     I am hungry.
> Хто [є] там?     Who is there?

The past and future tenses of the verb "to be" are expressed:

| | | |
|---|---|---|
| *Past:* | Я (ти) (він) був. (*m. sing.*) | I (you, *s.*) (he) was/were. |
| | Я (ти) (вона) була. (*f. sing.*) | I (you, *s.*) (she) was/were. |
| | Воно було. | It was. |
| | Ми (ви) (вони) були. | We (you, *pl.*) (they) were. |
| *Future:* | Я буду. | I will be. |
| | Ти будеш. | You (*s.*) will be. |
| | Він, (вона) (воно) буде. | He (she) (it) will be. |
| | Ми будемо. | We will be. |
| | Ви будете. | You (*pl.*) will be. |
| | Вони будуть. | They will be. |

**Past Tense.** The past tense is formed from the infinitive by dropping the ending *-ти* and adding the appropriate endings to the stem: *-в* for the masculine singular; *-ла* for the feminine singular; *-ло* for the neuter singular; and *-ли* for plural in all genders.

> думати (to think): думав  He was thinking.
> думала  She was thinking.
> думали  We were thinking.

**Aspects.** Almost every verb in Ukrainian has two different forms, called aspects. The imperfective aspect is used when expressing continuous, repeated, or uncompleted action. The perfective aspect is used when expressing a limited, isolated, or completed action. Typically, the perfective is formed by adding a prefix to the imperfective form. Almost all verbs have an imperfective infinitive (always given first in glossaries) and one or more perfective variations that express more specific or qualifying action:

| | |
|---|---|
| бачити, imp. (to see) | побачити, perf. (to catch sight of) |
| говорити, imp. (to talk) | поговорити, perf. (to have a talk) |
| питати, imp. (to be asking) | спитати, perf. (to ask once) |

When expressing the present tense, the imperfective aspect is used.

**Future Tense**. There are two ways to express the future tense in Ukrainian. For actions that are continuous or incomplete, combine the proper form of the verb "to be" with the infinitive of the imperfective verb:

| | |
|---|---|
| Я буду іти. | I'll be going. |
| Ми будемо це читати. | We'll be reading it. |

To express an action that will be completed in the future, use the present tense of the perfective aspect of the verb:

| | |
|---|---|
| піти:  Я піду. | I'll go. |
| прочитати:  Ми це прочитаємо. | We'll read it through. |

### Essential Phrases: The Most Basic Words

| | | |
|---|---|---|
| Yes | Так | tahk |
| No | Ні | nee͡ |
| Maybe | Можливо | moz͡h-LIH-vo |
| Please | Будь ласка | bood' LAHS-kah |
| | *or* Прошу | PRO-shoo |

*In the Lviv region, прошу is more common, while будь ласка is used in eastern Ukraine. Both will be understood everywhere.*

| | | |
|---|---|---|
| Thank you. | Дякую. | DYA-koo-yu |
| Thank you very much. | Дуже дякую. | |
| | DOO-z͡heh DYA-koo-yu | |
| Not at all. | Нема за що. | |
| | neh-MAH  zah  shcho | |

| Excuse me. | Перепрошую. | |
| | peh-reh-PRO-shoo-yu | |
| | *or* Вибачте | vih-BAHCH-teh |

*Перепрошую is more common in the Lviv region, while вибачте is used everywhere.*

| I can. | Я можу. | ya MO-zhoo |
| I can't. | Я не можу. | ya neh MO-zhoo |

## This, That, These, Those

| It is / this is / these are / those are | Це … | tseh |
| It isn't / this isn't / these aren't … | Це не … | tseh neh |
| Is it …? | Чи це …? | chih tseh |
| That is … | То є … | to yeh |
| That isn't … | То не є … | to neh yeh |
| There isn't/aren't … | Нема … | neh-MAH |
| Here it is. | Ось тут. | os' TOOT |
| There it is. | Ось там. | os' TAHM |

## Questions

| Who? | Хто? | khto |
| Which? | Який? (яка, яке) | yah-KIHY̌ (yah-KAH, yah-KEH) |
| Where? (place) | Де? | deh |
| Where? (direction) | Куди? | koo-DIH |
| Where is…? | Де є…? | deh yeh |
| When? | Коли? | ko-LIH |
| Why? | Чому? | cho-MOO |
| What? | Що? | shcho |
| What's that? | Що це? | shcho tseh |
| What do you call this? | Як ви це називаєте? | yak vih tseh nah-zih-VAH-yeh-teh |
| How? | Як? | yak |
| How much/many? | Скільки? | SKEEL'-kih |
| How long? (time) | Як довго? | yak DOV-ho |
| How far is it? | Як далеко? | yak dah-LEH-ko |

| | |
|---|---|
| What time is it? | Котра година? |
| | kot-RAH  ho-DIH-nah |
| Where can I buy …? | Де можна купити…? |
| | deh  MOZH-nah  koo-PIH-tih |
| Where can I find …? | Де можна знайти…? |
| | deh  MOZH-nah  ZNAHY-tih |
| Where's a telephone? | Де телефон?          deh  TEH-leh-fon |
| From where can I phone? | Звідки я можу подзвонити? |
| | ZVEED-kih  ya MO-zhoo pod-zvo-NIH-tih |
| Where can I buy an | Де можна купити англійські газети? |
| English language | deh  MOZH-nah  koo-PIH-tih |
| newspaper? | ahn-HLEEY-s'kee  hah-ZEH-tih |

## Want and Need

| | | |
|---|---|---|
| I want … | Я хочу … | ya  KHO-choo |
| I'd like … | Я б (хотів, *m.*) (хотіла, *f.*) … | |
| | ya  b  (kho-TEEV)  (kho-TEE-lah) | |
| We'd like … | Ми б хотіли … | mih  b kho-TEE-lih |
| What do you want? | Що ви хочете? | |
| | shcho  vih  KHO-cheh-teh | |
| I need … | Мені потрібно … | |
| | meh-NEE  po-TREEB-no | |
| We need … | Нам потрібно … | |
| | nahm  po-TREEB-no | |
| to be … | бути … | BOO-tih |
| to go … | іти … | EE-TIH |
| to have … | мати … | MAH-tih |
| I'm hungry. | Я хочу їсти. | |
| (I want to eat.) | ya  KHO-choo  YEES-tih | |
| I'm thirsty. | Я хочу пити. | |
| (I want to drink.) | ya  KHO-choo  PIH-tih | |
| I'm looking for … | Я шукаю … | ya  shoo-KAH-yu |

| | | |
|---|---|---|
| I can't find my way to … | Я не можу знайти дороги до … | |
| | ya neh  MO-zhoo  ZNAHЎ-tih do-RO-hih do | |
| It's important. | Це важливо. | tseh  vahzh-LIH-vo |
| It's urgent! | Це терміново! | |
| | tseh  tehr-mee-NO-vo | |
| It's impossible. | неможна | neh-MOZH-nah |
| Hurry up! | Поспішаймо! | |
| | pos-pee-SHAHЎ-mo | |
| Quickly. | Швидко. | SHVIHD-ko |
| It's dangerous. | Це небезпечно. | |
| | tseh  neh-behz-PEHCH-no | |
| Watch out! | Обережно! | o-beh-REHZH-no |

## Requests

| | | |
|---|---|---|
| May I, is it possible? | 1. Можна? | MOZH-nah |
| | 2. Чи можна мені? | chih  MOZH-nah meh-NEE |
| May I have …? | Можна мені мати …? | MOZH-nah  meh-NEE MAH-tih |
| May we have …? | Чи можна нам мати …? | chih  MOZH-nah nahm MAH-tih |
| Please tell me … | Прошу мені сказати … | PRO-shoo  meh-NEE skah-ZAH-tih |
| Please show me … | Прошу мені показати … | PRO-shoo  meh-NEE po-kah-ZAH-tih |
| Please help me. | Прошу мені допомогти. | PRO-shoo  meh-NEE do-po-mo-HTIH |
| Please give me … | Прошу мені дати … | PRO-shoo  meh-NEE DAH-tih |
| Please bring me … | Прошу мені принести … | PRO-shoo  meh-NEE prih-NEHS-tih |

## Size and Quantity

| | | |
|---|---|---|
| big | великий | veh-LIH-kihў |
| little | малий | mah-LIHЎ |
| a little bit | трохи | TRO-khih |
| a few (small quantity) | мало | MAH-lo |
| some | декілька | DEH-keel'-kah |
| much, many, a lot | багато | bah-HAH-toh |
| how much/how many | скільки | SKEEL'-kih |
| so much/so many | стільки | STEEL'-kih |
| more than | більше | BEEL'-sheh |
| less than | менше | MEN-sheh |
| enough | досить | DO-siht' |
| too much | забагато | zah-bah-HAH-to |
| each, every | кожний | KOZH-nihў |

## Emergency Phrases

| | | |
|---|---|---|
| HELP! | Допоможіть! | do-po-mo-ZHEET' |
| STOP THIEF! | зупиніть злодія! | zoo-PIH-neet' ZLO-dee-ya |
| WATCH OUT! | Обережно! | o-beh-REHZH-no |
| POLICE! | Міліція! | mee-LEE-tsee-ya |
| FIRE! | Пожар! | po-ZHAHR |

*While the Ukrainian word for fire, пожежа (po-ZHE-zhah), is used in normal conversation, in times of emergency, most Ukrainians will use the Russian word пожар.*

# CHAPTER 4.
# ARRIVAL AND DEPARTURE

*Ukrainian Proverb*: Тихше їдеш, далі будеш.
TIHKH-sheh YEE-dehsh DAH-lee BOO-dehsh
*The quieter you go, the farther you'll get.*

Getting in and out of Ukraine continues to become easier with increasing modernization of air and rail transportation and facilities. Boryspil Airport in Kyiv is modern, efficient and staffed with English-speaking customs officers. Airports in other cities are less modern with less English spoken, and check-in and baggage handling requires some patience.

**Passport control**    Паспортний контроль
PAHS-port-nihў kon-TROL'

On the plane or immediately upon arrival, you'll receive an immigration form that asks for your flight number and basic information in your passport. Present this form to the passport control officer, who will return part of it to you and check your passport and visa.

Here's my passport/my visa.   Ось мій паспорт/моя віза.
os' meeў PAHS-port / mo-YA VEE-zah

Here are some questions you may be asked:

| *What is the purpose of your visit?* | Яка ціль вашого приїзду? | |
|---|---|---|
| | ya-KAH tseel' VAH-sho-ho prih-YEEZ-doo | |
| Business. | Бізнес. | BEEZ-nehs |
| Tourist. | Турист. | too-RIHST |
| In transit to … | Проїздом до … | pro-YEEZ-dom do… |
| To visit relatives. | Відвідати родичів. | veed-VEE-dah-tih RO-dih-cheev |
| A conference. | На конференцію. | |
| | nah kon-feh-REHN-tsee-yu | |
| To study at … university. | Навчатись в … університеті. | |
| | nahv-CHAH-tihs' v… oo-nee-vehr-sih-THE-tee | |

| *Your passport, please.* | Ваш паспорт будь ласка. |
| | vash PAHS-port bood' LAHS-keh |
| *How long will you stay* | Як довго ви будете на Україні? |
| *in Ukraine?* | yahk DOV-ho vih BOO-deh-teh nah |
| | oo-krah-YEE-nee |

| One day. | Один день. | o-DIHN dehn' |
| One week. | Один тиждень. | o-DIHN TIHZ͡H-den' |
| One month. | Один місяць | o-DIHN MEE-syats' |
| One year. | Один рік. | o-DIHN reek |
| Several days | Декілька днів | DEH-keel-kah dneev |
| (weeks) | (тижднів) | (TIHZ͡HD-neev) |
| (months) | (місяців) | (MEE-syah-tseev) |

| **Baggage** | Багаж | bah-HAHZ͡H |

Most baggage arrives with the passengers. If you come in ahead of yours, there's a small room in the luggage claim area at Boryspil Airport staffed by several clerks who'll ask you about the contents of the missing luggage and give you a report form to fill out. When the luggage arrives it'll be delivered to your address.

Where do I claim my baggage?
  Де я можу отримати мій багаж?
  deh ya MO-z͡hoo ot-RIH-mah-tih meeў bah-HAHZ͡H
My flight number is …     Номер мого рейсу є …
  NO-mehr MO-ho REHŸ-soo yeh
Where can I get a luggage cart?
  Де я можу взяти возик для багажу?
  deh ya MO-z͡hoo BZYA-tih vo-ZIHK dlya
  bah-HAH-z͡hoo
I didn't get     Я не (отримав, *m.*) (отримала, *f.*) мого багажу!
my luggage!    ya neh (ot-RIH-mahv) (ot-RIH-mah-lah) MO-ho
  bah-hah-Z͡HOO
Where can I report missing luggage?
  Де я можу заявити про загубленний багаж?
  deh ya MO-z͡hoo zah-ya-VIH-tih proh
  zah-HOO-blehn-nihў bah-HAZ͡H

**Customs**   митний контроль
              MIHT-nihў kon-TROL'

**Declaration of Personal Items.** To expedite entry, travelers to Ukraine self-report whether they have something to declare. At the airport, list the goods and cash you must declare according to the signs posted in English. If you have nothing to declare, proceed to the green customs corridor or **green line**. You will not have to fill out a form and will be asked only a few simple questions by a pleasant customs officer. If your cash and valuables exceed the posted limits or if you're carrying certain items, pick up a declaration form in the luggage claim area after you've gone though passport control. List on the form only what you have that exceeds the limits and proceed to the **red line**. For example, you're permitted to carry up to US$10,000, but must declare the amount of cash exceeding US$1,000. You must also declare personal jewelry worth more than US$240; more than 1 liter of hard liquor, 2 liters wine; 10 liters beer, or 200 cigarettes, as well as any prohibited items, such as explosives and weapons (except those officially approved by Ukrainian authorities), drugs, artwork, antiques, and luggage sent separately. The red line moves slower than the green line because more questions are asked, customs officers may check your luggage, and duty is collected on expensive gifts you're carrying. Save any paperwork you're given, as you'll need to present it when departing.

**Customs Duty.** The list of items subject to duty is huge, complicated, and continually changing. Generally, you're allowed to carry in US$200 worth of gifts duty-free or a single item worth up to US$300. Anything above that is subject to a fee of 20 percent. Specific consumer items, such as electronics and furs, are subject to fees ranging from 20 to 30 percent of their value. Some items, such as chocolates or liquors, are subject to much higher duties. However, since Ukraine's distilleries and candy factories produce top-notch products and the shops are stocked with fine food, drink, and gift items from all over Europe at reasonable prices, you'll save money by buying the high-duty gifts you intend to give to your Ukrainian friends in Ukraine.

Certain consumer items have a designated value, regardless of what you actually paid. For example, 21-inch TV sets are valued at US$500. The duty on TVs and computers is 20 percent, with used ones assessed at their price when new, not at their market value. So if you want to donate a used computer to an associate in Ukraine, you may have to pay more than it's worth to get it though customs, and may opt to buy one in Kyiv.

Goods, property, and equipment intended for commercial use are also subject to duty, as are medical supplies, unless you've obtained a humanitarian aid permit in advance.

Here's my declaration form. Ось моя декларація.
os' mo-YA deh-klah-RAH-tsee-ya
Where can I get a declaration form in English?
Де я можу отримати бланк декларації по-англійськи?
deh ya MO-zhoo ot-RIH-mah-tih blahnk
deh-klah-RAH-tsee-yee po-ahn-HLEEY̆-s'kih

Here's my baggage. Ось мій багаж.
os' meey̆ bah-HAHZH

You may be asked:

| *Do you have* | Чи ви маєте щось об'явити? | |
| *anything to declare?* | chih vih MAH-yeh-teh shchos' ob'-ya-VIH-tih | |

| Jewelry. | Ювелірні вироби. | yu-veh-LEER-nee VIH-ro-bih |
| A necklace. | Намисто. | nah-MIHS-to |
| A ring. | Перстень | PEHR-stehn' |
| It's gold. | Це золото. | tseh ZO-lo-to |
| It's silver. | Це срібло. | tseh SREEB-lo |
| It's a diamond. | Це діамант. | tseh dee-ah-MAHNT |
| A camcorder. | Відеокамера. | vee-deh-o-KAH-meh-rah |
| A camera with lenses. | Фотоапарат з об'єктивами. | fo-to-ah-pah-RAHT z ob'yehk-TIH-vah-mih |
| A digital camera. | цифрова камера | tsihf-ro-VA KAH-meh-rah |
| A computer. | Комп'ютер. | kom-P'YU-tehr |
| Dollars. | Долари. | do-LAH-rih |
| Pounds. | фунти. | FOON-tih |
| Money. | Гроші. | HROH-shee |
| … bottles of whisky. | … пляшка віскі. | PLYA-shka VEES-kee |
| … packages of cigarettes | … пачка цигарок. | PAHCH-kah tsih-HAH-rok |

This is for personal use.
Це для особистого користування.
tseh dlya o-so-BIHS-to-ho ko-rihs-too-VAHN-nya

| | | |
|---|---|---|
| Where's the restroom? | Де туалет? | deh too-ah-LEHT |

Where can I find a porter?

Де я можу знайти носильщика (*or* носильника)?
deh ya MO-zhoo znahy̆-TIH no-SIHL'-shchih-kah
(*or* no-SIHL'-nih-kah)

| | | |
|---|---|---|
| PORTER! | НОСИЛЬЩИК! | no-SIHL'-shchihk |
| Please take my baggage. | Прошу взяти мій багаж. PRO-shoo BZYA-tih meey̆ bah-HAHZH | |
| I need to go to the … | Мені треба до … meh-NEE TREH-bah do | |
| taxi stop | таксі | tahk-SEE |
| train station | поїзду | PO-yeez-doo |
| bus station | автобусу | ahv-TO-boo-soo |
| exit | виходу | VIH-kho-doo |

How much do I owe you?

Скільки мені треба заплатити вам?
SKEEL'-kih meh-NEE TREH-bah zah-plah-TIH-tih vahm

**Ukrainian Medical Insurance.** In September 2001 the Ukrainian government reversed its policy of requiring foreigners to purchase at border entry points medical insurance covering emergency treatment at state hospitals. According to the amended degree, foreigners who are temporarily staying in the country are required to have insurance policies that guarantee the payment for any medical aid provided to them. Ukrainian insurance can be purchased at points where visas are processed or at state border crossing locations, but because most Westerners are already covered, the insurance counter maintains a low profile in Boryspil Airport. At less sophisticated border entry points, over-zealous border guards may try to sell insurance, and officials at various visa and registration offices (VVIR) may direct foreign travelers who request visa extensions to local insurance companies.

The insurance may make it easier to secure an ambulance should you need one, but most Westerners in need of medical care opt for private clinics (which are not covered by Ukrainian insurance) or carry overseas policies that include evacuation in case of illness. Be advised that you're within your rights to refuse Ukrainian health insurance if you're already covered.

**Leaving Ukraine.** Travelers tend to be distrustful of foreign customs and assume they'll be treated harshly, but most difficulties result from ignorance of regulations. Items forbidden to take out of Ukraine are those of great artistic, cultural, or historical value. These may include paintings, sculptures, engravings, crystal, ceramics, precious and semiprecious stones, relics, furniture, coins, books, and musical instruments. Antique icons are no longer allowed out of Ukraine. And it almost goes without saying that you are not allowed to export arms, ammunition, narcotics, toxic or radioactive materials.

If you buy an original work of art, such as a new icon, ask the artist or store that sold it for a signed receipt and a certificate affirming that it has no significant historical value. If you happen to buy a valuable piece of art from a source that's not authorized to sell it, or if you have doubts about exporting an item you've bought, take it to the Ministry of Culture office. Your purchase will be inspected, you'll be issued an export permit, and duties will be assessed based on value. In Kyiv, the Ministry of Culture is at 19 Ivan Franko Street (вулиця Івана франка, *vulytsya Ivana Franka*). In Lviv, a branch of the Ministry of Culture is in the city hall building in Market Square (площа Ринок, *ploshcha Rynok*) in the city center.

In addition to artworks and antiques, you'll need permission to export collections of fine, applied, or folk art, archeological and numismatic items, war medals, samovars, valuable music instruments, gold, silver, hand-woven carpets, manuscripts, books published before 1966, and furniture made before 1945. There is an export tax on these.

There's virtually no limit to the amount of souvenirs and consumer goods you can take out, so long as it doesn't appear that the items are for resale abroad. And you should not have to pay duty on your purchases so long as you exchanged your money at an authorized currency exchange. *Be sure to save all records of currency exchange, shopping receipts, and credit card receipts* in the unlikely event that you need to show that your total purchases are not worth more than the amount of money you declared upon entry. If you've made a gift of a substantial amount of cash or an expensive item that you declared upon entering Ukraine, it's a good idea to have a written receipt from the person you've given it to, to prevent any problems when leaving the country.

Generally Ukrainian customs officers at the airport in Kyiv are very professional, and wave through exiting green line tourists while checking more carefully the red-line individuals and anyone arousing suspicion. In more remote areas, there's less professionalism and customs workers may attempt to use their positions for personal gain. A worker, for example, might claim that an inexpensive souvenir is an antique and slap a large duty on it, which, of course, he or she has no intention of turning in to the government. While it's easier not to be intimidated if you're fluent in Ukrainian, you can nonetheless resist this unscrupulous practice by calmly refusing to give in. If you should find yourself in one of these situations, produce your receipt for the item in question, proving that it isn't as valuable as the custom official claims.

Here is my receipt for this. Ось мій чек. os' meeў chehk

If he or she persists, ask a receipt for the duty you paid:

I want a receipt for this. Я хочу чек. ya KHO-choo chehk

As a last resort, you might try the following phrase:

I want to contact the American consulate.
Я хочу звіязатись з Американським консульством.
ya KHO-choo zvee-ya-ZAH-tihs' z ah-meh-rih-KAHNS'-kihm KON-sool'st-vom

If you continue to be held at customs, and it appears you won't get your acquisition through without paying a fee you think is unreasonable, you may want to leave it with the person who brought you to the airport and retrieve it another time.

When shopping in Ukraine, it's a good idea also to keep in mind how much your home country will allow you to import. U.S. Customs, for example, allows duty free US$400 worth of imports, including both purchases and gifts. Only 1 liter of alcohol can enter duty-free, but when faced with the opportunity to buy inexpensive fine cognac in Ukraine, travelers may opt to pay a small import duty at home. Also, remember that travelers aren't allowed to bring certain foods — meat, for example — into the U.S. from abroad. Check the current USDA list of food products prohibited from entry on the Web site www.aphis.usda.gov/travel/.

**Money** Гроші HRO-shee

Soon after independence in 1991, Ukraine decided to call its currency hryvnya, after various examples of silver coins used in the ancient Kyivan Rus state. It was also the currency during the brief independence in 1918. The unstable economic situation, however, prompted the government to place the hryvnya on hold and adopt a series of rationing coupons, called *karbovantsi* (карбованці) as the official Ukrainian currency. In September 1996, inflation stabilized enough for the government to release the hryvnya Banknotes come in denominations of 1, 2, 5, 10, 20, 50, and 100 and there are also coins in denominations of 1, 2, and 5 hryvni. Coins, called *kopiyky*, come in 1, 2, 5, 10, 25, and 50-kopiyky denominations. One hundred kopiyky equals one hryvnya.

Ukraine is still largely a cash economy. Credit cards are accepted in the better hotels, Western-style restaurants, and stores in Kyiv and other larger cities. American Express, MasterCard, and Visa are the most commonly accepted cards. Traveler's checks are seldom accepted, but banks will cash them. There is also a surcharge for cash advances on a credit card. ATMs can be found in city centers in businesses patronized by Westerners. If you ask for a large sum, you'll probably receive it in bigger dominations than can be useful in normal business transactions. It's assumed that Westerners may be carrying large amounts of Western currency for business or to give away; be sure to wear a money belt under your clothes.

| **Currency Exchange** | Обмін Валют | OB-meen vah-LYUT |
|---|---|---|
| Ukrainian Proverb: | Хто міняє, той і має. | |
| | khto mee-NYA-yeh toў ee MAH-yeh | |
| | *Who changes money, has it.* | |

Obviously, someone other than you is going to profit every time you exchange money. However, businesses are prohibited from accepting foreign currency, so you will no longer get very far without changing your money. How much money you bring depends for the most part on your personal habits and choices. Your itinerary is also a big factor. A day in Kyiv can be expensive, with the prices of hotels and restaurants higher than comparable facilities in the U.S. You can find bargains, but they may be at lower standards or farther from the central city than you want. In Kyiv you can use a credit card in most hotels and Western-style restaurants. Hotels and eating establishments in small cities are much cheaper, but will probably require payment in cash. You'll need to pay for entertainment and domestic travel, whether by air or rail, with cash, but you can expect these to be quite inexpensive.

**Currency Exchange Kiosks.** There are numerous exchange kiosks (labeled Обмін Валют) located throughout cities as well as exchange counters in banks, airports, hotels, and stores. The exchange rate will be pretty much the same at all legal counters. Before you leave home, go to the Internet Currency Converter at www.uazone.net/Hryvnia/convert.html to check the exchange rate. Sometimes the official exchange counters don't have adequate hryvni to make the transaction, especially near the end of the business day. Watch that you don't exchange more than you can spend; you're not allowed to take more than 85 hryvni out of the country and it may be impossible to find a place to exchange it for dollars before your departure.

Where can I change some money?
Де можна поміняти гроші?
deh MOZH-nah po-mee-NYA-tih HRO-shee?

Can you cash this traveler's check?
Чи ви можете обміняти цей дорожній чек на гроші?
chih vih MO-zheh-teh ob-meen-NYA-tih tseў
do-ROZH-neeў chehk nah HRO-shee

Can you change (Canadian) dollars (pounds) (Euros)?
Чи ви можете поміняти (Канадські) долари (Фунти) (євро)?
chih vih MO-zheh-teh po-mee-NYA-tih
(kah-NAHDS'-kee) do-LAH-rih (FOON-tih) (YEHV-ro)

Can you give me bigger/smaller bills?
Прошу, дати мені в більших/менших коп'юрах?
PRO-shoo DAH-tih meh-NEE v BEEL'-shihkh/MEHN-shihkh
ko-P'YU-rahkh

Can you make change for this? [showing bill]
Чи ви можете розміняти це?
chih vih MO-zheh-teh roz-mee-HYsA-tih tseh

I think you made a mistake.
Я думаю що ви помилились.
ya DOO-mah-yu shcho vih po-mih-LIH-lihs'

## Banks      Банки      BAHN-kih

In 1991 the old state-owned banks became public and were restructured into a vast network of branches throughout the country. There are now thousands of banks in Ukraine, many occupying magnificent new buildings, but the majority do not provide the services of banks in Western Europe, such as transferring money from your bank back home. More advanced banking services can be found in the main branch of a bank in a larger city. All banks will change your money into hryvni. Banking hours are Monday through Friday from 9 a.m. to 1 p.m.

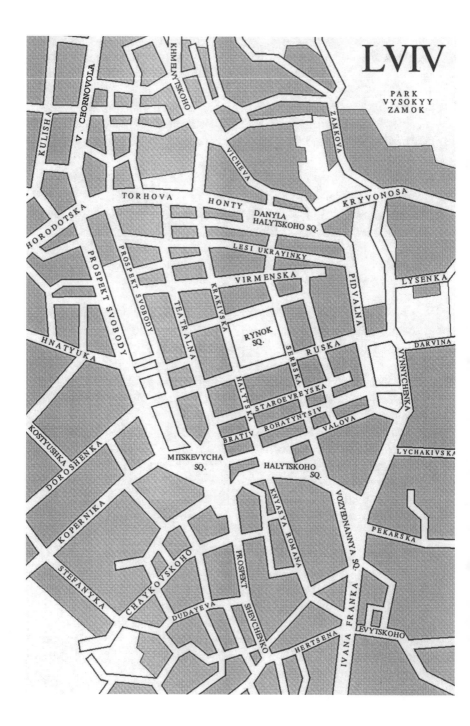

# CHAPTER 5.
# LVIV: "CAPITAL" OF WESTERN UKRAINE

ЛЬВІВ      l'veev

Imagine a couple who were born in Austria, married and raised their children in Poland, lived in Germany, died in the Soviet Union, and are buried in Ukraine. Yet during their entire lifetime, they never moved. That could have happened in Lviv, a fascinating city that has changed hands many times throughout its long history. Just in the last hundred years, it's also been known as Lemberg, Lwow, and L'vov.

**Name.** The Ukrainian name for the city Lviv ( Львів) literally means "of Lev." Lev, or Leo, was the son of Danylo, the city's founder. An enduring tribute to Lev are the numerous lions depicted in stone and metal throughout the city, while a new monument depicting Danylo on his horse is on ploshcha Halytska, facing the George Hotel.

**Location.** Sometimes referred to as the "Capital of Western Ukraine," Lviv is close to the Polish border, only some 73 km (45 miles) away. It's about 250 km (155 miles) from Chop, an access point from Slovakia and Hungary on the southwestern border. Lviv is the hub of the main roads that extend to major Ukrainian cities. It's 575 km (450 miles) from Lviv to Kyiv; to Ivano-Frankivsk, 135 km (85 miles); to Uzhhorod, 275 km (170 miles); to Chernivtsi, 275 km (170 miles); to Lutsk, 150 km (95 miles).

**Population.** Lviv has about 757,000 residents. About 90 percent are ethnic Ukrainians, with a diverse assortment of other ethnic groups. This represents a radical change from the ethnic composition before World War II, when Poles made up 50 percent of the city, Jews constituted over 30 percent, and Ukrainians less than 20 percent. Earlier in its history, however, Lviv was considered a second Babylon, with Armenians, Greeks, Jews, Italians, Scots, Hungarians, Czechs, Germans, Russians, Tatars, Saracens, and Karaims represented. Throughout the history of this cosmopolitan city, its various ethnic groups have, for the most part, lived together harmoniously. The city's architecture and culture show diverse influences, but despite shifting populations and foreign rule, the city has maintained a Ukrainian consciousness and shows a strong nationalistic fervor.

**Climate.** The climate is moderate continental. The average temperature in January is –4°C (24.6°F); June and July average 18°C (64.9°F). While winter or summer temperatures are never extreme, humidity that may cause slight discomfort. On average, Lviv has 66 cloudy days per year. December is the cloudiest month and August the clearest. The annual rainfall is about 26 inches, ranging from a January average of only one inch of precipitation to four inches in December.

**Business and Industry.** With 11 institutions of higher education, Lviv has the ambience of a college town. It has many publishing houses, and manufacturing includes buses, radios and televisions, machinery, and food products. *Svitoch*, t he candy factory, the *Lvivsky Pyvo* brewery, and a joint distillery enterprise, the Canadian-Ukrainian Seagram's, are located in Lviv.


## History

The first documented reference to Lviv was in a 1256 chronicle. Part of Halytsya (Galicia)-Volyn, a western principality of Kyivan Rus, Lviv was founded by Danylo, a crowned prince from the Rurikovych dynasty who ruled Halytsya (Galicia)-Volyn. Its strategic position as a stop on east-west trade routes and Carpathian passes resulted in an influx of diverse cultural influences and a cosmopolitan ambience, but also made it vulnerable to siege.

The onslaught of invaders started in the early part of the 14th century when the ruler Dmytro Detko and his forces successfully repulsed the troops of Polish King Kasimir. Soon, however, Lviv fell under Polish domination. A major consequence of this European influence was the establishment in 1596 of the Uniate Church. Also known as the Ukrainian Greek Catholic Church, the church was a compromise between Polish Roman Catholicismand Ukrainian Orthodoxy: the Ukrainians acknowledged the supremacy of Rome while maintaining the Orthodox Byzantine form of worship.

In 1772 the First Partition of Poland brought eastern Poland and western Ukraine (a region called Galicia) under the jurisdiction of the Austro-Hungarian Empire. Lviv became the administrative center of a newly created province dominated by Poles. With the collapse of the Hapsburg Empire at the end of World War I, a newly formed Ukrainian national *rada* (council) proclaimed an independent government known variously as Ruthenia, West Ukraine, or East Galicia. Lviv was the seat of this new government. Shortly thereafter, however, Polish troops occupied Lviv and returned western Ukraine to Polish rule. The 1939 German-Soviet nonaggression agreement (the Molotov-Ribbentrop Pact) transferred most of western Ukraine from Poland to the U.S.S.R. This transfer – against the will of its residents – marked the first time in its long history that Lviv was ruled by Moscow. The take over of the Red Army put a stop to Ukrainian cultural and political activity and ushered in a climate of severe repression, including mass arrests and executions. In 1941, Lviv was occupied by Germany and much of its large Jewish population was wiped out.

After the Nazis' retreat in 1944, Soviet forces regained Lviv and re-instituted their campaign of repression against the nationalistic Ukrainian people. Opposition to Soviet totalitarianism festered in western Ukraine, particularly in Lviv, and grew into dissident movements that were eventually instrumental in winning independence.

## Sightseeing

With its narrow cobblestone streets and its assortment of western architectural styles – Renaissance, Baroque, Rococo, and Neoclassical – that came with its various rulers, Lviv has an eclectic old European ambience. Although the city's 14th and 15th century Gothic architecture was destroyed by fire in 1527, it has the distinction of being the only Ukrainian city with original Renaissance structures. From the 18th to the 20th centuries, the city supported architects and sculptors of many nationalities, who left a fantastic legacy of work. Lviv's architectural heritage has been more fortunate than that of other Ukrainian cities. During World War II there was no fighting in its streets; the Nazis destroyed a few historic synagogues, but the Soviets arrived later than in other parts of Ukraine and did not bother to raze landmarks and initiate monumental building projects such as those that had disfigured Kyiv and other eastern cities.

**Tourism**. Lviv, a city of great beauty and charm, is on UNESCO's World Heritage List. Its central part, designated a national architectural preserve in the mid-1970s, is small enough to cover on foot. Even with a correct address and a good street map, however, finding the building you want is a challenge because of the ancient street layout. In the last few years, many streets and buildings have been restored to their original beauty, and the city

– always rich in cultural and intellectual life – experienced a cultural renaissance, with lively theater, music, art, and coffeehouse scenes. Shopping is good, with a blend of big-name brands, Western European goods, and Ukrainian-made items. Shopkeepers are friendly and helpful and there's little waiting in line. Prices for dining out and lodging are cheaper than in other large Ukrainian cities, and there's an abundance of stylish inexpensive restaurants serving delicious food. The Ukrainian language is universally spoken; Russian is usually understood although not encouraged, and English is beginning to be useful.

Currency exchange counters are throughout the city. Automatic cash machines are located in some hotel lobbies or in businesses that cater to Westerners, and credit cards are accepted in tourist hotels, restaurants and some businesses. Banks in the central area will cash personal checks for a small surcharge, and a few may cash traveler's checks.

Difficulties: The city's water supply is not adequate for its population, and until the problem is solved, water is available 24 hours a day only in limited areas, primarily near the central tourist area. In most residential districts the water flows for two hours in the morning and again in the evening. As in all of Ukraine, you'll need to boil water for 10 minutes before drinking it or buy bottled water. For conservation, electricity may be shut off for several hours each day in certain parts of town.

## The City Center

The main street, **prospekt Svobody** (проспект Свободи), or "Freedom Avenue," stretches 600 meters (about one-third of a mile) from the opera theater south to Mickiewicz Square or *ploshcha Mitskevycha* (площа Міцкевича). At the north end of prospekt Svobody is the **Solomiya Krushelnytska State Academic Theatre of Opera and Ballet**, built as the Lviv Municipal Theater by local architect Zigmunt Gorgolevsky. Before the completion of this masterpiece of neo-Renaissance architecture in 1900, a swampy marsh covered the site, and the river Poltva had to be diverted through a concrete duct directly underneath the building. Typical of the period's Austro-Hungarian Empire, the building's facade is opulently embellished with Corinthian columns, pilasters, cornices, bas-reliefs, and stucco garlands. At the top stand large copper statues representing Poetry, Glory, and Music. The interior is resplendent with beautifully colored marble lining the foyer and composing the wide main staircase. The multitiered auditorium, accommodating 1,800 spectators, is topped by a gilded ceiling with oil paintings. The theater, named after the renowned soprano who often performed, has permanent opera and ballet companies. The ticket office is just inside the main entrance.

Facing the theater is the city's central plaza. It contains a monument to Ukrainian national hero Taras Shevchenko and a 40-foot-high Wave of National Revival stele. Prospekt Svobody continues south, culminating in Mickiewicz Square (площа Міцкевича, *ploshcha Mitskevycha*) with its tall monument erected in 1904 in honor of Polish romantic poet Adam Mickiewicz. The chestnut tree-lined pedestrian walk in the center of the avenue is a popular Lviv gathering place. On Saturdays wedding parties pose for photos in front of the Shevchenko monument, while on evenings and Sunday afternoons families stroll the promenade, children drive little battery-powered cars, and chess players fill the benches.

A few blocks east of prospekt Svobody is ***ploshcha Rynok***, (площа Ринок) or **Market Square**, the heart of the old town area. This charming square was first noted in 1381 in the municipal acts of Lviv as the site of the first city hall. In the Middle Ages, the nobility built their homes here. The area became the trading center of Lviv and remained the commercial hub through the 19th century. The present structures were built during the 16th century to replace Gothic buildings lost in a fire, and were enlarged, restored, and rebuilt throughout the 18th century. The 44 buildings that ring the square, each with its own beauty and historical significance, reflect evolving architectural fashions.

Standing in the square's center is the **Town Hall** (*Ratusha*). The earliest version was built on this site in 1356. Following several reconstructions over the centuries, the present building was built between 1827 and 1835. The tower, rebuilt in 1851, stands 65-meter-high (210-foot), and is open for a panoramic view of the city. Tickets to the top are available in the underground office on the side of the Ratushka that faces the Latin Cathedral. A guide will lead you inside the building and up an elevator to the stairs, which take 15 minutes to climb and are not recommended for those not physically fit. For an extra fee the attendant will show you the mechanism of the 1848 Austrian clock.

Fountains with statutes of Roman deities — Neptune, Adonis, Diana, and Aphrodite — sculpted in 1793 by Hartman Witwer ornament the corners of the square. Ringing the square are historic buildings housing a blend of museums, small restaurants, and interesting shops.

## Monuments to Some Famous Sons

Lviv was home to scores of outstanding architects, artists, writers, musicians, churchmen, and statesmen who gave their names to streets and squares and inspired a wealth of monuments. Here are a few of the most significant:

**Ivan Fedorov**, a 16th-century Russian printer, was forced to flee Moscow in 1564 after he enraged the local clergy by publishing his *Book of the Apostles*, the first printed book in Russia. After arriving in Lviv, Federov established the first permanent printing shop on Ukrainian territory in 1573. The next year he published the first printed book in Ukraine, a new version of *Book of the Apostles,* now on display in the National Museum on Svobody Avenue. In 1583 Federov died and was buried in St. Onuphrius Church, which now functions as the Museum of Ivan Federov. A statue was erected in 1977 on Pidvalna (Підвальна) Street near the small outdoor market for old books and memorabilia in front of the Royal Arsenal building.

**Ivan Franko** (1856–1916), scholar of western Ukraine, is most noted for his poetry, but also wrote fiction, plays, and literary criticism, and translated literary masterpieces from 14 languages into Ukrainian. He spent 40 years in Lviv and is buried in Lychakiv Cemetery. The **Ivan Franko Literary Memorial Museum** at 152 Ivano Franko Street (вулиця Івана Франка, *vulytsya Ivana Franka*), south of Stryiskyy Park, is in the home that Franko built and where he lived his last 14 years. The museum contains manuscripts, photographs, first editions of his printed works, and personal effects. A large monument to Franko was erected in 1964 in a park named after him in the center of Lviv, opposite the city's leading educational institution, the **Ivan Franko Lviv State University**.

**Mykhaylo Hrushevskyy** (1866–1934), the most distinguished Ukrainian historian and a prominent scholar, was elected president of the short-lived Ukrainian National Republic in 1918. In 1994 Ukraine's first modern president, Leonid Kravchuk, unveiled a monument to Hrushevskyy. The monument, depicting a seated Hrushevskyy, is at Hrushevskyy Square, where Drahomanova intersects with prospekt Shevchenka. A Hrushevskyy house-museum is at 154 Ivano Franko Street, (near the Franko Museum) in the home where Hrushevskyy lived in 1902.

**Yahn Mateyko**, born Nykyfor Dvorniak, was a folk artist and painter who died in 1968. His allegorical painting of the development of science lines the conference room of the main building of the Lviv Polytechnical Institute, 12 Bandera Street (вулиця С. Бандери, *vulytsya S. Bandery*). The street named for Mateyko (вулиця Матейка, *vulytsya Mateyka*) is a short distance east, heading toward the center of town.

**Adam Mickiewicz** (1798–855) was the leading poet of Polish Romanticism and a lifelong advocate of Polish national freedom. His works have had a marked influence on Ukrainian literature, particularly on Taras Shevchenko. Although Mickiewicz had no real association with Lviv, a monument to him erected in 1904 dominates Mickiewicz Square, an area of hotels and shops.

**Ivan Pidkova** (died 1578) was a legendary Ukrainian Kozak who led the struggle for the liberation of Ukraine and Moldova from Turkish domination. Pidkova was captured by Poland, an ally of Turkey, and executed in Market Square in Lviv. To the northwest, in the very center of the city, is **Ivan Pidkova Square**. Reconstruction of the square in 1978 turned up foundations of a medieval poor asylum. A monument to Pidkova, sculpted by Petro Kulyk, was dedicated in 1981.

**Taras Shevchenko.** Ukraine's greatest hero had no actual association with Lviv, but soon after independence, the city rushed to replace the Lenin monument with one of Shevchenko. After some debate on location, a large bronze statue of Shevchenko, financed by the Ukrainian diaspora in Argentina, was sculpted by Andriy and Volodymyr Sukhorsky and erected in 1996 in the pedestrian mall at Svobody Avenue. Although some say that artistic merit was sacrificed in the rush to honor Shevchenko, the monument is frequently honored by groups of schoolchildren commemorating patriotic events. A street and an avenue in the city center are also named for Shevchenko, but neither is adjacent to the monument.

**Vasyl Stefanyk** (1871–1936) was a noted western Ukrainian short-story writer and political activist. The research library of the National Academy of Sciences of Ukraine, one of the largest libraries in Europe, is named for him. A statue of Stefanyk was erected in 1971 in front of the library at 3 Stefanyka (Стефаника) Street, just off Kopernika near the city center.

**Ivan Trush** (1869–1941) was an impressionist painter and artist from the Lviv region who became a master of Ukrainian landscape painting and portraiture. Many of his works are displayed at the **Ivan Trush Memorial Art Museum** in his former residence at 28 Trush Street (вулиця Труша, *vulytsya Trusha*) in a neighborhood of lovely villas on the southwestern edge of the city. His works are also in the National Museum. In 1997 a life-sized sculpture depicting a dapper Trush dressed for a stroll was erected on the square at the crossing of Parkova and Ivano Franko Streets east of Stryysky Park.

## Churches

Lviv's churches reflect centuries of evolving architectural styles as well as the ethnically diverse populations that built them. In the city's early days, many were lost to fires, but for the most part they survived the turmoil of recent centuries. Following Ukrainian independence, a big shift in the use of the churches occurred. Many were restored and reopened, and a major shift in denominations occurred: Roman Catholic churches became Greek Catholic and Russian Orthodox were reborn as Ukrainian Orthodox. A few of the most noteworthy:

**St. George's Cathedral** (Собор Святого Юра, *Sobor Svyatoho Yura)* at *ploshcha Svyatoyurska* (площа Святоюрська), was constructed on a hill west of the city center between 1744 and 1770 to replace a medieval church of the same name. The cathedral is a fine example of Ukrainian Baroque architecture, complete with a turret sculpture of St. George the Dragon Slayer. In 1990, the historical seat of the Ukrainian Greek-Catholic Church, the cathedral reverted – with great pomp and ceremony – to the Ukrainian Catholic faithful from the jurisdiction of the Russian Orthodox Church which had taken it in 1946. The complex contains the Metropolitan's Palace and a courtyard bell tower. In the lower church are crypts containing the remains of Metropolitan Andrey Sheptytsky, the highest-ranking clergyman in all of Europe to speak out against the Nazis, and his successor, Patriarch Yosyf Slipyj, who died in exile in Rome after spending 18 years in a Siberian prison.

The **Latin Cathedral** at 1 Kafedralna (Кафедральна) Square is the popular name for the **Roman Catholic Cathedral of St. Mary** . It was constructed between 1360 and 1479 after Poland gained control of the city. Some of the original Gothic features were later replaced with Baroque architectural elements. It's a functioning Roman Catholic church. **Boyims' Chapel** was added to the southeast corner in 1615. The chapel, originally one of the burial vaults that surrounded the Latin Cathedral, was constructed from local limestone and alabaster for George Boyim, a Lviv patrician. Fresco portraits of Boyim and his wife are on the east wall; on the west are the sculptural reliefs, notably the *Pieta* by Johann Pfister. The exterior facade consists of stone carvings of Biblical themes, including Ss. Peter and Paul and the Passion of Christ. Run by the Lviv Art Gallery, the Chapel is open daily except Monday from 11 a.m. to 4 p.m.

The **Chapel of the Kampians** was added to the north side of the church in 1619. Its interior is black, white, and pink marble, and its exterior is noted for stone carvings depicting Biblical scenes.

The **Armenian Cathedral** (Вірменський собор, *Virmenskyy sobor*) at 7 Virmenska (Вірменська) Street is one of the oldest buildings in the city. Originally constructed between 1363 and 1370, it was the center of the local Armenian community that included a monastery, an archbishop's residence, a nunnery, a printing press, a bank, and a cemetery. The white cut-stone cathedral combines Armenian architecture with the local style; it features three apses and a twelve-sided tent-shaped dome. A Renaissance gallery was added to the south side in 1437, and over the centuries there have been many enlargements and restorations following fires, with extensive renovations in the early 1900s. In 2001, before the visit of Pope John Paul II, the church reopened and now serves Lviv's small Armenian community. The interior artwork ranges from the oldest frescoes in Lviv to 20th-century wall paintings. Of special interest is a 15th-century sculpture depicting St. Thomas with St. Sophia and her daughters. The entrance to the church is on Krakivska Street.

**Transfiguration** (Преображенська, *Preobrazhenska*) Church at 21 Krakivska (Краківська) at the intersection with Lesya Ukrayinka Street is an elegant, white Baroque church typical of 19th century Ukrainian style. The church hasn't changed since completion in 1898 by architect Sylvester Havryshkevych. Its interior is splendid. Decorated by outstanding Ukrainian painters of the late 19th and early 20th centuries, its scores of paintings are lovingly draped with blue-embroidered *rushnyky*, or ceremonial towels. A functioning Ukrainian Greek Catholic Church, it also hosts lovely concerts.

The **Uspenska (Dormition) Church Complex** is three blocks east at 9 Pidvalna (Підвальна) Street at the corner of Ruska (Руська), just east of *ploshcha Rynok*. The church was built for the Dormition Brotherhood at the beginning of the 17th century to replace a wooden church destroyed by fire. The Brotherhood originated in Lviv in the mid-16th century and became the center of Lviv's Orthodox community. Dedicated to promoting education, culture, and publishing, they constructed a stone library, a high school, a publishing house, and an archive. Uspenska Church is one of the finest examples of a harmonious blend of Renaissance architecture with the traditional Ukrainian tripartite wooden church. Built from large white stone blocks, its interior walls are embellished with Tuscan pilasters and Greek Doric stone friezes. Its 17th-century icons and early 20$^{th}$-century stained glass are noteworthy. It's a functioning Ukrainian Autocephalous Orthodox church.

The **Kornyakt Bell Tower** is part of the Uspenska Church complex. From its beginning, this 180-foot tower has dominated Lviv's skyline and served as the architectural symbol of the city. Constructed between 1572 and 1578, it was named after the Greek wine merchant who financed it, Konstantin Kornyakt. The tower was destroyed in 1672 when the city was besieged by the Turkish army. It was rebuilt at the end of the 17th century with an added fourth story ornamented with Baroque features.

Adjoining the west face of the tower, and accessible through a small courtyard, is the three-domed **Three Prelates' Chapel**. A fine example of Renaissance architecture, the chapel was originally constructed between 1578 and 1591 as a small church by Lviv master builder A. Pidlisnyy. It was integrated with the Uspenska Church in the mid-19th century. The chapel's stone portal, with carvings of grapevines and lions, is especially worth seeing, and inside, its painted ceiling depicts bunches of grapes.

**The Dominican Church** at 1 Museyna (Музейна) Square, one of Lviv's most splendid Baroque buildings, is recognizable for its huge green dome. Replacing a nearly 15th-century Dominican church, the structure was designed by Dutch fortifications engineer Jan de Witte and built between 1749 and 1764. Following a fire, it was restored by the sculptor Klemens Fesinger between 1792 and 1798. The interior contains alabaster and marble monuments and tombs embellished with gold statuary. The complex encloses a 16th-century monastery and 1865 bell tower. The church now functions as a Greek Catholic church, the **Church of the Holy Eucharist**, with 9 a.m. and 11 a.m. Sunday services that include choir performances.

It also holds concerts of sacred music. The **Museum of the History of Religion,** occupying the old monastery, contains objects from Christian, Jewish, Buddhist, and Muslim worship. Of special interest are 18th-century Torah scrolls. On exhibit in the basement are gold and silver liturgical jewelry and coins. The museum is open from 10 a.m. until 5 p.m. daily except Thursdays. Phone (0322)72-02-32.

On Bohdan Khmelnytsky Boulevard(бульвар Богдана Хмельницьког*о*, *bulvar Bohdana Khmelnytskoho*) are three of Lviv's oldest churches. **St. Nicholas Church** (Святого Миколая, *Svyatoho Mykolaya*),28 Khmelnytsky, was the first church built in Lviv and is the oldest stone structure in the city. Built by Prince Lev in the 13th century as the family church of the Halychyna princes, the founders of the city, it was designed in the cruciform shape typical of Kyiv-Rus church architecture. The two chapels and the three naves give the church a pleasing pyramidal appearance. Restoration took place following fires in the 17th and 20th centuries.

To the north is the **Church and Monastery of St. Onuphrius** (Святого Онуфрія, *Svyatoho Onufriya*), 36 Khmelnytsky. Constructed in the princely era as a wooden church, it was rebuilt or restored in each subsequent century, becoming a stone church around 1550. In 1574 Ivan Fedorov published the first book in Ukraine in the monastery here; Fedorov's tomb is inside the church. The church is used by the Basilian Order of the Ukrainian Greek Catholic Church.

Continuing north to Number 77 Khmelnytsky, at the foot of Castle Hill, is **St. Paraskeya-Pyatnytsya Church** (Параскева- П'ятниця церква, *Paraskeva-Pyatnytsya tserkva* ). It was first built in the 15th century, financed by Moldovan prince Vasyl Lupul. Several Moldovan rulers are buried in the church. Reconstruction in 1644 gave it a fortress-like look with thick stone walls and small, high windows. The interior is well preserved. The ornately ornamented wooden iconostasis made about 1740 by Lviv craftsmen of the Senkovych workshop is outstanding. The iconostasis consists of 70 icons arranged in six tiers and united by filigree wood carvings.

The **Ensemble of the Bernardine Monastery,** at Soborna Square, was built between1600 and 1630 as a replacement for a 15th-century wooden church. Constructed in the Renaissance style from funds donated to the Bernardine order by a Polish magnate, the architectural ensemble includes a monastery building, a bell tower, and a well with a rotunda. Because the monastery served as a defense outpost, the church is surrounded by massive walls that were integrated into the city wall.

In the 17th century, the ringing of the bells of St. Bernadine's at 6 p.m. signaled the closing of all gates to the city wall. The story is told that once a monk on top of the 38-meter (about 120-foot) tower at 5:55 p.m. spied a Tatar army about to enter the city. He pushed the hand of the clock in the tower forward five minutes so that the bells would ring and the gates would close. To commemorate the city's close call, the clock was kept five minutes fast until Soviet times.

The church's Baroque interior consists of three naves containing 15 gilded wooden altars, wooden sculptures, and frescoes depicting scenes from old Lviv. Today the church functions as the Greek Catholic Church of St. Andrew and also houses the **Central Historical Archives** in Lviv.

**Ss. Peter and Paul Church** (Святого Петра і Павла, *Svyatoho Petra i Pavla),* is at 82 Lychakivska (Личаківська) Street at the corner of Mechnikov. This little jewel of a church was built in 1786 in the Baroque style; the atrium and bell tower were designed by Klemens Fesinger in 1798. The church is decorated from ceiling to floor with white linens embroidered in monochromatic blue nature motifs. The church belongs to the Ukrainian Autocephalous Orthodox Church.

### Museums

Most museums in Lviv, while worthwhile, are not very large and provide a pleasant diversion during a sudden cloudburst. A small fee is charged, with guided tours available at a small additional cost. These are the most significant museums:

The **Lviv Historical Museum** comprises several buildings in the picturesque Market Square. The main holdings are in the building at 24 ploscha Rynok (площа Ринок), which has a facade with interesting stone heads. This collection contains some 270,000 items depicting the history of Lviv beginning in the 13th century and of western Ukraine from the 15th to 18th centuries. At 4 ploscha Rynok is the **Black Stone House,** *Chorna Kamianytsia,* a gem of 16th century Renaissance architecture with exhibits on the struggle of the Ukrainian people for independence. Dominating the square is **Kornyakt's Palace** at 6 ploshcha Rynok, a palazzo built in 1580 for a wealthy Greek merchant. After his death in 1603, it became the property of the father of the future king of Poland, Jan III. To the left of the street entrance is Gothic Hall, a shop selling antique metalwork and jewelry. Don't miss the view from the rear door of the Gothic-ceiling hallway of a lovely courtyard with a three-tiered Italian Renaissance columned arcade. The courtyard, Italian Yard, has a coffee shop and occasional performances of classical music. On exhibit in the museum are jewelry, precious metals objects, and furniture. The exhibit halls are open daily except Wednesdays from 10 a.m. to 5 p.m. in winter and 10 a.m. to 6 p.m. the rest of the year. There's a fee for photography.

The **National Museum in Lviv** (Національний музей у Львові, *Natsionalnyy muzey u Lvovi*) has two branches. The original museum is at 42 Drahomanova (Драгоманова) Street in a highly ornamented building. Originally established in 1905 by Greek-Catholic Metropolitan Andrey Sheptytsky for the display of ecclesiastical art, the museum now houses handicrafts and fine art. Examples of Ukrainian glasswork, ceramics, textiles, clothing, rugs, embroidery, woodcarving, and metalwork are on display. There's also 19th-century to contemporary landscapes, portraits, graphics, and sculpture by Ukrainian artists. Hours are from 10 a.m. until 6 p.m. daily except on Thursdays and Fridays. Phone (0322)72-57-45.

The newer branch of the National Museum is at 20        prospekt Svobody, across from the Grand Hotel, in an imposing exhibition hall built in 1904 as a polytechnical museum. In Soviet days it became a Lenin museum and now houses church antiquities. Icons dating from the 14th through 18th centuries, old books, including those printed by Ivan Fedorov, and art from the 11th to the 18th centuries are on display. The museum is open 10 a.m. to 5:30 p.m. daily except Friday. Photography is permitted, but flash is not allowed. Phone (0322) 74-22-82 or 72-89-60.

**Lviv Art Gallery**, 3 Stefanyka (Стефаника) Street, first opened in 1907. One of the biggest art museums in Ukraine, it features European paintings, sculpture, graphics, and decorative arts in an overcrowded display. Highlights include works by Rembrandt, Rubens, and Goya. Museum hours are 10 a.m. to 5 p.m. Tuesday through Saturday and 11 a.m. to 5 p.m. on Sunday. Phone 74-40-47. The **Palace of Arts**, a block away at 17 Kopernika Street, was built in 1996 as a new wing of the Art Museum. The arts palace is easily recognized by its white color, classic arcade, and a large sculpture of St. Luke, the patron saint of painters, on its corner wall. Ukrainian modern art and temporary exhibits are on display inside. There's a fine lobby, a conference hall, and an elegant café, *Simex*, that serves good Ukrainian and European cuisine. Adjoining the Palace of Arts, the imposing **Potocki Palace** has been beautifully restored and is used for official receptions of the Art Gallery. Built for Polish nobility in 1880 in the French classic style, the palace interior is strikingly ornamented with brightly-colored walls, stucco molding, murals, and stained glass windows. The **Museum of the Art of the Ancient Ukrainian Book**, a branch of the Art Gallery, is at 15a Kopernika Street, behind the Potocki Palace. Among the exhibits are works by Ukrainian medieval printers and engravers, European Renaissance publications, and a 17th-century printing press. A highlight is the frontispiece of the first book published in Ukraine, Ivan Fedorov's *Book of the Apostles*. Open daily except on Monday from 11 a.m. until 4 p.m. Phone (0322)72-25-36.

The **Museum of the Ancient Relics of Lviv**, another branch of the Art Gallery, is at 3 ploscha Rynok. Dating from the 13th century and rebuilt in 1887, the building now houses art, historical documents, and archeological exhibits from the city's earliest days. The museum is open every day except Monday from 11 a.m. until 5 p.m.

The **Lviv Museum of Ethnography and Handicrafts** makes a striking first impression in its Renaissance-Baroque building at 15 prospekt Svobody (проспект Свободи). Built in 1891 as the Galicia Savings Bank, the building's cupola is ornamented by what locals call a "Sitting Statue of Liberty," but is really an allegorical symbol of the Austrian Empire. The first floor has farm implements from the 19th and 20th centuries and costumes from various parts of Ukraine. Upstairs are ceramics, embroidery, and glass. Highlights include the *pysanky* or decorated eggs collection; a large collection of *rushnyky* or embroidered ceremonial towels; icons from Kyiv and Poltava; and church woodcuts of the 17th to 19th centuries. The museum's gift shop sells more expensive but better quality embroidery than found at the nearby crafts market. Open 10 a.m. to 5 p.m. daily except Thursdays. Phone (0322) 72-70-12.

The **Museum of Furniture and China** at 10 ploshcha Rynok (Market Square) in the former Count Lyubomirsky Palace, is a branch of the Museum of Ethnography. It has three floors of furniture, tapestries, and porcelain from the 15th to the 20th centuries. Especially interesting are the 18th century Chinese furniture, 18th and 19th century clocks, Italian majolica, English Wedgwood, and 18th-and 19th-century Austrian and French china. Museum hours are 10 a.m. to 5 p.m. Wednesday through Sunday. Phone (0322) 74-33-78.

**Pharmacy Museum** is at 2 Drukarska Street, across from Privatbank, just off ploscha Rynok. Constructed in 1735, the building has been used as a pharmacy since 1775. A modern drugstore is upstairs, but go behind the counter immediately to the right of the entrance for the museum. Follow the green arrows downstairs to the cavern rooms to see a fascinating exhibit of early pharmaceutical items and medicines. Pharmacy hours are weekdays 9 a.m. until 7 p.m. and weekends from 10 a.m. until 5 p.m. Phone 72-00-41.

The **Museum of Weapons**, 5 Pidvalna (Підвальна) Street, a branch of the Lviv Historical Museum, is housed in an arsenal built about 1575. The rectangular structure was built with eight-foot-thick walls that are stone on the outside and brick inside. Originally built as a municipal defense structure from donations of Lviv's citizens, over the years the arsenal was also used as a granary, a foundry, and a prison. After restoration in 1981, it was opened as a museum of arms and ammunition. On display are weapons from more than 30 countries from the 11th through 20th centuries. The museum is open in the winter from 10 a.m. to 5 p.m. every day except Wednesdays and until 6 p.m. the rest of the year. The circular stone building with the conical roof adjacent to the arsenal at 4 Pidvalna Street is the **Gunpowder Tower**. Built between 1554 and 1556, the tower served as a warehouse for gunpowder and ammunition and in peacetime, grain. It now houses the Lviv branch of the Union of Architects of Ukraine. The **Royal Arsenal**, at 13 Pidvalna Street, was also part of the city fortifications. Financed by the Polish king, it was built in the early 17th century to store weapons for anticipated battle with Turkey. The style is Baroque with an ornamented facade over the south entrance and fine courtyard inside. It now functions as the Regional State Archive.

The **Museum of Folk Architecture and Rural Life**, commonly called *Shevchenkivsky hai* (grove), is at 1 Chernecha Hora, 1½ miles northeast of the city center. This open-air museum consists of approximately 100 old wooden buildings spread out over 150 acres. The museum is divided into miniature villages representing historical-ethnographic areas of western Ukraine: Polisia (the northern area bordering Belarus); Volhynia, the area north of the Lviv region; the Lviv region; the Hutsul, Lemko and Boiko groups of the Carpathian Mountains; Zakarpaty, the region bordering Slovakia and Hungary; Bukovina, the region bordering Romania; and Podilia, a large area in west-central Ukraine. Each village features 15 to 20 buildings: churches, a school, a windmill, cottages, and farm buildings. Household utensils, farm implements, tools, and articles of clothing are displayed. The 1763 St. Mykola Church from Kryvka in the Boiko region is outstanding. The museum is open daily except Monday, from 11 a.m. to 6 or 7 p.m., depending on the season. Phone 71-80-17.

### Other Sights Worth Seeing

**Castle Hill** (Замкова гора, *Zamkova hora*), northeast of the center, offers a fine panorama of the city. Reputed to be the site where Lviv was founded, the 90-acre park was planted in 1853 with 45 species of trees and shrubs. At the apex are the ruins of **High Castle**, ( Високий замок, *Vysokyy zamok*), a 14th-century fortress barely visible from the lookout point below. There's also a cross and a flagpole flying the Ukrainian flag.

**Lychakiv Cemetery** (Личаківське кладовище, *Lychakivske kladovyshche*) is considered one of the most beautiful cemeteries in Europe. It was established in 1786 after Austrian authorities forbade the further use of church cemeteries in the city. Designated a state historical landmark in 1991, the densely wooded, hilly terrain covers 110 acres and contains some 3,600 monuments and sculptures by prominent artists and architects. A stroll along its lovely, winding, tree-lined walks is a passage through the history of Lviv. Markers in several different languages reflect the many cultures that have influenced the city and note the burial sites of scores of distinguished Lviv residents. Take Tram 7 to the main entrance on Mechnikova (Мечнікова) Street. There's a small admission charge.

The **Botanical Gardens of Lviv State University** , 44 Cheremshyna (Черемшина) Street, are just southeast of the cemetery. Founded in 1911, the 46-acre gardens have 1,200 species of plants. **Lviv State University** is located a few miles to the northwest of the gardens at the east end of **Ivan Franko Park**, not far from the city center. The university, one of the oldest in Ukraine, was founded in 1606 as a Jesuit college. The majestic main building was built in 1877 as the Galician assembly. Opposite the university's main entrance is a park with a large monument to Ivan Franko. The park, first designated a municipal park in 1773, is a pleasant place to stroll, sit on a bench, or watch people. In contrast to this urban park is beautiful **Stryyskyy** (Стрийський) **Park**, located a little more than a mile southwest of the city center off vulytsya Stryyska. Designed in the first half of the 19th century by landscape architect Arnold Rering, the park covers 140 acres of fir and beech forests. Near the main gate is a pond with black and white swans. Winding paths lead through shady glades, past formal gardens, and to a greenhouse with subtropical plants and cacti. The large Modernist-style building at the south end of the park is Cinema Lviv, built in the 1920s. Take Tram 4 or 5 in the direction of vulytsya Mushaka and get off at the Parkova stop.

Heading north of the opera theater on V. Chornovil Avenue (formerly 700-richchia Lvova), about a mile past the city center is a small park with a **Monument to the Victims of the Lviv Ghetto 1941–1943**. Designed by sculptor Luiza Schternstein, it was erected in 1992 on the site of the former gates of the city's Jewish ghetto to commemorate the 100,000 victims of the Nazi occupation. The monument consists of a large statue of the prophet Ezekiel, a tablet inscribed with a verse from the Book of Ezekiel in Hebrew and Ukrainian, and a large granite menorah.

## Lviv Environs

Just 10 km (4 mi) west of the center in the suburb **Bilohorshcha** is the **Museum of Roman Shukhevych**. Shukhevych, born Taras Chuprynka in 1907, was commander-in-chief of the Ukrainian Insurgent Army from 1940 to 1950. The museum displays artifacts of the Ukrainian underground resistance, including objects that belonged to the partisans. The mud bunker, or *skhron,* where Shukhevych was killed in 1950 has been reconstructed. Take the Lviv–Bilohorshcha *marshrutka* from Halytska Square.

**Bryukhovychi** (Врюховичі), an attractive small resort town about 3 miles northwest of Lviv, offers lakes, pinewoods and a relaxed tree-shaded town. Driving into town, one passes the imposing new church of St. Olha and Volodomyrska. Overlooking a lake, the excellent restaurant *Kolyba* is part of a residential resort which was refurbished for a Lviv summit meeting of the heads of European states. The attractive new *Motel Olena* (Олена) at 5 Balabanivska Street is a good choice for lodging.

Continuing northwest, you'll come to **Khrekhiv**, a village founded in 1456. Khrekhiv is the site of a 17th and 18th-century Basilian monastery that was restored in 1991 and is fully functioning. Situated at the foot of Mount Pobiyna, the monastery includes St. Mykola Church, first built in 1721; a theological seminary; three buildings housing 18th- century cells; nicely preserved fortifications; and a beautiful garden. Religious pilgrims climb Mount Pobiyna to visit the 15th–and16th-century cave church; the spring with holy water, and the cross at the apex planted by the monks at the spot where the Virgin Mary appeared. The walk to the top requires two hours.

**Zhovkva**, a village about 12 km (7 mi) east of Krekhiv and 23 km (14 mi) north of Lviv , was designated a  historical and architectural preserve in 1994. Its history dates to 1588 when it became part of the land holdings of Polish magnate Stanislaw Zholkevsky, who began construction of a Renaissance fortress-castle with ramparts and moats in 1594. King Jan Sobieski occupied the castle in 1678, and the town flourished as a home to painters and craftsmen during the 17th and18th centuries.  In addition to the castle, there's a market square with an arcade and noted churches, including several wooden churches and a synagogue constructed in   1692 with Renaissance and Baroque features. One of the biggest and most beautiful in Europe, the synagogue's lavish interior was destroyed by fire during World War II, but partially restored in 1956. To get to Zhovkva, catch the Zhovkva marshrutka from downtown Lviv.

**"The Golden Horseshoe"** is a scenic stretch of the Lviv-Kyiv Highway dotted with castles  northeast of Lviv. Several  have restored interiors and are now museums administered by the Lviv Art Gallery.

   Approximately 72 km (about 45 mi) east of Lviv on this highway, you come to **Olesko Castle** (Олеський замок, *Oleskyy zamok*). Built as a fortress in the 14th century, its early 17th-century reconstruction gave it an Italian Renaissance look. Olesko was the birthplace of Polish king Jan Sobieski III, an avid art collector. The castle displays furniture, tapestries, icons, canvases of great battles, and a large number of 14 th through 18th-century sculptures. Exhibits are displayed in a sequence of rooms to suggest a walk though a functioning manor. The view of the surrounding countryside is lovely. The castle is open from 10 a.m. to 5 p.m. six days per week. The day it closes varies. Flash cameras are permitted. A short distance east is **Pidhirtsi Castle**, constructed between1635 and 1640 in late Renaissance style. Set in an Italian-style park with a Baroque Roman Catholic church, the castle is under restoration by the Lviv Art Gallery. Nearby, in Pidhirtsi village, is the 1820 wooden Church of St. Michael, and an old inn and brewery.

A short distance south of Pidhirtsi, is **Zolochiv Castle**, which dates to the 1630s. The castle was occupied by the Sobieski and Radziwill families in the 17th and 18th centuries. The ensemble includes a citadel. The interior has been turned into a museum, a highlight of which is the Chinese pavilion. Continuing south, 27 km from Zolochiv is the village **Pomoryany.** A castle was constructed here in the early 16th century and improved more than a century later by King Jan Sobieski III. To the west, back towards Lviv, you reach the village **Svirzh** and its scenic vistas. On a hill overlooking a river and lake are the remains of **Svirzh Castle**, dating from the 14th through the 17th centuries. A restored 1541 Roman Catholic church is open to the public. Continuing west, 18 km outside of Lviv are the remains of the **Stare Selo Castle**, which dates from the 16th and 17th centuries.

## Hotels

Hotels in Lviv run the gamut from subdued luxury for the discriminating traveler to clean, "no frills" lodging for bargain hunters. Prices for a standard double room range from about US$20 nightly to about US$100, with about US$50 as the median. Hotels are listed in order of decreasing price.

The *Grand* (Гранд) *Hotel*, 13 *prospekt Svobody*, (просп. Свободи), across from the Shevchenko Monument in the heart of Lviv, is the most upscale hotel in the city. Built in1898, it's been restored to its Austro-Hungarian splendor with carved molded ceilings, murals, and stained glass. The 60 guest rooms are modern and tasteful, but offer little elbow room. A professional and courteous staff provide many guest and business services. Phone (0322) 72-12-22; fax (0322) 76-90-60.

The *Hotel Lion's Castle* (Замок лева, *Zamok leva)*, 7 Glinka Street, is a 14-room hotel occupying two villas in a quiet, shady neighborhood adjacent to Bohdan Khmelnytsky Park, is a 20 to 25 minute walk to the city center. Built for magnates during the Austrian era, the later hotel once served Communist Party bosses, including Mikhail Gorbachev. The rooms and baths are large, the management friendly, and the food good. Phone (0322) 35-11-00, fax (0322) 35-11-02, or e-mail lions_castle@org.lviv.net.

*Hotel Dnister* (Дністер)at 6 Mateyko Street (вул. Матейка), overlooking the 30-acre Ivan Franko Park on the west edge of the city center. Modernized and sleek with marble, this large Soviet-era tourist hotel lacks its former Ukrainian charm but compensates with amenities. It has three restaurants, a lively night bar with a discotheque, a tourist bureau, gift shops, meeting rooms, and secure parking. Guest rooms have local and international TV. Phone (0322) 72-07-83; fax (0322) 97-10-21.

*Hotel George* (Жорж) at 1 Mickiewicz Square (площа Міцкевича, *ploshcha Mitskevycha*) in the heart of the city, is on the site of a 19th-century hotel where French author Honoré de Balzac honeymooned with a Polish countess. The present hotel was constructed in 1900 by Herman Helmer and Ferdinand Fellner, the Viennese architects who designed the Odesa opera. Recently renovated, the spacious guest rooms with private bath, phone, and TV are under US$100. A restaurant and service bureau are on the premises. Phone (0322) 72-59-52; fax (0322) 97-11-44.

The small *Hotel Eney* (Еней), 2 Shmzeriv Street, is at the end of Perkarska Street, southeast and not within walking distance of the center (take Tram 7). Eney is comfortable with faux-Greek elegance and lots of amenities including its own water-purifying station. Phone (0322) 76-87-99.

The *Hotel NTON* (НТОН), 154 Shevchenka Street, is 5 km (3 mi) northwest of the center. A small well-run hotel, it offers satellite TV, an Internet café, and a pizzeria. Phone (0322) 33-31-23.

The *Hetman* (Гетьман),a 12-story boxy concrete structure at 50 Volodymyra Velykoho, opened in 1976 as the *Karpaty* to serve tour groups. Located 5 km (3 mi) from the center in the southwest part of the city, it's on a major bus line. Guest rooms have private baths, phones, and TVs, and amenities include a currency exchange, hair salon, a good restaurant, and secure parking. Phone (0322) 64-84-67; fax 64-84-72.

*Suputnyk* (Супутник) is a large newly-renovated hotel at 116 Knyahyni Olhy Street, about a 20-minute tram ride southwest from the center. Suputnyk offers a wide range of amenities, including a private guarded parking lot. A tourist agency operates in the hotel. Phone (0322) 64-58-22.

For no-frills hotels try **Hotel Nezalezhnist** (Незелність), 6a Tershakivtsiv Street, near the medical university and a 10-minute walk to the center, phone (0322) 75-72-14; **Lviv** (Львів) **Hotel**, 7 Chornovil Avenue, in the center, phone (0322) 79-22-70; and **Vlasta** (Власта), 30 Kleparivska Street, in the southwest part of the city, phone (0322) 33-34-30.

**Dining Out.** The city's Viennese influence shows in the strong coffee and rich desserts found in numerous coffee shops. Pizza is very popular and cafés abound, many with a wide range of menu choices. The **Korona Café** at 7 prospekt Svobody specializes in ice cream. **Knyazhyy Lviv Café**, around the corner at 11 Hnatyuka Street, has Ukrainian decor and traditional dishes. **Na Soborniy** (На Соборній), at 2a Soborna Square, serves tasty and inexpensive dishes in a Ukrainian folk setting. The cozy **Tsukernia** on Staroyevreyska Street has delectable desserts and confections. **Coffee World** at 6 Kateldralna Square near the Latin Cathedral has a great selection of coffee.

**Kastelyari** near the juncture of Pidvalna and Lychakivska Streets has some of the best pizza in the city, as well as very good ice cream upstairs. For quick counter service with traditional Ukrainian cuisine at unbeatable prices, try **Domova Kukhnya** , at 5 Shevchenko Street, next door to McDonald's.

The popular **Café Veronika** is at 25 Shevchenko Street. You can breakfast on croissants, great omelets, and real cappucino, take an afternoon break in its second floor European-style patisserie (or take some pastries home), and choose from its large menu for a special evening in the elegant downstairs dining hall.

Many cafés are clustered in an area west of prospekt Svobody near Ivan Franko Park and the central building of Lviv University, mainly on two streets that run parallel to the park, Petra Doroshenka (Дорошенка) and Sichovykh Striltsiv Streets. **Lisova Pisnya** at 5 Sichovykh Striltsiv is recommended.

Lviv is full of good, inexpensive restaurants, which generally offer evening entertainment. Hours are 11 a.m. until 11 p.m. unless noted. Reservations usually aren't necessary.

**Amadeus**, (Амадей) on Katedralna Square at Teatralna Street, behind the Latin Cathedral, is a tiny, pretty restaurant with good food and live jazz in the evenings. Phone (0322) 97-80-22.

*Kavkaz* (Кавказ) is at 2 Shota Rustaveli Street (near Zelena), across from the bus stop and park. It serves excellent Georgian cuisine at reasonable prices in a rustic stone-and-wood setting. Phone (0322) 76-20-44.

*Kupol* (Купол), 37 Tchaikovsky Street, creates a plush, elegant, homey pre-WWII ambience with cuisine to match. Patio dining in the summer. Open 9 a.m. until 11 p.m. Phone (0322) 74-42-54.

*Mushketer* (Мушкетєр) or *Le Mousquetaire*, the "little French restaurant" at 7 Hrushevskoho Street, has a subdued French ambience which allows somewhat higher prices than is typical of Lviv restaurants. The French dishes, however, suggest Ukrainian cuisine. Phone (0322) 74-30-76.

*Oselya* (Оселя), 11 Hnatyuka Street, serves good Ukrainian cuisine in an attractive village home decor. An English menu is available. There's an evening folklore show. Phone (0322) 72-16-01.

*Videnska Kavyarnya* (Віденська кавярня), 12 Svobody Avenue, serves cuisine of Galician Austria with live music in the evenings. Phone (0322) 72-20-21.

**Dining in the suburbs.** If you have access to a car and a hankering for delicious traditional Ukrainian cuisine, try these two restaurants that are open around the clock. *Ukrayinsky Kray* (Українсий край) is 7 km (4 mi) east on the Lviv-Kyiv Highway between the villages of Dublyany and Hamaliyivka . A large, homey luncheonette with an adjoining gas station, the diner's decor sports a fantastic collection of mounted wild game, and the kitchen serves freshly made Ukrainian fare at very reasonable prices. The menu includes a variety of meat and mushroom dishes, home-baked buns, pastries, and *pampushky*, a deep-fried, filled pastry. Phone (0322) 72-37-19.

The restaurant *Kolyba* (Колуба) is part of an attractive resort in **Bryukhovychi**, (Врюховичі), about 4 miles west of Lviv. Overlooking a lake, this traditional restaurant resembles a wooden shepherd's hut, with seating either in the main restaurant or outdoors in attractive mini-huts overlooking the lake. Specialities are Hutsul-style fish, meat, and game dishes, some cooked on an open fire. Live music in the evenings. Phone (0322) 59-31-41.

**Shopping.** Some pricey Western brand names can be found in the central district, but bargain hunting in the city's authentic Ukrainian shops is more fun. Shops are centered around prospekt Svobody. Horodotsk Бфродоцка)

Street, which runs to the northwest of prospekt Svobody, has a number of interesting shops.

**Arts and Crafts.** Lviv is a great place to buy art, whether traditional or modern. Ask a travel agent to arrange a visit to a factory that produces woodcarvings, ceramics, or linens, or to an artist's studio. For locally crafted souvenirs and art try the following:

**Khudozhnyk** (Художник) is at 5 *ploshcha Mitskevycha,* directly off prospekt Svobody. This is an especially nice shop with a selection of out-of-the-ordinary handcrafted jewelry, pottery, glasswork, and embroidery; a hardwood walking stick with a carved wolf's head handle cost the equivalent of US$8. Immediately around the corner to the right at 2 Voronoho Street, is the art gallery section of the store. Open Monday through Saturday 11 a.m. until 5 p.m. Phone (0322) 72-66-83.

Other fine arts galleries are *Art Gallery of V. Pylypiuk* at 14 Shevchenko Avenue, *Gerdan* at 4 Ruska Street, and the *Dzyha Art-Cultural Center* at 35 Virmenska Street, at its east end. Dzyha, run by an art association, occupies a former Dominican monastery and consists of a number of picturesque galleries showing contemporary art and antiques. A coffee shop is on the premises. Open from 10 a.m. until 10 p.m. daily. Phone (0322) 75-21-01 or 76-74-20.

A large outdoor artists' market, *Vernisazh,* operates every day at ploshcha Teatralna, just east of the opera theater on prospekt Svobody. Oil paintings and graphics predominate, with landscapes, Lviv cityscapes, still lifes, and florals among the most popular subjects. Ceramics, woodcrafts, beadwork, and embroidered linens and blouses are also sold.

**Book and Music Stores.** For pretty Ukrainian-made porcelain tea sets, glassware and figurines, check out *Sklo, Farfor Fayans* at 2 Lesia Kurbasa Street, just west of Svobody Avenue. Stores for books and music are clustered around the Mickiewicz Square area at the south end of Svobody.

Across from the Hotel George is *Budynyk Knyhy* (Будинок книги) or House of Books, a corner building that occupies a block and contains a number of bookshops selling maps and a variety of books such as travel guides, language books, and cookbooks. Across the street to the west, *Ukrayina knyharnya naukovoho* (Україна книгарня наукового) at 8 Shevchenko Street, has a good selection of history, modern literature, and scientific literature.

**Department Stores and Malls.** The Central Department Store (*Tsentralny univermah*, Центральний універмаг), popularly called *TSUM* (ЦУМ), is at 1 Shpytalna (Шпитальна) Street. The new *Lviv Department Store* is in a striking building on Knyahynya Olha Street in the new residential district southwest of the center. *Roksolyana* is in a passage in the old French Hotel at 5 Mitskevych Square and *Na Rynka* is at 32 Rynok Square.

**Food Shops.** Svobody Avenue and the streets running off it are a good place to find pastries, bread, excellent chocolates and other candies. *Svitoch Candy Factory*, a local company specializing in fine chocolates, has outlets throughout the city. *Khvylya* is at 30 Svobody Avenue; *Delicacies* is at 4 Doroshenko; *VAM*, a new supermarket is at 100 Vyhovskoho; *Mini Market* is at Doroshenko and Bankivska Streets.

**Open markets** are an authentic way to enjoy the color of the city and participate in the everyday life of its residents. The oldest and most popular market at Halytska Square was replaced by a widened road and new shops, but many new *rynky* have opened. Check out *Dobrobut*, near the Zankovetska Theater behind the opera house; the *Central Market* at 11 Bazarna Street; *Pivdennyy*, a very large clothes and household market, at 36 Shchyretska Street; *Pryvokzalnyy*, the best food market in town, at 2 Horskoye Street; *Stryyskyy* at 81 Ivan Franko Street; *Pidzamche* at 120 B. Khmelnytskoho; and the *New Market* at 2 Petlyura Street.

## Transportation

**Local.** Lviv is served by a number of bus, trolleybus, and tram lines. Most convenient are the newer marshrutky, or "pick-up" minibuses that provide extra transportation on busy routes. Buy your tickets directly from the driver or conductor; it's not necessary to cancel them in the box in the car. Public transportation is best avoided during rush hours, as the crowding is unbelievable.

**Long-Distance Bus.** Buses link Lviv to various cities in western Ukraine, Poland, Hungary, Germany, Great Britain, Italy, Greece, France, Russian and Moldova. The long-distance station at 109 Stryyska (Трийська) Street is in a modern triangular building with concave sides. Take Trolleybus 5 from the terminal stop at Shota Rustavelli Street, near ploshcha Ivana

Franka. Schedules change frequently; for information, phone (0322) 63-25-31 or 63-24-73. There's a ticket outlet at **Mandry Company** at 4 Rynok Square.

**Rail.** Lviv is an important rail link between Central and Eastern Europe. There are daily trains to major international cities, among them Budapest, Prague, Belgrade, Sofia, Riga, and Moscow. There's also good service to cities throughout Ukraine, including several trains a day to Kyiv. Call 005 for information on arrivals and departures. Buying tickets in advance is recommended; it's easiest, though more expensive, to go through a hotel service bureau. Tickets are also available at the booking office on the ground floor in the railway station or at the Railway Booking Office at 20 Hnatyuka Street in the center. The Railway Station, at 1 ploshcha Dvirtseva at the end of Chernivetska (Чернівецька) Street, offers some tourist amenities. Tram 9 runs between Doroshenka Street in the center and the railroad station. To catch a train to cities in the Lviv oblast, go to the local railway station, **Prymiskyy Vokzal**, near the center at the intersection of Horodotska and Chernihivska Streets.

**Air.** Lviv Airport is an elegant jewel, as pretty as a small church with its classic style and fine woodwork. Most of the time it's also as empty and quiet as a church, with few planes using it. The small number of personnel don't speak English, and there are no baggage carousels or luggage carts, but friendly porters will carry your baggage from the customs area to your taxi.

The airport is located at the end of Liubinska Street at the southwest edge of the city. Trolleybus 9 and marshrutka service run between the airport and the university. For airport information, call (0322) 69-21-12 and for international flight information call (0322)72-78-18.

Among the limited flights into the city are Lot Polish Airline from Warsaw and Aeroflot from Moscow, which arrive nearly every day. Ukraine International Airlines (0322) 69-27-44) runs flights between Lviv and Frankfurt in the winter, and adds London, Manchester, and Amsterdam in warm weather. Domestically, it flies to a number of cities including Kyiv, Odesa, Donetsk, and Simferopol. Ticket offices for Ukraine International Airlines are located in the airport, in the Grand Hotel, and in travel agencies Elita-Business on Lesi Ukrainky Street and Pilgrim on Kopernika Street. Tickets can be reserved in advance on Internet and picked up at one of the Lviv offices. Tickets are cheaper if purchased more than three days before departure.

## Useful Addresses

**Communication Services.** Post office branches throughout the city sell phone cards for local calls from public phones as well as providing mailing services. The **Main Post Office** is at 1 Slovatskoho (Словацького) Street, between Doroshenka and Kopernika Streets. Phone 065. Hours of operation are Monday through Friday from 8 a.m. to 8 p.m., Saturday from 8 a.m. to 6 p.m., and Sunday from 8 a.m. to 2 p.m. A Western Union office and banking services, including cashing traveler's checks, are in the post office.

**Internet.** *Cybercafé* at 3 Shevchenko Avenue right in the center is open 10 a.m. until 7:30 p.m. Phone (0322) 72-45-23. The *Internet Café* at 14 Zelena Street is open 24 hours every day.

**Pharmacies.** Pharmacies are found throughout the city. In the center there are pharmacies at 18 Rynok Square and at 15 Doroshenka Street. Pharmacy No. 24 at 1 Kopernika (Коперніка) Street is an interesting old shop stocked with a variety of medicinal herbs.

**Medical Services.** Dial 03 for an ambulance. One of the best hospitals in the city is *Clinic Hospital* at 3 Ohiyenka ( Огієнка) Street, just northwest of Lviv University, but tourists often use *Hospital Bohdan* in Bryukovychi. An *Emergency Hospital* is on Hetman Myzery Street.

**American Fast Food.** For a quick, familiar meal, *McDonald's* restaurants can be found at 7 Shevchenko Avenue, facing the restaurant in Hotel George; on V. Chornovil Avenue, less than a mile from the opera; on Volodymyra Velykoho Street, and near the *New Department Store* on Knyahyna Olha Street.

**Public Restrooms.** Public restrooms are fairly clean, but may not be up to American standards, especially if no fee is charged, and you can't count on finding toilet paper. It's best to use the rest- rooms in restaurants and cafés.

**Banking Services.** Hotels, restaurants and some businesses accept credit cards. ATMs in McDonald's and in a few other businesses in the central area can supply cash in hryvni using your bank or credit card. Banks will give an advance on your credit card for a small percentage. *Prominvetsbank*, 2

Hnatyuk Street, just off Svoboda Avenue across from the Museum of Ethnography, was designed as a bank in 1912 by Czech artisans and has preserved its interior. Also try *Pryvatbank* at 21 Hutsulska Street or *Inko* at 67 V. Chornovil Avenue. *Bank Aval* in the main post office at 1 Slovatskoho Street is the most likely to also cash traveler's checks. Typical banking hours are 9 a.m. until 1 p.m.

**Tourist Services.** The Lviv city tourist bureau is located at 1 Pidvalna (Підвальна) Street, just east of the center. To hire a city guide, visit historic sites outside the city, or to rent an apartment, try the tourist service bureaus in the large hotels or check these agencies: *Algol Travel* at 16a Melnyka (Мелника) Street; *Leo Tour*, 8 Virmenska (Вірменська) Street; *Lvivtourist Company*, 12 Stryiska (Стрийська) Street; *Mandry* at 44 Rynok Square (площа Ринок); *Mist-Tour* at 34 Shevchenka (Шевченка) Avenue; *Navkolo Svitu* at 5/2 Saksahaskoho (Саксагаского) Street; and *Travel Ukraine Agency* at 38/9 Drahomanova (Драгоманова) Street.

**Government Offices.** To export art, go to the Commission of Exports of the Western Regional Customs Administration at 1 Kosyushko Street at the corner of Doroshenko. Phone 72-85-13. To extend a private, business, or tourist visa, the Ministry of Internal Affairs *(VVIR)* is at 3 Voronoho (Вороного) Street in the center. You'll need documentation supporting your request and will be charged a small fee. The VVIR is open Tuesday through Thursday, from 9 a.m. until 6 p.m. and Saturday from 9 a.m. until 11 a.m.

# CHAPTER 6.
# WESTERN UKRAINE

A charming memorial complex honoring distinguished Ukrainian poet and writer Ivan Franko is in the **Lvivska oblast**. Located in **IVANA FRANKA** (formerly called Nahuyevychi), the village of Franko's birth, the memorial is 12 km (7 mi) east of Drohobych on local road T 1419. It consists of the restored homestead where Franko grew up, including farm buildings. Across the road is the Franko Walk, a path through the woods past wooden sculptures carved with selections of his writings.

Following road T1419 south from Ivana Franka, you come to **TRUSKEVETS** (Трускевець), one of the leading health resorts in Ukraine. This bustling little town is about 12 km (7 mi) south of Drohobych in the foothills of the Eastern Carpathian mountains. It's been a source of salt since the 11th century. In 1847 it opened its first health resort based on its 14 mineral springs, and today there are numerous sanatoriums and hotels that have modernized to "European standards" for the 200,000 visitors who flock to this picturesque resort town yearly for treatment and relaxation. The town's most famous product is Naftusia, a sulfur spring water said to relieve liver, gallbladder, urological, and metabolic disorders.

The **Art Museum of Mykhailo Bilas,** 3 maydan Kobzaria, displays the weavings, appliques, and embroidery of this contemporary fabric artist. The museum is open from 10 a.m. until 6 p.m. daily except Monday. Phone (03247) 5-00-02 or (03247) 5-42-35.

Sanatoriums, hotels, shops, and reasonably priced restaurants abound. At the Kafe-Bar Zhadka (Згадка), 1 vulytsya Shevchenka, a delicious two-course lunch, including beverage costs about US$5 per person. Restaurant Komandor (Комадор) at 20 vulytsya Sukhovolya serves delicious seafood in a pretty setting for similar prices.

The **Ukrainian Carpathian Mountains** (Карпати, *Karpaty*) are in the southwest corner of Ukraine, bordering on Romania, Hungary, Slovakia, and Poland. Transcarpathia (Закарпацька, *Zakarpatska*) is Ukraine's most mountainous region, and parts of the Lvivska, Ivano-Frankivska, and Chernivetska oblasts are also in the Carpathians.

Several ethnic groups closely related to Ukrainians are indigenous to the area. The Lemkos and the Boikos are agricultural people who built villages at low altitudes, while the Hutsuls, who occupied higher elevations, were traditionally engaged in cattle breeding and shepherding. The Hutsuls are noted for their rich cultural traditions and fine woodcrafts, which are sold in the area's resort towns.

The Carpathians are young mountains of medium elevation. An extension of the Alps, they're composed of deciduous and coniferous forests that alternate with rolling hills and Alpine meadows dotted with charming villages. The climate is a tourist's dream. Spring is long, summer is pleasant, fall is warm, and winter is mild (sometimes snow melts more quickly than a skier desires). Its tranquil beauty, invigorating air, and natural mineral springs make Karpaty Ukraine's second most popular resort and recreation area after Crimea. Recreational opportunities include festivals, hiking, mountain biking, mountain climbing, camping, horseback riding, boating, rafting, fishing, hunting, skiing, tobogganing, and enjoying the therapeutic benefits of the waters.

A Carpathian vacation is ideal for those who want to "rough it" a bit. Hiking trails are not well developed and camp sites are primitive. Bringing your own sporting equipment is advisable; rental camping equipment is not widely available and rental winter sports equipment is hard to find and may not be up to Western standards. Dining and lodging is comfortable, with new hotels and restaurants springing up along the main roads and in the resort towns in the mountain region. Intercity buses and marshrutky run frequently through the mountain area, and it's always easy to find a taxi.

The Lviv-Uzhhorod Highway, a popular route to the mountains, passes through the mountain town of **SKOLE** (Сколе), 103 km (64 mi) south of Lviv. Skole was first mentioned in documents dating to 1397; today it's a ski resort. Located on the Opir River, Skole boasts impressive waterfalls. Going south up the Opir valley is the Ukrainian Carpathian's most accessible ski resort, **SLAVSKE** (Славське). Lodging is inexpensive: the *Perlyna Karpat* starts at the equivalent of US$11 per night, including breakfast. Phone (0322) 97-15-16.

The most picturesque of the Ukrainian Carpathians are the "Hutsul Alps," a group of mountains between the Bila Tysa (Біла Тиса) and Ruskova (Рускова) river valleys in the **Transcarpathian Oblast**. **RAKHIV** (Рахів), a town of 16,000 on the Tysa River in the heart of the mountains is the geographical center of Europe, according to a marker on the banks of the Tysa River just off the Uzhhorod-Rakhiv (Ужгород-Рахів) Autoroute.

In the 17th and 18th centuries, Rakhiv was a major livestock trading post; it's now a resort and Hutsul cultural center with an annual Brynza Festival in early September. Besides *brynza,* a cheese from the local sheep's milk, expect to witness song and dance and lots of sheep.

In the Rika River valley, not far from the town of **KHUST**, is a spectacular mountain phenomena. The **Valley of Narcissus** is one of the world's largest natural displays of the rare species of *Narcissus angustifolius,* a narrow-leafed variety, that carpets the valley with fragrant white blossoms in late April and May.

The **Carpathian Biosphere Reserve** is an 18,000-hectare (54,700-acre) reserve established in 1968. The Biosphere Reserve is Europe's only remaining virgin beech forest and is a protected environment for many species of plants and animals, such as deer, mountain goats, lynx, and brown bears. The terrain ranges from stalactite caves to an Alpine vegetation belt with a large rhododendron area. Hiking in the reserve ranges from moderate to difficult. Accessible from the reserve is **Mt. Hoverla** (Говерла). At 2,061 meters (6,679 feet) high, Hoverla is Ukraine's highest mountain and a symbol of Ukrainian independence. A growing tradition is to climb it on August 24, Ukrainian Independence Day.

The nearest town to Mt. Hoverla is **YASYNYA** (Ясиня), just north of the reserve in a broad valley on the Chorna Tysa (Чорна Тиса) River. For the hiker, Yasynya has food shops, cafés, and lodging. A little more than a mile south of town by the river is an 1824 wooden church with a central dome and a separate bell tower.

For an authentic Carpathian experience, the Rakhiv district has a bed and breakfast program which arranges lodging for tourists with local families and local cuisine. Contact the Carpathian Agency for Regional Development, phone (3132) 2-14-06.

**Synevyr National Park** is about 160 square miles and contains several villages among the peaks. The highest peaks are **Nehrovets**, 1,712 meters (5,617 feet) high, and **Strymba**, 1,719 meters (5,640 feet). The area has a number of *kolyby,* or small shepherd cottages, that have been turned into cafés specializing in *shashlyk,* roasted meat on a stick. *Hotel Kamyanka,* perched on a mountain overlooking the park, is very inexpensive and serves good food. To get to Synevyr National Park, take Highway P03 from

Uzhhorod to Khyst, then go north east to **MIZHHIYA**, which is 154 km (92 mi) from Uzhhorod, and an access point to the park with several resorts. **Synevyr Lake** (Синевирске озеро, *Synevyrske ozero*),is considered the gem of the Carpathians. Sitting 989 meters (3,240 feet) high in a spruce forest, this beautiful small lake is a popular tourist destination because there are practically no other lakes in the Carpathians. In past centuries a dam was constructed on the lake, raising the water level needed to float timber from the mountains down to the valley for processing. The **Museum of Timber Rafting** is based on a reconstruction of the old dam.

**Uzhanskyy National Park** (formerly Stuzhytsya Regional Landscape Park) is between Lviv and Uzhhorod on the Lviv-Uzhhorod Highway. The park is on Ukraine's western border at its juncture with Slovakia and Poland. As a result of numerous 20th-century border shifts, the region shows the influence of its Slovakian, Hungarian, and Czech past. The folk traditions of the area's highland Lemko and Boyko population are distinctive and their Ukrainian dialect borrows many words from Slovakian and Hungarian.

Uzhanskyy National Park is part of the International Biosphere Reserve, a UNESCO-supported project designed to protect Europe's largest beech forests, mountain pastures, natural vegetation, and rare species of wildlife. The park also preserves traditional agriculture, shepherding, folklore, and religious traditions. A train runs inside the park with stops at the various villages. The villages **Sil**, **Kostrino**, **Uzhok**, **Sukhyy**, and **Khusnyy** are noteworthy for their well-preserved 17th-century wooden churches, now used for Ukrainian Orthodox or Ukrainian Catholic services. A friendly person with the key will usually come along to aid a tourist who attempts to peek inside a church. The more remote villages of **Lubnya** and **Verkhovyna Bista** are worth a visit for their traditional wooden homes, hiking and horseback-riding trails, trout streams, as well as for breathtaking views of the Ukrainian and Polish mountains.

The Uzh river runs through the park, fed by local mineral springs. There's a network of hiking trails and several ski bases. The most developed is the *Krasiya* ski area outside the village of Kostrino. Krasiya is open all year round with bus access in winter. *Lissovets*, outside the village **STAVNE**, is another ski lodge. The leading hotel in the area, *Hotel Krasiya*, is very inexpensive. *Dubovy Hai* is a new hotel with some good rooms at a reasonable rate. Outside of **VELYKYY BERESNYY** on *Yavirnik* mountain, is a traditional Czech-built tourist hut with three rooms that each sleep up to ten people. The cost of a night's lodging with a traditional Carpathian breakfast costs several dollars. For information on recreation and lodging in Uzhanskyy National Park, call (03135) 2-10-37.

**Carpathian National Nature Park**, the largest park in the mountains, is in the **Ivano-Frankivska Oblast**. The area's leading resort town, **YAREMCHA** (Яремча), is set amidst the vertical cliffs of the Prut (Прут) river valley. Yaremcha has several tourist centers and numerous rest homes, sanatoriums, and spas, many up to Western standards. In the spring fearless adventure lovers come to ride kayaks and inflatable rafts over the slalom route of the Prut rapids. A footbridge crossing the Prut River affords a view of a small waterfall; adjacent to the bridge is *Hutsulshchyna*, a picturesque wooden restaurant. Its interior is furnished with wooden tables and chairs, intricately carved pillars, and delicate lanterns. Its tall windows flanked by carved wooden shutters offer a panoramic view of the valley and hillsides. The restaurant serves delicious meals, and specializes in mushroom dishes. On the other side of the bridge local residents sell traditional crafts at a large bazaar. A popular hike is from Yaremcha to the top of **Mount Hoverla**. The scenic view overlooks the boundary markers of Ukraine's borders in the 19th and 20th centuries.

About 3 kilometers (1.8 miles) north of Yaremcha in the town of **DORA** (Дора) is a 17th-century wooden Hutsul church constructed without nails. Upstream amid fir forests, **VOROKHTA** (Ворохта) is known for its winter sports. Most popular are its cross-country and downhill skiing facilities. There are several chair lifts and a ski jump facility used to train Olympic athletes. One chair reaches a height of 1,100 meters. Accessible by train, Vorokhta is also popular for its sanatoriums. It has some interesting wooden churches, including one dating to 1615.

Among the many resorts, one of the most luxurious is the *Karpaty Resort Complex*, near Yaremcha, which offers full board for about US$65 daily for a double room. Fax (03434) 2-21-34. For a more traditional experience, **The Rural Green Tourism Association** in the Ivano-Frankivsk oblast maintains a list of hospitable families in several mountain villages who will provide lodging, home-cooked meals, and an authentic glimpse of lifestyles rooted to tradition and nature. Homestays are available in Yaremcha, Vorokhta, Kosiv, Kryvorivnya, and other mountain towns. Amenities vary, but generally the homes lack indoor toilets and the hosts don't speak English. The Association urges interested tourists to view the photos and descriptions of the homes on its attractive Web site at http://members.aol.com/chornohoro. Interested tourists negotiate directly with the homeowner and agree on a fee. The cost is extremely low, with all revenues going directly to the host family.

Because of its location on the northeast edge of the mountainous region, **IVANO-FRANKIVSK**, the capital of its oblast, is known as "The Gateway to the Carpathians." Its population is 264,000. The city began as a fortress to protect the inhabitants from Crimean Tatars' raids, and by the 17th century it had become a village on the trade route between Lviv and the mouth of the Danube river. A stronghold of the Polish Pototski family, the city came under Magdeburg law in 1662 and was called Stanyslaviv. In the 18th and 19th centuries it was a trade center of Poland, and later Austria. It was a place of strife during World Wars I and II, and then fell under the Soviet Union. In 1962, to celebrate its 300th anniversary, Stanyslaviv was renamed after the famous writer and public figure Ivan Franko, who had a close association with the city. Natives refer to it simply as "Frankivsk."

Ivano-Frankivsk is an attractive city, vibrant culturally and economically. Among its manufactured products are machines and tools, computer hardware, mini-tractors, and consumer items such as washing machines, furniture, clothing, and processed foods. The city's oldest institution of higher learning is the Vasyl Stefanyk Pre-Carpathian University, which now offers a liberal arts curriculum. Other post-secondary schools are the National Technical University of Oil and Gas, the state Medical Academy, an institute of economics and law, an institute of management, and several seminaries. The city is accessible by train and plane. The railroad station is a short distance east of the center at Pryvokzalna Square. The airport is a 20-minute taxi ride from town. Formerly a military airport, it has a good runway, but sees practically no traffic other than a weekly flight to and from Kyiv.

In the center of the city, numerous modern shops and cafés blend with hundreds of well-preserved late-19th-and early-20th-century buildings ornamented with spires, towers, and caryatids. The main street is **Nezalezhnosti** (Незалежності), a long pedestrian mall lined with rows maple trees. Streets fan out from **Rynok Square**, where the city originated. The focal point of the square is the city hall. Reconstructed between 1929 and 1932, it makes a striking impression with its high tower in the center of its crossed-winged halls. Inside the city hall building is the **Ivano-Frankivsk Regional Museum**. Fully air-conditioned, the museum exhibits the region's ancient history (Neolithic and Bronze Age items), modern history, natural history, and crafts. Folk art displays include wood carvings, weaving, embroidery, leather, and ceramics. Located at 4-a Halytska Street, the museum is open from 10 a.m. until 5:30 p.m. every day except Monday. Phone (0342) 2-21-22.

Just west of Rynok Square across Halytska Street is Andrey Sheptytsky Square with two striking 18th century church buildings. **The Church of the Holy Resurrection**, built between 1753 and 1763 in a Baroque style with twin spires, was restored in 1988 and functions as a Ukrainian Greek Catholic church. At the north end of Sheptytsky Square is the oldest building in Ivano-Frankivsk, the former Roman Catholic Parish Church, built between 1672 and 1703 in Renaissance style. The building now houses an **Art Museum**. Established in 1980, the museum has a splendid collection of Western Ukrainian icons from the 15th through 19th centuries, paintings and drawings by prominent Western Ukrainian artists, baroque sculpture, and artwork by Austrian, German, Polish, and Italian painters of 18th through 20th century. Phone (0342) 4-40-38.

**The Ivan Franko Drama Theater** was constructed in 1981 at 42 Nezalezhnosti Street. The main entrance hall is worth a look; under the wood-carved ceiling, ceramic motifs from folk tales, folk songs, and proverbs cover the two-story walls. The theater is a venue for drama and all sorts of concerts. Phone (0342) 2-39-81. The Philharmonic Society is at 1 Lesya Kurbas Street, phone (0342) 23-11-46; and the Puppet Theater is at 1 Shevchenko Street, phone (0342) 2-35-81.

**Restaurants and Hotels.** There are good places to eat all over the center. *Slovan* (Слован), at 2 Shashkevycha Street, is a very popular restaurant with pleasant outdoor seating in the summer. Phone (0342) 22-25-94. *Pegasus* (Пегас) is an attractive café at 3 Vahylevycha Street. Phone (0342) 55-25-05. Café-Bar *Count Monte Kristo* (Граф Монте Крісто), north of the city hall at 60 Vasyliyanok Street, is regarded as one of the city's finest, with entrees costing about US$5. Quail eggs wrapped in pork and served with brown sauce is recommended.

*Hotel Auskoprut* (formerly Roxolana), a small deluxe hotel, is in a 1907 Secessionist building renovated in 1992 with an Austrian partner. Large and comfortable rooms contain nice baths, cable TV, and direct-dial telephones. Amenities include an Austrian-style breakfast buffet, room service, porters, an efficient multilingual concierge desk, business services, and a tourist desk. Auskoprut is at 7-9 Grunwaldska Street. Phone (0342) 24-31-35; fax (0342) 24-32-69. *Hotel Nadiya*, (formerly the Ukraina), 40 Nezalezhnist Street, is a 385-room hotel that's been renovated to European standards. Phone (0342)53-70-75; fax (0342) 53-70-76. An official Ivano-Frankivsk tourist information center is in a wooden stall in the central square near the city hall. Open from 10 a.m. until 6 p.m. daily, the center provides limited information only in Ukrainian.

**Ukrainian crafts** are sold in a shop on 4 Shashkevycha Street, on the corner adjacent to Slovan Restaurant, and also in a craft shop on Nezalezhnosti Street across from the Hotel Nadiya.

Southwest of Ivano-Frankivsk, in the village of **DZVYNYACH** in the district of Bohorodchanyy, there's a new inn resembling a Swiss chalet. *Lisova Pisnya* is an ideal vacation retreat, with mountain views, attractive rooms, a good restaurant, and leisure activities such as sauna and horseback riding. Phone (03471) 3-03-56; e-mail tgts@ukr.net.

The village **MANYAVA** is also in the Bohorodchanskyy district, about 10 km (6 mi) south of Dzvynyach. The first wooden church of the Manyavsky Skyt Monastery was built in 1612. The monastery was destroyed by Turks in 1676, rebuilt, but closed in the 18th century. In the 1970s it was restored as the **Historical and Architectural Museum of Manyava**. Nestled in a pine grove, the Skyt Manyavskyy monastery includes an entrance bell tower, stone and wooden cells, a refectory, and a rampart tower. On display are preserved frescoes, icons, sculptures, and vestments.

About 115 km (71 mi) south of Ivano-Frankivsk, is **KOSIV** (Косів), with a population of about 9,500. In the 19th century the town was noted for its production of painted tile stoves. Today it still turns out the crème de la crème of Hutsul folk arts with the Kosiv State Institute of Applied and Decorative Arts training future artisans in wood and metal working, leather craft, weaving, embroidery, ceramics, and painting. Set in the piney woods of the Carpathian Mountains, Kosiv has long been a perfect setting for health spas and sanatoriums, and today tourism is developing rapidly with construction of hotels, restaurants, and a casino.

The biggest attraction, however, is a 20-minute walk from the center of the city. At the bustling open market, under the large wooden "Косів" sign just west of the bridge, you can buy anything from a pig to pastries to peony plants. Make your way past the mélange of colorful booths, through a wooden gate to the **Hutsul craft market** in the rear. There you'll find skillfully carved and inlaid wood, metal and leather works, *kylyms* (small woven rugs), embroidery, and pottery from local artists, sold at wholesale prices. The general market is open daily, but hours for the famous craft market are flexible, operating generally on Saturday from 7 a.m. until 2 p.m (closing earlier in bad weather) and on Thursday only until 10 a.m.

The town center is pretty and colorful. Stop first at the **Kosiv Information and Welcome Center**, 55 Nezalezhnosti Square, diagonally opposite the pink administration building. The tourist office occupies the first floor of a beautiful yellow and cream two story building. Open Monday through Saturday from 9 a.m. until 1 p.m., the office maintains an updated listing of lodging, health spas, restaurants, craft shops, and entertainment and recreation opportunities. It can arrange guided tours to the Carpathian Biosphere Reserve as well as to other outdoor activities such as fishing, hunting, skiing, horseback riding, or a flight in a small plane over the picturesque mountains. Cultural options available include visiting local craft makers in their studios, a guided tour through classrooms of the applied art institute, and witnessing a Hutsul wedding. English interpreters can be recruited from willing high school students. Phone the Kosiv tourist information office (03478) 2-45-86 or (03478) 2-03-21.

On the second floor of the information and welcome center is the **Kosiv Museum of Hutsul Folk Art**. Open every day from 10 a.m. until 6 p.m., its exhibits include indigenous embroidery, weaving, and decorative household arts. Phone (03478) 2-16-43.The **Museum of the Kosiv Institute of Applied and Decorative Arts** is a five-minute walk west of the central square. In a museum shop, students sell their wood, leather, and jewelry crafts. Hours for the museum and shop vary, but in the summer they're usually open from 10 a.m. to 5 p.m. Phone (03472) 2-11-53.

*Bayka,* a nice new hotel at the edge of the forest is a short taxi ride into town. Rooms go for about the equivalent of US$25, depending on the season, and include breakfast. Phone (03478) 2-36-33 or 2-36-58.

**KOLOMYYA** (Коломия) is a lovely small city (population about 70,000) at the southern entrance to the Carpathians in the Ivano-Frankivsk region, known for its woodcarvers, master-ceramicists, embroiderers, and weavers. The focal point of the town, the central plaza adjoining Teatralna Street, is the site of two popular museums and a good new hotel. The splendid **Museum of Hutsul and Pokuttya Folk Art,** 25 Teatralna Street, displays outstanding wood and fabric crafts, ceramics, metal, leather, icons, and folk instruments in 20 halls. A small gift shop stocks a fine selection of *pysanky* (batik-dyed Easter eggs) and beaded jewelry. The museum is open daily except Mondays from 10 a.m. until 6 p.m. Phone (03433) 2-39-12. Across the street and a short walk south through the green is the fantastic **Pysanka Museum**, easily recognizable by the gigantic colorful egg that houses its galleries. Pysanky from various eras and regions are artfully displayed. Phone (03433) 2-39-12.

Adjacent to the plaza is **Vidrodzhennya** Avenue, a pretty pedestrian mall with nice shops and many restored buildings. At 41 Vidrodzhennya is *Hotel Pysanka*. Built in 2000, this attractive hotel has independent heating and water systems and very reasonable rates. Phone (03433) 2-03-56. The tall structure visible down the street at Vidrodzhennya Square is the **Town Tower**, part of the city hall.

The museum area has a number of very good places to eat. *Zgarda* (Зґарда), 23 Vidrodzhennya Street, serves very fine cuisine in an elegant subdued interior of marble and granite with wood trim. Phone (03433) 3-29-71). *Karpaty*, 15 Teatralna, to the right of the folk arts museum and down several blocks, offers very good meals in a modern setting. Phone (03433) 2-78-90. For tasty tortes and other pastries, try the *Café Kaska* at 26 Renaissance Prospect, open daily from 9 a.m. to 7 p.m.

To purchase folk art, try the gift shops in the folk arts and *pysanky* museums. There's also *Khudozhnyk Salon*, a wonderful shop on the corner of Teatralna Street across from the folk arts museum that's crammed full of embroidered blouses, weavings, carved wood and diverse area crafts. Hours are 9 a.m. until 6 p.m. weekdays; 10 a.m. until 3 p.m. weekends.

West of the center on Karpatska Street, on the road that goes out to Yaremcha, is the enlarged and restored wooden **Orthodox Church of the Annunciation**, dating from 1587.

Several larger cities in the Carpathians make a good base for mountain area excursions. **UZHHOROD** (Ужгород) is the center of the **Transcarpathian Oblast**, the southwesternmost region of Ukraine. With a population of 125,000, it's the smallest regional capital in Ukraine. Its name literally means "city *(horod)* on the Uzh (grass-snake)" because the serpentine River Uzh (Уж) winds through it from west to east. Once the westernmost outpost of the Kyivan state, Uzhhorod was devastated by the Polovtsi in 1080. Under Hungarian rule from the 11th through 13th centuries, it was also ruled by Transylvanian princes and Austrian Hapsburgs. Under Czechoslovakia in the 1920s and 1930s, Uzhhorod was ceded to Hungary until Soviet troops took the city in 1944. In independent Ukraine, the city is a peaceful blend of many ethnic groups: Ukrainians, Hungarians, Russians, Romanians, Roma, Slovaks, Germans, Jews. Russian is the most common language, but street and business signs are in Ukrainian.

The main road into town passes miles of stucco homes surrounded by vine-covered iron trellises. Viticulture is noticeable everywhere, even on apartment balconies in the center. The region is known for its dry white wines (look for the outstanding "Rose of Transcarpathia"). Uzhhorod is a beautiful city with a relaxed ambience. A footbridge links the historic city center on the north side of the river to the university, drama theater, hotels, railway and bus stations on the south side. In the center there are a number of small squares linking pedestrian malls lined with numerous shops stocked with the latest Western goods. Narrow streets and an eclectic mix of architecture with a good measure of stucco Baroque buildings give Uzhhorod a Mediterranean feel. The natural beauty of the seasons adds to its charm, with spectacular blossoms in the spring and colorful trees and a grape harvest in autumn.

The castle-fortress on the hill at the end of Kapitulna (Капітольна) Street in the town center was built on the site of the earlier palace of the Ukrainian Prince Laborets, who was executed by the Hungarian army in 896. In use between the 13th and 17th centuries, the castle was repeatedly rebuilt after battles and today it has a crumbling 16th-century facade. Inside is the **Museum of Local Lore**, with a fine archeological collection of area Bronze Age objects and folk art collections of musical instruments and costumes from different parts of Transcarpthia. The castle museums are open from 10 a.m. until 6 p.m. daily except on Mondays. Adjacent to the castle is the **Transcarpathian Museum of Folk Architecture and Life**, a collection of several dozen old wooden buildings containing traditional furnishings, costumes, and crafts of the indigenous ethnic groups including Hutsuls, Romanians, Hungarians, and Boikos. A highlight is the pagoda-like 1777 St. Michael Church from the Mukachevo district. A cultural center at the entrance displays seasonal exhibits of regional arts and crafts. The outdoor museum is open 10 a.m. until 6 p.m every day except Tuesdays. The **Fine Arts Museum**, at 3 Zhupanatska (Жупанатська) Square, exhibits works from artists of Ukraine, Hungary, Czech Republic, and Russia. The grounds of the museum contain interesting sculpted figures depicting known artists.

The tall buff-colored, twin-spired cathedral near the top of Kapitulna Street (Капітульна) was built by the Jesuits as part of a monastery in 1640 and became a Ukrainian Catholic church in 1770. During Soviet times it was Russian Orthodox, but is again a functioning Ukrainian Catholic Cathedral. Beautifully restored, its Baroque interior features a spectacular four-tiered icon screen.

There are numerous cafés in the bustling center, many featuring a blend of Ukrainian and Hungarian or Slovak cuisine, such as *Toranado* with its Western American decor. *Tortilla* at 16 Korzo Street is a large café with a prominent aquarium. Continuing down Korzo Street toward the river, *Kaktus* (**Кактус**), a cowboy-themed bar and restaurant, serves good food and coffee. Evenings are a lively, smoky scene with a band playing American country songs and classic rock. On the south side of the river is the more elegant *Karpaty Art*, at 12 Ferents Rakotsi Street. The lovely interior showcases original fine art, patio seating overlooks a peaceful garden, and there's evening dancing.

South of the river are several Soviet-era hotels with restaurants. *Hungarian Restaurant*, one of several restaurants and coffee shops in the huge hotel *Zakarpattya* (Закарпаття), serves moderately spicy dishes accompanied by a band or floor show. The restaurant in the *Hotel Uzhhorod* on Khmelnitsky Square, just over the west vehicular bridge, is a better place to eat, according to some. There are several nice small hotels in the heart of the old town. *Eduard* is a new hotel at 22a Bachynskyy Street, a 10-minute walk from Koryatovych Square. It offers a guarded parking lot and a 24-hour restaurant and bar. *Korona* is a recently-renovated hotel right in the old town square. Very desirable is *Atlant*, centrally located at 27 Koryatovycha Street, across from the **Koryatovych Bazaar**, a large multi-cultural flea market with Hungarians, Ukrainians, Slovaks, and Poles selling all kinds of Western goods at bargain prices. For a good selection of Transcarpathian crafts, visit *Diamont* at 18 Voloshyn (Волошина) Street.

Not far to the south is **MUKACHEVE** (Мукачеве), the second largest city in the Transcarpathian region, with nearly 120,000 inhabitants. Inhabited since prehistoric times, its strategic position in the picturesque Lyatorytsya (Ляториця) River valley near the border separating Ukrainians, Slovaks, and Hungarians makes for complicated political history. Part of Kyivan-Rus Ukraine in the 10th and 11th centuries, Mukacheve was later captured by Hungary. In 1393 the Hungarian king presented the city to Prince Koryatovych of Podillya, who established a monastery and expanded the fortress that stands on a rocky hill towering high over the town. Later building and rebuilding gave **Palanok** (Паланок) **Castle** a blend of several architectural styles, but it retains medieval features in its thick walls, bastions and tower, a moat and two inner yards. Over the centuries, the castle was the residence of Old Slavic, Hungarian, and Transylvanian princes; the hiding place of the Hungarian crown from Napoleon; and during the Soviet period, a prison, an agricultural school, and a technical school. The beautiful castle was restored in 2001 and now houses a historical museum. Phone (03131) 24 -71. Open 10 a.m. until 6 p.m. On a mountain overlooking the Lyatorytsya river is the **Mykolayivska** (St. Nicholas) convent, founded in the 11th century. Highlights are the 1804 St. Nicholas Church and the cells built in 1786. The convent is at 2 vulytsya Pivnichna.

The Carpathian mountains taper off into foothills in the Chernivtsi region in southwestern Ukraine and eventually form a broad plateau. This area, which borders Romania and Moldova, was historically known by its ethnographic name, Bukovyna. It's about 70 percent Ukrainian, with substantial numbers of Romanians, Moldovans, and Russians. The region is famous for its wood carvings, rug (*kylym*) weaving, and embroidery.

In **VYZHNYTSYA** (Вижниця) on the Cheremosh (Черемош) River (just southeast of Kosiv and about 86 km [50 mi] west of Chernivtsi) is the **Cheremosh Tourist Resort**. The resort is open year-round. From it you can take a bus tour through the picturesque mountain roads or a walking tour in the footsteps of Oleksa Dovbush, an 18th-century local hero known as the "Ukrainian Robin Hood." The town is a woodcarving center and a good place to buy crafts. The Applied Arts Building, a branch of the *technikum* in Kosiv, teaches wood carving, but it also instructs weavers, embroiderers, and designers.

**CHERNIVTSI** (Чернівці), population 260,000, is the political and cultural center of **Chernivetska Oblast**. Located on both banks of the Prut (Прут) River close to the Romanian border, the area was inhabited as far back as the Paleolithic period. Remnants of the Trypillian, Scythian, and early Slavic cultures have been uncovered. In more recent times Chernivtsi was known as Czernowitz under Austro-Hungarian rule, Cernauti under Romania, and Chernovtsi by the Soviets. The contributions of these ruling powers plus those of the substantial Jewish population that once inhabited the city give it a cosmopolitan character. Once an important Jewish cultural center, Chernivtsi's Ghetto still exists: There's an active synagogue and cultural center, and a large Jewish cemetery whose memorials are a who's who of renowned Jewish families. Nevertheless, a Ukrainian feel pervades the city today, and Ukrainian is the leading language.

Chernivtsi has a university, a medical school, an art school, a theater, a philharmonic orchestra, many squares and parks, and a botanical garden. The city bustles with reconstruction projects and shopping. It's accessible by air from Kyiv and by train and bus from many points.

In Chernivtsi's historical district, Byzantine architecture blends with the Baroque and Gothic styles of Central Europe, reflecting the city's 150 years as an outpost of the Hapsburg Empire. The heart of the district is Tsentralna Square, with the 1847 *ratushka,* or town hall. Also on the square is the renovated **Art Museum,** displaying regional folk art and a collection of rare religious books. East of the central square, on Ruska (Pyc'ka) Street, is **St. Nicholas Cathedral** (Миколаївська, *Mykolayivska*), built by the Romanians in 1939 as a copy of a 14th-century royal Romanian church. Its four oddly twisted cupolas earned it the nickname "drunken church." Just north of the cathedral, off Sahaydachnoho (Сагайдачного) Street, is **St. Nicholas Church,** a little wooden church dating from 1607 that was constructed without a single metal nail. Reputedly the oldest building in the Chernivtsi region, the church was restored in 1954.

Going southeast from the central square is the tree-lined main pedestrian street, vulytsya Kobylyanska (вулиця Кобилянска), named after the Ukrainian writer Olha Kobylianska. The street starts with a turn-of-the-century Art Nouveau building containing the worthwhile **Regional History Museum.** Also on Kobylyanska Street is the magnificent **Cathedral of the Holy Spirit** and some noted German and Polish houses. Among the charming shops and cafes are *Vienna Café*, 49 Kobylyanska, the city's most popular restaurant, phone (3722) 2-39-23; and the attractive *Café Maestro* at 30 Ukrayinska Street, phone (3722) 2-81-47. A local dish is *banush,* cornmeal cooked in milk and garnished with bacon pieces, mushrooms, and butter.

Next go south to Shevchenko Street and back up vulytsya Ukrayinska, past the 1869 **Armenian Church**, now a concert hall with excellent acoustics. West of the central square, a few quaint streets lead to Teatralna Square with the **Kobylyanska Theater of Music and Drama**. The theater was built in 1904 by Herman Helmer and Ferdinand Fellner, the Viennese architects who designed the Vienna and Odesa opera houses and other noted theaters throughout central Europe. The square also contains the Jewish community center, which reopened after Ukrainian independence. Universytetska Street is close by and runs west to the most impressive structures in the city, the main building of **Chernivtsi University**, constructed between 1864 and 1882 as the residence of the

Bukovynian metropolitans. The university's Romanesque and Byzantine architecture is embellished with motifs of Ukrainian folk art, such as tile roof patterns that duplicate the geometric designs of weavings. **The Chernivtsi Museum of Folk Architecture and Folkways** is an outdoor museum consisting of two village streets with 40 fully furnished households and public buildings representing Bukovynian settlements of the mid-19th and early 20th centuries. The museum is at 80 Moskovsko Olimpiada Street. Phone (03722) 6-29-70. The leading hotel is *Cheremosh* at 13A Komarova Street, 4 km (2.5 mi) from the center, phone (03722) 4-84-00. Closer to the center is the *Bukovyna,* 141 Holovna Street, phone (0372) 58-56-25 or 3-06-38.

**TERNOPIL**, the capital of the **Ternopilska Oblast**, a picturesque city of 235,000 residents, is a quiet town in an agricultural area, with no heavy industry. The city takes pride in having served as the capital of the independent West Ukraine National Republic for several months in 1918 to 1919. Ternopil is the only oblast capital built around a lake. **Ternopilskyy Stav**, a man-made lake, is surrounded on three sides by forest and parkland. The main park is Shevchenko Park, on the east side of the lake. Summer pastimes are bathing at one of two beaches, paddle and sail boating, and even wind surfing. At the south end of the park is the city's oldest structure, the ruins of a castle originally built in 1540 and rebuilt by a Polish count in the 19th century. South of the castle, across the main thoroughfare, Ruska Street, is a nice children's park, **Topilche**.

The attractive center of the city and a good shopping street is Shevchenko Boulevard near the **Shevchenko Theater of Music and Drama**. The theater faces Teatralnyy Maydan, the central plaza, which is bordered by Valova Street, a pedestrian mall lined with outdoor cafés, souvenirs, artists, and local craft vendors. Valova extends north to the statue of Ivan Franko where it intersects another pedestrian street, Sahaidachnoho. Going west on Sahaidachnoho is the immense Greek Catholic Church of the Dominican Monastery and Cells, a Baroque basilica built between 1749 and 1779. Today it functions again as a monastery for men. The **Ternopil Local Lore Museum**, 3 Mystetstv Square, south of Ruska Street, is in a large modern building. Exhibits include historical documents, 17th- century military objects, and folk clothing and crafts.

**Hotels and Restaurants.** *Hotel Ternopil*, 14 Zamkova Street, on a hill overlooking the lake, has a very good Ukrainian restaurant. Phone (0352)

22-42-63. *Halychyna*, 1 Chumatska Street, on the opposite side of the lake, is smaller and newer. Phone (0352) 43-57-92. There are many good places to eat in the center. *Stare Misto* (Old Town), on the south side of Sahaidachnoho Street toward the Greek Catholic Church, serves tasty, inexpensive dishes with outdoor seating in summer. *Khutir* offers traditional food in a forest setting on the west side of the lake. *Yevropa*, on the north side of Sahaidachnoho, past Verlova, serves food in its bar and in a classy restaurant. Its "Drunk Cherry" ice cream is a local favorite. *Flamingo*, south of the center next to the bus station on Zhyvova Street, makes some of the best pizza in town; a specialty is green *borshch* served in a freshly baked bread bowl. It's worth the ride east of the center to the colorful *Staryy Mlyn* for excellent *shashlik, kovbasa, borshch,* potato pancakes and other Ukrainian dishes. Take Marshrutka 27, 28, or 30 to the first bus stop after the railroad underpass and look for a three-story building on the northeast side of the circle.

**Pochayiv Monastery** (Почаївська лавра, *Pochayivska lavra*) is approximately 75 km (45 mi) north of the city Ternopil. The second largest Orthodox monastery in Ukraine, after the Kyivan Cave Monastery, its first recorded history dates to 1527. Legend has it that it was founded by monks from the Cave Monastery who fled the Tatar invasion of Kyiv in 1240. In 1261 the monks saw an apparition of the Mother of God. From the imprint of her right foot on the rock on which she stood, there flowed an eternal spring with healing powers.

The monastery grew from the donation of benefactors. In 1597 a Ukrainian noblewoman, A. Hoyska, donated a large estate as well as a miraculous icon of the Mother of God that had been brought to the area by a Greek metropolitan. This icon reputedly healed many who prayed to God before it, and in 1675 it saved the monastery from an attack by Turks and Tatars. The complex flourished and grew despite a complicated history of being buffeted among churches and states. In 1730 it was transferred to the Ukrainian Greek Catholic Church, and under the Basilian monastic order became an important cultural and publishing center. In 1831 the Russian government gave the monastery to the Russian Orthodox church and in modern times the Soviet regime all but closed it. Fully functioning again with about 70 monks in residence, it draws hordes of faithful pilgrims.

The most noteworthy building in the complex is the **Dormition Cathedral** (Успенський собор, *Uspenskyy sobor*), built on a cliffside terrace between 1771 and 1783 and renovated in 1876. The vast Baroque cathedral has eight large and seven smaller cupolas and can accommodate 6,000 people. Surrounding the cathedral are monks' cells. Nearby are a bishop's residence, a large bell tower, and several other churches of differing architectural styles, including a cave church with the remains of the first Father Superior in 1604, Saint Iov.

Pochayiv is one of Ukraine's primary pilgrimage sites. At the 5 a.m. daily service, worshipers revere the miraculous icon, which, according to Ukrainian custom, is draped with an embroidered towel and lowered for veneration. The gold cloth of the healing "footprint" spring is alsounveiled. Visitors arriving later can receive a sample of the spring's holy water. Each year on August 5, thousands of faithful gather to commemorate the anniversary of the deliverance from the Turks. The city of Pochayiv also contains an ethnographic museum; a wooden church dating from 1643, the **Church of the Holy Protectress** (Покровьска, *Pokrovska*); and **All Saints Church** (Всіхсвятська церква, *Vsikhsvyatska tserkva*), a Baroque church from 1773.

**KAMYANETS-PODILSKYY** (Кам'янець-Подільський) is in the **Khmelnytska oblast**, east of the Ternopil region. The town sits on a sheer rock bluff carved out of the steppe by the Smotrych (Смотрич) River below. Continuously occupied since the Kyivan-Rus period, Kamyanets-Podilskyy has 100,000 residents today, but during the 15th through the 17th centuries it was one of the largest cities in Ukraine. Historically it straddled the boundary between European and Asian empires, between Christianity and Islam, and between Catholicism and Orthodoxy. An important commercial center on the route from Kyiv to the Balkans, Kamyanets-Podilskyy shows the influence of several ethnic groups. Ukrainians first settled the area in the sixth century, followed by Armenians, who in the 13th century built the St. Nicholas Armenian Orthodox Church, the oldest Armenian church in Ukraine. In the middle of the 15th century Polish colonists took over. Each community maintained one of the city gates and was represented on the city council. The city also had a large Jewish minority. In 1672, when the city was conquered by the Ottoman Turks, there were eleven Orthodox churches, a Catholic cathedral, five Catholic religious houses, and three Armenian churches. In the late 19th century, under Russian control, a resettlement policy encouraged Jews to move to the area. By 1880 the city's Jewish population was nearly 70 percent.

The composer Mykola Leontovych, while a student at a theological seminary in Kamyanets-Podilskyy, wrote his world-famous Epiphany carol *Shchedryk,* known in English as the "Carol of the Bells."

The **Kamyanets-Podilskyy Historical Museum and Preserve** covers about 30 hectares (12 acres) and contains almost 100 architectural monuments and other artifacts that played a significant role in the complicated history of Kamyanets-Podilskyy. The centerpiece of the preserve is the large stone citadel that guarded access to the city. With its towers, dungeons, turrets, and underground passages, the fortress is a good example of military architecture of the feudal era. Inside is a fine ethnographic museum with costumes, embroidery, art, and religious artifacts from Podillya. It's open 9 a.m. to 5 p.m. daily.

Besides the fortress there are other remnants of diverse cultures – a Polish town hall, a number of Roman Catholic monastic buildings, and Armenian warehouses. Layers of civilization are strangely juxtaposed. Next to the Roman Catholic Cathedral of Ss. Peter and Paul stands a Muslim minaret, for example, topped with a bronze statue of the Virgin Mary. On-going excavations are conducted by international archeologists in cooperation with the Kamyanets-Podilskyy Foundation, a nonprofit organization devoted to the study and preservation of the Old City's cultural heritage. The historical sites are largely unrestored, with the exception of the fortress.

Leaving the fortress, you cross over a bridge to the old town square, **ploscha Virmenskyy**, with Armenian structures dating from the 14th through the 19th centuries. An Armenian restaurant, ***Pid Bramoyu***, which serves good, spicy cuisine of the Caucasus, is set in the ancient walls. About 300 meters (1000 feet) north of the fortress, at 3 Zhvanetske Shose is *Ksenia*, a new good motel with a restaurant, phone (03849) 2-03-79; fax (03849) 2-86-13; e-mail: ksenia@kp.km.ua.

**KHOTYN** (Хотин), is just 23 km (14 mi) south of Kamyanets-Podilskyy on Khmelnytsky (Хмельницький) Road. The town is noted for a large fortification system built on the steep right bank of the Dnister River by the Genoese in the second half of the 13th century. The site of many battles, the fortress was rebuilt in the 15th and 16th centuries. The fiercest struggle was the Khotyn Battle of 1621, when Zaporizhski Kozaks joined the Polish to defeat a 150,000-strong Turkish army, thus checking the Turks' westward conquest of Europe.

The fortress complex includes defensive towers from 1480, a commandant's palace, and a church. Some of the towers are as high as a 12-story building and the grayish-white limestone walls are embellished with red brick ornamentation. The fortress has been the location of a number of films because of its remarkably good condition and its classic castle appearance.

North of Kamyanets-Podilskyy on Road M20 and east on M12 is **MEDZHYBIZH,** a town of 2,000 inhabitants on the Buh river. The town has a striking 14th-century stone fortress with a well-preserved castle and towers and some 16th-century churches. The majority of visitors, however, come on pilgrimage to honor Israel Baal Shem Tov, the founder of Hasidism, an important Jewish religious movement. Born Israel ben Eliezer in 1700, Rabbi Israel settled in Medzhybizh in the middle of the 18th century and became a renowned teacher, attracting thousands of followers by teaching that those leading ordinary, humble lives can experience God. He and some of his disciples are buried in the Jewish cemetery in Medzhybizh.

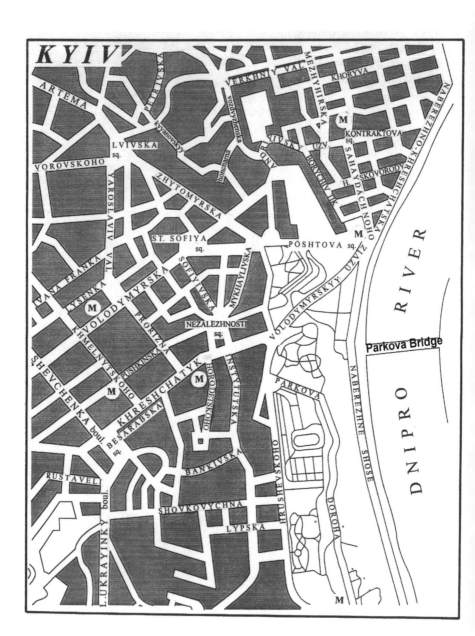

# CHAPTER 7.
# KYIV: UKRAINE'S CAPITAL CITY

КИЇВ    KIH-yeev

**Name.** Legend has it that the city was founded by Kyy (Кий), prince of a Slavic tribe, with his two younger brothers and sister. The name Київ (KIH-yeev) is the possessive adjective form of the word Кий – literally, it means "of Kyy." Kyiv is known as the Golden-domed City (*Zolotoverkhyy*) because of the numerous church cupolas covered with gold leaf, estimated at as many as 1,000 domes during the peak of the Princely Era.

**Location.** According to an old Ukrainian saying, all roads lead to Kyiv. Situated on the bank of the Dnipro River in north central Ukraine, Kyiv is indeed a major road and rail junction and a port city. By highway, it's about 480 km (300 mi) from Odesa, 544 km (338 mi) from Lviv, and 487 km (302 mi) from Kharkiv.

**Population and Language.** Kyiv is Ukraine's most populous city, with 2.6 million residents. The city is growing rapidly, as well-educated, jobless young people from around the country relocate for the greater opportunities it offers. Eighty-one percent of the residents are fluent in Ukrainian while 92 percent can speak Russian. Ukrainian literacy is increasing as more and more schools have begun to conduct classes in Ukrainian.

**Climate.** Summers are moderately warm, with an average July temperature of 19.3°C (66.7°F) and an average July high of 22.7 °C (73°F). Generally, air-conditioning is not missed. Winters are moderately cold, with the average January temperature -6°C (21°F). There's usually snow from mid-November until the end of March. For current weather conditions in Kyiv, you can go to the Web site weather.yahoo.com/forecast/UPXX0016-f.html.

**Business and Industry.** As the administrative center of its oblast and the capital of Ukraine, Kyiv has a great number of government workers. It's the seat of the Ukrainian Academy of Sciences and has numerous research and educational institutions. It's rich with cultural and entertainment opportunities, from classical music, theater, and folk dancing to a lively nightclub scene and sports events.

The major economic activity is heavy industry, especially machine building, metalworking and the manufacture of chemicals and wood products. Electronics and printing are also important. Nevertheless, Kyiv is a very green city, with an official count of 300 parks and gardens.

## History

Archeological discoveries date human habitation in the Kyiv vicinity to the Stone Age (40,000 to 10,000 BCE). A settlement existed in some form as far back as the first century CE, but historians traditionally date the founding of Kyiv to 482 CE. According to an 11th-century chronicle, when Prince Oleh ascended the throne he asserted his dominion over all the Kyivan principalities by calling Kyiv the seat of great princes and proclaiming "This will be the mother to all the Rus' cities." The word "Rus," thought to be of Scandinavian origin, was an ancient term for Ukraine as well as for much of Eastern Europe.

Its site on the Dnipro River gave Kyiv access to the Black Sea. It developed into a regional trade center and a gateway for economic relations with countries of western Europe, the Baltics, Asia Minor, and Byzantium. As a crossroads of the East and West, the city grew in wealth, power, and influence. By the time Volodymyr came to rule in 980, Kyiv-Rus was a leading power in Europe. It occupied the territory from the Baltics and the Carpathians to the Black Sea and the Volga. Volodymyr's search for a religion for his people and his choice of Byzantine Christianity is legendary.

Under the reign of his son Yaroslav the Wise (1017−1054), the city continued to flourish. It became a great cultural center, with the development of a written language, literature, and art. Magnificent structures were built, and by the 12th century, the city had approximately 400 churches.

During the last half of 12th century, Kyiv was weakened by internal conflicts among members of the ruling family. The final blow was the invasion of the Tatars (Mongols) in 1240. They held the city for 80 years, it then passed into Lithuanian and Polish rule. Kyiv experienced a revival in the early 17th century and became the great political, religious, and cultural center of Ukraine, but was ravaged by the Polish-Lithuanian army in 1651.

In order to free Kyiv and Ukraine from the Polish, the Kozak leader Bohdan Khmelnytsky turned to Tsar Aleksei of Russia (then known as Muscovy) for help. While it's unclear whether their agreement in 1654 was understood as a simple military alliance or a submission to Russian authority, this desperate act placed Kyiv under Moscow's control. Russia subverted the Kozak autonomy, and war between Russia and Poland devastated Ukrainian lands.

After the Second Partition of Poland in 1793, Poland retreated from Right-Bank Ukraine. All of Kyiv (as well as much Ukrainian territory to the east) passed to Russian rule. Kyiv grew in importance as the capital of Ukrainian Russia, but tsarist policies suppressed Ukrainian culture and language and promoted Russification, including the encouragement of Russian settlement in Kyiv.

Reconstruction following a great fire in 1811ushered in a policy of urban planning. The city grew rapidly in the second half of the 19th century. A new railroad line linked Kyiv to Odesa and Moscow, strengthening its role as a center of industry, commerce, and administration. Communication and transportation were modernized and the population grew. By the eve of the First World War, Kyiv's population was 626,000, almost ten times greater than before the railroad.

The Revolution of 1905 was followed by a period of liberalization. Kyiv became the focal point of Ukrainian cultural, scholarly, publishing, and political activity. After the tsarist empire was overthrown in 1917, forces promoting Ukrainian autonomy − always ready to surface − proclaimed an independent Ukrainian National Republic on January 22, 1918. It was a period of great chaos, however, and Ukrainians were not able to maintain firm control. The next few years saw a continual struggle between Ukrainian, White, and Red forces. Frequent battles for control of the city caused much destruction. In a single year the population dropped by almost 200,000 residents; many died, others fled because of hunger and terror.

Kyiv became part of the Ukrainian Soviet Socialist Republic in 1920, but because of its Ukrainian activists, the capital was temporarily moved to Kharkiv. In the twenties and thirties, the Kyiv intelligentsia was persecuted and Ukrainianization stamped out. In 1934, the capital was returned to Kyiv and the city was again built up; new machine tool, electrical, and chemical industries were established. The intensive industrialization was fueled by impoverished peasants who flocked to the city from the countryside.

The German invasion of 1941 and its two and a half years of occupation of Kyiv brought severe suffering and devastation. Forty percent of Kyiv's buildings and three-quarters of its industrial enterprises were destroyed. By the time the Red Army retook the city on November 6, 1943, hundreds of thousands had lost their lives, including most of the city's large Jewish population. Eighty percent of the survivors were homeless. The post-war period saw an industrial boom and growth of the suburbs. The Ukrainian Helsinki Monitoring Group, a watchdog committee for human rights, was founded in Kyiv in 1976. In the late 1980s, the democratic movement culminated in the establishment of Rukh, the Popular Movement in Ukraine for Restructuring. Independence was declared in Kyiv on August 24, 1991.

### Sightseeing

Kyiv's lovely historic architecture that accents its vast green areas, and its spacious boulevards, lined with chestnut, poplar, and linden trees, give it an ambience of peaceful elegance that doesn't suggest the turbulence and destruction that took place during the first half of the 20th century. When the Soviet government switched Ukraine's capital from Kharkiv back to Kyiv in 1934, over two dozen ancient churches and historic landmarks in the old city were senselessly destroyed to make way for new government buildings. Especially singled out were those churches built in the Ukrainian Baroque style by Hetman Ivan Mazepa, who sided with Sweden against Russia in 1709.

The devastation was even greater during the German capture and occupation. Much damage was caused by the retreating Soviets who destroyed buildings on Khreshchatyk and adjacent streets.

The three decades following the war saw the construction of massive edifices that catered to popular culture. The Palace of Sports, Palace of Culture, and Central Stadium were built, as well as the large tourist hotels. The victories and heroes of the war are commemorated in bronze, granite, and concrete throughout the city.

While there's a reverent attitude toward the monuments honoring brave soldiers, others have not been well received. To many, the massive works of "socialist monumentalism" that tower over the city with their excess of concrete and steel undermine the delicate beauty of the golden-domed churches. Furthermore, many feel no enthusiasm for the events commemorated by these monuments. For example, the gigantic arch resembling a steel rainbow that rises from the park behind the Philharmonic Building was supposed to commemorate the "union" of Russia and Ukraine, but Ukrainians often referred to it as "The Yoke."

Following the Ukrainian declaration of independence in 1991, changes took place at a dizzying pace. Statues of communist heroes were toppled and religious monuments restored. Historic buildings that vanished during Soviet days were rebuilt and a glut of nationalistic monuments were erected, not always enhancing their location. Streets, squares, and avenues were renamed, with the shuffling of names like a cartographical version of musical chairs; the prominent square named for Bohdan Khmelnytsky was given its old name, Sofiyivsky Square, while the name of Bohdan Khmelnytsky went to the street named for Lenin.

Kyiv's livability has been enhanced with the modernization of railway and air terminals, transportation, and public utilities. A huge number of good restaurants and cafés, serving both international and local cuisine, sprang up in the city. Foreign money brought about a modern renaissance and modern skyscrapers transformed the skyline. Kyiv is one of the most vibrant cities in Europe, although it sometimes appears that Western culture has arrived with a vengeance. The commercial areas have lost their sleepy local character to the glitzy, expensive name-brand shops found in every modern capital city. Kyiv won the dubious honor of erecting the world's biggest billboard, which promoted a shampoo, and later of constructing the largest underground shopping mall in Europe. Nevertheless, it remains a city of beauty and elegance, in which history, culture, and art are important and where temporary difficulties are met with acceptance and forbearance.

**Tourism.** Detailed maps of the center city are easily found in hotel lobbies and newsstands, but not all of them are printed in English. *What's On*, a weekly English-language publication of culture and entertainment in Kyiv, is distributed free in selected restaurants, hotels, and businesses around the center. The English-language *Kyiv Business Directory,* published by the *Kyiv Post,* is a treasure trove of local information and is snapped up quickly when it appears quarterly around the city center.

Kyiv is a wonderful city to visit for its sightseeing and cultural opportunities. The residents are friendly and the city center is relatively crime-free; a visitor feels safe wandering around the city and riding the metro at night. Nevertheless, a few cautions are necessary. Exercise extreme caution in crossing the street. Traffic can be abominable; drivers speed and don't give pedestrians the right of way. Whenever possible, use the pedestrian underpasses. Driving in the traffic-clogged city is not recommended, but the relatively small size of the center and good public transportation make it unnecessary. Beware also of homeless dogs in the streets. Not all of them have been vaccinated and some are rabid.

The Chornobyl nuclear power station is only about 100 km (60 mi) north of Kyiv. While medical experts agree there's no danger to short-term visitors in the Kyiv area, the consequences of long term residency are not completely known. The Chornobyl Information Service hotline will give the current radiation levels: 8-293-4-34-24.

**Orientation to Kyiv.** Kyiv straddles the Dnipro River, which divides it into two unequal parts. The western or right bank — as the river flows from north to south — is the larger of the two. This side is the primary tourist interest, containing the modern city and the historical old town built on a hilly terrain. The eastern or left bank of the city is on an extensive flat plain with a 10-km (6-mi) stretch of fine beaches and a lovely recreational area that merges into drab industrialized suburbs with large housing developments.

The most efficient way to see Kyiv is a sightseeing tour of the whole city when you first arrive, in order to get a feel for the layout. An individually guided motor tour of Kyiv, costing about US$50 for three hours, can be arranged through the service bureaus of hotels. You can then choose which attractions you want to see in depth, and walk to many of them or easily zip from one to another on the metro system.

For sightseeing purposes, Kyiv can be divided into sections according to the separate settlement areas that historically grew around the city's hilly terrain. The main street of the **Modern City** is **Khreshchatyk Street** (вулиця Хрещатик, *vulytsya Khreshchayk*). According to one account, its name comes from the word *khreshchennya* (хрещення) meaning "baptism," because it was the eastward route of Volodymyr's subjects to the Dnipro where they received the Christian faith. The **Old Town** (Старий город, *Staryy horod*), also known as Upper Town ( Верхний город, *Verkhnyy horod* ), contains most of the city's surviving historical and architectural monuments. North of the Old Town, down below on the flat land along the Dnipro, is **Podil** (Поділ). This area contains the river port. To the south, on top of the riverbank, is **Pechersk** (Печерськ), the site of Ukraine's largest monastery.

## The Modern City

After World War II, **Khreshchatyk Street** was totally rebuilt. In 1998 it was given a major facelift, and again in 2001. Today the city's main street, with attractive landscaping and classy boutiques, can compete with the best of international thoroughfares. Khreshchatyk's mile-long stretch, from European Square to Besarabian Square, is 70 to 100 meters (230 to 328 feet) wide with a tree-lined pedestrian boulevard on the east side. On weekends the street closes to vehicular traffic and is used for diverse public events and entertainment.

At the northeast end of Khreshchatyk Street, is the city's main square, **Independence Square** (площаНезалежності, *ploshcha Nezalezhnosti*). *Maydan Nezalezhnosti*, as it's commonly called, has long been a favorite gathering place of Kyivites. In 2001, to commemorate ten years of independence, the square was redone with a mishmash of monuments and architectural features, highlighted by an ornate 62-meter (200-foot) column sporting the gilded figure of a woman representing independent Ukraine. On either side are the domed entrances to the gigantic two-level underground mall full of the standard pricey European boutiques. Though it's difficult to find a Kyivite who prefers the new design, city residents come out in large number on nice weekends to stroll, meet friends, and photograph themselves. The *Maydan* is also a lively gathering place for musicians, artists, poets, stand-up comics, roller bladers, and activists.

Side streets along Khreshchatyk did not suffer much during the war and have preserved much of their turn-of-the-century appearance. About half way down, to the south, is **Lyuteranska (Лютеранська) Boulevard**, where late-19th and early-20th-century mansions and luxurious apartment buildings now serve as apartments for the newly rich and as government offices. Lyuteranska joins **Bankivska (Банківська) Street**, characterized by Art Nouveau-style architecture with floral and animal motifs.

At the junction of Bankivska and the attractive **Ivan Franko Square** is **Architect Horodetsky (Архітектора Ґородецького) Street** with the quintessential Art Nouveau building of the neighborhood. **House with Chimeras**, at 10 Horodetskoho Street just above the square, was built by renowned architect Vladyslav Horodetsky in 1902–03 as an apartment for himself. Lavishly embellished with gigantic concrete fantasy creatures – mermaids, elephants, fat bullfrogs on gigantic lily pads – the bizarre-looking residence was Horodetsky's homage to the new building material of his day, concrete. The building was used as a polyclinic for government officials, but is currently serving as the official president's residence during the renovation of Mariyinskyy Palace. Heading back toward Khreshchatyk down **Instytutska Street,** one notices more fine old apartments and office buildings as well as movie theaters and some posh Western shops.

At the west end of Kheshchatyk Street is **Bessarabian Square** (площа Бессарабська, *ploshcha Bessarabska*), site of the first covered market in Ukraine. **Bessarabskyy Rynok** (Бессарабский ринок) was established in 1910. Attractively renovated, it's still the major farmers' market in Kyiv for produce, meat, cheese, and flowers. Open daily, its prices are high but the produce is the freshest in town and beautifully displayed.

Running northwest from Bessarabian Square is poplar-lined      **Taras Shevchenko Boulevard** (бульвар Тараса Шевченка, *bulvar Tarasa Shevchenka*). The boulevard begins with a Soviet-era monument of Lenin; several blocks west it passes lovely **Shevchenko Park**, where a 5.8 meter (19-foot) bronze statue of Shevchenko, the great poet-patriot, stands on a red granite pedestal. The park, between Volodomyr and Tereshchenko Streets, is a gathering place for students who attend Kyiv University.

Two worthwhile art museums are on the east side of Shevchenko Park. The **Museum "Tereshchenko Gallery"** (formerly called Museum of Russian Art) is at 9 Tereshchenko Street (вул.Терещенківська, *vul. Tereshchenkivska)*, in a mid-1880s house built by sugar magnate and patron of the arts, Fedir Tereshchenko. The museum features Ukrainian art from all periods. Old icons, Kyivan Rus artifacts, porcelain collections, and paintings are among its highlights. Hours are 10 a.m. until 5 p.m. Closed on Wednesday and Thursday. Phone (044) 224-62-18.

   **The Art Museum of Bohdan and Varvara Khanenko** ( Музей мистецтв ім. Бодана та Варвара Ханенко, *Muzey mystetstv im Bohdana ta Varvara Khanenko*), 15 Tereshchenkivska, was established in 1908 by archeologist and arts patron  Bohdan Khanenko in a mansion he and his wife, daughter of collector Fedir Tereshchenko, constructed to showcase their art collection. Formerly known as the Museum of Western and Oriental Art, it includes works by Italian, Flemish, and Spanish masters; works from Central Asia, the Near, Middle, and Far East; and ancient Greek, Roman, and Byzantine art. Recently restored, the museum is noteworthy for the elegance of its interior and the depth of its collection. Hours are 10:30 a.m. to 5 p.m. from Wednesday through Sunday. Phone (044) 235-32-90.

Across Shevchenko Boulevard at number 12, the      **Taras Shevchenko Museum** (Музей Т.Г. Шевченка) contains some 800 paintings, drawings, and prints by the great poet as well as mementos of his life. The museum is open daily except Monday from 10 a.m. to 5 p.m. Phone (044) 224-25-

23. The house in which Shevchenko lived and worked in 1846 is    at 8a Shevchenko Lane, about three blocks north, behind Independence Square. Landscape paintings Shevchenko completed while living here are on display, and some of his personal belongings are in the room upstairs. The **Shevchenko House-Museum** is open 10 a.m. to 5 p.m. every day except Friday. Phone (044) 228-35-11.

The striking red-painted Classic-style building on the west side of Shevchenko Park at 64 Volodymyr Street is the main building of Taras Shevchenko University, also known as **Kyiv University**. Founded in 1834, it was destroyed during the Nazi occupation of Kyiv and rebuilt between1946 and 1952. Today it's one of the most prestigious institutes of higher education in Ukraine.

The **A. Fomin Kyiv University Botanical Gardens** are behind the University's main building on Shevchenko Boulevard and extend south to Lva Tolstoho Street. The 23 hectares (56 acres) of neatly arranged and well-kept plots contain some 10,000 plants, shrubs, and trees arranged by habitat. Just northeast of the gardens at 20 Boulevard Shevchenka is the massive **St. Volodymyr Cathedral** (Володимирський собор, *Volodymyrskyy sobor*). The church was built in the late 19th century in the pseudo-Byzantine style to commemorate the 900th anniversary of Christianity in Kyiv. Especially noteworthy are the frescoes. This is the head church of the Kyiv Patriarchate of the Ukrainian Orthodox Church. Daily liturgy is at 9 a.m. and 6 p.m.; Sunday morning services are at 9 and 12 with the Patriarch presiding at the noon service. The choir is excellent.

## <u>Old Town</u>  Старий Город  *Staryy Horod*

**Volodymyr Street** (вулиця Володимирска, *vulytsya Volodymyrska*), is the main street of the old town. **The Golden Gate** (Золоті ворота, *Zoloti vorota*) is at 40a in front of the Golden Gate Station, possibly the city's most beautiful metro station, with mosaic work and candelabra. The Golden Gate, Kyiv's oldest structure, was immortalized in Mussorgsky's piano piece, *Pictures at an Exhibition*. Located in the center of Kyiv during the reigns of princes Volodymyr the Great and Yaroslav the Wise, the Golden Gate was constructed in 1037 as the main triumphal entrance to the city as well as a watchtower. The original structure was of brick and stone and consisted of a tower with a vaulted passageway topped by a platform for guards and a small church. The doors and cupola of the gate-church were covered with gilded copper sheets, giving the gate its name.

The arch was damaged in 1240 during the Tatar-Mongol raids, but continued to serve as the city's entrance until the 17th century. Eventually the arch fell into disuse and became buried. In 1837 the ruins – consisting of some brick and stone columns and portions of the arch – were excavated and reinforced. In 1982 the Golden Gate was restored according to scholarly research to commemorate the city's 1,500th birthday. The reconstruction consists of a tower over the vaulted passageway with the **Over the Gate Church of the Annunciation of the Holy Mary**. A monument of Yaroslav the Wise holding a model of St. Sophia Cathedral was erected in 1997.

At the north end of Volodymyrska, is one of the city's major squares, **St. Sophia's Square** (площа Софійска, *ploshcha Sofiyska*). In the center of the square is the 10.85-meter- (36-foot-) high monument to the Kozak leader, Bohdan Khmelnytsky. The 10-ton bronze sculpture was erected in 1888 on the spot where Kyivites gave Khmelnytsky a triumphal welcome after he defeated the Polish invaders in 1648.

Near the square is **St. Sophia Cathedral** (Софійський собор, *Sofiyskyy sobor*), a masterpiece of world architecture, with beautiful mosaics and frescoes of religious and secularthemes that blend harmoniously with mosaic floors and marble decorations. It was established by Yaroslav the Wise in 1037 to commemorate his victory on the site over the invading Pechenegs. St. Sophia's became the center of official state ceremonies and commemorations as well as a library and center of writing. The early Kyivan princes were entombed here but the only remaining tomb is that of Yaroslav the Wise, who was entombed in 1054 in a six-ton carved marble sarcophagus.

The cathedral and monastery complex was built over a period of nine centuries. The basic structure of the church is original. Its thousands of square feet of mosaics and frescoes in combination are a Kyivan interpretation of the Byzantine style. Especially noteworthy are the color gradations of the mosaic stones, including 25 tons of gold and silver alone. Of the one-third of the original mosaics that survive, the most noted is that of the Christ Pantokrator high overhead in the central dome. In addition to the religious subjects, murals depict hunting scenes, the family of Yaroslav the Wise, and other secular themes.

During its long history, the cathedral was repeatedly gutted by fire and rebuilt, so that the bulk of what there is to see comes from restorations and additions over the centuries. Nevertheless the 11th-century interior has been preserved in the original Romanesque style and decoration, though the exterior architecture took on a Baroque style in the late 17th to early 18th century when the cathedral was enlarged. About 260 square meters of mosaics and 3000 square meters of frescos from the 11th century have been cleaned and restored. In 1990 the St. Sophia Cathedral together with its monastery buildings was included on the UNESCO World Heritage List. Except on rare occasions, the cathedral is not used for services. It functions as a museum of the cathedral's history and the architecture of Kyivan Rus. The restored upper level dates from the 18th century and is used for an exhibition gallery of 11th-century mosaics and frescos from the original St. Michael's Golden-Domed Cathedral walls. Exhibits are well-labeled in Ukrainian, English, and Russian. **St. Sophia Cathedral Museum** is open 10 a.m. to 5 p.m. on Wednesday and 10 a.m. to 6 p.m. on all other days. Admission tickets are sold next door with an extra fee for photographing the cathedral interior. The 76-meter (250-foot) **Bell Tower** is southeast of the cathedral. Built in the 18th century and rebuilt in the 19th, the tower's four stories reflect the evolution of Ukrainian architecture.

Just east of St. Sophia Square is a promenade leading to the newly built **Mykhaylivska Square**, considered by many the center of spiritual life in Ukraine. Along the promenade is a monument of saints Olha, Andrew, Cyril and Methodius. Constructed in 1996 to replace the original monuments destroyed during the Soviet era, they're a popular backdrop for Kyivites who want to be photographed on special occasions. The walkway continues to the brilliant blue cathedral church of **St. Michael's Golden-Domed Monastery** . The original early-12th-century church, second in importance to St. Sophia Cathedral, was blown up in 1937 on orders of Stalin to build a government center in the country's new capital. The massive colonnaded building west of the St. Michael's monastery complex is the only government building constructed on the site. Today it houses the Ministry of Foreign Affairs. The monastery was reconstructed in the 1990s, with the huge cathedral church rebuilt in its 19th-century Ukrainian Baroque style, with six gilded blue and white cupolas. As you approach the church, you pass a bell tower containing a modern carillon system with an 84-ton bell; a chapel dedicated to the victims of the 1932−33 Great Famine; and a museum with a history of St. Michael's Golden-Domed Monastery. St. Michael's Golden-Domed Monastery is under the Kyiv Patriarchate of the Orthodox Church and includes a seminary. Gift shops are on the grounds.

Northeast of St. Michael's Golden-Domed Monastery is **Volodymyr Hill,** a bluff near the highest point of the city. The terraces and parks surrounding the hill constitute Central Park, which was laid out in the 1830s and 1840s. In 1853, a 4.5-meter (15-foot), six-ton statue of the prince-saint was erected in the park. This solitary bronze figure – perhaps the quintessential image of the city – is dressed as an ancient warrior who, with cross in hand, overlooks the flowing river in which he had his subjects baptized.

To the northwest, at the beginning of Volodymyrska Street is the **National  Historical Museum of Ukraine**      (Національний музей історії України, *Natsionalnyy muzey istoriyi Ukrayiny*). Founded in 1899, the museum contains archeological and ethnographical discoveries from prehistoric times, from the Tripillia culture, the Scythians, the early Slavs, and the Kozaks; as well as coins, works of art, and old books. The museum is open from 10 a.m. to 5 p.m. daily except Wednesday; phone (044) 228-29-24. Adjacent to the museum is Old Kyiv Hill, the location of the earliest important structures of Kyiv-Rus. Vestiges show **Desyatynna Church** ("the Church of the Tithes"), the city's first great stone church. Built by Prince Volodymyr brtween 989 and 1015, the church was destroyed by the Mongol invasion in 1240. Historical markers in English are very helpful.

To the right of the museum is one of the most familiar landmarks of Kyiv, **St. Andrew Church** (Андріївска, *Andryivska*). This rococo church with a turquoise facade and green domes accented with ornate golden trim was built between 1747 and 1753 at the place where in 50 CE St. Andrew the Apostle is believed to have erected a cross and predicted that a great city would be founded. The architect was Bartolomeo Rastrelli, the Paris-born Italian who originated the Russian Baroque style. The tall, graceful church is a variation of the traditional Ukrainian five-domed church with a central dome flanked by four slender towers topped with small cupolas.

Under repair for many years, the interior has been meticulously restored to the original Rastrelli plans that were located in Vienna. Its stunning rococo red and gold iconostasis is decorated with carved gilded ornaments, sculptures, and icon paintings. Entry tickets are sold at the *kasa* (каса) near the bottom. The terrace surrounding the church is a vantage point for a fine view of the river and the Podil district below.

On the west side of St. Andrew Church begins the city's most popular tourist street, **Andriyivskyy Uzviz** (Андріївський узвіз). On this long, steep, winding cobblestone street a great many artists and craftmakers sell their works, and galleries and cafés flourish. The tall, sand-colored building with the steep spire that stands out at 15 Andriyivskyy Uzviv is a 1904 apartment house, "Castle of Richard the Lion-Hearted." At number 13 is the **Mikhail Bulgakov Museum**. Bulgakov, a Russian satirical writer, author of *The Master and Margarita,* lived here from 1906 to 1916 and again from 1918 to 1919. The seven-room apartment has been restored with the author's personal effects and family photos.The apartment is a vision in white, inspired by his first major work, *The White Guard.*

Other museums on the street are the **One Street Museum**, 2B, which displays a reproduction of early 20th century Andriyivskyy Uzviz and some temporary exhibits (open 12 to 6 p.m. except Monday); and **Kavalerisdze Museum-Studio** (open 11 a.m. until 7 p.m. daily, closed Monday).

## Podil  Поділ  po-DEEL

At the bottom of Andriyivskyy Uzviz is the Lower Town, or the Podil neighborhood. Extending from the foot of Volodymyr Hill north along the river flats, Podil was settled by fishermen, merchants, and artisans while the Upper Town was home to the nobility and ecclesiastics. Nevertheless, the area is full of historic churches and educational institutions, many which were rebuilt following Ukrainian independence.

From the foot of Andriyiskyy Uzviz, turn right and go a block to the large **Prokovska Church**, built in 1766 in the Ukrainian Baroque style. Turn around on Prokrosvka Street and walk a few blocks down to the heart of Podil, **Contract Square** (площа Контрактова, *ploshcha Kontraktova*), where in olden days international merchants came for trade fairs.

The large white rectangular building in the center of the square is **Hostynnyy Dvir** (Гостинний Двір), or "Hospitable Courtyard," built as a trade building in 1809 and restored from 1983 to 1987 with shops and a restaurant. Immediately to the west is the tall, single-domed **Bohorodytsya Pyrohoshcha Church**. Originally built from 1134-36, the church became the cathedral church of Kyiv following the Mongol-Tartar invasion. City archives were kept in the church, and festivals took place on its plaza. Over the centuries it saw much reconstruction, until in 1935 it was totally demolished by the Soviets. In 1998 it was re-created in a Kyiv-Rus style. The front of Pyrohoshcha Church faces Prytysko-Mykilska and Frolivska streets, location of the **Florivsky Monastery** (Фролівський монастир, *Frolivskyy monastyr*) founded in the 15th century. Daughters of the most aristocratic Ukrainian and Russian families took the veil here and their talents established its fame as a center of gold embroidery. Most of the architectural ensemble was constructed in the 18th and 19th centuries and includes the 1732 Church of the Ascension, the 1824 Resurrection Church, several other churches, a bell tower, and dormitories. Today it's a functioning convent again.

Next to the Prytysko-Mykilska Street entrance gate to the monastery is one of Kyiv's oldest pharmacies, established in 1728 and still operating. Since 1986 the pharmacy houses an **Apteka Museum** (Аптека-музей) with a large number of thematically arranged exhibits detailing the pharmacology history of Kyiv.

The **National Chornobyl Museum** is north of Hostynny Dvir at the corner of provuluk Khorevy and Spaska Street in the fawn-color building under a tower. The museum, established in 1992, details the world's worst nuclear disaster. Open daily except Sunday. Phone (044) 471-54-22.

In the green adjacent to Hostynny Dvir are two monuments. The **Samson Fountain** is a re-creation of an 18th-century fountain that combines art with hydro-technology. Under an arched pavilion the figure of Samson tearing apart the lion's mouth constituted the central section of Kyiv's watermain, inspiring the legend that whoever drank water "from the lion" would forever remain in Kyiv. At the other end of the green is a monument to philosopher, educator, and poet **Hryhoriy Skovoroda**, known as the Ukrainian Socrates. Across the street and facing the monument is the 1815 **Contract House**, a beautiful large two-story yellow building in a Classical style, where the traders signed contacts.

Just to the west of Contract Square, across from the Skovoroda monument, the block between Illinska and Skovorody streets is occupied by two historic institutions. The **Kyiv-Mohyla Collegium** is the large semi-circular building. Constructed between 1822 and 1825, it served as a classroom of the Kyiv-Mohyla Academy which was established in 1632. The academy functioned under the supervision of the Kyiv Brotherhood, an Orthodox order founded by wealthy burghers, nobles, clerics, and Kozaks to protect the Orthodox faith from the onslaught of Polish rule and Roman Catholicism. This prestigious institute educated Ukraine's scholars, statesmen, clergymen, writers, and historians. It was persecuted and closed many times over the years for its liberalism. In 1615 the Brotherhood founded the **Bratsky Monastery** on this site. Much of the monastery was ruined by the Soviets, but the remaining buildings are now part of the **National University of Kyiv-Mohyla Academy**, which reopened as a private liberal arts college in 1992. On the university campus is an 18th century sundial by the French mathematician Brullion. To visit these Podil landmarks, take the metro to ploshcha Kontraktova.

The Podil district's main street, **Sahaydachnoho**, unlike much of the heart of Kyiv, is as flat, straight, and wide as a Midwestern small town main street. Sahaydachnoho Street is undergoing urban renewal, with much apartment renovation and shops and cafés springing up. On weekends, the short street becomes a pedestrian mall with loads of neighborhood college students out for a stroll. Sahaydachnoho ends at the metro stop at **Post Office Square** (площа Поштова, *ploshcha Poshtova*).

The Classic-style church squeezed in between the east side of the metro entrance and the river is the **Nativity of Christ Church**, originally built from 1810–14. In 1861 the church served as the temporary resting place of Taras Shevchenko until his body was shipped down the river to Kaniv for burial. Completely destroyed in 1935, the church was rebuilt in 2003. Across the street is the **funicular railroad**. Originally built in 1905, the funicular has all-metal cars and accommodates 80 passengers in the steep ride up or down Volodymyr Hill, linking Podil in the lower town to Mykhaylivska Square in the upper town.

Across from the Poshtova Metro stop is the River Terminal. The street running north along the river, **Naberezhne-Khreshchatytska**, blends businesses and popular restaurants. Two old churches are in the neighborhood. **St. Elias's Church**, built in 1692, is the single-domed Ukrainian Baroque church with the bell tower. It's believed to stand on the spot where the city's first Christian church with the same name was built in 944 by Christian Varangians. Just to the north at the corner of Pochaynynska and Skovoroda Streets is **St. Nicholas Naberezhna Church** or "Church of the Embankment." This late Ukrainian Baroque church (1772–75), has an elegant facade highlighted by the colonnade ornamentation of the drum supporting the cupola. In 1863 a church with a belfry was added on to the earlier church.

**St. Cyril Church** (Кирилівьска, *Kyrylivska*) **Museum**, 12 Oleny Telihy Street, about 4.8 km (3 mi) northwest of the city center, is an important example of Kyivan-Rus architecture of the 12th century. Its original form and some 800 meters of mural paintings from the 12th, 17th, and 19th centuries have been preserved. The church was commissioned by the wife of the Prince of Chernivhiv around 1146 to serve as the cathedral of an ancestral monastery. The rectangular structure was built according to a cruciform construction with three naves and apses, six pillars, and a single dome. In the 12th and 13th centuries, it was a royal burial place. In the mid-18th century, exterior reconstruction gave it a Ukrainian Baroque appearance. Closed on Friday. From Podil, take Frunze Street north to Oleny Telihy Street.

**Babyn Yar** (Бабин яр) is better known by its Russian name, *Babi Yar.* This memorial to Kyivites slaughtered by the Nazis during World War II is in a tranquil wooden park about 3.2 km (2 mi) northwest of the city center on Oleny Teliha Street between Melnykov and Dorohozhytsky Streets. Several monuments commemorate the horrific event. In 1976 a monument consisting of 11 bronze figures was erected in memory of "Soviet citizens" who were "victims of fascism." The central figure was a communist resistance fighter. The monument ignored the fact that Jews constituted the majority of the 100,000 victims. Other victims were Roma, Soviet prisoners of war, Ukrainian nationalists, and anyone considered a threat to German authority. Following independence, the Ukrainian government invited the government of Israel to erect a new monument. The 1991 monument consists of a 10-foot high bronze menorah that was erected about three-quarters of a mile across the park from the first one, closer to the actual site of execution. Take the metro to the Dorohozhychi station. When you exit (passing a large Western-style supermarket in the metro station) you'll be standing at the beginning of the park and see a new small monument to the children killed at Babi Yar. For the 1991 menorah monument, turn right and walk past the tall tower (380 m) of the Kyiv TV center. To see the 1976 Soviet monument, and several small new monuments, turn left at the metro exit, go around to the other side of the metro station, and cross over to the field.

## Pechersk   Печерськ   peh-CHEHR'SK

Pechersk gets its name from the **Pecherska Lavra** (Печерська лавра), literally "The Cave Monastery," a complex of 40 structures representing eight centuries of art and architecture. This section of the city contains a large riverfront stretch of parkland that extends about 5 km (3 mi) from St.

Andrew Church near Podil as far south as the Academy of Sciences Botanical Garden. The parks are enjoyable to stroll and observe the residents of Kyiv in their leisure, to take in concerts, or stop for snacks. Monuments, restaurants, and a large amphitheater are in this area. There are also government buildings, notably the glass-domed Parliament, in which the country's independence was declared on August 24, 1991, and the ten-story block that houses the Council of Ministers.

**Mariyinskyy Palace** (Маріїнський палац), 5 Hrushevskyy Street (вул. Грушевського, *vul. Hrushevskoho*), is behind the Parliament building just over half a mile from the art museum. The blue and white palace was designed in the rococo style by Bartolomeo Rastrelli, the Italian architect who also designed St. Andrew Church and many of St. Petersburg's great buildings. It was originally built in 1750 as a tsarist palace. Used sporadically, it was renovated in 1870 for the visit of Emperor Alexander II and Empress Maria, for whom it's named. Today it's the official residence of the president of Ukraine (who doesn't actually live in it) and is used for official state meetings and receptions. It's been open only for those who make arrangements with the **Kyiv History Museum** in the Klovsky Palace at 8 Pylypa Orlyka Street (phone 293-13-44), but will close in 2004 for renovation. Trolleybus No. 20 and Bus No. 62 go to the palace.

The **National Art Museum of Ukraine** (Національний художній музей України, *Natsionalnyy khudozhniy muzey Ukrayiny*), 6 vul. Hrushevskoho, is housed in a stately building styled after a Greek temple, complete with lions flanking the entrance. Designed by famous Kyiv architect Vladislav Horodetsky, the museum was constructed with pubic funds and first opened in 1899. It has a large collection of Ukrainian icons, paintings, drawings, and sculpture from the 12th century to the present. The museum contains sections on old art, 19th and early 20th-century art, and contemporary art. Take Trolleybus No. 20. Open 10 a.m. until 6 p.m. daily and 11 to 7 p.m. on Friday. Closed Mondays; free on the last Sunday of the month. Phone 228-74-54.

**The Pecherska Lavra** covers 28 hectares (70 acres) of riverfront parkland between the Metro Bridge and the Paton Bridge. It originated in 1051 when two monks, Antoniy and Feodosiy (Theodosius), founded a monastery in natural caves and built a church above it. Supported by the

Kyivan princes and boyars, the monastery prospered and grew into one of the largest religious and intellectual centers in the Orthodox world. Noted chroniclers, scholars, architects, painters, and physicians lived and worked at the monastery. From the 11th through the 20th centuries, 86 buildings were constructed. For centuries, hundreds of thousands of Orthodox faithful have come to visit the relics of Antoniy and Feodosiy, who were canonized in 1643, and of the later saints entombed in the caves. In 1926 the Soviet government made the complex the **Kyivan Cave Historical-Cultural Preserve**. In recent years the monastery was returned to the Moscow Patriarchate of the Ukrainian Orthodox Church, and today functions both as an active monastery and a museum complex, with a variety of interesting museums. The Church, however, would like control of the entire complex. Several of the churches on the grounds hold services, while others are just for viewing. Touring the caves and a couple other highlights can be done in three hours, but at least a day is necessary to do the complex justice.

The Pecherska Lavra complex is open daily from 9:30 a.m. to 6 p.m. The caves close at 4 p.m. and each museum is closed once a week, most on Tuesday. Also, museums close over the lunch hour, from 1 to 2 p.m. The ticket office at 25 **Sichnevoho Povstannya** (Січневого повстання) **Street**, outside the Trinity Gate Church, sells general admission tickets. Inside, tickets are sold for a few of the individual attractions with extra fees charged for photographing building interiors. A small cafeteria *Kalvarna* (Калварна) is near the bell tower; restrooms are located near the entrance to the caves. There are a few small gift shops on the grounds, most near the entrance. Take Trolleybus No. 20 to the Pecherska Lavra. Phone (044) 290-30-71 if you wish to book a special excursion.

The first church you notice as you approach the Lavra is the **Church of the Savior at Berestove**. Located just north of the Lavra outside its walls, the church is considered part of the monastery preserve. It's generally believed to date to the second half of the 11th century with major rebuilding in the Ukrainian Baroque style in the 17th century. Frescoes and murals from the 12th to the 17th centuries are preserved in the interior. Originally thought to be the burial place of the ruling family of ancient Kyiv, only the tomb of Yuri Dolgorukiy, the founder of Moscow, remains.

**Upper Lavra.** The majority of the architectural structures are situated on the flat plateau that constitutes the Upper Lavra. Over the centuries many of the buildings suffered periodic looting or destruction by invaders or damage from fire. Reconstruction in the 17th and 18th centuries, funded by Kozak hetmen and officers, give the complex a Ukrainian Baroque feel. Later construction in the 19th and 20th centuries was in a Russian synodal style. A number of beautiful historic churches are in the Upper Lavra:

**Holy Trinity Gate Church** (Троїцька надбрамна церква, *Troyitska nadbramna tserkva*) is a narrow, four-tiered, single-domed church located above the main entrance to the Lavra. Originally built from 1106 to 1108, it's not been changed since its early 18th-century reconstruction. The church is a good example of Ukrainian Baroque art and architecture. Outside, embellished stucco moldings frame the icons. The interior features an openwork gilded iconostasis made by Lavra woodcarvers, wonderful painted murals, and a floor of molded cast-iron slabs.

The **Great Bell Tower**, 96.5 m (316.6 ft) high, was built by architect Johann Shädel between 1731 and 1745 in the Classical style, and topped by a gilded cupola. Each of its four octagonal tiers are adorned with columns, pilasters, and cornices. A stairway with 239 steps takes you to the top, where you can view the extent of the Lavra grounds and enjoy a magnificent vista of every corner of the city. There's an extra charge for the bell tower and another fee for a guide to the very top and a look at the clockworks.

Just beyond the Bell Tower is the new **Uspensky (Dormition) Cathedral**. First constructed from 1073 to 1078, this was the first stone structure of the lavra complex and the primary church. Over the years the cathedral was damaged, rebuilt, and enlarged several times, and finally destroyed in 1941, reputedly by mines laid by Soviet forces retreating from the Germans. In 1991 the Cabinet of Ministers of Ukraine passed a resolution to rebuild it, and a splendid reconstruction of a white seven-domed Ukrainian Baroque cathedral reopened in 2001. (See cover photo.)

The church of **All Saints** (Всіх святих, *Vsikh svyatykh* 1695–98), is on the north edge of the Lavra complex or to your left as you face the Dormition Church. Situated above the Economic Gate, the administrative and service office, All Saints is considered one of the great gems of Ukrainian Baroque architecture. Modeled after Ukrainian two-storied wooden, cruciform churches, it has five gilded domes and contains a carved and gilded wooden iconostasis from the 18th century and brilliant interior murals painted in 1905 by students of the Lavra icon painting school. The exterior is delicately ornamented with pilasters, ledges, cornices, and moldings.

In the center of the Upper Lavra is the **Refectory Church**, so-called because it's adjacent to the two-story refectory (dining hall). The church was built in 1893-1895 in the official Russian synodal style. It has a large flat central dome painted with gold rays that is topped by a small cupola and surrounded by four gilded cupolas. The spacious interior is splendid. The church is the head church of the Moscow Patriarchate of the Ukrainian Orthodox Church. Liturgy is performed daily at 7 a.m. and 5 p.m. and Saturdays at 4:30 p.m.

Museums in the Upper Lavra are open daily except Tuesdays at 10 a.m. and close in the mid-to-late afternoon. They require an additional admission fee. If you have time for only one, be sure to see the **Museum of Historical Treasures** (Історичний музей коштовностей, *Istorychnyy muzey koshtovnostey*) in building 10, the former monastery bakery. On display are precious stones or metals excavated or made in Ukraine, organized according to historical era. Exhibits include prehistoric cultures, the Scythian period, the Kyivan Rus era, 14th to 18th century Ukraine, and 19th and 20th century Ukraine. The highlight is the ornate jewelry collected from 4th century BCE Scythian burial mounds in the Dnipropetrovska and Zaporizhska regions. The star of the museum – and perhaps the most renowned museum exhibit in all Ukraine – is a gold pectoral from the Tovsta Mohla burial mound. The large chest cover is elaborately embellished with animal figures. A numismatics section displays coins of ancient Greece, Rome, and Kyiv-Rus, and there's also an impressive exhibit of Judaic ritual objects. Photography is not permitted. Phone (044) 290-13-96.

The **State Museum of Books and Book Printing** is adjacent to the Historical Treasures Museum. Housed in the monastery's original early-17th-century print shop, the museum is devoted to the history of printing in Ukraine. On display are a variety of early books, including those of Ivan Fedorov, the first printer in Russia and Ukraine; graphics; printing equipment; miniature books, and much more of interest to book lovers. Phone (044) 290-22-10.

The **Ukrainian Decorative Folk Arts Museum** is in Trapezna Hall, the former residence of the Kyivan Metropolitan, which is attached to the

Refectory Church. The museum covers the historical development of each type of folk art from the 16th to the 20th century. On display are printed and woven textiles, dress, embroidery, ceramics, glass, porcelain, woodcarving, and fabrics from the past as well as from contemporary masters. There's an especially good collection of old carpets woven in different parts of Ukraine and samples from major porcelain producers.

Near the Ukrainian Decorative Folk Arts Museum (to the right of the bell tower after you enter the main gate) is an offbeat but fascinating **Museum of Miniatures** featuring micro-miniature art of all sorts — paintings, carvings, and engravings — so small they can be seen only with a microscope. The world's tiniest book, a copy of Shevchenko's *Kobzar* with a carved portrait of the poet, is on display as well as various works of art on fruit and vegetable seeds. All the miniatures are the creation of contemporary artist Mykola Syadrysty from Kharkiv.

The **Museum of Theater and Cinema Arts** (Музей театрального та кіномистецтва, *Muzey teatralnoho ta kinomystetstva*), in buildings 24–26, displays costumes, stage decorations, posters, drama manuscripts, musical scores, and all sorts of memorabilia from outstanding Ukrainian actors, directors, film makers, playwrights, and composers dating back to the early part of the last century. Phone (044) 290-16-22.

The **Caves** (Печери, *Pechery*) are situated in the **Lower Lavra**, the hilly southern half of the complex. They consist of two underground labyrinths of tunnels ranging from 5 to 10 meters (16 to 33 feet) deep with corridors up to 1.5 meters (5 feet) wide and 2 meters (6 ½ feet) deep. Excavated in these soft sandstone catacombs are small burial niches containing the remains of monks and saints that have been naturally mummified due to the chemical composition of the soil and the cool, constant temperature. The caves are divided into the Near and Far Caves.

The **Near** or **St. Antoniy Caves** are 228 meters (750 feet) long. They contain 75 burial niches, including those of Antoniy and of the monk Nestor, the first Ukrainian historian, who died in 1115. Interspersed among the crypts are frescoes and three churches: the Church of the Presentation in the Temple (Введенська, *Vvedenska*); St. Antoniy Church (Антонівська, *Antonivska*); and St. Varlaam Church (Варлаамська, *Varlaamska*). A gilded iconostasis is in each church.

Just west of the entrance to the caves is the exquisitely decorated church of the **Elevation of the Holy Cross** (Хрестовоздвиженська, *Khrestovozdvyzhenska*), dating from 1700. The church has three apses and a Baroque-style wood-carved and gilded iconostasis built in 1769. The southern portal is richly decorated with stucco work.

The **Far** or **St. Theodosius Caves** extend for 280 meters (920 feet). Their entrance is in the **Conception of St. Anne Church** (Аннозачатіївська, *Annozachatiyivska*). The church dates back to 1679. It features a tent-shaped cupola and a carved oak iconostasis. The cave beneath contains 45 burial niches and three churches: **Nativity** (Різдва, *Rizdva*); **St. Theodosius** (Феодосіївська, *Feodosiyivska*); and the **Annunciation Church** (Благовіщенська, *Blahovishchenska*).

The underground passages of the caves go deep into the ground. They are narrow, and, in places, dimly lit and a bit slippery. You can buy a candle from the attending monks, but a tiny flashlight would be more dependable. Rubber-soled walking shoes are also recommended. Many Orthodox make pilgrimages to the caves; visitors should remember that they are in an Orthodox holy place and maintain an attitude of reverence. Women should cover their heads and men should wear long pants.

At 29 Sichnevoho Povstannya ( Січневого повстання) Street, not far down from the Lavra entrance, is the **Ivan Honchar Museum**. (Take the left fork of Sichnevoho Povstannya and when you reach the Afghanistan memorial in the park to your right, enter the courtyard through the arch in the brick wall.) The museum is based on the early-20th- century folk art acquisitions of artist Ivan Honchar, who attempted to document the national character and mentality of Ukraine. Nationalism was suspect during the Soviet period, and a museum wasn't established until 1993. On display are 17th to 20th-century paintings, engravings, sculpture, folk art, and traditional costumes collected from all over the country. Of special interest are 16th to early-20th-century folk icons from different regions. The museum is closed weekends; phone 573-92-68.

A short walk south of the Caves Monastery, up a hillside to 4 Sichnevoho Povstannya Street, is *The Motherland*, a gigantic steel statue of a woman raising a sword and shield. In a city fueled by rumors, many concern this controversial Soviet-era monument that has marred the city's elegant architecture since it was erected in 1981. There's skepticism about official statistics that rank the combined pedestal and female statue 5 to 10 meters taller than the Great Bell Tower at the Caves Monastery. (The woman's figure is 62 m tall and, with its base, the structure totals 108 m or 356 ft high.) Local lore has it that Kyivites objected to anything taller than the bell tower, so the sword was shortened. Urban myth     – motivated by wishful thinking, say some — also had the monument slowly and unevenly sinking into the cavelike foundation beneath it to topple over one day. A geodesic commission that carefully examined the structure, however, concluded that the monument is sound. In 2003 an observation deck in the palm of the Motherland's hand was constructed. Accessible by a special elevator, it gives tourists a spectacular view of the city and contributes to the revenues of the **Museum of the History of the Great Patriotic War**, situated directly beneath the monument. The museum consists of 14 rooms depicting various aspects of Soviet participation in World War II, plus a display of tanks on a plaza outside. Hours are daily except Monday from 10 a.m. until 6 p.m. Phone (044) 295-94-57.

The Perchersk Landscape Park surrounding the controversial monument is a gathering place for large public events. A staircase descends down to Naberezhne Shose. Along the river is the small Navodnitsky Park with its graceful landmark, **Memorial to the Founders of Kyiv** depicting the four founding siblings standing in a Viking-style boat. It's traditional for wedding couples to lay flowers at the base of the monument.

Just past the large highway, *Bulvar druzhby narodiv*, Naberezhne Shose becomes Naddnipryanske Shose. About a half mile south is a charming little complex, **St. Vydubytskyy Monastery** (Видубицький монастир), originally established in the 11th century and restored through the 18th. Its centerpiece is the elegant Ukrainian Baroque **St. George Cathedral** (Георгіївський собор, *Heorhiyivskyy sobor*, 1696–1701). Built in a cruciform design with nine chambers, the cathedral's tall, narrow towers are topped by five cupolas set on polygonal drums, giving it the vertical appearance typical of wooden churches of the Dnipro region. There's also a refectory, a belfry with a pretty top dotted with gold stars, and a remnant of the **St. Michael Cathedral** (Мигайлівський собор, *Mykhaylivskyy sobor,* 1070–1088), with a fragment of an 11th or 12th century fresco, *The Last Judgement.* Take Trolleybus No. 14 or 15 to 40 Vydubytska Street.

**The National Botanical Garden** of the Ukrainian Academy of Sciences is on a bluff overlooking the Vydubytskyy Monastery. Construction of the gardens began with German prisoner-of-war labor in 1944, but the gardens weren't completed and opened until 1964. The academy uses the gardens for horticultural research, and five continents are represented in its 13,000 varieties. The lilac collection, in bloom in May, is particularly noteworthy. The fragrance of lilacs, the song of the nightingale, and the view of the river behind the beautiful church below make this garden a lovely walk. Hours are from 9 a.m. until 4 p.m. every day. A small entrance fee is charged. Take the metro to the Druzhby Narodiv stop or take Trolley No. 15 or Marshrutka 238. Besides using the main gate, you can also access the garden from the southeast through a small gate at the edge of the Vydubytskyy Monastery. There's a small admission charge.

## In the Suburbs

The **Museum of Folk Architecture and Folkways** is worth the 19-km (12-mi) drive down Odesa Road south of the city to the village of Pyrohiv (Пирогів). The 150-hectare (375-acre) outdoor display recreates 16th-to 20th-century village life in different regions of Ukraine. More than 300 restored cottages, granaries, barns, wooden churches, schools, and other village structures are meticulously preserved and furnished with period furniture, utensils, and embroidered linens. The exhibits are organized into farmsteads and villages representing diverse regions of Ukraine and show the variations in their folk art. Of special interest is the exhibition southeast of the entrance depicting fully furnished village homes from the 1960s and 1970s from each of the country's 24 regions, plus Crimea. A stroll through the well-tended hilly terrain past the farmers, housewives, and craftspeople at work is a step back into the past. Exhibits are widely spaced, so that a fair amount of walking is required.

Traditional Ukrainian meals are available in the *Yarivtsi Tavern* and in the alehouse, and handcrafted items are sold in several cottages. On religious holidays and historical memorial dates, there are special festivals and shows and many visitors wear traditional Ukrainian costume. Take Bus No. 24 or No. 61 from the grand National Exhibition Center (Національни центр виставок і яармарків) at prospekt 40-richya Zhovtnya. The museum is open from 10 a.m. to 5 p.m. daily. Between November and May the hours are shortened and some of the buildings are closed.

## The Arts and Recreation

Entertainment runs the gamut in Kyiv, from high culture to sports. Check *What's On,* the *Kyiv Post* or a hotel concierge for current activities and events. Tickets are available at hotel service bureaus, directly from the box office, or from special ticket kiosks around the city. Main box offices are the Teatralna Kasa at 21 Kreshchatyk Street, 26 B. Khmelnytskoho Street, and 16 Velyka Vasylkivska Street, (also called Chervonoarmiyska Street).

**Music.** The **Taras Shevchenko National Opera** (Театр опери і балету im. Т. Г. Шевченка), 50 vul. Volodymyrska ( Володимирська), was built in 1901 by architect Victor Shreter. This fine company produces many classical and new Ukrainian and foreign operas as well as ballets. Phone (044) 224-71-65 or 229-11-69.

The **National Philharmonic**, 2 vul.Volodymyrskyy Uzviz at European Square, is in the historic Merchants Assembly Building. This home of the National Philharmonic Symphony Orchestra of Ukraine has been gloriously restored to its original 19th-century splendor. Its acoustics, among the best in Europe, attract world famous musicians. The Symphony Orchestra has an extensive repertoire of world classics and of early and 20th-century Ukrainian composers. The Philharmonic also has a world-class Chamber Orchestra and a number of high-quality ensembles specializing in traditional and folk music. Phone 228-16-97.

**National House of Organ and Chamber Music**,77 vul.Velyka Vasylkivska (also called *vul. Chervonoarmiyska*) in the beautiful early 20th century pseudo-gothic St. Nicholas Cathedral, is a venue for wonderful regularly scheduled classical music performances. Phone (044) 268-31-86.

**Drama.** Kyiv has a lively theater scene with more than 20 theaters. Here are a few of the most notable. **Ivan Franko Drama Theater** at 3 I. Franko Square ( площа Івана Франка, *ploshcha Ivana Franka)* is a leading Ukrainian drama theater; it also hosts musical performances. Phone (044) 229-59-91. The **Lesya Ukrayinka Theater** at 5 Khmelnytskyy Street (вулиця Хмельницького, *vulytsya Khmelnytskoho*) is a major theater of Russian works. Phone (044) 235-50-87. The **Drama and Comedy Theater on the Left Bank,** 25 Brovarska Avenue, is the city's leading experimental theater, featuring comedy and drama of Ukrainian and foreign playwrights. Phone (044) 517-19-55. **Bravo Drama Theater**, 79 O. Honchara Street, is Kyiv's first private theater and attracts the city's leading actors. Phone (044) 216-40-22.

**Art Galleries**. The **National Union of Artists of Ukraine**, 1−5 Artema Street, sponsors exhibitions of contemporary artists. Phone (044)212-05-35. The **Folk Art Masters Union** exhibits works of leading traditional artists throughout Ukraine in its new gallery at 27a Reytarska Street, near

St. Sophia Cathedral. Hours are Monday through Saturday, 11 a.m. until 6 p.m. Phone (044) 228-56-25.

**Sports and Fitness. Dynamo Stadium**, 3 Hrushevskoho Street, is used by Kyiv's championship soccer team, Dynamo, for matches against other Ukrainian teams. The country's largest stadium, the 83,000-seat **Olympiyskyy National Sports Complex**, 55 Velyka Vasylkivska Street, is used by Dynamo for international matches. Phone (044) 246-70-30. Behind the stadium are the **Central Tennis Courts** with a number of indoor and outdoor courts. For reservations, phone (044) 246-70-53. For a Russian-style sauna, *Tsentralni* at 3 Mala Zhytomyrska Street, close to Independence Square, is state of the art. Bring your own towel. Phone (044) 228-03-78. Fitness club *Planet Fitness* accepts drop-in customers for its modern sauna and other health facilities at 10 Kropyvnytskoho Street, near the Bessarabskyy Market. Phone (044) 254-62-00 #1.

The **Kyiv State Circus** performs in a 2,000-seat amphitheater located at 2 Peremohy (Victory) Square (площа Перемоги). When the circus or a visiting circus is in town, acrobats, gymnasts, clowns, and animal trainers perform weekdays at 7 p.m. and on Saturday and Sunday in matinee and evening performances. Phone (044) 216-39-27.

**Beaches.** Literally hundreds of miles of sandy beaches stretch along the banks and islands of the river Dnipro, most easily accessible by a short metro ride from the city center. **Hidropark**, the most popular and crowded recreation area is on a large island halfway under the Metro Bridge. This popular summer place for boating and sunbathing has a number of beaches and grounds for volleyball, tennis, and gymnastics. There are also food kiosks, beer bars, and cafés. Take the metro to the Hidropark Station.

**Trukhaniv Island**, north of Hydropark, is a short walk from European Square over the Parkovyy pedestrian bridge. This is another popular, crowded beach for swimming or water sports. Changing area and toilets are available and plenty of opportunity for *shashlyk* and beer. For serious sunbathers, there's a nude beach on the bay on the east side of the island facing Hydropark.

**Cautions about swimming:** Cautions about the possibility of post-Chornobyl radioactive silt at the bottom of the river are no longer emphasized, but you should avoid areas that appear to present physical danger or seem chemically contaminated or polluted. Be sure to bring plenty of insect repellent.

**Boat Cruises.** From April through October, the River Station (Річний Вокзал, Richnyy Vokzal) runs cruises on the River Dnipro. A boat ride around the city's environs is 90 minutes long, but if the boat is not more than half full, it won't leave the shore. Cruises to port cities to the south are also possible, but adequate information is not posted at the River Station, so for English-speaking tourists, the help of a travel service or a native Kyivite may be needed. Take the metro to ploshcha Poshtova (площа Поштова) and go to Pier 3 of the River Passenger Terminal or take the funicular down from Volodymyrska Hill

The **Day of Kyiv,** a celebration of the birthday of Kyiv, takes place the last weekend of May. The festival originated in 1982 as a celebration of the 1500th anniversary of Kyiv. The chestnut trees lining city streets and lilacs in the parks are in full bloom, and the rainy weather that often occurs during the festival doesn't dampen the genuine attitude of merriment that pervades the city. Snack and souvenir vendors set up shop among parades and performers in the Khreshchatyk Street area. The highlight is the gigantic art market on Andriyivsky Uzviz with booths of artists and craft makers from all over the country lining the long street in three-deep rows.

### Hotels and Other Accommodations

Kyiv hotels have been renovated and provide nice rooms and a wealth of amenities. Many are owned by the city, which intends to open more top-level hotels in coming years. Generally hotels in Kyiv are quite pricey. Even "budget" hotels that are far from the city center may well run close to US$100 per night.

Individual hotels often offer a wide price range, reflecting room-to-room differences in size, modernization, decor, and amenities. Generally, the less you pay, the simpler the breakfast you'll receive; a mid-price hotel will provide a small breakfast, while an upper-price-end hotel will provide a large and lavish breakfast buffet with hot dishes.

You can book a Kyiv hotel through a travel service, directly with the hotel, or through Internet hotel reservation services such as www.hotelsukraine.com or www.hotelkiev.com. Checking the Internet is a good way to learn more about the hotel and see photos. And a speedy response in English to your initial inquiry can be very reassuring.

Hotels are listed according to proximity to the center. Prices are indicated by $ representing the hotel's usual going rate for a standard double room per night. $ = less than US$100; $$ = US$100 to $200; $$$ = US$200 to $300.

*Ukrainia* (Україна) *Hotel*, 4 Institytska Street, is centrally located in the city, right in Independence Square, over the gigantic underground mall. Formerly called *Moskva*, the 370-room hotel has 24-hour room service, satellite TV, and direct-dial phone. $. Phone (044) 229-03-47.

*Kozatskyy* (Козацький) *Hotel*, at 1/3 Mykhylivska Street, at the opposite end off Independence Square, offers a great view of the city center and is within walking distance of two metro stations. $. Phone (044) 229-49-25.

*Dnipro* (Дніпро), 1/2 Khreshchatyk Street, is one of Kyiv's most popular hotels. Its central location on European Square next to the Philharmonic can't be beat. It has a river view, air-conditioning, a very good restaurant with a great breakfast buffet, 24-hour room service, and outstanding business services. $$. Phone (044) 254-67-77 or e-mail sale@ dniprohotel.kiev.ua.

*Khreshchatyk* (Хрещатик), at 14 Kreshchatyk Street in the heart of the city, opened in 1988 for the 1,000th anniversary of Christianity in Kyivan Rus. Popular with tourists, its comfortable, spacious rooms are a good value. $$. Phone (044) 229-71-93.

*Premier Palace* (Премьєр палац), 5—7/29 T. Shevchenko Blvd. at the corner of Pushkinska Street, was originally built in 1909 as the Palace Hotel and until the recent reconstruction was the *Ukraina Hotel*. Touting itself as the first Kyiv hotel with upscale European standards, the super modern complex is elegant and replete with services. A beautiful swimming pool under a vaulted glass roof, exercise facilities, a computer room, and a rooftop restaurant with a great view add to the exclusivity. $$$. Phone (044) 244-12-01; Fax (044) 229-87-72; www.premier-palace.com.

The *President* (Президент) *Hotel*, at 12 Hospitalna Street, is a large, new hotel that was refurbished in 1999 to become one of the most luxurious in the city. Among the amenities are conference facilities, three restaurants, a pool beauty and health center, and an underground garage. $$–$$$. Phone (044) 294-39-50 or 294-31-57.

The less upscale *Rus* (Русь), next door at 4 Hospitalna Street, provides a wealth of tourist amenities, including safe deposit, souvenir shop, on-call doctor, car rental and airline desk. $–$$. Phone (044) 294-

30-20 or 220-42-55. The President Hotel and the Rus are situated on hilly terrain; city views from their windows are magnificent, but the walk back from the shopping district is a bit arduous. Reservations can be made at its Web site: www.hotelrus.kiev.ua.

*Lybid* (Либідь) Hotel Complex, 1 Peremohy Square, near the city center, is close to the central train station and across the street from a large department store. This large block served Intourist during Soviet days, but renovation has added much charm. The air-conditioned rooms are small but nice, and the lobby offers many tourist services. $ –$$. Phone (044) 236-00-63 or 236-63-36; www.hotellybid.com.ua.

Northwest of the center are several small, charming hotels. *Hotel Andriyivksy* (Андріївський), at 24 Andriyivskyy Uzviz (access from 60 Vozdvyzhenska Street), in a quiet and picturesque location, is a bargain compared to large hotels in the center. $. Phone (044) 416-22-56.

Adjacent to it at 60 Vozdvizhenska Street is *Hotel Vozdvizhenska* (Воздвиженска),a small hotel of great charm. It offers air conditioning, 24-hour service, laundry and other amenities. $$. Phone (044) 462-58-43.

In the Podil neighborhood are two small European luxury hotels with especially good business service: *Hotel Domus* (Домус) at 19 Yaroslavska Street is pleasant and peaceful. $$. Phone (044) 462-51-20. Even smaller is the 17-room *Impressa* (Імпресса), 21 Sahaydachnoho Street. $$–$$$. Phone (044) 417-00-27.

*Hotel Dniprovskyy* (Дніпровський), 10a Naberezhna-Khreschatytska Street, moorage #2 at the River Station, is a 22-room hotel in a new two-story barge on the Dnipro river. Beds are king-sized and rooms are air-conditioned with satellite color TV and international telephone. There's a currency exchange, an Internet room, and a safe deposit box at the desk. The Dniprovskyy is very close to a metro station. $. Phone (044) 490-90-55.

*Kyiv* (Київ)*Hotel*, 26/1 Hrushevskoho Street, is a 20-story white tower, reconstructed in 2002, just southeast of the center. Close to government offices, the hotel's dining rooms offer a large choice of excellent Ukrainian dishes with very good service at reasonable prices. Evenings, there's live music for dancing. In the lobby are a currency exchange, souvenir shop, newsstand, and reception desk safe deposit box. $. Phone (044) 253-01-55 or 253-64-32.

Beyond the center, the *Hotel Bratyslava* (Братислава) at 1 Andriya Malyshka Street is a serviceable alternative. Rooms cost about half the average price of hotels in the business district and the metro ride across the bridge to the Darnitsa stop is convenient and picturesque. $. Phone (044) 559-69-20.

Very reasonably priced is *Hotel Myr* (Мир), 70 Holosiyivskyy Avenue, located in a picturesque neighborhood near Holosiyivskyy Park on the city's south side. The hotel has attractive rooms with private baths and refrigerators, satellite color television, and telephone. Amenities include a restaurant, cafés, currency exchange, casino, hairdresser, and business services. $. Phone/fax (044) 264-96-51; e-mail hotelmir@ ambernet.kiev.ua; Web site www.hotelmir.kiev.ua.

*Prolisok Tourist Complex*, 139 *Prospekt Peremoha*, is 19 km (12 mi) west of the city center in a 60-acre pine forest with oak and birch groves. The complex includes two new hotels as well as shops, bars, and car service. Prolisok caters to groups and offers a variety of reasonably priced package tours around central Ukraine and Crimea as well as hunting excursions. Phone (044) 451-90-37; 451-80-38. Three restaurants on the premises serve very good Ukrainian cuisine in traditional decor: *Prolisok, Yaroslaviv Dvir*, and the most expensive, *Kara's House* (Хата Карася, *Khata Karasya*).

**Apartment Rental** can be a more comfortable and thrifty alternative to hotels. Fully furnished apartments with hot water in the center of the city, range from about US$50 to US$120 per day, depending on size and amenities. Services available include cleaning, laundry, meals, car rental and parking.

The **Sherbourne Guest House** has several small apartment buildings in the Perchersk area. Attractive apartments cost under US$100 per night with cleaning service. Service is prompt and efficient, and doorman and desk are on duty 24 hours. The lack of an elevator may be a problem for those with heavy luggage. Phone (044) 490-96-93.

For additional rental possibilities, contact a travel service that specializes in Ukraine, or check out Web sites on Kyiv apartment rentals. *Kiev Apartment Express* at www.autoexpress.kiev.ua/serv/apartments.htm has a large listing; also try *Kiev Apartments* at www.lodgingkiev.com.

## Restaurants and Nightlife

Restaurants and cafés featuring a wide variety of cuisines from around the world have sprung up all over the central business district. Whatever your taste, from posh restaurants with doormen and other pretensions of grandeur (French generally means very expensive) to McDonald's (there are at least 17 in the city), you'll have no trouble finding satisfactory dining. Ambience is very important in Kyiv restaurants with decor ranging from tasteful understated modern to historical fantasy. Restaurants are usually open from noon until late evening.

**Ukrainian-Style Restaurants.** To sample local cuisine, consider the following: ***Hostynyy Dvir*** (Гостуний Двір) or "Welcoming Court," is an airy elegant dining room at 4 Kontraktova Square in the Podil district. Specialties include mushrooms in a cream sauce, potato or berry *varenyky,* and a variety of broiled or boiled fish. Wine is from Crimea. Waiters are costumed and musical entertainment in the evenings include Ukrainian folk songs and international favorites. Prices are higher than in many Ukrainian cuisine restaurants, and food and service are very good. Open daily from noon until 1 a.m. Phone (044) 416-68-76.

***Khutorok*** (Хуторок), 1 Spasky Pier off Naberezhno-Khreschatytska Street, is a large colorful barge on the Dnipro River. In a setting crammed with Ukrainian country motifs, diners sit in either the "cellar" or "attic" and choose from tasty house specialties prepared in the brazier such as *varenyky, holubsti,* blood pudding, and sausage. Open noon to midnight. Live music 8 p.m. until 11 p.m. Reservations recommended. Phone (044) 416-80-39 or 463-70-19.

***Kobzar*** (Кобзар), 25 Khreschatyk Street, is a Ukrainian village transplanted to the heart of Kyiv's busiest street. The outdoor seating area is great for people-watching. Specialties include pork rolls with mushrooms, chicken Kyiv, and baked apples with cheese.Reservations are recommended. Phone (044) 234-09-35.

***Kozak Mamay*** (Козак Мамай), 4 Prorizna Street, on the south side of the Main Post Office, offers a quiet respite from the bustling Khreshchatyk Street. Costumed wait staff serve outstanding out-of-the-ordinary Ukrainian cuisine, such as rabbit stewed with vegetables in sour cream, veal rolls stuffed with cheese and mushrooms, and fish specialties such as trout baked in pastry. Menus include English translation, and you can choose to sit indoors or on the patio facing a small park. Musical entertainment. Open 9 a.m. until 11 p.m. Phone (044) 228-42-73.

***Pervak*** (Первак), 2 *vul. Rohnidynska* , close to Lva Tolstoho Square, is the place to go for a large selection of excellent Ukrainian specialties without the over-the-top village decor. The large attractive restaurant fancifully combines such diverse decorative elements as antiques, fluttering angels, Communist leaders, and the U.S. West. Open 10 a.m. until 12 p.m. Phone (044) 235-09-52 or 246-77-84.

*Skhidtsi* (Східці) or "The Stairs," one of Ukraine's first private restaurants, is on the lower floor of the House of Architects at 7 Borysa Hrinchenka (Бориса Грінченка) Street close to Independence Square. Specialties in this very popular basement restaurant include beef stew with smoked plums served in ceramic pots and fish rissoles. Skhidtsi (or *Skhody* in Russian) is open from noon until 11 p.m. every day; phone 229-86-29 several days in advance for reservations.

*Taras* (Тарас), in Shevchenko Park on Volodymyrska Street, serves traditional Ukrainian cuisine daily from 10 a.m. to 2 a.m. Phone (044) 235-21-32.

*Tsarske Selo* (Царське Село), 42 Sichnevoho Povstannya Street, just south of the Lavra, goes over the top with its 18th-century Ukrainian country decor. Popular with tourists, the restaurant serves very fine dishes based on traditional family recipes, using a charcoal and firewood oven. Costumed staff meet visitors at the door and wandering minstrels entertain on a private balcony. Tsarske Selo is open from 11 a.m. until 1 a.m. on Sunday through Thursday or until 2 a.m. on Friday and Saturday. It has a parking lot. Reservations are suggested; phone (044) 573-97-75.

*U Seni i Gogy* (У сені і гоги), 4 Shota Rustaveli Street, near the Great Synagogue, was named by *Kyiv Post* readers as their favorite Ukrainian cuisine restaurant. Its decor is typical country rustic, but its dining area smaller than many Ukrainian-style restaurants. Phone (044) 234-06-92.

**International Restaurants** abound in Kyiv, with pizzerias and American cuisine, such as Tex-Mex, particularly popular.

*Osteria Pantagruel,* at 1 Lysenka Street, near the Golden Gate, is a popular country-style tavern offering traditional Italian cuisine with homemade pasta and a large selection of wine. Its patio seating area is among the prettiest in the city. Open 11 a.m. until 11 p.m. Phone (044) 229-73-01.

For upscale Italian cuisine with great views, there's *Da Vinci* at Evropeyska Square, near the Dnipro Hotel. Open 8 a.m. until 12 p.m. Phone (044) 229-00-59.

*Apollo*, in the Passage off 15 Khreshchatyk Street, is an elegant upscale Italian restaurant, with outstanding cuisine and a good selection of French and Italian wine. Phone (044) 229-0437.

*Himalaya,* 23 Khreschatyk, is a conveniently located Indian restaurant with an authentic tandoor oven. Open 12:30 p.m. or until the last customer leaves. Phone (044) 462-04-37.

*Mylyy Avgustyn,* one level down at 18 Velyka Vasylkivska Street, just off Tolstoy Square, as the first German restaurant to open in Kyiv. It simulates a Bavarian beer hall with very good German and Ukrainian dishes. Phone (044) 224-91-29.

*Svitlytsya* (Світлиця), 13b Andriyvsky Uzviz, serves Breton cuisine and European wine in an attractive wooden cottage decorated with a collection of miniature lighthouses. Recommended are the crepes or steak with a wine sauce and French fries. Open 11 a.m. until 11 p.m. Phone (044) 416-31-86.

*Arizona BBQ,* the waterfront, is a popular Southwestern sports bar serving ribs, steaks, fries, and American-style breakfast in a very faux-Western decor. Open 8 a.m. until the last customer leaves. Phone (044) 416-24-38.

*San Tori* (Сан Топі), at 41 Sahaydachnoho Street in Podil, is a highly reputed Japanese and Thai restaurant. Open daily from 11 a.m. until 1 a.m. Phone/fax (044) 462-49-94 or 462-49-95.

**Fast Food.** When sightseeing takes precedence over a leisurely meal, you'll have no trouble locating fast food. *McDonald's* has about 17 outlets throughout the city; *Mak Smak* is a popular competitor with 8 locations serving pizza and sandwiches around the clock. According to a *Kyiv Post* poll, when it comes to traditional deli fare, nothing beats *Furshet* for its breads, meats, cheeses, prepared foods, and fresh-squeezed juices. Located in the basement of the new Madarin Plaza next to the Besarabska Market, Furshet is open from 10 a.m. to 10 p.m. Phone (044) 230-95-22. *Ripriza,* 40/25 B. Khmelnytskoho, is an outstanding takeout or dine-in bakery with a small non-smoking dining room in the back serving delicious menu items, including omelets and quiche for breakfast. Phone (044) 246-49-00.

If you'd rather eat Ukrainian on the run, *Shvydko* (Quickly)*,* a Ukrainian knock-off of McDonald's, serves the most quintessential national dishes in a hurry. Shvydko has several outlets around the city including the Globus Mall food court and the *Kvadrat* shopping malls in the underground metro passages at Slavy Square and Druzhby Narodiv.

A bigger choice is offered at the trendy **Ukrainian cuisine cafeterias**: The popular (and crowded at meal times) *Domashnya Kukhnya,* at 22 B. Khmelnytskoho in the center, also has a second location at 2a Kostyantynivska in Podil. ***Puzata Khata*** (Home of the Big Belly), at 1/2a Baseyna is across the street from the Bessarabska Market in a two-level restaurant, and ***Dva Husya*** (Two Geese) is nearby at 42 Khreschatyk.

**Nightclubs.** The nightlife scene in Kyiv is thriving, with an abundance of bars, nightclubs, discos, cabarets, strip joints, and casinos throughout the center of town. They're easy to spot. Among the most popular is ***The River Palace***, a classy entertainment complex on a boat on the Dnipro River where foreign businesspersons and men on wife-hunting expeditions mingle with the locals. A sports bar with a British pub atmosphere on the lower deck features live music, dancing, and informal dining; on the middle deck is a night club and Le Jardin, an elegant restaurant with a mix of delicate seafood dishes and classic European appetizers and desserts. A huge casino is on the upper deck. Credit cards are accepted and parking is available. River Palace is open from 3 p.m. until 8 a.m. and is at Naberezhne Shosse on the waterfront. Take the metro to the Dnipro stop. Phone (044) 240-72-63 or 416-82-04.

## Shopping

Bright new shops filled with luxury foreign goods have popped up all over the city. The most-sought-after Western brand names compete with lower-priced Ukrainian shops and with the vast selection at the city's some 115 thriving open markets. **Khreshchatyk** is the city's main shopping street. The Kreshchatyk on-street shops offer a variety of interesting merchandise, but far more is packed into the two floors of shops in the gigantic mall stretching underneath the length of the street.

The ***Globus Mall Complex*** at Independence Square, one of Europe's largest underground shopping malls, is a popular gathering place during the cold winter months. The ambience and stores, however, are generic European and provide little reminder what country you're in. For a more authentic Ukrainian shopping experience, stay above ground or patronize the vendors in the kiosks in the metro stops.

Halfway down Kreshchatyk, on the south side of the street, is a narrow arched passage, *Pasazh* (Пасаж), with cafés and restaurants and specialty shops full of Western high-tech goods. Across the street and to the west is **Bohdan Khmelnytskoho**, another good shopping street with many attractive stores. At the west end of Kreshchatyk, ploshcha.Tolstoho turns into **Velyka Vasylkivska Street**, (often called by its former name, Chervonoarmiyska). This area is a good place to find bargains in traditional crafts, books, or gifts.

**Open Markets** or *bazaars* are numerous throughout the city and offer the thrill of the hunt along with the best prices. Among the some 115 open markets are special ones for cars, home appliances, fishing gear, pets, wedding apparel, and electronics. For tourists, two of the most interesting are the *Volodymyrska Market*, which sells spices, nuts, meat, vegetables, clothing, toys, and miscellaneous items (take the metro to Ukraine Palace and go two blocks south and one block west); and *Petrivka*, a large book and clothing market in Podil near the Petrivka metro stop.

**A Few Interesting Stores.** The *Central Department Store* (Центральний універмаг, *Tsentralnyy univermah),* commonly called *TSUM* (ЦУМ) is at 2 Khmelnytskoho, just off Khreshchatyk. If you've visited TSUM in the past, check to see how it's changed. When tired of browsing through household items, clothing, and accessories sold at better prices than the foreign boutiques, stop for coffee and a sandwich or pastry at the coffee shop on the second floor. TSUM is open from 9 a.m. until 8 p.m. daily except on Sunday when the hours are 11 a.m. until 7 p.m. Phone (044) 224-95-05 or 221-30-68. West of the center at 3 Peremohy Square at the beginning of Shevchenka Blvd., the huge *Ukrayina* department store has been renovated and transformed into the modern *Yunist* (Юніст). Phone (044) 236-59-15.

There are a number of Western-style supermarket chains in the city, including *Billa, MegaMarket, Silpo,* and *Furshet*. The Ukrainian *Central Gastronome*, 40 Khreshchatyk, across the street from TSUM, is a worth a stop for the great selection of Kyiv-made tortes, chocolates, and fresh foods.

*Farfor-Fayans* (Фарфор), at 34 Khreshchatyk, is two floors of china and gifts from leading European makers. For tea services, figurines, and crystal from factories throughout Ukraine, turn left at the entrance and go to the end. A complete tea service for six costs about US$40. The store is open 10 a.m. to 7 p.m. Monday through Friday and 10 a.m. to 6 p.m. on Saturday.

Also on Khreshchatyk, down the street at No. 24, is the *Mytetstvo Bookstore,* selling Ukrainian general interest books, such as cookbooks, travel books, and children's books. For second-hand English language novels, head around the corner up B. Khmelnytskoho Street to   No. 39 where the trendy *Baboon Book Coffee Shop* combines book browsing with an art gallery and café.

**Traditional Ukrainian Crafts**are sold in shops scattered about the city center: *Suveniry* (Сувеніри), 32 Khreschatyk Street, across from the metro entrance, sells a variety of hand-crafted items, including amber jewelry, lacquer wood, icons, and embroidery. *Ukrayinski Suveniry* (Українські Сувеніри), 23 Velyka Vasylkivska Street, (formerly Chervonoarmiyska), just off Tolstoy Square ( площа Льва Толстого, *ploshcha Lva Tolstoho*), has an especially nice selection of crafts and linens.

The most enjoyable souvenir browsing, however, are the outdoor stalls lining **Andriyivskyy Uzviz**. A number of galleries on the street deal in signed art. One of the most interesting is *Gonchari* (Гончарі) at 10a for its diverse media. Phone (044)116-12-98. *L-Art*, at 2b close to the bottom of the street, sells framed art; it's open 11 a.m. until 8 p.m. except Monday.

Look in gift shops in museums and at historical sites for souvenir books, postcards, and even some fine art. Artists sell their prints at the *Pecherska Lavra*, for example, and there's an icon shop at St. Michael's Golden-Domed Monastery.

## Transportation

**Air.** Two domestic airlines are AeroSvit Ukrainian Airlines, at 58a Taras. Shevchenko Blvd., phone (044) 246-50-73, and Ukraine International Airlines, at 14 Peremohy Avenue, phone (044) 216-70-40. These airlines fly out of Boryspil Airport to major Ukrainian cities and foreign countries.

**Boryspil Airport** (Бориспіл Аеропорт) is about 39 km (24 mi) southeast of the city center on a rare stretch of four-lane road, Kharkhiv Highway (Харківському Шосе, *Kharkivskomu Shose*). Dozens of international carriers land at Boryspil. Upgrading technology and major refurbishing has put it on par with other European airports, though it's due for enlargement. Customs officials are fluent in English, there are luggage carts, modern clean restrooms, a coffee shop, several bars, and a duty-free shop with a superb selection of Ukrainian vodka as well as many gift items.

*Boryspil Hotel*, just 200 meters (660 feet) down a tree-lined street to the airport entrance, is a good choice when making an early departure. Efficient and pleasant English-speaking personnel provide wake-up calls and continual free shuttle rides to and from the terminal. *Olga*, a good restaurant on the ground floor, is open around the clock. Phone (044) 296-71-05 or fax (044) 296-79-53.

**Transportation to Boryspil.** A taxi between Boryspil Airport and Kyiv center costs from US$10 to US$20. A red express bus from Peremohy Square (площа Перемоги, *ploshcha Peremohy*) in the center runs to the airport every forty minutes. The ride takes one hour and costs the equivalent of several U.S. dollars.

Airport shuttle buses run from the Rus and Dnipro hotels during midday; a return shuttle bus runs on the hour from Boryspil and will drop passengers off at any area in Kyiv. Cost is about US$10 one way, US$20 for a round trip. It's advisable to allow several extra hours when checking into the airport. The airport's phone number is (044) 296-72-43. For information call (044) 296-76-09.

**Kyiv Zhulyany** (Жуляни) **Airport**, just 11.3 km (7 mi) southwest of the city, is used for domestic flights by regional Ukrainian air companies, for example Odessa Airlines, Lviv Airlines, and Crimean Airlines. During the day buses run to and from Independence Square and Zhulyany. Trolleybus No. 9 from ploshcha Peremohy takes 40 minutes to get to Zhulyany. The airport phone is (044) 272-12-01 or (044) 272-12-02.

**Rail.** The train station is at 2 ploshcha Vokzalna (площа Вокзальна), right next to the Vokzalna metro station on the western edge of the city center. Completely renovated, among its excellent amenities are a computer screen listing departure times and ticket availability in English. Trains go daily to major cities of eastern Europe, and all over Ukraine, with plush new fast trains running to Kharkiv and Odesa. The advance ticket office for domestic travel is at 38/40 Taras Shevchenko Blvd., ( бульвар Тараса Шевченка, *bulvar Tarasa Shevchenka*). Phone 050.

**Bus.** The Central Bus Station serving intercity bus travel is at 3 ploshcha Moskovska (площа Московська). Take trams No. 9 or 10 or trolleys 1, 11, or 12 to get to the long-distance bus terminal. Throughout the city are additional depots for shorter-distance travel. For advance bus tickets to all destinations, go to 74 Lesya Ukrayinka Blvd. (бульвар ЛесіУкраїнки).

**City Transportation.** Kyiv has an efficient network of bus, streetcar, trolleybus, and marshrutni taxis (minivans). Buses and trolleys cost 50 kopiyky a trip, and marshrutky cost about twice as much. Public transportation runs frequently and is crammed full of riders. Purchase tickets at yellow kiosks around the city, or from the controller – not the driver – on a bus or trolley. Tickets are good for one ride only; no transfer passes are given. Passengers form queues to board, so those near the end of the line may not be able to squeeze in. Tourists are well advised not to try for a bus during the rush hours. Vehicles operate from 6 a.m. until 12 p.m. daily.

**Metro.** Three subway lines run east–west, north–south, and northwest–southeast through the city and connect at several main transfer points, such as the Kreshchatyk station in the center of the city. A single-use token costs 50 kopiyky and allows you to transfer from line to line. A monthly pass for the equivalent of about US$5 is available at any metro station during the last week of the previous month through the first week of the new month. The metro is clean and safe and some stations are attractively decorated to illustrate a nearby monument or building. The metro runs from 6 a.m. to 12 a.m. daily.

The stations on Kyiv's three metro lines are listed in order on the next page. (Additional stations on these lines are planned for the future.) The three lines are: (1) the Sviatoshyno-Brovarska line running west-to-east, (2) the Syretsko-Percherska line running northwest-to-southeast, and (3) the Kurenivsko-Chervonoarmiiska line running north-to-south. The lines meet each other at three transfer stations whose names are shown connected by dashes. At a transfer you can walk from one line's station to the connecting line's station.

### Personal Needs

**Embassies.** The **United States Embassy** building is at 10 Yurya Kotsyubynskoho (вул. Юря Коцюбинского) Street, phone (044) 246-97-50, but the Consular Department is at 6 vul. Mykoly Pymonenka (Миколи Пионенка) off of Artema Street, a 10-minute walk northwest of the Embassy. Consulate hours are Monday through Friday from 8:30 a.m. until 12:30 p.m., but for an emergency, the office is open anytime. Phone (044) 490-44-22.

The **Canadian Embassy** is at 31 Yaroslaviv Val (Ярославів Вал) Street, phone (044) 464-11-44, and the **British Embassy** is at 4 Hlybochitska (Глибочіцька) Street, phone (044) 494-34-00.

## KYIV METRO STATIONS

| **WEST END** | **NORTHWEST END** | **NORTH END** |
|---|---|---|
| AKADEMMISTECHKO | | |
| (Академмістечко) | | |
| ZHYTOMYRSKA | | |
| (Житомирська) | | |
| SVYATOSHYN | | |
| (Святошин) | | |
| NYVKY | | HEROIV DNIPRA |
| (Нувки) | | (Героїв Дніпра) |
| BERESTEYS'KA | | MINS'KA |
| (берестейська) | | (Мінська) |
| SHULYAVS'KA | | OBOLON |
| (Шулявська) | | (Оболонь) |
| POLITEKH NICHNIY | DOROHOZHYCHI | PETRIVKA |
| INSTYTUT | (Дорогожичі) | (Петрівка) |
| (Політех нічний Інститут) | | |
| VOKZALNA | LUKYANIVS'KA | TARASA SHEVCHENKA |
| (Вокзальна) | (Лукянівська) | (Тараса Шевченка) |
| UNIVERSYTET | L'VIVS'KA BRAMA | KONTRAKTOVA PLOSCHA |
| (Університет) | (Львівська брама) | (Контрактова Площа) |
| TEATRALNA ------------- | ZOLOTI VOROTA | POSHTOVA PLOSHCHA |
| (Театральна) | (Золоті Ворота) | (Поштова Площа) |
| KHRESCHATYK -------------------------------------- | | MAYDAN NEZALEZHNOSTI |
| (Крещатик) | | (Майдан Незалежності) |
| | PALATS SPORTU ------- | PLOSHCHA LVA TOLSTOHO |
| | (Палатс Спорту) | (Шлоща Льва Толстно) |
| ARSENAL'NA | KLOVS'KA | RESPUBLIKANS'KYY STADION |
| (Арсенальна) | (Кловська) | (Республіканський Стадіон) |
| DNIPRO | PECHERS'KA | PALATS "UKRAINIA" |
| (Дніпро) | (Печерська) | (Палатс "Україна") |
| HIDROPARK | DRUZHBY NARODIV | LYBIDS'KA |
| (Гідропарк) | (ДружбиНародів) | (Либідська) |
| LIVOBEREZHNA | VYDUBYCHI | |
| (Лівобережна) | (Видубичі) | |
| DARNYTSYA | SLAVUTYCH | |
| (Дарнится) | (Славутич) | |
| CHERNIHIVSKA | OSOKORKY | |
| (Чернігівська) | (Осокорки) | |
| LISOVA | POZNYAKY | |
| (Лісова) | (Позняки) | |
| | KHARKIVS'KA | |
| | (Харківська) | |
| **EAST END** | **SOUTHEAST END** | **SOUTH END** |

**Communications.** Post office branches are located all around the city, but the **Central Post Office** is at 22 Khreshchatyk Street, near Independence Square. It's open seven days a week for postal services, international and intercity phoning, fax, and telegrams. It also has an Internet center and a cash machine. Phone 065.

**E-mail** access is available at many hotels; otherwise try the post office or the numerous Internet cafés in the center, for example, *Cyber Café* at 21 Prorizna Street, open from 10 a.m. until midnight. The *Lybid-Kyiv* tourist agency in the Hotel Lybid at ploshcha Peremohy offers e-mail services and has a **Western Union** office, open from 9 a.m. until 7 p.m.

**Money.** Currency exchange counters are all over the center. **Cash machines**, called "bankomats," are located in hotels, in the main post office and in the central department store, both on Kreshchatyk Street, in the McDonald's restaurants, and in Western-style grocery stores. These give cash in either dollars or hryvni on a variety of credit cards and some will recognize ATM bank cards as well.

Most **banks** are open from 9 a.m. to 1 p.m. Generally, the more central its location, the more services a bank will provide. Some banks, such as State Savings Bank of Ukraine at 6 Khreshchatyk Street, will cash traveler's checks (businesses do not accept them) and will advance cash on a credit card for up to a five percent surcharge.

**Medical Services.** For a public ambulance, with no English spoken, dial 03. You can also call 432-88-88 or 294-70-09 for a private ambulance with English spoken. Private ambulances will be expensive.

An *American Medical Center* is located at 1 Berdychivska Street, opposite the Lukianivska Metro Station. Phone 490-76-00.A receptionist is on duty 24 hours a day and can arrange for emergency medical or dental care. A pharmacy is on the premises. Payment is by cash or credit card; paperwork can be provided for you to apply for reimbursement by your U.S. health insurer. (Medicare can not be used outside of the United States.)

*Medikom Private Clinic*, 8 Kondratyula Street, works 24 hours per day and is equipped for emergencies and wide-ranging diagnostic and treatment. Phone 234-03-03; Web site www.medikom.ua.

**Dental services** are numerous. *Cabot Dental Clinic* has a number of locations including an office at 8/16 Khmelnytskoho Street, phone (044) 224-04-68.

Several **pharmacies** have numerous locations thoughout the city: *7X7*; *Biocon* ; and *Falbi* are the major chains, and private clinics also contain pharmacies. Dial 067 for pharmacy information.

**Church Services.** Most of the functioning churches in Kyiv are Orthodox, but several other denominations have working churches. There are 30,000 Greek Catholics in Kyiv. **Ukrainian Greek-Catholic Church** services are held in the church of **St. Mykola** (Nicholas) in the small rotunda at Askold's Tomb. Originally built by architect A. Melenky in 1810, the church was reconstructed in 1998.

The **Cathedral of the Resurrection of Christ** , is a huge new Byzantine-style church on Mykilsko-Slobidska Street close to the Livoberezhna metro stop, is destined to serve as the head church of Greek-Catholic worshipers in Ukraine when the seat is transferred from Lviv to Kyiv.

Roman Catholic Masses are held at **St. Nicholas Polish Roman-Catholic Church** , 61 Velyka Vasylkivska Street. With its gingerbread Gothic spires, the church – a neo-Gothic recreation of a medieval cathedral – is quite striking in a city full of Ukrainian Baroque church architecture. It was designed by architect V. Horodetsky and built from 1899 to1909. Take Trolleybus No. 11 or 12.

**St. Oleksandr's Roman Catholic Cathedral**, was built in 1817 in the Classic style. Converted to a planetarium in the Soviet era, it was restored to a Roman Catholic church in 1990. Some services, including the 8:30 a.m. Sunday Mass, are in English. The church is at 17 Kostyolna Street. Phone (044) 295-09-47.

**The Great Synagogue of Kyiv**, 13 Shota Rustaveli Street, is also known as the Central Synagogue, the Brodsky Synagogue, or the Choral Synagogue. It was designed by architect H. Schleifer and built in 1898 with a Roman-style exterior. Shut down by the Soviets in 1926, it served a variety of uses, most recently a puppet theater. After being returned to the Jewish community in 1992, the synagogue was beautifully restored and rededicated in 2000. Phone (044) 246-60-64.

**Podil Synagogue,** 29 Shchekovytska (Щекавицка) Street, is Kyiv's oldest synagogue, built in 1895. Closed by the Soviets in 1929, it reopened in 1945. Phone (044) 463-70-87.

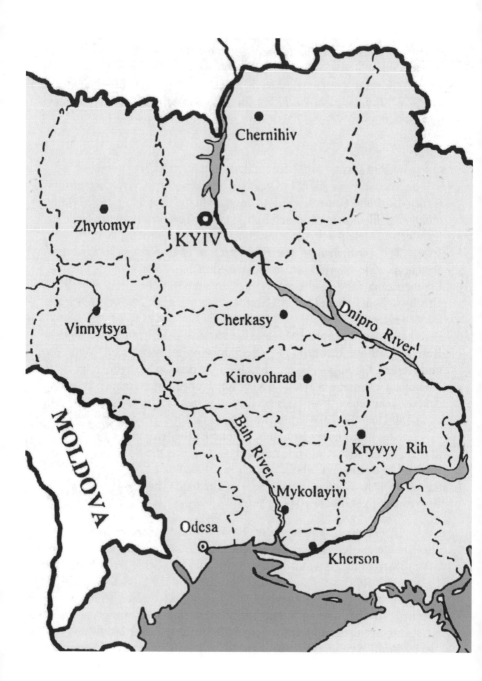

# CHAPTER 8.
# CENTRAL UKRAINE

**CHERNIHIV** (Чернігів), population 301,000, is the principal city of the **Chernihivska oblast**, which borders Russia and Belarus. Just 140 km (84 mi) northeast of Kyiv on the right bank of the river Desna (Десна) River, it's ideal for a day trip. A train and numerous buses make daily trips from Kyiv to Chernihiv, and it's an easy drive on the modern divided highway.

According to archeological discoveries, Chernihiv attracted settlers as early as 2000 BCE. The city is believed to have been established as a trading center by a Slavic tribe, Silveriany, in the 7th century CE. The Silveriany were one of the eight tribes that made up ancient Kyiv-Rus, and Chernihiv, second in size to Kyiv, was an important principality. Several of the tribe's *kurhany* (burial mounds) remain on **Boldyn Hill**, the original center. From a lookout point on Boldyn Hill, beautiful golden domes peek through chestnut and oak trees. Though the smokestacks of Chernihiv's industries are visible in the skyline, the city is clean and attractive, and luxuriant parkland adds to its charm.

Chernihiv is noted for its impressive church architecture, particularly those erected during the 11th and 12th centuries. Many are part of the **Chernihiv State Architectural and Cultural Reserve**, located at Chernihiv's early fortress settlement, the **Dytynets**. The most notable Dytynets structure is the *Spaso Preobrazhensky Sobor* or **Transfiguration Cathedral**. One of the oldest churches of Kyivan Rus, it was built about 1017 by Mstyslav, the younger brother of Yaroslav the Wise. Adjoining it is a church of impressive Byzantine Kyiv-Rus architecture, the 12th-century **Boroyso-Hlibsky Cathedral**. Inside the church are "the Royal Doors," wooden icons once constituting the gates to an iconostasis that depict Boris and Hlib, the first Ukrainian saints. The icons were commissioned by Hetman Ivan Mazepa in the 17th century. A historical display is also in the church.

At the east end of the reserve, the neo-Classical palace at 4 Gorky Street is the **Chernihiv Regional Historical Museum**. Founded in 1896, it's one of the oldest and most popular regional museums in Ukraine. Highlights are archeological finds from the Chernihiv kurhany, Kozak weapons, and everyday objects from the Kyivan Rus period. Phone (04622) 7-26-50.

**St. Kateryna Church** sits on a hill along the edge of the old fortress. It was completed in 1715 in the Ukrainian Baroque style to commemorate the heroism of the Kozaks of Chernihiv in the storming of the Turkish fortress of Azov in 1696. The church contains a Museum of National Decorative Folk Art of the Chernihiv region.

**The Yeletsky Uspensky Monastery** on Proletarska Street was founded by Chernihiv Grand Prince Svyatoslav in the mid-11th century. It includes the 12th-century Uspensky (Dormition) Cathedral, which has a five-tiered iconostasis that is one of the largest in Ukraine, and a 17th-century convent.

**Troyitsko-Illinsky** (Holy Trinity and St. Elijah)**Monastery** on vul. Lva Tolstoho (Leo Tolstoy), is one of the finest architectural complexes of its kind in Ukraine. It includes several churches, a 58-meter-high bell tower, a printing house, monks' cells, and three underground wooden churches and catacombs. It was founded in 1069 by the monk Antoniy Pechersky, who co-founded Kyiv's Monastery of the Caves. Destroyed by invading Mongols in 1269, it was rebuilt in 1649 and became a center of Ukrainian chronicle-writing. Two of the churches are outstanding: the **Troyitsky Cathedral** (1679–95) and the **1677 Church of the Presentation** (Введренска, *Vvedrenska*), with its five-tiered bell tower.

**BATURYN,** a farming village of 4,000, is southeast of Chernihiv on route M-02. It became the Kozak capital of Ukraine in 1669, when Bohdan Khmelnytsky's forces took it from the Polish. Under Hetman Ivan Mazepa, it flourished until Tsar Peter I ordered Russian troops to destroy the city and murder some 15,000 inhabitants in retaliation for Mazepa's siding with the Swedish in the Great Northern War. In 1750 the last hetman, Kyrylo Rozumovsky, was given permission to rebuild the city. Among other numerous structures, he built a Classical-style palace, still standing today. The **Hetman Capital State Historical and Cultural Preserve** is the site of archeological excavations conducted by Ukrainian and Canadian teams. The digs have turned up weapons and tools, gilded copper icons, bronze and silver jewelry, pottery and glassware, and remnants of buildings.

**CHORNOBYL** (*Chernobil* is from the Russian spelling), the site of the world's worst nuclear power plant accident, is 20 km (12 mi) south of Prypyat, now a ghost town close to the Belarus border. The accident took place on April 26, 1986 when one of the four reactors at the Chornobyl Atomic Energy Station blew up, hurling nearly nine tons of radioactive material into the sky. The major fallout zones were to the north and west, contaminating large parts of Belarus and many regions in Ukraine, especially Rivne, Volyn, Zhytomyr, Kyiv, and Chernihiv.

A new city, **Slavutych**, was hastily built about an hour's ride northeast of Chornobyl to house the workers after Prypyat became uninhabitable. However, without a commercial base, unemployment in Slavutych is very high.

The Ukrainian government made a massive attempt at clean-up but simply was not equipped for the enormity of the job. The damaged reactor No. 4 was encased in a gigantic steel-and-concrete sarcophagus, but even with the obvious horrors of Chornobyl and pressure from the world community, the government balked at closing the power plant, citing the country's lack of fuel sources and inability to pay market prices for gas and oil. Two of the remaining reactors were eventually shut down for safety reasons, but the last working reactor, No. 3, wasn't closed until December 2000. Ukrainian authorities blame more than 8,000 deaths on the accident, and hundreds of thousands people have suffered from radiation-related illnesses. Birth defects have risen sharply and thyroid cancer rates among young children have increased tenfold.

Radioactive isotopes will continue to contaminate the arable soil and drinking water for centuries. Meat and dairy products, wild berries, and especially mushrooms from exposed areas were tested and found to have unacceptable levels of radiation. While the cesium-137 and plutonium content in the soil can be measured, sufficient equipment and expertise is not available to continuously monitor the radiation in live animals, farm products, and forests. It's particularly difficult to monitor food sold in farmers' markets.

Ukraine is asking for assistance from the West to decommission the plant; to build a new ecologically safe sarcophagus over the damaged reactor; to build two Western-style replacement nuclear reactors – one in Rivne and the other in Khmelnytskyy; and to retrain and relocate the Chornobyl workers living in Slavutych.

Chornobyl is 100 km (60 mi) north of Kyiv. For many years, the exclusion zone was accessible only to foreign experts, journalists, and public figures working though official government channels. Now several travel agencies offer a one-day guided tour from Kyiv with a safety guarantee. Price is about US$190. Contact *Sam Travel* at ukraine @samcomp.kiev.ua, phone (044) 238-69-57; or *VsuduBudu Travel* at igo@everywhere.com.ua or phone (044) 254-3252.

For the less adventuresome, the **Ukrainian National Chornobyl Disaster Museum** is in Kyiv, near Kontraktova Ploshcha Metro Station at the corner of Spaska Street and provuluk Khorevy. Phone (044) 416-30-68. To learn more about Chornobyl, check the Ukrainian Ministry of Emergency's official Web site, which has an English-language option: www.ic-chernobyl.kiev.ua.

**PEREYASLAV-KHMELYTSKYY** (Переяслав-Хмелнитскии), 80 miles downriver from Kyiv in the **Kyivska oblast**, makes another easy day trip. One of the oldest cities in Ukraine, it dates back to 907 as a strategically important fortress in the defense of Kyiv Rus against the steppe nomads. Centuries later, it served as a center of the Kozak state. The Treaty of Pereyaslav, which united Ukraine with Russia, was signed here in 1738.

In addition to its political and military importance, some of Ukraine's greatest writers and thinkers, including Skovoroda and Shevchenko, found their inspiration in Pereyaslav and its neighboring villages. Yiddish writer Sholom Aleichem was born here in 1859 and drew his inspiration from *shtetl* life. Pereyaslav was the model for the town Anatevka in *Fiddler on the Roof*.

Several churches were built during the Ukrainian Baroque period. **Mykhailivska** (St. Michael) **Church** (1646–66) was constructed on the site of a medieval church of the same name that was destroyed by the Tatars. One of the finest examples of Ukrainian archetecture, the **Voznesensky (Ascension) Cathedral** (1695–1700), a monastery church, was financed by Ukrainian Kozak leader Ivan Mazepa. Its bell tower was constructed from 1770 to 1776. Ruins of a 12th century castle are nearby.

Mostly, however, Pereyaslav-Khmelnytskyy is a museum town. Mykhailo Sikorskyy, a historian (b. 1923), founded most of the town's 20 or so museums and personally collected much of their holdings. The **State Historical-Cultural Preserve in Pereyaslav-Khmelnytskyy** includes a historical museum with four branches whose huge collections range from a second-century chess set to Bohdan Khmelnytsky's sword. Among the branches are a picture gallery; an archeological museum, the Hryhory Skovoroda Museum, and a diorama of the battles for the Dnipro in 1943 in the Peryaslav-Khmelnytsky region. Built in the former sacristy of the old Ascension Church, the lifelike diorama depicts the fierce battle in which approximately 250 thousand Ukrainian troops lost their lives regaining a Nazi stronghold.

The Pereyaslav-Khmelnytskyy preserve also includes an open-air museum of architecture and folkways showing traditional rural architecture and folk arts. The preserve contains a number of small museums including a museum of *kobza* (bandura) playing, a bread museum, a beekeeping museum, a medicinal plants museum, and a Sholom Aleichem museum.

**BERDYCHIV** is 180 km (108 mi) southwest of Kyiv in the **Zhytomyr oblast** in north central Ukraine. Its population is approximately 90,000. Remnants of Bronze Age and the Chernyakhiv cultures indicate that the area was settled as far back as the first century BCE. The name Berdychiv is believed to have originated from the first settlers, likely the Berendeyis, a late 10th century BCE nomadic steppe people who protected Kyiv-Rus from invaders. Mongol invasions of the 13th century wiped out the town, but it was rebuilt and came under Polish and Lithuanian control. Starting in the 14th century, the town was occupied by Polish nobility, the Tyszkevych family. They built a fortification that was impenetrable to the invading Tartar-Mongol hordes.

In 1627 the Tyszkevych family built a monastery dedicated to the Virgin Mary and gave it to the "barefoot Carmelite" order. The monks exploited the local population of Ukrainian peasants, who, with Kozak help, stormed and ruined the monastery during the 1648 War of Liberation. The Polish rebuilt it in 1663 with financial help from the Vatican.

Berdychiv was at the intersection of many trade routes. With the encouragement of the Polish kings who ruled Ukraine, it became a major trade center, with an annual fair. The commerce attracted merchants and craftsmen, and many Jews settled the area. After seven Jewish cloth merchants were granted the monopoly of the Bedychiv cloth trade by Polish Prince Radziwill in 1797, Jews began to dominate commerce in Berdychiv, establishing scores of trading companies and banks, and serving as agents of agricultural products of the neighboring estates of the nobles.

In the 19th century, the castle and monastery were Polish and Roman Catholic, while almost the entire city was Jewish and the outskirts were inhabited by Ukrainian Orthodox. From the 19th century until after 1917, Jews accounted for as much as 50 to 90 percent of the population of Berdychiv, but due to the declining economy Jewish families began to relocate to Odesa. In 1941 the invading Nazis conducted mass exterminations.

Today, Berdychiv's Jewish population is small, but the city has a new synagogue and it's a pilgrimage destination for followers of Rabbi Levi Yitzhak, a major Hassidic *zaddik* or leader who preached in

Berdychiv. He died in the city in 1810, and his grave is in an imposing new mausoleum in the Jewish cemetery on the main street, Lenina. Not to be missed are the city's churches, synagogue, and museums. The old **Carmelite Monastery** is a large fortified complex overlooking the river Hnylopat. Again functioning, it serves the city's sizable Roman Catholic community. Other than Sunday services, however, the monastery is not very active. Among its churches are the **Mariyinska Church** (1634, 1739−54), a Baroque church that was destroyed in WWII and later rebuilt. In the underground chapel is the miraculous icon of the Holy Mother of God of Berdychiv. The icon is a copy of an icon given to the church by an Orthodox Ukrainian who converted to Catholicism. It's reputed to restore health and to answer prayers.The local history museum and a gallery of local art are also on the Carmelite Monastery grounds.

French novelist Honoré de Balzac married a local Polish countess, Evelina Hanska, in **St. Vavera's** (Barbara's) **Church**in 1850. The **Balzac Literary and Memorial Museum** is in the village **VERKHIVNIA** where Balzac lived between 1847 and 1850. The three-room museum with beautiful grounds is near the city **RUZHYN**, several hours southeast of Berdychiv.

In 1857 novelist Joseph Conrad was born as Jósef Teodor Konrad Korzeniowski in **TEREKHOVA**, just outside Berdychiv. The building in which he was born is now an agricultural college and contains the interesting **Conrad Museum**. About a 15-to 20-minute drive from Berdychiv, the museum is on a city bus route.

In 1903 famed concert pianist Vladimir Horowitz was born in Berdychiv. He went on to the Kiev Conservatory and performed in Ukraine and Russia, later emigrating to the United States.

Despite its historic interest, Berdychiv is in an economically depressed area. Water is rationed and hot water flows only in winter, even in the city's leading hotel, *Druzhba*, at 82 Karl Libknekhta Street. Phone (0414) 32-10-37.

Restaurants and tourist destinations are all on Berdychiv's three major streets, Lenina, Karl Libknekhta, and Sverdlova. Among the better restaurants is *Blahodat* in the House of Culture just down the road from the bus and train station on Karl Libknekhta Street. Operated by a Swedish Pentecostal church, it's smoke- and alcohol-free with an attractive atmosphere and good service. Other acceptable restaurants are *Kazka* at 35 Libknekhta Street and *Prestige* on Sverdlova Street.

**Vinnytska oblast** lies on the right (west) bank of the Dnipro in the forest-steppe region of south central Ukraine. Vinnytska is a major agricultural region, and a leader in sugar production and food processing. Natural resources abound, with kaolin and colorful granite as well as some rarer minerals such as garnet. Ethnographers call the region Podilya; it's known for folk handicrafts including pottery, embroidery, weaving, and carpet-making. It's also a region of renowned writers, among them the modern dissident poet Vasyl Stus, who died in the Soviet Gulag, and the late 19th- and early 20th-century writer Mykhailo Kotsiubynsky, whose works include *Shadow of Forgotten Ancestors,* a psychological novella of Hutsul life that touches on folk customs and witchcraft.

**VINNYTSYA** (Вінниця) the administrative, economic, and cultural center of the oblast is a city of 379,000 straddling the southern Buh River. Its recorded history dates back to a Lithuanian fortress in the 14th century, but archeological excavations reveal signs of ancient Slavic tribes. The city was continuously under Tatar attack, then struggled for two centuries against Polish rule, and was finally annexed by the Russian Empire in 1793. Twentieth-century Vinnytsya also suffered much. The Soviet regime murdered thousands of ethnic Ukrainians in the city and its environs in 1937−38. As a strategic city on the Eastern Front and the location of Hitler's easternmost command, Vinnytsya was occupied by the Germans from 1941 through 1944, who murdered the Jewish population.

Although it's an economic and industrial center, Vinnytsya has many trees, parks, and gardens. It's a quiet and livable city, with an abundance of open-air markets filled with fresh produce and wild edibles gathered from the countryside. **Vulytsya Sverdlova**, the main street in the business district, follows the meandering Buh River. With its interesting souvenir shops, it's a pleasant street to walk. For a good meal, try the *Kumbasi* restaurant on Ivana Bohuna Street, north of the center. A daily sightseeing excursion boat, the *Nikolai Pirogov,* sails the Buh River. Another amusement option is a seven-day trip down the Buh on inflated rafts, past picturesque villages, fields, pastures, and fruit orchards.

Among the significant 17 th and 18th century architecture are the **Dominican Cathedral** (1624), **Jesuit Monastery** (1610), and the wooden church of **St. Nicholas** (1746). The large church visible from Khmelnitskyy Highway at vul. Maksimova, west of the center, is the new First Baptist Church. Combining Byzantine and Western church architecture, it's one of the largest Baptist churches in Ukraine, seating 2,500 people.

The **Vinnytsya Regional Studies Museum,** 1 pl. Museyna, at the juncture of Sverdlova and Kotsiubynskoho streets, is outstanding. Besides large numismatic and ethnographic collections, it includes stunning objects from a 1st-century CE Sarmat burial mound. The **Vinnytsya Regional Museum of Art,** in an adjoining wing of the building, displays paintings and engravings of Western and Eastern European masters; 17th-century Italian majolica; 18th-and 19th-century porcelain of Ukrainian, Russian and Western European workshops; various handicrafts; primitive art and Podillya folk icons. The **Mykhailo Kotsiubynsky Literary Memorial Museum** is in the house of the writer's birth at 15 vul. Bevzi    , off of Kotsiubynskoho.

A museum devoted to **Nikolai Pirogov** is at 155 vul. Pyrohova in his estate in the southwestern corner of the city. Born in Moscow in 1810, Pirogov was a prominent surgeon, professor of anatomy, and educational leader in the Russian Empire. His *Atlas of the Human Body* was so accurate that only recent computer techniques can duplicate his drawings. Pirogov pioneered many medical advances, notably army surgery. The first to use anesthesia on the battlefield, Pirogov created the concept of triage. Losing favor with the Tsar, he settled in the area in 1866, where he consulted and wrote. The museum is fascinating and the surrounding Botanical Gardens beautiful. On display in the crypt of a nearby church is Pirogov's preserved body, a project undertaken by his students upon prior instruction.

Hotels in the center of Vinnytsya are *Podillya*, 4 Pushkin Street, phone (0432) 32-75-96; *Savoy*, 36 Kozicky Street, phone (0432) 32-17-71; and *Vinnytsya*, 36 Soborna Street, phone (0432) 32-49-64.

**BAR** (Бар) is on the P-100 road, 66 km (40 miles) west of Vinnytsya. A small agricultural town (population 18,600), Bar is a restful place with a rich history and offers opportunity to witness authentic folklore, song and dance of rural life. Locally made crafts are paintings on wood, handmade dolls, and Vinnytsya-area embroidery.

Bar was named in 1537 after Bari, the southern Italian birthplace of Bona Sforza, wife of Polish King Zygmunt Stary (Sigismund the Old). The king built a castle with a fortress next to the Riv river. The structure is long gone, but the stone outline constitutes a park and the castle is now the site of a Roman Catholic Church, **Castle Saint Ann.** A Benedictine women's monastery is also in the town. Seven miles north of town in the village of **Kharmaky** are the ruins of a Ukrainian WWII bunker. Restaurants in Bar are *Aldiz* on Lenina Street next to the bazaar, and *Marafon* on Saint Mykola Street, which has dancing in the evening.

*Podolyanka* **Green Tourism Center**, 14 Dzershinskyy Street, gives Bar tourist information and arranges bed-and-breakfast accommodations from a database of local lodging. Cost per night is 15 to 40 hryvni in Bar and 5 to 15 hryvni in nearby villages, depending on availability of running and hot water. Families speak Ukrainian and Russian, but no English. A number of traditional folk and church special days are observed. The center is open Monday through Friday from 9 p.m. until 5 p.m. Phone (04341) 2-45-42 or call (04341) 2-20-95 weekends and after hours. E-mail Podolyanka@ ukr.net.

The scenic **Cherkaska oblast** straddles the Dnipro in the forest-steppe belt in the heart of Ukraine. The first human settlement dates from the 7th to 3rd century BCE. Part of Kyivan-Rus, the region was later devastated by the Tatars, fell under Lithuanian rule in the second half of the 14th century, and served as an important Ukrainian political center in the Zaporizhskyy Kozak struggle against Poland between 1648 and 1654. Ukraine's two most famous historical figures, Taras Shevchenko and Bohdan Khelmnytsky, were born and are buried in the the the Cherkasy region, which commemorates their lives with a number of historical museums and displays.

A cruise from Kyiv 162 km (100 mi) down the Dnipro River to **KANIV** (Канів), is a popular summertime day trip. Kaniv's recorded history dates to 1144, but excavations have uncovered dwellings and artifacts of an ancient settlement of Slavic farmers and herders in the area. The construction of the Kaniv Hydro-Electric Power Station brought it into the modern era.

Kaniv is known primarily as the final resting place of the great Ukrainian poet and patriot, Taras Shevchenko. The **Shevchenko National Reserve in Kaniv** (Шевченківський національний заповідник у м. Канів, *Shevchenkivskyy natsionalnyy zapovidnyk y m. Kaniv*), is located atop Tarasova Hora, a high bluff overlooking the Dnipro. A climb up 400 steps leads to the burial site and monument to Shevchenko, who expressed the wish in one of his most-loved poems, *Zapovit* (Testament), to be laid to rest above his beloved Dnipro river. The site is a pilgrimage destination for those of Ukrainian roots. Near the gravesite is the **Shevchenko Memorial Museum**, which details Shevchenko's life and works. The beautiful building was designed by noted early 20th-century architect Vasyl Krychevskyy. A library, souvenir shop, and restaurant are part of the reserve. In the town is the **Heorhiyivsky Uspensky Cathedral**, built by Prince Vsevolod in the Kyiv style in 1144.

The **Kaniv Nature and Historical Reserve** (Канівський природничо-історичний заповідник, *Kanivskyy pryrodnycho-istorychnyy zapovidnyk* is about 16 km (10 mi) south of Kaniv. This forest-steppe preserve is approximately 2,000 hectares (5,000 acres) of forests and hills containing more than 5,000 different native plant species and a wealth of wildlife, including 275 species of birds. Views of the river are beautiful,and fossils and artifacts from the late Paleolithic and Neolithic eras and the Trypillian and Scythian cultures are noticeable.

**CHERKASY** (Черкаси), is a port city on the right bank of a wide expanse of the Dnipro, 240 km (150 mi) downriver from Kyiv. Originally an outpost on the southern frontier of the Kyivan State, it later became a Kozak defense point against Tatar and Turkish raids. It also played an important role in Kozak insurrections against Polish rule, but in 1783 fell under the Russian Empire.

Cherkasy's population is 308,000, including military retirees who are looking for a pleasant place to live on a pension and are attracted to the spacious parks, scenic river vistas, and cultural opportunities. The wide main street, **Shevchenko Boulevard**, extends the eight-mile length of the city. The main department store, ***Budynok Torhivli***, at 202 Shevchenko, is in the central square of the city. It contains a modern supermarket, boutiques for flowers and jewelry, and domestic items. For a snack and a cup of coffee, try the ***Café Magnolia*** next to the department store or the ***McDonald's*** across the square. A good place for people watching is the ***Café Sladkarnitsa*** on Shevchenko next door to ***Ruben***, a gift and jewelry shop. The café serves excellent pastries and offers outdoor seating in a French-like ambience.

A monument to Taras Shevchenko and the handsome **Shevchenko Music and Drama Theater** are at 234 Shevchenko Boulevard. Here a repertory company performs Ukrainian plays during the school year, and other groups, such as the renowned Cherkaski Kozaki singers and dancers, use the theater for cultural performances.

A nice street to stroll is **Khreshchatyk**, which begins a block north of Shevchenko at Lenin Street and runs west. The street is lined with large, colorful concrete murals painted by the city's schoolchildren to screen the construction site of the future Cherkasy Philharmonic building. Khreshchatyk Street has two museums, the **Kobzar Book Museum** at the corner of Bayda-Vyshnevtsky, which shows the works of Taras Shevchenko in various languages, and the **Cherkasy Art Museum**, 259 Kreshchatyk, with both fine and folk art works and special exhibitions.

The blue castle-like building at the corner of Kreshchatyk at 20 Dashkevych Street was originally a puppet theater but now functions as the *Ursotsbank*. Another pre-WWII building is the wedding palace at the southeast end of Kreshchatyk where it meets Lenin Street; on Saturdays the wedding parties are lined up outside.

The two-acre Bohdan Khmelnytsky Park is on a hill near the river. To the left of the park, the street culminates at **Glory Hill**. Atop the hill is the striking **Motherland Monument**, a gigantic figure of a woman holding a bowl with an eternal flame overhead in honor of those who lost their lives defending the city from the Nazi invasion. The names of those commemorated are inscribed on a wall below the hill. The view from the hill includes the majestic wide river and the lovely Valley of Roses, a walkway through rose gardens along the river.

The large modern building across the street from Glory Hill at the beginning of Slavy (Слави) Street is the **Cherkasy Regional Museum**. The museum contains a comprehensive display of the region's cultural, political, and natural history, from dinosaur bones to ancient Scythian and Trypillian artifacts to Kozak costumes. About a mile north from the center on Shevchenko Boulevard is a popular recreation area, **Jubilee Park**, located in **Sosnovka** (Сосновка) or **Pine Woods**. The park has shady walkways, footbridges, man-made lakes and waterfalls, and a Ferris wheel that provides an excellent view of the river and countryside. Take Trolleybus No. 1 or 7 to the park.

Shopping is good in Cherkasy, with many modern boutiques downtown and a sprawling outdoor market southeast of the center square on Engels Street between Zhovtneva and Ilina Streets. An outdoor and covered farmers' market is close to the center at Smilyanska and Gogol Streets; adjacent to it is a block-long flower market that's open into the evening.

The best hotel in town, with nice rooms and good service is *Hotel Dnipro* at 15 Frunze Street, just two blocks from the center of town. Phone (0472) 47-23-60; fax (0472) 54-03-04.

Among many good restaurants in town, two that serve traditional Ukrainian cuisine are *Stare Misto* (Old Town), across from the department store on Smilyanska Street between Shevchenko and Khreshchatyk, and *Taras Bulba* at 218 Shevchenko.

About a 15-mile drive across the river from Cherkasy, outside the town of **ZOLOTONOSHA**, is **Krasnohorsky Monastery**, a fully functioning convent. Situated on a hill overlooking the peaceful countryside, the monastery's main church, the **Transfiguration** (*Preobrazhenska*) **Church**, was built in 1767 in the Ukrainian Baroque style. Painted deep blue with white embellishment, the church is an architectural gem. The nuns in residence can be seen tending gardens and livestock, and going about their daily chores. Women visitors should wear skirts and head coverings.

**KORSUN-SHEVCHENKIVSKYY** (Корсун-Шевченківський) population approximately 25,000, is on the Ros River, a tributary of the Dnipro. The site of two huge decisive battles which occurred three centuries apart, the town grew out of a fortress, **Korsun**, established in 1037 by Kyiv-Rus Prince Yaroslav the Wise. In 1240 it was destroyed by Mongols. The Polish built a fortress in 1584 and began to rule. In 1648 the ever-festering Kozak-Polish hostilities resulted in a battle near Korsun in which 15,000 Kozaks and 4,000 Tatars defeated 20,000 Polish. The victory encouraged the national uprising against Polish domination.

In 1944, another gigantic battle took place when the Red Army encircled and destroyed 80,000 invading Germans. Also in 1944 "Shevchenkivskyy" was added to the town's name, but it's still commonly called simply "Korsun."

The **Korsun-Shevchenkivskyy State Historical and Cultural Reserve**, a 97-hectare (250- acre) park overlooking the Ros River, contains a palace and several museums. The palace and the surrounding beautiful landscape park were designed by noted European architects Muntz and Lindsay and constructed over a number of years. Originally built for the nephew of the king of Poland in the late 18th   century, the palace was presented in 1799 by the Russian tsar to the Grand Duke Lopukhin, who was the General Procurator. Among the prominent visitors to the palace was the mother of Tsar Nicholas II, who planted a blue fir tree that's still growing. The reserve includes a museum of the history of the 1944 battle, which displays WWII tanks and armaments outside. There's also a historical museum and an art gallery featuring the works of area masters of decorative arts.

**CHYHYRYN** (Чигирин) is approximately an hour's drive southeast of Cherkasy on the main highway. In the early 1500s, it was a fortified winter Kozak settlement. From 1648 to 1657, hetman Bohdan Khmelnytsky resided in Chyhyryn, and later it became the capital of the first Ukrainian Kozak state, with a population of 200,000. From here Khmelnytsky welcomed ambassadors of many European countries. A monument to Khmelnytsky stands at the site of the historical military fortress atop an escarpment in the center of Chyhyryn, which provides a commanding view of the countryside. The newly built museum below "Bohdan's Hill" is dedicated to the life of Khmelnytsky and features exhibits of Kozak history.

A few miles to the northwest is the village **SUBOTIV**, where the hetman spent his childhood on his father's estate. **Illinska Church**, which he commissioned in 1653, was built in the Ukrainian Baroque style and later became Khmelnytsky's final resting place.

**UMAN** (Умань), a charming city of 93,000, is about 188 km (117 mi) west of Cherkasy. During its centuries under Polish rule, the city gained its outstanding landmark, **Sofiyivkyy Park** (Софіївкий Парк). Built in 1796 by Polish Count Potocki in honor of his wife, Sofia, a former Turkish slave, Sofiyivka, is considered one of the finest parks in Europe. It was constructed by thousands of serfs on a picturesque site on the outskirts of Uman. The original landscape design covered more than 150 hectares (370 acres) of land and included entrance grottoes, waterfalls, and a system of waterways and lakes with footbridges, fountains, and sculptures. Over time, assorted pavilions and temples were added.

The park was restored between 1966 and 1972; a new entrance was built in 1996 to observe the park's 200 th anniversary. Now a functioning arboretum with nearly 500 varieties of trees and shrubs, the park is a popular day trip for tourists from Kyiv.

If you're staying overnight, the *Hotel Muzey*, next to the main entrance of the park, has a friendly, English-speaking staff and reasonable rates. Phone (0474) 45-62-75.

Also in Uman is the **Uman Regional Studies Museum** (Уманьський крайезнавчий музей, *Umanskyy krayeznavchyy muzey*) on Zhovtnevoyi Revolyutsiyi Street. Its large archeological and ethnographic collection ranges from prehistoric and Scythian cultures through the Kozak period.

Uman is the burial place of Rabbi Nahman ben Simheh of Bratslav, who developed the Bratslavite form of Hasidism. Borrowing motifs from Ukrainian folktales, Rabbi Nakhman improvised allegorical tales and recited them in the Yiddish vernacular rather than in Hebrew, the language of the educated elite. After he died in 1810, his grave became a pilgrimage site for Bratslavite Hasids who visit in great numbers during the holy days of Rosh Hashanah.

In **TALYANKY**, 15 km (9 mi) northeast of Uman, is an excavation of the largest and most developed site of Trypillian civilization in the world.

Trypillian was a neolithic farming culture that flourished in many areas of the territory of present-day Ukraine from 7,400 to 4,740 years ago. Peaceful and family-oriented, the Trypillians worshiped female gods, built spacious houses, domesticated animals, cultivated land with metal picks and axes, and made clay pottery. By the beginning of the Bronze Age, 2500 BCE, the culture had disappeared. In 2002 archeologists completed the excavation in Talyanky of a 1,000-acre town dating back to a thousand years before the Egyptian pyramids. The oval-shaped town consists of approximately 2,000 buildings converging in a circular pattern to a central square. A small museum is across the river from the excavation site.

**Mykolayivska oblast** in south-central Ukraine extends from the steppes to the Black Sea, where it occupies several hundred kilometers of the shoreline. Its fertile land and temperate continental climate make it ideal for vegetable and fruit growing and livestock breeding. The fertile land, moderate climate and three rivers emptying into the sea were a magnet for prehistoric tribes, and the area was first settled during the Paleolithic period nearly 250,000 years ago.

The region's capital, **MYKOLAYIV** (Миколаїв), is 80 km (48 mi) from the Black Sea, on the left bank of an estuary of the southern Buh River. The area was first inhabited in the Neolithic period. In the 4th and 5th centuries CE, it was the southernmost province of Kyivan Rus. Founded in 1789 as a shipbuilding center, Mikolayiv was named after St. Nicholas, upon whose feast day the Kozaks captured a Turkish fortress. It later became the shipbuilding center of Russia and an important commercial center.

Today Mikolayiv is a modern commercial seaport with a population of 518,000. Although street signs are written in Ukrainian, the Russian language is the vernacular and the streets are commonly referred to by their Russian names.

The main street, **prospekt Lenina**, is a tree-lined boulevard running east−west through the city. The street is dotted with war monuments and statuery, including a tank in a Peace Garden at the corner of Konsolmolska Street. At 259 Lenina is the main department store, the *Pivdenny Buh*. The **Museum of Regional Ethnography** is at 32 Dekabrystiv Street, just south of where it crosses Lenina. At 38 Dekabrystiv, behind the gates, is **Kazka Children's City**, a fanciful park for children.

The center is focused around Radyanska Street (usually called by its Russian name, Sovietskaya), a north − south street that crosses Lenina. At this intersection, in front of the McDonald's, is the monument to shipbuilders, a large sphere surrounded by helmsmen and navigators. Diagonally across the street is a good Turkish restaurant, **Lasunka**, with attractive outdoor seating in summer. Stretching about seven blocks north from here to Lenin Square are a mixture of shops and outdoor cafés and "Pensioners' Park," where artists and craft makers sell their wares.

Lenin Square extends to Admiralska Street and culminates at the Inhul River. This is a pretty neighborhood, with numerous shade-covered outdoor cafés, a river view, men playing chess, and boys skateboarding. A footbridge leads to **Patriot Park**, an area of cafés and a few stony beaches.

At 27 Admiralska is the newly renovated **Russian Dramatic Arts Theater**. On the east end of Admiralska is the **Shipbuilding Museum**. One room of the fascinating museum is devoted to the memory of shipbuilders who were killed for their knowledge of ships. An English-speaking guide is recommended to appreciate the exhibits.

The **Vereshchahin Art Museum** at 47 Velyka Morska Street, consists of 10 galleries of Ukrainian, Russian, and Western European paintings, drawings, icons, sculpture, crafts, and numismatic items of the 17th to 20th centuries. Phone 35-23-67.

The **City Zoo** is reputed to be the best in Ukraine, though the concept of natural habitat has yet to arrive. The zoo is close to the main bus station, about a 15-minute trolleybus ride east from the corner of Radyanska and Lenina. Nearby is **Kolos**, the city's largest outdoor market.

The city's best hotel is **Inhul** at 34 Admiralska Street, 1 km north of the center; phone (0512) 35-55-57.

Restaurants in the center are  **Natasha's** on Radyanska, one block south of Admiralska, and **Staryy Nikolaev** on Pushkinska, several blocks west of Radyanska. For good coffee, try **Svit** (Світ) on prospekt Lenina near McDonald's. A large self-service grocery is on prospekt Lenina, behind the tank at the Konsolmolska trolleybus stop.

The **Olvia** (Ольвіа) **National Preserve** is in the village of **PARUTYNE**, 30 km (18 mi) southwest of Mykolayiv, across the Dnipro-Buhsky Estuary. The preserve consists of the ruins of the oldest Greek settlement in the Black Sea area. Olvia appeared in the early 6th century BCE and existed for a millennium. International archeologists continue to excavate the 270-hectare area. The preserve includes a small museum that displays artifacts which haven't gone to major museums or to looters. The preserve opens at 8 a.m. Phone 2-24-53 or 2-26-80. A taxi from Mykolayiv to Olvia takes an hour and-a-half and costs under US$10. An early morning bus to Parutyne takes two and-a-half hours and costs about US$5. Continuing south another 33 km (20 mi), you come to the town **OCHAKIV**, in an area of sandy beaches.

Directly east of the Mykolayivska region is the **Khersonska oblast**, which also lies in the steppe belt of the Black Sea Lowland. The region straddles the lower Dnipro River, where it flows into the Black Sea. Human settlement dates back to the Paleolithic era. By the 8th to 7th centuries BCE, Scythians ruled the region. Early Slavic tribes appeared in the 2nd century CE, and by the 10th to 13th centuries, the area was part of Kyiv-Rus Ukraine. Kozaks arrived in the 16th century and opposed the invading Turks and Tartars. Under Russia in the 19th century, the Kherson region was settled by people from modern day Ukraine and Germany.

The capital of the region, **KHERSON** (Херсон), is the southernmost Ukrainian city on the River Dnipro, located where the river empties into the Black Sea. Both a river and a sea port, Kherson is a center of commerce and of shipbuilding with a population of about 360,000. The **Kherson Museum of Local Lore**, 9 vul. Lenina , has large displays of nature with dioramas of local species. Its archeology exhibits include ancient marble sculptures and precious metal artifacts, including Scythian gold.

*Fregat*, 2 Ushakova Street, a large hotel in the center, is Kherson's leading hotel. Fregat is a lively place with amenities including a currency exchange, shops, and a nightclub. Phone (0552) 24-11-17.

A 4-hour drive east of Kherson is Ukraine's premier nature preserve, the huge **Askaniya-Nova Biosphere Reserve**. In 1875 a German settler, F. Falz-Fein, established a zoo and botanical garden on the land owned by his father. In 1921 it became a government-supervised reserve whose purpose was to preserve the wild flora and fauna of the virgin steppe and to study, acclimatize, and breed plants, animals, and birds. The huge reserve includes some 28,000 acres of virgin fescue-feather grass steppe, a research farm, an acclimatization zoo, and a botanical park. Hundreds of species of birds and animals nest or roam among the stone    *baba*. Among the international animals bred are Przewalski horses, bison, and zebras. About 200,000 tourists visit Askaniya-Nova each year. The best travel plan is to drive from Kherson with an English-speaking guide.

# CHAPTER 9.
# ODESA: PEARL OF THE BLACK SEA

ОДЕСА        o-DEH-sah

Odesa (spelled *Odessa* in Russian) is a city of contrasts. Its stately 19th-century Classical architecture, set on orderly planned streets surrounded with green space, give it an air of elegance. Strikingly ornate buildings of the late 19th and early 20th century are reminiscent of the Right Bank in Paris. It's also a seaport resort with bathing beaches, boardwalks, and health spas. With its balmy climate, seaside vistas, sandy beaches, and year-round lively street life, Odesa has a carefree and relaxed ambience more Mediterranean than Slavic.

The city is also an important scientific and academic center, with 14 institutes of higher education, including I. Mechnikov University, the state economic and polytechnic universities, the Conservatory, the Medical Institute, and the Institute of Naval Engineers. Odesa's artistic and cultural contributions are outstanding. Many great writers are associated with the city, among them native sons Isaak Babel (1894–1941), a Jewish writer of Odesa stories, and Mikhail Zhvanetsky, a modern satirist. Odesa has a strong tradition of performing arts, with many theaters and a world-class philharmonic. In the 1920s the city was the leading Ukrainian filmmaking center, and today there's an annual film festival at the end of summer. The city also hosts international contemporary music festivals and numerous exhibits, conferences, and symposia. Sports and recreation are also important. Odesa is the hometown of 1992 Olympic men's figure-skating gold medalist Viktor Petrenko.

Along with its considerable educational and cultural achievements, Odesa is a bustling commercial port with its share of urban blight and pollution. The dependence on the industrialized waterfront gives it a large blue-collar population as well as a reputation as a place where you can buy anything.

Odesa has always shown more color, spunk, and irreverence than other cities of the former Soviet Union. There's an excitement, a verve, an anything-is-possible feeling in its streets. The city has such a reputation for its cheeky and irreverent humor that it observes each April 1 as its city holiday with a big festival called Humorina. A few years ago, Odesa commemorated April 1 by erecting a monument of a chair in the city park, after the book *Twelve Chairs,* by early-20th-century native Odesa satirists, Ilya Ilf and Yevgeny Petrov. Another year, the local candy company produced chocolate-covered *salo* (pork fatback, a common Ukrainian delicacy).

**Location.** Odesa is situated on a high plateau overlooking a bay in the Black Sea-Azov Sea Basin, near the mouths of the Danube, Dnister, Boh, and Dnipro rivers. By road Odesa is 480 km (290 mi) south of Kyiv and 180 km (110 mi) southeast of the Moldovan capital, Chisinau.

**Population and Language.** The city's population of 1,027,000 consists of Ukrainians, Russians, Bulgarians, Moldovans, Jews, and other ethnic groups, making it one of the most cosmopolitan in Ukraine. With one of Ukraine's largest and most cohesive Jewish communities, numbering about 40,000, Odesa is a center of modern Yiddish and Hebrew literature.

Odesa's multi-ethnic legacy has evolved and changed over time. The Jewish population with its rich cultural life grew rapidly in the late 19th and early 20th centuries and by the turn of the last century, some 33 percent were Jewish, more than half were Russian, and only six percent were Ukrainian. Odesa's Jewish population was decimated by the Nazis, while the Ukrainian population grew during the rebuilding period following both world wars when people from the countryside moved into the city. During the post-WWII period until the mid-1970s, Ukrainians predominated. The newcomers usually tried to conform to the dominant Russian culture and many of them lost their ability to speak in their native tongue. Today there's no clear distinction between who is Russian and who is Ukrainian because no one born in Odesa claims to be anything but Odesan. And besides, issues of nationality and politics have never much bothered the residents of Odesa − the *Odesity.* They are more interested in the weightier concerns of love and money.

While the Russian language was nearly exclusive before independence, Ukrainian is taking over so quickly that Russian, not Ukrainian, is now a foreign language choice in schools. City documents are written in Ukrainian (which many residents can't read), new signposts with Ukrainian names mark the major streets in the center of town, while the population speaks, reads, and writes in Russian, with a unique Odesa dialect. The two languages co-exist comfortably in the city, but the sudden switch from one to another has led to speech patterns in the younger generation that blend both languages in an unpleasant and ungrammatical way.

**Climate.** May to September is the best time to visit, with average highs between 20° and 27°C (68° to 81°F). In July, the warmest month, the temperature averages 22.1°C (71.8°F), but can get as warm as 35 C (95°F). Winter temperatures hover around freezing, with the coldest month, January, averaging -2.8°C (27° F).Although Odesa averages only 351 mm (13.8 inches) of precipitation a year, mostly in rain, humidity is high year-round.

**Business and Industry.** Odesa is Ukraine's leading Black Sea port city, but was relieved of some of its cargo handling when a new port was built in 1957 at Illichivsk, 20 km (12 mi) to the southwest. Together they handle almost half the freight moving through Ukrainian ports. Major items of trade are grain, sugar, machinery, steel, petroleum products, coal, cement, metals, jute, and timber. Odesa is also a naval base, the home port of a fishing and antarctic whaling fleet, and a stop on the itinerary of many cruise ships.

Odesa was industrialized during the Soviet period. Metalworking and machine building account for more than a third of the industrial production. A chemical industry makes fertilizers, paints, dyes, and other materials. Shipbuilding, oil refining, food processing, and the manufacture of clothing and products from jute, wood, and silk are also important. Most factories lie along the waterfront north of the port.

## History

Odesa observed its two hundredth birthday on September 2, 1994. The site of the present-day city had, however, been occupied by various peoples and tribes since prehistoric times. In1415 the Ottoman Turks established a settlement called Khadzhibei. It was captured by the Russian army aided by a Ukrainian division of Kozaks during the Russo-Turkish War of 1787 to 1791. The Russians rebuilt it from 1792 to 1794 as a fortress and naval port and named it "Odessa" because they mistakenly believed that it was the site of an ancient Greek colony, Odessos.

In 1803, a French nobleman, Armand-Emmanuel du Plessis de Richelieu, became governor of Odesa, and transformed it into a modern city by developing its trade and agriculture and encouraging foreign immigrants.

Because of its strategic location, Russia considered Odesa "the southern window to Europe," and developed it as a port and an administrative center. Its duty-free status in the early part of the 19th century encouraged trade, and by 1850 Odesa was the largest wheat

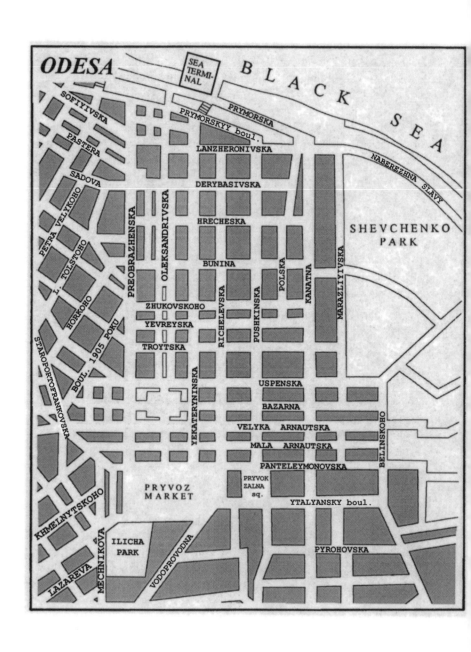

exporter in the Russian Empire. The city grew rapidly; in 1861 it was the largest city on Ukrainian lands, with 116,000 inhabitants.

By the 1880s Odesa was the second biggest port in the Russian Empire after St. Petersburg. Its primary exports were grain, sugar, and other agricultural products and its imports were tea and coal. The railroad stimulated further growth. The first industries processed agricultural products and imported raw materials.

Unemployment in years of bad harvest led to unrest. Odesa became a hotbed of political ferment. It was one of the chief centers of the 1905 workers' revolts, but demonstrations were ruthlessly suppressed. Between 1917 and 1920, many factions struggled to control Odesa — Bolsheviks, Whites, Ukrainians, Germans and Austrians, French and allied forces. The city suffered heavier losses than any other in Ukraine.

Under the Soviet regime, foreign trade lost some importance while heavy industry was emphasized. In 1941, despite a heroic resistance, Odesa was captured by the Germans and administered by Romanians. Before it was recaptured by the Soviet Army in 1944, it suffered heavy loss of life and property. It did not regain its prewar population of more than half a million until 1956.

## Sightseeing

**Tourist Concerns..** Odesa is a delightful city to visit and you should not be discouraged by a few necessary cautions. The city is rife with opportunism, corruption is said to permeate official circles, and bribery is an art form. However, there's no problem with violent crime, and you should feel safe day or night in the center of the city. But while assaults and muggings are rare, thievery is not, and you need to watch your wallet or purse, especially if riding public transportation or shopping in open markets.

Also, pay attention to where you step. Odesa's cobblestoned streets are irregular; pavements are badly in need of repair, and roads have potholes. In addition, street and sidewalk drainage is poor, resulting in dusty and muddy conditions.

The city's water system is old and low pressure sometimes affects supply. Hot water is not always available outside of the central district, but leading hotels and many residents rely on their own water heaters. As everywhere in Ukraine, you need to boil tap water before drinking it. Bottled water, usually carbonated, is easy to find. Swimming in the public beaches is not recommended since raw sewage is dumped into the sea.

**Orientation to the City.** *Names of streets and tourist sites are given in Ukrainian unless noted.* Legend has it that Duke Richelieu wanted to build a new city more beautiful than his native Paris. Although the modern city shows a faded grandeur that would benefit from a coat of paint and sandblasting of limestone facades, Odesa is kept clean and tidy, allowing Richelieu's dream of the splendor and elegance of Paris to shine through.

One of the few planned cities in Ukraine, Odesa's central core is laid out on a grid whose spacious avenues are paved with granite and lined with acacia trees. Old Odesa contains a number of lovely early 19th-century neo-Classical style two-storied limestone buildings that house cultural and scientific institutions and governmental offices.

The main street, **Derybasivska** (Дерибасівська) **Street**, was named after the Frenchman De Ribas, who led the capture of Odesa from the Turks in 1789. Derybasivska is a pedestrian mall shaded by linden trees. Numerous shops, pubs, and cafés with outdoor seating make it ideal for people-watching. On the west end of the street is the City Garden whose thriving Souvenir Market is the best place in the city to buy authentic art and crafts directly from the artists.

To the north is the focal point of the city center, **Prymorskyy** (Приморський) **Boulevard**, a shady seaside promenade with many historic landmarks and interesting monuments. Here Odesans sit on chestnut-shaded benches, enjoy the sea breeze, and gaze at the 180-degree panorama of the bay with its numerous ships, boats, and yachts. At the west end of the boulevard is the **Vorontsov Palace**, built between 1824 and 1829 by F. Boffo for the wealthy Count Mikhail Vorontsov, who was Governor of New Russia, the region surrounding Odesa. It now serves as the Palace of Youth. Its garden, with a striking Grecian colonnade, overlooks the harbor. On the square in the center of the boulevard, the toga-clad figure on the pedestal is Duke Richelieu, sculpted by I. Martos in 1828. The monument leads directly to Odesa's most recognizable landmark, the great Potomkin stairway which descends from Prymorskyy Boulevard to the port. At the bottom of the steps, across the road, is a new passenger ship terminal with a convention center and banking, lodging, and entertainment facilities. Continuing down Prymorskyy Boulevard to the east end, you'll come to the pink and white colonnaded **Odesa City Hall**. A British cannon from the Crimean War stands in front of the building.

A city stroll should also include **Pushkinska** (Пушкінска) **Street**. This pretty, tree-lined major cross street of Derybasivska has interesting shops and stately architecture. It was named for Alexander Pushkin, the great Russian poet who spent a few years in exile in Ukraine. The house at 13 Pushkinska Street in which he lived for 13 months is now the **Pushkin Museum**, open daily except Monday from 10 a.m. to 5 p.m. In the summer of 1999 in honor of the 200th anniversary of his birth, the city erected a monument to the poet on the sidewalk in front of the museum. The whimsical life-size bronze statue depicting Pushkin in a tuxedo with top hat and cane, placed right on the sidewalk, is a favorite photo opportunity for strolling Odesity.

To the west of the city center is an industrial district. To the north – beyond a strip of dense railway and tram lines, ship repair yards, factories, and warehouses – are flat, sandy beaches. A plateau to the south and southwest of the port is covered with gardens and parks. Going south along the parkland is **Frantsuzskyy Boulevard**. This cobblestoned boulevard, lined with acacia (locust) trees, was once the home of wealthy merchants of Old Odesa. Now it's home to hospitals, rest homes and sanatoriums, educational institutions, and the well-tended botanical gardens. South and west of the city along the coast are the more picturesque beaches and resorts.

**Maritime Stairs** (Приморські скгоди, *Prymorski skhody* ), link Prymorskyy Boulevard to the seaport on the north edge of the city. The stairs were designed by architect F. Boffo and constructed from 1837 to 1842. Its 192 steps are wider at the bottom than the top, so that when viewed from the bottom looking up, they give an illusion of being steeper than they actually are. Popularly known as the Potomkin or Potemkin Steps, the stairs were immortalized by Sergei Eisenstein's 1925 film, *Battleship Potemkin*. The film is a fictionalized account of the1905 mutiny of the ship's crew, and the massacre depicted on the steps was cinematic invention.

**Shevchenko Park** occupies 91 hectares (225 acres) on a plateau to the southwest of the port and offers a breathtaking view of the Black Sea. The park contains a monument to Taras Shevchenko, an obelisk with an eternal flame dedicated to the Unknown Sailor, a sports stadium, an open-air theater, a bathing beach, and an observatory. On the northeast corner of the park are the remains of the Odesa Fortress, built in 1793.

**Museums.** Museums in Odesa are good and not overwhelmingly large. Admission fees are low, but there's an extra charge for still and video photography. Museum guides usually speak only Russian. Hours are subject to change; most museums keep shorter hours during the non-tourist season.

**Odesa Fine Arts Museum** (Одеский художній музей, *Odeskyy khudozhniy muzey*) is at 5-a Sofiyivska (Софіевська) Street. It's housed in the imposing Count Pototskiy Palace, an 1805 —1810 Classical-style building with ornamented ceilings, parquet floors, and marble mantlepieces. Founded in 1899, the museum collection occupies 26 halls arranged chronologically, from 14th- and 15th-century icons to masterpieces of the Russian and Ukrainian realistic school of the 19th and early 20th century. Seascapes by I. Aivazovskiy and his followers, and etchings of Taras Shevchenko are on display as well as a good representation of modern painting, drawing, and sculpture from Ukraine and other former Soviet countries. The museum is open daily except Tuesday and the last Friday of the month from 10 a.m. until 5 p.m. Phone (0482) 23-72-87.

**Literary Museum** (Літературний музей, *Literatyrnyy muzey* ), 2 Lanzheronivska (Ланжеронівська) Street, opened in 1984 in a beautifully restored mansion built in 1842 by architect Ludwig Otton for Count Gargarin. The museum's 24 halls are chronologically divided into six collections that trace the literary history of Odesa, paying tribute to famous writers who lived and worked in the ci — Pushkin, Gogol, Chekhov, Tolstoy, and Gorky, to name a few. It's open daily except Monday from 10 a.m. until 4:30 p.m. English-speaking guides are available for about US$9 per hour. Phone (0482) 22-00-02 or (0482) 22-33-70.

**Odesa Museum of Archeology** (Одеский археологічний музей, *Odeskyy arkheolohichnyy muzey*), 4 Lanzheronivska (Ланжеронівська) Street, was designed in the Classical style by F. Gonsiorovskyy in 1883. It's a major archeology museum covering the area's human history up to the emergence of the Kyiv-Rus state. Collections come largely from excavations of Black Sea Greek colonies including Olvia, Khersonesus, Pantikapeum, and Tyras. Also on display are Egyptian, Roman, Trypillian, and late Bronze Age artifacts including ornaments and jewelry from the 6th to the 1st centuries BCE, and ancient coins from many periods and places. A highlight is the Gold Depository (*Zolota kladova*) with jewelry and coins from the early Greek Black Sea colonies to the 20th century. The museum is open daily except Monday from 10 a.m. until 5:00 p.m. English-speaking guides are available for under US$5. Phone (0482) 22-63-02.

**Naval Museum** (Музей морського флота, *Muzey morskoho flota*), 6 Lanzheronivska (Ланжеронівська) Street, is housed in the completely renovated English Club, a beautiful 1842 building designed by G. Toricelli in the Classical and Renaissance style. On display are 10,000 exhibits, including paper and scale models that illustrate shipbuilding and navigation from ancient times through the Kozak era to modern nuclear-powered submarines. The museum is open daily except on Thursdays from 10 a.m. to 5 p.m. No photography is allowed. Phone (0482) 24-05-09.

**Odesa Regional Museum** (Одеский краєзнавчий музеи, *Odeskyy Krayeznavchyy muzey*) at 4 Gavanna Street, right by Derybasivka Street, covers the history of the Odesa region from the 14th century until the present. The display includes sections on "Old Odesa," "World War II," "the Culture of Odesa," "Multinational Odesa," and "Sister-Towns." No video cameras are allowed. Open daily except Friday from 10 a.m. until 4:30 p.m. Phone (0482) 22-84-90; (0482) 25-52-02.

**Odesa Museum of Western and Oriental Art** (Одеский Музеи західного та східного мистецтва, *Odeskyy muzey zakhidnoho ta skhidnoho mystetstva* ), 9Pushkinska Street, was founded in 1920. Its collection of ancient art includes Greek and Roman sculpture, pottery, and glass. European art is represented by masterpieces from Italy, Holland, France, Spain, and Flanders spanning the 14th to 19th centuries; and oriental art comes from China, Japan, India, Mongolia, and Tibet. Several halls are set aside for exhibitions of local artists. The museum is open daily except Wednesdays from 10 a.m. to 6 p.m., with no tickets sold after 5:30 p.m. An English-speaking guide costs about US$10. Phone (0482) 24-66-46 or (0482) 22-48-15.

**Bleshchunov Municipal Museum of Personal Collections**, 19 Polska (Полска) Street, is located in the apartment of Odesa native son Alexander Bleshchunov, an early-20th-century collector of art and cultural objects from around the world. Bleshchunov had many interests and hobbies, among them mountain climbing, and his flat became a *salon* for the poets, artists, and actors of Odesa. Nearly 100 years old when he died, he willed his flat with his entire collection to the city. Arranged by theme rather than chronology, the exhibits include an Oriental room; a Western European room with Germanic porcelains and unique fans; Central Asia room with Persian carpets; a Christianity room with icons and church utensils; a Ukrainian room with icons painted on canvas and folk arts; and rooms devoted to the history of Odesa and life in 19th and early 20th centuries.

The museum is open from 9 a.m. to 5 p.m. daily except Wednesday. Phone (0482) 22-10-81.

**The Catacombs.** Underneath and throughout the city is a 580-mile labyrinth of tunnels that were carved out in the 19th century when the sandstone beneath the city was quarried for use in construction. The tunnels and caves attracted those who needed a place to hide, both heroes and criminals. During World War II, anti-Nazi resistance fighters and some Jewish residents were hidden in the caves. The area they used is a public museum, the **Museum of Partisan Glory,** located in the village of Nerubayske, 12 km (7 mi) northwest of Odesa on road M-20. Check at a hotel service bureau for a tour or take bus No. 84 (ask for *katakomby*). Open 9 a.m. until 4 p.m. Monday through Friday and 9 a.m. until 2 p.m. on Saturday. Navigating the network of dark, humid tunnels is not for the claustrophobic and not wise without an experienced guide.

**Churches, Synagogues, and Mosques.** Although religious life is not generally associated with Odesa, the city does have a number of places of worship of architectural significance:

**St. Nikolay Church** at the Passenger Ship Terminal was built in 1994 from a design by V. Kalinin.

**Preobrazhensky Cathedral,** Soborna Square, is the newly rebuilt copy of a church of the same name destroyed during Soviet times.

**Uspenska (Assumption) Cathedral** 70 Preobrazhenska Street, was designed by Shapin in 1845 and built in 1869. This five-domed cathedral with a magnificent Russian and Byzantine-style facade is the head Russian Orthodox church in Odesa.

**Roman Catholic Church of the Assumption,** 33 Katerininska Street, was built in 1853 by Morandy and Gonsiorovsky.

**Svyato-Troyitskyy (Holy Trinity) Church** 55 Katerininska Street, was built by Tedorov in the Classical style. The first stone was laid in 1795.

**Polish Roman Catholic Church of Saint Peter,** 5 Gavanna Street, was built in 1913 by Vassal.

**Svyato-Illinsky Cathedral,** 79 Pushkinska Street, built in 1895, is recognizable by its pretty blue facade. Adjoining it is the Illinsky male monastery.

**Panteleymonivskyy Cathedral** 66 Panteleymonivska Street (across from the train station) was built in 1888 by L. Prokopovych and M. Nikonov. Used as a planetarium for many years, it was renovated and reopened for worship several years ago.

**The Former Central Synagogue**, 25 Yevreyska Street. Built in 1853 by Morandy, the building needs restoration. The Jewish Religious Community, *Or Sameath,* meets in the building. Phone (0482) 24-36-94.

**Central Synagogue of Odesa**, 21 Osipov Street, is the only remaining synagogue of three originally on the street. Dating back to the late 19th or early 20th century, it has been fully restored and is functioning today. Phone (048) 221-88-90.

**Moblish Erulim Synagogue** at 46 Mala Arnautska Street, was built at the beginning of the 19th century.

**Mechet Mosque** is at 128 Balkivska Street.

**Svyato-Uspenska Monastery and Seminary** at Dacha Kovalevskoho, built in 1940, is one of a handful of seminaries that remained open during the Soviet era. Visitors can see monks at work in their gardens, selling holy water, and blessing crosses. Women visitors should wear a conservative skirt and head covering. A taxi ride from the city center to the monastery takes a half-hour; Bus No.127 from the railroad station will take about 40 minutes.

## Arts and Recreation

Recreation and entertainment abound in Odesa. Performing arts are strong with seven resident theater companies, a philharmonic orchestra, and a circus. In addition, the city hosts many visiting theater companies, musicians, and performers. There's a wealth of visual art, with some 3,000 professional artists and dozens of well-established galleries and significant exhibitions.

Odesans are also fond of sports and games, and have organized clubs for chess, bicycling, tennis, diving, and yachting.

The Odesa Port Authority runs a US$5 million yacht club at the sea terminal, complete with power hook-ups, slips, and a showroom of expensive motor and sailboats. Nightlife here is more vigorous than ever, with many hard-currency casinos for roulette and blackjack, a dance club on the roof, and shows and discos until the wee hours of the morning. Here are a few of the leading cultural opportunities:

**Odesa Theater of Opera and Ballet** (Одеский театр оперу та балету, *Odeskyy teatr opery ta baletu*), 3 Tchaikovsky Lane, was built in 1884 to 1887 in the Viennese neo-Renaissance style, according to a design by Herman Helmer and Ferdinand Fellner, the architects who designed the Vienna Opera. The rococo interior includes a ceiling decorated with scenes from the works of Shakespeare, and over five tiers containing 1,560 red-velvet seats. The Odesa Opera has always been one of the leading music theaters of Europe, hosting such stars as Pyotr Tchaikovsky, Nikolay Rimsky-Korsakov, Enrico Caruso, and Anna Pavlova. While the quality of performances is reputed to have declined a bit in recent years, the beauty of the theater is not to be missed. Tickets for performances cost under US$10, and are available at the ticket office adjacent to the opera. Formal tours of the building, conducted in Russian, are offered to concert goers for a very small fee an hour before performances.

**Philharmonic Hall**, 15 Bunina (Буніна) Street, on the corner of Pushkinska, was designed by A. Bernardazzi and G. Lonsky and built from 1894 to 1899 as the New Stock Exchange. The building's Florentine Restoration facade is decorated with ceramic plate, marble, and stained glass windows. Inside, is a sculpted wood ceiling symbolizing trade and industry. The conductor of the Odesa Philharmonic Orchestra is an American, Hobart Earle, whose enthusiasm and good humor have revived Odesans' interest in their Philharmonic, and home performances are a sell out. If this world-class orchestra is not away on tour when you're in Odesa, you shouldn't miss it. Phone (0482) 25-15-36 to check on performances or to order tickets, or buy tickets inside the entrance during the day.

**Odesa Theater of Musical Comedy** (Одеский театр музичноі комедіі, *Odeskyy teatr muzychnoi komedii*), 3 Panteleymonivska Street, features the operettas of Ukrainian and Russian composers. This very popular company is directed by a gifted ballet master who incorporates ballet stars in the performances. Rock concerts, comedians, and touring shows also appear here. Phone (0482) 25-09-24.

**Russian Drama Theater** , 28 Greece Street (vulytsya Hrecheska), was established in 1927. It has excellent performances of Russian-language dramas and comedies. Phone (0482) 22-72-50.

The **Ukrainian Music and Drama Theater**, at 15 Pasteur Street (vulytsya Pastera), was established in 1925. It performs Ukrainian language cultural programs. A puppet theater is at the same location. Phone (0482) 23-55-66.

**Beaches.** Odesa's beaches, stretching both to the north and the south, are separated from the city by a steep hill. This is a green area, closed to vehicular traffic, and a favorite destination for picnicking. Paths and stairs go down to the beaches, and there's also a nice skylift, **Kanatna Doroha** (Конатна Дорога), below Frantsuzskyy Boulevard, at the corner of

Kanatna and Pyrohovska Streets. The cable cars are a convenient and inexpensive way to get down to **Lazheron Beach** below.

Besides soaking up some sun, you can rent a rowboat, skiff, or catamaran; windsurf or fly on a hang glider; or have a meal at one of the small cafés. Beaches near the city are the most crowded. North of the city, the popular **Luzanovka** (Лузановка) **Beach** has many amusements, but beaches on the southern shore are nicer. Particularly attractive is **Arkadiya** (Аркадія), the largest and most developed of the beaches, with numerous cafés and restaurants, and lively nightlife. Going farther south is **Zolotyy Bereh** (Золотий Берег); **Velyka Fontanka** (Велика Фонтанка) or *Bolshoy Fontan* in Russian; and **Chornomorska** (Чорноморска). Bathing season is from early May until the end of September.

**Health Resorts.** Odesa's reputation as a health resort dates back to the 1820's. Therapeutic ingredients in the waters and muds along with the mild climate and beautiful beaches attracted vacationers and patients seeking a cure from various ailments, from arthritis to tuberculosis to skin disorders. Today numerous resorts, beauty spas, and sanatoriums dot a 50-mile stretch of coast from the village of Fontanka north of Odesa to Lebedivka to the south. These resorts attract hundreds of thousands of vacationers and medical patients yearly who seek health and beauty in hydro and mud treatments. For the most part, their Soviet-style orientation and the quality of the experience make them undesirable for Westerners, but a number of private resorts have opened.

   *Chabanka*, owned by the Sea Port, is popular with European tourists and sea terminal workers, who receive a large discount. This very attractive and well-managed resort offers good food, service, and lots of amenities. It's located at Chabanka Posyolok, about 25 km from Odesa on the road to Mykolayiv. Cost per night is about US$30 with full board, but no treatments. Phone (048) 729-41-86.

**Cruises.** Luxury cruises up the Dnipro River and to Black Sea ports are easily arranged between May and September. At least half a dozen ships are available for a 12-to-15-day cruise to Kyiv with stops in Crimea and several cities along the Dnipro River. Also, the newly seaworthy *T.G. Shevchenko* cruises to Bulgaria, Moscow, and St. Petersburg as well as around Crimea and up the Dnipro River. To arrange a cruise, contact *London Sky Travel* at the Sea Passenger Terminal; phone (048) 729-31-96; fax (048) 729-31-83; or e-mail lstravel@te.net.ua.

## Accommodations

**Hotels.** Hotel growth in Odesa has been on the upper end, with a number of new expensive luxury hotels. There are also some good mid-range hotels, and not-as-nice, but acceptable, bargain hotels, in which the water does not run during the night and may run cold when it flows. Note that, in the cheapest-priced rooms in budget hotels, baths are shared, so for maximum privacy choose the hotel's US$35 rather than its US$12 per night room. Prices also vary according to season, size and quality of room. Hotels are listed in order of decreasing cost and amenities for a standard double room in season. $$$$ = US$200 to US$300; $$$ = US$150 to US$200; $$ = US$75 to US$150; and $ = under US$50 nightly.

*Hotel Odessa*, 6 Prymorska Street, in the seaport, is the city's most luxurious and expensive hotel. It occupies the 19-story modern skyscraper that has given a jarring accent to the tranquil bay. All of the hotel's 158 spacious European-decor rooms have a sea view, a room safe, and electronic lock. The hotel offers every sort of amenity, including the rare ice machine. Breakfast is included. $$$$ Phone (048) 729-48-08; fax (048) 729-46-23.

*Arcadia-Plaza* (Аркадія-плаза), 1 Posmitnoho Street, is a lovely deluxe 24-room hotel in the Arkadiya Park area, about 5 km and a 15-minute ride south of the center. Among the amenities are Internet access in each room. $$$$ Phone (048) 234-17-70.

*Mozart Hotel*, 13 Lanzheronivska Street, is conveniently located near the opera theater. This four-story 40-room hotel occupies a 1794 building reconstructed in 2001 with elegant Austrian-style decor and furnishings. $$$ Phone (0482) 37-69-00, 37-69-00; fax (048) 237-98-94. E-mail office@mozart-hotel.com.

*Palace Del Mar Hotel and Spa Resort*, 1 Khrystalny Lane, occupies a 6-acre garden in the desirable Arcadia neighborhood. About a 15-minute drive from the center, it's accessible by public transportation. The hotel's 34 rooms occupy a renovated 4-story mansion with a grand marble staircase. Facilities include a fitness center, medical center, gourmet restaurant, swimming pool, and tennis courts. $$$ Phone (0482) 30-19-34.

*Hotel Londonskaya* (Лондонська), 11 Prymorskyy (Приморський) Boulevard, occupies a reconstructed handsome 1867 building near the seafront, close to the tourist attractions. The small hotel has some wonderful 19th-century features — wide corridors, grand marble staircase, charming courtyard, and large rooms with view of the harbor. Its very good restaurant serves European and Ukrainian cuisine. It has a coffee shop, bar, casino, business center, hairdresser, laundry, parking, currency exchange, and ATM. $$. Phone (048) 221-05-10; fax (482) 21-04-31.

*Hotel Krasnaya* (Красная), 15 Pushkinska (Пушкінска) Street at the corner of Bunina, is not far from the harbor. Originally constructed between 1894 and 1899 as a private mansion, it was designed by A. Bernardazzi, the same architect who designed Philharmonic Hall. Starting its hotel life as the Bristol, it later became the Krasnaya, meaning "red" or "beautiful" in Russian, from the rose-colored sandstone in its red and white exterior. Classical statuary and white marble columns add to the grandeur. It has a currency exchange; laundry; doctor on call; parking; and air and railway booking desk. Rooms are large and some are furnished with antiques. Long one of Odesa's leading hotels, the Krasnaya was closed in 2003–04 for renovation, and new prices may be higher than $$. Phone (0482)28-89-06; fax (482) 28-89-05.

*Frapolli* (Фраполлі) *Hotel*, 13 Derybasivska Street, is a new 26-room hotel. Rooms are furnished with a computer with Internet access; a safe; minibar; satellite and cable TV. In the lobby are a conference hall and a good restaurant. $$–$$$. Phone (0482) 35-68-00.

*Chorne More* (Чорне Море), 59 Rishelevska ( Рішелевська) Street, is located in the center of the city, a short walk to the railroad station and within walking distance of tourist sites and the seaport. The hotel is a recently renovated 1970s11-story Intourist hotel that is accustomed to serving large groups. All rooms have private bath, phones, TV, and minibar. There's 24-hour room service, an air-conditioned restaurant, a night club, beauty parlor, health club, post office, newsstand, and business services. $ to $$. Phone (482) 30-09-05; fax (482) 29-46-23.

*Hotel Victoriya* (Вікторія), 4a Henuezka Street in Arkadiya is a 15-minute drive from the center. This large (204-room) hotel is a short walk from a public beach. Rooms have a bath or shower and a phone. Some rooms have been renovated and have air-conditioning and hot water, but water may not be available at all times. $. Phone (0482) 61-89-03.

*Hotel Tsentralna*, ( Центральна) 40 Preobrazhenska Street, opposite the flower market, was built in 1886. Some rooms have a private bath, a TV, and a telephone. A hairdresser, a bar, and a small café are in the hotel. There's no water from 12 a.m. to 6:30 a.m. $. Phone (0482) 26-84-06.

More charming – though definitely showing signs of age – is the centrally located *Hotel Pasazh* (Пасаж), 34 Preobrazhenska, adjacent to an elegant baroque shopping arcade. Rooms are large but furniture is outdated, and there's no water from 12 a.m. until 6 a.m and no hot water from spring to fall. $. Phone (0482) 22-48-49.

**Other Lodging.** An alternative option during the tourist season when hotel rooms are hard to find is to rent a private apartment in the center; e-mail *Unipress* at travel@travel-2-ukraine.com. Other less expensive lodging options include staying with a host family or at a boarding house at Arcadia beach. For the cheapest room, about US$10 per night (which may include meals), follow the *babuskas* who hang out at the train station looking for boarders.

For those who are roughing it, there's *Camping Delfin* (Кемпінг Делфін), 29 Kotovsky Road in Luzanovka, 11 km (7 mi) north of Odesa center. This is a huge campground with campsites and bungalows, restaurant, bar, sauna, beach, and English-speaking service bureau. Camping Delfin is open June through September. Phone (0482) 55-22-23 or (0482) 55-50-52.

## Shopping and Dining

**Shopping.** With its mild climate and its entrepreneurial spirit, Odesa has always encouraged street vendors, and an ambience of an open-air bazaar pervades the whole city. On the western edge, south of Ovidiopilska (Овідіопільска) Road, shortly before the ring road, is an enormous weekend flea market where you can find all sorts of Western goods. Daily, a thriving open air artists' market is in      *Gorsad*, the city gardens on Derybasivska Street adjacent to Preobrazhenska Street.

*Pryvoz*, the central produce market, is near the train station. This sprawling market covers the area within Preobrazhenska, Panteley-monivska, Vodoprovodna, and Nevoshchepnoy Streets. At Pryvoz you can find grapes and peaches as large and luscious as any you've ever seen, as well as all sorts of exotic fruits and vegetables, fresh and dried herbs, dairy products, and sausage. One of the largest farmers' markets in the world, Pryvoz also has a huge amount of clothing and consumer goods. Bargaining is expected and payment is in cash only. Open daily except Monday from 6 a.m. to 3 p.m.

Although some of the most interesting merchandise is sold on the street, the heart of Old Odesa is full of modern shops. Most stores are open from 10 a.m. until 7 p.m. every day except Sunday, with a lunch hour from either 1 to 2 p.m. or from 2 to 3 p.m. The main street is **Derybasivska** (Дерибасівська) **Street**, a pretty, cobblestoned pedestrian mall with many cafés and stores selling simple local products to pricy Western clothing brands. *Dom Knigi* (Дом Кнігі) at 27 Derybasivska is one local store that remains. The biggest book market in town, Dom Knigi occupies a whole block with separate stores for books, maps, postcards, stationery, and music.

At the west end of the street at 33 Derybasivska is *Pasazh* (Пасаж), a baroque passageway connecting to Preobrazhenska Street. This picturesque alley was once Odesa's most exclusive shopping area; today it's the site of trendy shops, cafés, and restaurants. Katerininska and Pushkinska Streets, which run north–south off Derybasivska, are also good shopping streets.

*TSUM* or the *Central Department Store* ( Центральний універмаг, *Tsentralnyy univermah*) at 72 Pushkinska Street is open until 10 p.m.

A number of **art galleries** specialize in contemporary works of local, Ukrainian, and Russian artists. *Accent*, 2 Torhova Street, run by the Ukrainian Union of Artists, displays a wide spectrum of art; phone (0482) 23-26-97. *Alfa Design* at 55 Mala Arnautska Street, run by the Odesa branch of the Ukrainian Cultural Fund, encourages creativity and new artists; phone (0482) 25-39-61. The *Salon of the Union of Artists*, 18 Yekaterininska Street, features paintings of established artists; phone (0482) 25-46-67. *Liberty*, 24a Lanzheronivska Street, is a private gallery specializing in noted artists from the early 20th century and the '60s; phone (0482) 22-48-67. *Artis*, an art gallery at 62 Pushkinska, sells antiques as well as modern paintings and other art media. Phone (0482) 21-76-46.

**Food and Dining.** Food shops may be open around the clock, without a lunch break, and cafés and restaurants usually provide service from 11a.m. or noon until the last customer leaves in the evening.

The *Tsentralny* supermarket is on Preobrazhenska Street, at the corner of Derybasivska. Open daily from 9 a.m. to 11 p.m., Tsentralny carries a good selection of produce, meats, cold, and frozen foods.

For imported food from Scandinavia, there's *Troitsky* at 54 Troitska Street. The store includes a liquor department, a deli, a coffee shop, and a currency exchange. Visa cards are accepted. Troitsky is open from 9 a.m. to 8 p.m. Phone 24-90-40.

**Restaurants.** There's a lot of good eating in Odesa, averaging about the equivalent of US$10 to US$20 for a three-course meal. The more upscale restaurants accept credit cards, but others take payment only in cash. New international restaurants offer a wide range of non-traditional cuisines: pizza, barbeque, burgers, Chinese, Japanese, and Middle Eastern. For authentic Ukrainian cuisine, try *Ukrayinska Lasunka* at 17 Derybasivska Street. Recommended are the veal with cognac and garlic and the sour cherry *varenyky*. Phone 25-84-12. It can be hard to get a table at the very popuar *Kumanets* on Lanzheronivska at the corner of Gavana Street. *Khutorok* in Shevchenko Park at Lanzheron serves large portions of Ukrainian dishes in a 19th-century ambience.

A more expensive choice is *Deja Vue*, 1 Yekaterininska Square, by the statue of the Duke at the Potomkin Stairs. Deja Vue (named for a humorous Soviet film about Odesa) serves very good Odesa cuisine in a dining room recreating early 20th century Odesa and in another lampooning the Soviet era, down to the hammer and sickle on the red menu cover and the "*Gazata Pravda, use appropriately*" toilet paper in the restroom. Price of a full-course dinner is about US$40.

Hotel restaurants shouldn't be overlooked. The restaurant in the *Londonskaya Hotel* at 11 Prymorksyy Boulevard, serves well-prepared dishes among the fountains and ferns in its beautiful, renovated courtyard. Phone 7-38-01-28. The new hotels, *Mozart*, *Frapolli*, and *Palace Del Mar*, also have good restaurants. For an unbeatable view with Mediterranean or excellent Ukrainian cuisine, try *Panorama* at the top of the *Hotel Odessa* in the seaport.

A popular restaurant on Derybasivska Street is *Mick O'Neill's*, an Irish bar with Guinness beer on tap and a large beverage menu, plus well-prepared international pub food and some authentic Ukrainian dishes. A block west, an attractive *McDonald's* uses real stained glass in its decor and offers welcome air-conditioning.

## Transportation

A comprehensive network of bus, tram, and trolleybus lines covers the city and goes within walking distance of the beaches. They operate from 6 a.m. until 1 a.m. Buses, trams, and trolleys are inexpensive, only 50 to 70 kopiyky to 1 hryvnya. *Marshrutni* taxis, at a slightly higher cost, run from every 10 minutes to once an hour – depending on the route – and are a preferable alternative to buses and trams.

**Taxi.** Look for cabs at stands in front of hotels and at major intersections throughout the city, or phone 070 for an English-speaking dispatcher. However, in Odesa it's easy to find an unofficial cab just by standing near the road and putting out your hand to hail a private car. The best way to insure a reasonable fare is to have a Ukrainian friend engage the car and negotiate the price beforehand. The standard rate for a five- or ten-minute trip within the city is the equivalent of less than two dollars and about twice that for a 20-minute ride to the suburbs. But don't expect your driver to know English or to obey traffic laws.

**Bus.** Avtovokzal (Автовокзал), the long -distance bus terminal, is at 58 Kolontayivska Street, west of the center. Bus travel is cheap; buses go to major Ukrainian cities every day for no more than US$15 per person. International destinations are Hamburg, Athens, Varna, and Sophia. Call (0482) 004 for information.

**Rail.** The railroad station is the striking light-pink colored building on Pryvokzalna Square (площа Привокзална, *ploshcha Pryvokzalna*) at the south end of Pushkin Street (вулиця Пушкінска, *vulytsya Pushinska*). There's daily service to major cities. A new fast train goes daily to and from Kyiv; a one-way trip takes 5 to 6 hours and is inexpensive. The Odesa Express to Moscow takes less than 24 hours. Trains from Odesa also go to Warsaw, Prague, Bratislava, Berlin, and Saint Petersburg. To call the station, dial 005. Purchase your tickets either at the railway station or make an advance booking at 12a Serednyofontanska Doroho by showing your passport. A registered travel agency can also purchase your tickets for you.

**Air.** Central Airport is 12 km (7 mi) southwest of the city center off Ovidiopilska Road. Bus No. 101 runs to and from Hrecheska Square in the city center. The airport has been renovated and modernized, but not enlarged. Domestic airlines fly daily between Odesa and Kyiv's Borispil Airport. International flights go to Moscow, Vienna, Warsaw, Istanbul, Athens, Aleppo, Dubai, Yevrevan, Larnaca, Tel Aviv, Tbilisi, and Chisinau. For airport information, phone 39-33-12.

**Sea.** *Morskyy Vokzal* (Морський Вокзал), the Sea Passenger Terminal, is off Prymorska Street, at the bottom of the Potomkin steps. From here you can cruise up the Dnipro river to Kyiv or by sea to ports in Russia, Turkey, Bulgaria, or Israel. The *Gloria* and the *Caledonia* are catamaran ferries which sail weekly between Odesa, and Istanbul. Contact *Unipress* at (0482) 21-05-16 or e-mail travel@travel-2-ukraine.com. To book *The Crimean*

*Arrow,* a high speed catamaran to Sebastopol and Yalta or Varna Bulgaria, contact *London Sky Travel* by phoning (0487) 29-31-96 or e-mailing lstravel@te.ne.ua.

The terminal offers currency exchange and banking services; ticket windows for sea, rail, and air travel; and contains restaurants, bars, shops, parking, and a yacht marina.

**Rental Car.** Check at your hotel service bureau or at city travel services for a car rental company. You can rent a car with or without a driver. Road service stations are at 27 Leningrad Highway (Ленінградське шосе, *Leninhradske shose*) and 20 Promyslova (Промислова) Street.

## Useful Addresses

**Phone Card Calls.** MTTS, the inter-city telephone and telegraph station, is at 100 Balkivska (Балківська) Street. International phone booths are available at the main post office at 10 Sadova (Садова) Street, which also sells phone cards. A convenient place to make a phone card call is the Sea Passenger Terminal at the bottom of the Potomkin stairs.

**Internet Connections.** For sending e-mail messages home, go to the travel service bureaus of the leading hotels. In the city center, there's also *Neo@Club*, an Internet club and café at 58 Rishelyevska Street, which offers fast connections in either a smoking or nonsmoking room, and the *Internet Café* at 16 Sadova Street and *Internet Club* on Katerininska Street between Bazarna and Velyka Arnautska. Internet use in Odesa costs about the equivalent of US$1.50 to US$2 per hour.

**Banking Services.** Currency exchange booths are scattered throughout the city and many are open until late at night. For cashing travelers' checks and withdrawing cash on your credit card, banks will charge a 2 to 3 percent fee. *Aval Bank* at 9 Sadova Street in front of the central post office, charges a 2 percent commission on travelers' checks. Its hours are from 9 a.m. to 1 p.m. and from 2 to 3 p.m. every day except Sunday. At the Sea Passenger Terminal, the *Pivdenny Bank* charges 2 percent for a minimum of US$10 exchanged. It's open daily from 9 a.m. until 6 p.m. Better still, *Privatbank*, at 1 Hrecheska Square, has an ATM that will give you cash – either dollars or hryvni – on several credit cards as well as on your bank debit card. Open 10 a.m. until 4 p.m. Monday through Friday.

**Medical Services.** Into-Sana, 2a Varnenska Street, is the only satisfactory medical clinic in the city, though English is not spoken well. Phone 10-62 within the city; the long-distance and mobile phone number is (0482) 22-23-25.

**Toilets.** If you don't have access to a private toilet, your best bet in the central city is to use the restrooms in some of the restaurants in the center, for example, Mick O'Neil's on Derybasivska Street. McDonald's restaurants are on Derybasivska Street and near the railway station.

**Travel Agencies.** Travel services are usually found in the major hotels. A small, enterprising, reliable agency is *Unipress BTD*, at 5 Tiraspolska Street, second floor. Phone (0482) 21-05-16 or (0482) 21-07-13; fax (0482) 21-06-21; e-mail travel@travel-2-ukraine.com.

*Abundant old churches and Middle European architecture add to the great charm of Lviv.*

*Park benches along Svoboda Avenue in Lviv are often filled with men playing chess.*

Villages nestle among the tranquil green valleys of the Carpathian Mountains.

The art of bandura playing has been passed down to the younger generation.

*One of the best places to find Hutsul arts and crafts is the Kosiv craft market in the Ivano-Frankivsk oblast.*

*The Bessarabskyy Market on Kyiv's main street has the best selection of fresh produce in the city.*

*The St. Michael church in the Transcarpathian Museum of Folk Architecture in Uzhhorod was originally built in 1777.*

Destroyed during the Soviet era, the main church of St. Michael's Golden-domed Monastery in Kyiv has been completely rebuilt.

Baroque architecture in Odesa dates back nearly 200 years and lends a French look to the city.

*A large two-story mall was built under Kyiv's main street.*

*Plush new fast trains are serving major cities in Ukraine.*

*A seashore on the Black Sea, nearby mountains, and a perfect climate all make Yalta a tourist's dream.*

*A fascinating new tourist attraction is the Pysanka Museum in Kolomyya.*

*In mid-May Kyiv residents enjoy the annual display of lilacs and the river view from the Botanical Gardens.*

# CHAPTER 10.
# EASTERN UKRAINE

The **Poltavska oblast** lies on a lowland plain on the left (east) bank of the Dnipro River. Part of Kyiv Rus in the 10th to 11th centuries, it belonged to the Pereyaslav principality in the 11th to 13th centuries, then was controlled by the Tatars and later by Lithuania and Poland. A series of peasant-Kozak uprisings against the occupying forces culminated in 1648 in war. Under the leadership of Hetman Bohdan Khmelnytsky, the struggle for national liberation freed Ukraine of Polish rule.

The region was a battleground during the period of the Great Northern War between Sweden and Russia (1700 to 1721). The turning point of the war was the Battle of Poltava in 1709. After assurance that Ukraine would not be annexed to Poland in the event of a Swedish victory, Hetman Ivan Mazepa and his troops sided with Charles XII of Sweden against Peter I. Their defeat resulted in Russian military rule in the Hetmanate and a decrease in its autonomy. Ultimately, serfdom was introduced into Ukraine.

The Poltavska region is particularly rich in Ukrainian culture and lore. Taras Shevchenko lived here from 1843 to 1846. The Ukrainian composer Mykola Lysenko (1842–1912) was born and spent his early years in the village **Hrynky** (Гринки). The philosopher and poet Hryhoriy Skovoroda was born in the village of **CHORUKHY** (Чорнухи) in 1722. His family's estate was reconstructed and now houses a historical-ethnographic museum.

Nikolai Gogol (1809-52), who is usually considered one of the great Russian writers, was born Mykola Hohol in the village **VELYKI SORO-CHYNTSI** (Великі Сорочинці) on the Psel (Псел) River in the Myrhorod (Миргород) district. Gogol, an ethnic Ukrainian who used Ukrainian themes and settings in many of his works, wrote in the Russian language in order to be published. Gogol spent his childhood and adolescence outside of Myrhorod in a village now named **HOLOLEVO** in his honor. His family estate was reconstructed in 1984 and today is a cultural preserve, including a house, pavilion, park, and a museum

Worth seeing in Velyki Sorochyntsi is the **Gogol Literary Museum** and the 1732 baroque **Church of the Transfiguration** (Преображенська, *Preobrazhenska*) with a magnificent large wood-carved icon screen. The village of 5,000, however, is most famous for its annual fair. Each year near the end of August, the town hosts the famous **Sorochyntsi Fair** , immortalized in a Gogol story. Several acres are packed with booths selling local pottery, embroidery, carpets, and wood crafts, as well as a vast array of vegetables, fruits, cured meats, honeys, and prepared dishes. There's even livestock and farm machinery, since in recent years the fair has become the venue for a huge national trade show. Musicians perform, while Gogol and some of his fictional characters come to life and stroll among the crowds.

**OPISHNYA** ( Опішня),a village on the Poltava-Hadyach (Полтава-Гадяч) Road, 43 km (27 mi) north of the city Poltava, is famous for its earthenware. The area clay is superior, and archeological excavations have unearthed semi-pit dwellings with clay ovens dating from the late 8th to 9th century BCE.

The **National Museum of Ukrainian Ceramics** opened in Opishnya 1991, dedicated to preserving and reviving the ancient traditions. It includes an art school, research center, a large library dedicated to arts and crafts, and children's ceramic arts schools. Also, a ceramics factory makes tableware with traditional decorations, animal figurines, and clay toys. Each year on a Sunday in June, the village celebrates its potters, with local masters demonstrating such techniques as *filigranova porcelyana,* edging the ceramics with a lacelike filigree.

The administrative center of the Poltavska oblast is**POLTAVA**(Полтава), a city with approximately 320,000 residents. Situated on three hills over the Vorskla (Ворскла) River, Poltava is on the Kyiv-Kharkiv Road, about 350 km (210 mi) east of Kyiv and 135 km (84 mi) west of Kharkiv. The fast train from Kyiv to Poltava takes four and a half hours.

Poltava is one of the oldest settlements in the recorded history of Ukraine. Recent archeological discoveries date it to the year 899, surpassing previous findings that dated it to the year 1174. A major highway and railway crossing, the city has a reputation as an important cultural center with a long theatrical tradition and a prominent role in the 19th-century Ukrainian literary renaissance. Poltava was under German occupation from 1941 to 1943; it suffered heavy damage and is largely reconstructed.

Eight broad city streets converge upon a large circular plaza, **Round Square** (площа Крула, *ploshcha Kruhla*).The public garden in the central "square" is **Petrovsky Park**, a venue for public gatherings and concerts. In the very center, the tall iron column topped with an eagle was erected in 1809 for the 100th anniversary of the Battle of Poltava. The surrounding street is ringed with stately early-19th-century Classical-style buildings including a school of art, the city hall, a military training academy, and a technical university. Just beyond Round Square is the 1994 Monument to the Fallen Kozaks, honoring the Kozak casualties of the Battle of Poltava.

**Zhovtneva** (Жовтнева) Street, which intersects Round Square, is the city's main thoroughfare. The east end of the Zhovtneva between Frunze and Gogol streets is a shady brick-paved pedestrian mall with an assortment of shops.

The main department store is on the north side of Zhovtneva at the corner of Kotlyarevskoho Street. Hours are 9 a.m. to 8 p.m. on weekdays, 9 a.m. to 6 p.m. on Sundays.

*Khudozhniy Salon* (Художній Салон) 27 Zhovtneva Street, at its west end, sells work by local artists. It's open Sunday through Friday from 10 a.m. until 6 p.m., and Saturday from 11 a.m. until 4 p.m. Gogol Street going north of Zhovtneva is particularly attractive, with 19th-century buildings that survived the Second World War. The beautiful **Gogol Music and Dance Theater** is at 23 Zhovtneva, where it intersects Gogol going south.

The **Gallery Museum,** at 7 Frunze Street, adjacent to the central park, is worth seeing. Constructed in 1999 to commemorate the 1100th anniversary of Poltava, it contains 16th-to19th-century European art and 17th-century to contemporary Ukrainian and Russian art, from icons to modern tapestries. Among the painters represented are E. Delacroix, L. Cranach, G. van Eyk, and I. Repin. Labels are in Ukrainian and English. There's a recital hall with exhibits of area artists. The museum adjoins the *Gallery Hotel* and is open 10 a.m. until 6 p.m. every day except Monday.

The simple, elegant, white-walled squarish church accented with green at the southeast end of Zhovtneva Street doesn't look like an 18th-century wooden church. But the **Spaska** (Спаська) or "Savior" Church, 1705–6, is really the only example of old wooden church architecture in the Poltavska region. Because so many of Poltava's old churches had already been destroyed, the city built an outer church around the wooden structure to protect it from the elements.

A few blocks north at Lenin Square (площа Леніна, *ploshcha Lenina*) is the **Regional Studies Museum**. The museum is housed in the provincial county council building or *zemstvo,* originally built from 1903 to 1908 by architect Vasyl Krychevskyy. The building's Art Nouveau "Ukrainian Moderne" style gained Krychevskyy the reputation as the father of Ukrainian architecture. Its facade is embellished with crests of the region's towns and contains ceramics and majolica from historic area pottery factories. The interior tile work is dazzling.

The building was destroyed during the Second World War and reconstructed in the 1960s. The museum is one of the largest in Ukraine with over 200,000 exhibits, including valuable archeological objects; historical documents and manuscript books; and folk arts, including *kylyms* (carpets), costumes, embroidery, wood carvings, ceramics, and old *pysanky* (colored eggs). A mammoth skeleton stands in the natural history hall. Closed on Wednesday, the museum's hours are 9 a.m. until 5 p.m. daily except Monday, when it opens at 10 p.m.

Southeast of the center is **Ivana Hora**, or Ivan's Hill, the popular name of ploscha Mayden Soborna. The hill offers a panoramic view of the city and a spectacular 17th-century cathedral. Wedding parties pose for photos and pop bottles of champagne at the Friendship Rotunda on the bluff.

On the hill is the homestead of **Ivan Kotlyarevsky**, the well-known 19th-century writer whose classic works *Naltalka Poltavka* and *Eneida* were written in the Ukrainian language. Reconstructed in 1969 from a Shevchenko drawing, the homestead includes a pretty garden, and some thatched roof outbuildings.

The **Poltava Battle Field Historical and Cultural Preserve**is at Shvedska Mohyla (Шведська Могила) on the site of the battle, about 7 km (4 mi) north of the city center. Take Zhovtneva Street north from the Column of Glory, and at the end bear right on Zinkivska (Зінківська) Street. The Battle of Poltava Museum, though in need of renovation, is very well organized. A member of the International Military Museums Association, it's a must for military history buffs. Its fascinating exhibits detail the life and culture of the battle's participants through outstanding artwork, period artifacts, and dioramas. Galleries include a Peter the Great Room, Swedish Room,Turkish Room, and since 1991, a Ukrainian Room with Kozak household items and clothing. The museum is closed on Mondays.

Also on the site is the church of St. Sampson; a monument constructed in 1894 over the common grave of 1,385 Russian soldiers who lost their lives fighting Sweden and the Ukrainian Kozaks; and a monument to the fallen Swedes.

Just outside Poltava, near the village of **Chervonyy Shlyakh** (Червоний Шлях, the **Elevation of the Cross Convent** (Хрестовоздви-женський, *Khrestovozdvy-zhenskyy*) is set high on a hill above the River Poltavka and offers a fine view of the old part of Poltava. The main church was built from 1689 to 1709 from Kozak funds following a victory over Polish forces. The only existing seven-domed Ukrainian Baroque structure in Ukraine, the church is considered a flower of Kozak church architecture. The four-tier 47-meter-high bell tower was added in 1686. Closed twice in the last century under the Soviets, it reopened in 1992 as a Russian Orthodox convent.

A small, good hotel in the center of Poltava is **Gallery**, 7 Frunze Street. Phone (0532) 56-16-97; fax: (0532) 56-31-21.

The restaurant *Ivanova Hora*, *2* Maydan Sobornyy, on the hill where the city was founded, offers a lovely interior or a magnificent view of the city from veranda seating. The excellent dishes are presented with flair. Hours are 2 p.m. until 1 a.m. daily; 5 p.m. until 1 a.m. Sunday. Dancing nightly. Phone (0532) 56-32-21.

Try *Café Khutorok* for very tasty regional dishes, including *borshch* with *halushky* (noodles), mushroom soup, and strawberry *varenyky* (dumplings) with honey. Open daily from 11 a.m. until 11 p.m., it's at 118 *vul. Lenina*.

**DNIPROPETROVSK** (Дніпропетровськ) is the country's third largest city with a population of approximately 1,153,000. It was founded in 1787 by Prince Potomkin on the site of the Zaporozhian village Polovysia, and was known as Yekaterinoslav until 1926. Industrial development began with the laying of a railroad line in the 1870s linking the city with the industrial centers of the Donets Basin. From the early 20th century, it's been the major steel industry center. Other large industries are machine-building, chemical, and oil-refining. It's also a major trade and finance center and an important river port and railway junction.

Dnipropetrovsk is the birthplace of Oksana Baiul, the 1994 Olympic women's figure skating gold medalist. Under the Kuchma government, scores of Ukraine's top politicians called this city home, and their influence is seen in the high proportion of Ukraine's foreign investments. The money pouring in has turned Dnipropetrovsk into a boom town; an underground subway system opened in 1995; there are new tram lines; an upgraded phone system; a modernized airport and train station; and new hospitals.

Despite its pollution, Dnipropetrovsk is very attractive. Overlooking the river Dnipro, it contains extensive expanses of parks and green areas. The city is bisected by the wide river and its center is on the right (west) bank. **Shevchenko City Park** lies below on the slopes of the riverbank. The park contains the reconstructed palace of Prince Potomkin. Originally built in 1787, in modern times it's used as a culture palace for students.

A footbridge and a skylift link the park to **Monastyrskyy Island**, a large recreation area in the Dnipro surrounded by white sandy beaches. The first recorded history of this island was in the ninth century when Greek monks established a cloister, which was destroyed by Tatars in the 13th century.

The city's main thoroughfare is the **Avenue of Karl Marx**, a beautiful wide east–west street lined by acacia trees. This is a lively area of shops and cafes. *TSUM*, the Central Department Store, is at 52 Karl Marx Avenue; the place to buy souvenirs is *Exhibition*, across the boulevard from TSUM; and there's good shopping on nearby streets and squares as well.

At the east end of Karl Marx Avenue, the **Yavornytsky Museum of History** is worth a visit. Highlights are its archeological department with the largest collection in Europe of Polovtsian stone *baba* figures; its Kozak-era objects; and its *Battle for the Dnipro* diorama, depicting the 1943 battle of the armies of five Soviet fronts against the Nazi invaders. Tapestries and paintings are in a separate building. Museum hours are 10 a.m. to 5 p.m. daily except Monday and the last Friday of the month. Phone (0562) 43-34-22 or (0562) 46-05-12.

The **Dnipropetrovsk Fine Arts Museum,** at 21 Shevchenko Street, displays paintings of Russian and Dnipropetrovsk area artists as well as Petrykivka decorative paintings.

Cultural attractions include an opera and ballet theater; children's and youth theater; puppet theater; T. Shevchenko Ukrainian Music and Drama theater; M. Gorky Russian Drama Theater; a philharmonic; an organ and chamber music hall; a circus; and a large freshwater aquarium.

Dnipropetrovsk is dotted with architectural gems of the 19th and 20th centuries. Though many historic churches and buildings were destroyed either by Stalin in the 1930s or during WWII, neighborhoods of untouched fine architecture still exist. Of church architecture, the **Transfiguration** (*Spaso-Preobrazhensky*) **Cathedral** is the most outstanding. The cornerstone was laid in 1787 by Empress Catherine II, who intended the cathedral to be larger than St. Peter's in Rome, but lack of funds resulted in a structure only one-sixth the size of the original plan. The church was designed in the Classical style by architect A. Zahkorov and built from 1830–35.

Also noteworthy is the **Cathedral of the Holy Trinity** (*Sviatro-Troitsky*), the central cathedral of the Dnipropetrovsk eparchy of the Ukrainian Orthodox Church. It was built in 1855 by St. Petersburg architects Viskonti and Sharleman.

**Hotels.** Among the city's best hotels is *Grand Hotel Ukraine* at 2 Korolenko Street. Located in the city center, this 70-room hotel was built in 1904 in a Gothic style by architect P. Fetisov and recently was completely renovated to its former majesty. All rooms are air-conditioned and contain king-sized beds. The restaurant serves Ukrainian, Chinese, and Japanese cuisine. Prices start at US$120 per night. Phone (0562) 34-10-10; fax: (0562) 34-02-00; e-mail admin@grand-hotel-ukraine.dp.ua.

*Astoria Hotel*, 66-A Karl Marx Avenue in the center, is a fine small hotel with lovely decor. Rates start at US$118 per night. Phone (0562) 37-42-70.

For a cheaper alternative, the 11-story *Dnipropetrovsk Hotel*, 33 Naberezhna Lenina, is in the city center, overlooking the river. It was built in 1968 and renovated in 1998. Phone (0562) 45-53-27.

On the left bank of the Dnipro, about 50 km northwest of Dnipropetrovsk is the village **PETRYKIVKA** (Петриківка), recognized since the 18th century for its distinctive ornamentation of traditional stoves, whitewashed house walls, and door and window frames. Today Petrykivka decorative painting is applied to dishes, boxes, vases, and other souvenir items by craftsmen of the **Museum of Applied Art in Petrykivka**.

The **Zaporizhska** (Запоріжська) **oblast** in southeastern Ukraine extends south to the Sea of Azov. The name comes from the phrase *za porohamy* (за порогами), or "beyond the rapids," referring to the spot past a series of rapids on the Dnipro where navigation was possible. The name has a special place in Ukrainian national lore because it's associated with the territory inhabited by a particular group of Kozaks from the mid-16th century to 1775. The Zaporizhian frontier grew as a result of Ukrainians fleeing serfdom. They established homesteads and built fortified camps called *sichi* (січі) to defend themselves against Tatar raids. The camps were later united to create a central fortress, the Zaporizhska Sich (Запоріжська

Січ). The Sich was the embryonic form of the independent Kozak state, which was the first state established on Ukrainian territory, as well as the first democratic form of rule in modern Europe.

**ZAPORIZHYA** (Запоріжжя), the capital of the region, is a city of about 887,000 residents on the left (east) bank of the Dnipro. It dates back to Kozak origins in 1553. Rebuilt after World War II, the city's architecture is modern and its wide streets are tree-lined.

Despite its scenic and cultural attractions, Zaporizhya's overwhelming impression is that of a dirty, polluted city, with huge smokestacks spewing out black clouds of smoke. The city's gigantic industrial complex owes its existence to the massive steel and concrete Dnipro Hydro Power Station dam. Built from 1927 to 1932 with the help of Canadian and American engineers, the dam was the USSR's first hydroelectric dam and provided energy for Zaporizhya's extensive industrial growth. Partly destroyed in World War II, it's been rebuilt and expanded.

The city is also the site of Europe's largest nuclear power station. It's a major home of Ukraine's auto industry, Zaporizhya Auto Works, in joint venture with German Opel and a Swiss firm that bought out the bankrupt South Korean Daewoo. Other factories make aircraft engines, steel, agricultural machinery, and chemicals.

The main street, **Lenin Avenue** (просп. Леніна, *prospekt Lenina*), commonly referred to as the Prospekt, runs 12 km (7.2 mi), making it one of the longest city streets in Europe. The Prospekt is lined with glitzy new shops selling all sorts of expensive consumer goods and is well served by public transportation. The main department store is the four-story *Ukrayina* at 147 prospekt Lenina. Very affordable cafés serving Ukrainian cuisine are on almost every block. **Festivalna Square** is in the very heart of the city, located just off the main street. The *Tsentralny Shopping Center*, across from the main government building in the square, contains several good restaurants including an excellent pizzeria that also serves Ukrainian-style salads.

The city's leading open market is the large *Angolenko Bazaar* off Angolenko Street. Stretching for blocks, the bazaar sells both clothing and food. It operates until 5 p.m. daily and is closed on Mondays. For hand-crafted souvenirs, try the department store; the gift shop, *Podarunky*, at 148 Lenina, a block down the street behind the department store; and the craft market in Festivalna Square, near the *Intourist Hotel*. The hotel is within the **Zaporizhya** business complex at135 prospekt Lenina in Festivalna Square. Visitors favor this centrally located 195-room hotel with many English-speaking staff and lots of amenities. Phone (0612) 34-12-92.

**Khortytsya (Хортиця) Island,** southwest of Zaporizhya, is the largest island in the Dnipro River, covering some 3,000 hectares (7,400 acres). The scenic island attracts those wanting to escape the city noise and pollution and, in the summer, enjoy some shade or a beach.

Khortytsya Island was designated a national reserve in 1965 because of its important role in Ukrainian history. Ancient stone idols dot the island and ruins of an 11th-century Slav fortress have recently been excavated. In the 12th century, the Ukrainian princes launched a successful campaign against the Polovtsians, a Turkish tribe also known as Cumans, but soon the Slav state was conquered by the Tatar-Mongols.

In the late 15th century, freedom-loving Kozaks, attracted by the natural fortress formed by the island's steep and rocky perimeter, established Khortytsya as their base camp against various invaders. From this island they ruled south central and northeastern Ukraine for over 150 years. Hetman Bohdan Khmelnytsky launched his anti-Polish war from Khortytsya in 1648, and in the 1660s and 1670s the Kozak otaman Ivan Sirko used the island as his military base. The Kozaks held the island until the Zaporizhska Sich was destroyed in 1775 by the Russian Army on orders of Catherine II.

The rocky north end of the island contains most of the Kozak remnants. Remains of the Sich fortifications include a fortress and a shipyard built in 1737 during the Russo-Turkish War. Natural rock formations hold many legends: **Durna Skelya** (Дирна Скеля) is the cliff where Kozaks were punished; Black Rock or **Chorna Skelya** (Чорна Скеля) is a cliff where the Grand Prince of Kyiv Svyatoslav was killed by the Pechenegs in 972. On **Mala** (Small) **Khortytsya Island**, 10 km (6 mi) north, are remains of some of the earliest Kozak fortifications, dating from the 1550s.

In 1983 a **Kortytsya National Preserve** was built near the northern rocks of Khortytsya Island, close to the picturesque Black Rock. The very attractive **Kozak Museum** shows the history of the island, starting from Bronze and Stone Age artifacts. Most of the displays concern Kozak life, from their naval weapons to their farm implements and kitchen utensils, but there are also World War II dioramas. A restaurant is on the premises. The museum is closed Mondays.

Next to the museum is a recent memorial mound honoring all those who died for Ukraine's freedom, and a hill outside the museum's main door leads up to a beautiful view of the city. Marshrutky run all day from the Metalerhov bus stop next to McDonald's to the island. Follow the Музей" signs to the museum.

Travel services can arrange participation in special Kozak cultural events, for example a gala traditional dinner with folk performances at the *Hotel Zaporizhya*. Outside of the city you can sail in a *chayka* or "seagull," a canoe-like Kozak boat; visit the Orlovaky horse-breeding farm; see a Kozak equestrian show; or make a several-day excursion down the Dnipro on a large, motorized chayka, stopping at villages and historical sites.

Across the Dnipro from Zaporizhya, heading west to the village of **VERKHNYA KHORTYTSYA** (Верхня Хортиця), is the site of a 700-year-old oak tree that died in 1995. The historic tree stood about 36.5 m (120 ft) high with a trunk diameter of almost 7 m (23 ft) and was said to have sheltered Bohdan Khmelnytsky and his Kozak troops while they planned their battle strategy.

In **MELITOPOL** (Мелітополь), 110 km (67 mi) south of the city of Zaporizhya, a Scythian royal burial mound from the 4th to 3rd century BCE was excavated in 1954. The remains of a noble couple and a slave, as well as 4,000 artifacts, including much gold and silver, were uncovered. The collection is in the Museum of Historical Treasures of Ukraine in Kyiv.

The **Melitopol Museum of Local Lore**, 18 Karl Marx Street, gives an overview of the various ethnic groups which inhabit the region. World War II memorabilia and battlefield history are displayed in another hall. The museum is open daily from 9 a.m. until 4 p.m. except Mondays.

**Kamyana Mohyla** (Rock Mound) **Historical and ArcheologicaPreserve** is a sandstone knoll resembling a large burial mound with caves. Located 2 km outside the village **MYRNE**, about a 20-minute drive from Melitopol, Kamyana Mohyla dates from the Paleolithic (20,000 to 16,000 BCE) to the Bronze Age. The 37-acre site in the middle of a wheat field contains many stone *baba*, the matronly-shaped stone idols of the prehistoric civilizations that inhabited the swampy site. Etched in boulders buried in the sand are numerous petroglyphs – depicting mammoths, horses, hands and feet – believed to be the oldest stone carvings in the world. A one-room museum displays some carvings, pottery and other artifacts.

According to legend, **KHARKIV** (Харків) was founded in 1654, by Kharko, a Zaporizhyan Kozak. Today it's Ukraine's second-largest city with 1.6 million residents. Although not a major tourist destination, Kharkiv is worth a visit. Known for its heavy machine-building, chemical and pharmaceutical plants, Kharkiv is nevertheless pleasant, spacious, and attractive, with more than 100 parks within its 272 square kilometers (105 square miles). It has more than 20 institutes of higher learning, many with international reputations, such as the Institute for Low Temperature Physics. *Kharkivyany* are highly educated and cultured. The city has the highest student/population ratio in Ukraine, outstanding professional theaters, museums, and scores of libraries,

From 1919 to 1934, when it served as the capital of Soviet Ukraine, Kharkiv was intensely developed. Numerous industries were established, apartments built, and public transportation extended. Ukrainian academic and cultural life also flourished during this period: important scientific institutions were established; museums and theaters erected; and writers' and artists' associations formed. With the rise of Stalin, not only was Ukrainian cultural life suppressed in Kharkiv, persecution against the intelligentsia began. Much historic architecture – including Ukrainian Baroque churches – was senselessly destroyed to make way for government buildings. By the time the capital was transferred to Kyiv in 1934, Kharkiv had lost much of its Ukrainian character.

During World War II, the city was hotly contested and suffered extensive damage. The Germans occupied it for 22 months, during which time they killed 100,000 people and forcefully sent another 60,000 to Germany as laborers. After the war, the city was rebuilt with broad streets, large gray concrete apartment blocks, and massive administrative and office buildings.

Only 40 km (25 mi) from the Russian border, Kharkiv today is a highly Russified city. About 94 percent of the residents speak Russian, while some 71 percent are fluent in Ukrainian. Russian is the language heard most often in public, although street signs are now mostly in Ukrainian.

Kharkiv's main thoroughfare – and street for strolling – is **Sumska** (Сумська) Street, an old cobblestoned street with many beautiful buildings, lovely parks, lots of small cafés, some restaurants and souvenir shops. North of the city center and extending west to Klochkivska (Клочківська) Street is **Shevchenko Garden**. First planted in 1804, the 25-hectare (62.5-acre) garden contains thousands of trees, shrubs, and

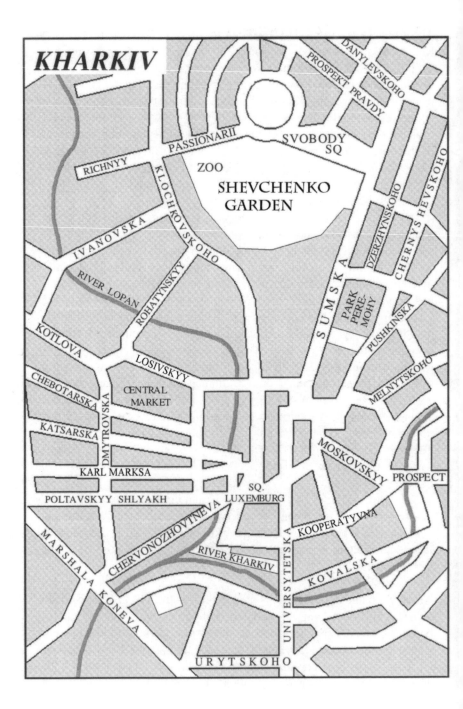

bedding plants. On the park's western slope, a lovely waterfall cascades down to Klochkivska Street and a lookout platform offers a panoramic view of the city. A fountain with built-in colored lights and music is in the center of the park and a beautiful chestnut-lined central path leads from a monument of Taras Shevchenko. to the north edge of the park. Within Shevchenko Garden are the **Kharkiv Zoo**, the university astronomical observatory, and the 1,850-seat **Movie and Concert Hall Ukrayina**.

On its north edge, the garden meets the massive **Freedom Square** (площа Свободи, *ploshcha Svobody*), one of the largest in Europe and a locale for concerts, fairs and other Kharkiv public events. The collection of tall blocklike buildings facing the park is *Derzhprom,* the State Industrial Building, built from 1925 through 1928 as the first high-rise in the country. It's still largely occupied by government offices along with non-government organizations and enterprises. At the east end of Derzhprom, the huge crescent-shaped building facing the square is **Kharkiv National University**, the city's leading educational institution.

**Churches.** While church architecture doesn't dominate Kharkiv, several churches are worth noting. The **Cathedral of the Holy Protectress** (Покровська, *Pokrovska*) is at 8 Universytetska ( Університецька) Street, close to Constitution Square. Built in 1689 as part of the original Kharkiv fortress settlement, **Pokrovska Church** with its bell tower is the oldest remaining structure in Kharkiv. The white stone church is in the style of a typical three-domed Ukrainian wooden church. The church became part of the Pokrovskyy Monastery, which was built in 1726 within the fortress. Adjacent to the church is the former bishop's residence, built in 1820 in the Classical style. In the Soviet era, the buildings of the monastery were used as storehouses and offices and during WWII they were severely damaged. They were restored in the early 1990s. Considered one of the most beautiful structures in Kharkiv, Pokrovska is now a functioning Orthodox church under the Moscow Patriarchate.

Farther down the street is a Kharkiv landmark, an 89.5-m-high (292- ft) gold-domed bell tower designed by architect Yehen Vasilyev and built from 1821 to 1844. The melodious chimes of the tower's clock can be heard hourly throughout the city. Adjacent to the tower at 11 Universitetska Street is the brick **Uspenskyy Cathedral**, built in the Baroque style from 1771 to 1778 to commemorate the victory of Russia over Napoleon. With its pipe organ and fine acoustics, the cathedral functions as an **Organ and Chamber Music Hall** for scheduled concerts and recitals.

As you go west across the Lopan (Лопан) River to Karl Marx Square, you'll notice the striking principal cathedral of the Russian Orthodox Church in Kharkiv. **Blahovishchenskyy** (Blessed News) **Cathedral** was constructed from 1881 to 1901 of dark red and cream bricks in an alternating striped pattern. Architecture and motifs were based on the Hagia Sofia Cathedral in Istanbul. The church is worth a visit for the beauty of its interior as well as its choir.

**Other sights.** In 1977 the city erected **Glory Memorial**, a WWII memorial in the park on Belgorodske Shose, a continuation of Sumska Street after it passes Gorky park going north. The memorial consists of a huge statue representing the Motherland with the sound of her heart beating and an eternal flame.

Following independence, the city erected a Holocaust memorial, **Drobytsky Yar**, devoted to the Jewish victims during 1941and 1942. The monument consists of a large menorah-like structure and a white arch with the inscription *Here the dead teach the living, do not kill.* To visit Drobytsky Yar, take the Rostov highway, turning left just after passing the police checkpoint outside the city.

Another impressive new monument is the burial site of captive Polish military officers and Ukrainian citizens killed from 1938 to 1941 by the NKVD, the secret police. Opened in 2000, the memorial is located in the wooded park along Belgorodske Shose, closer to Pyatykhatky.

**Arts and Recreation.** The **Kharkiv Fine Arts Museum**, at 11 Radnarkomivska (Раднаркомівська) Street, is one of the leading art museums of Ukraine. Founded in 1920, the museum holdings are nearly 20,000 works, with 25 halls of exhibits. The painting division is the strongest, with medieval murals;16th-to 19th-century icons, portraits, and folk paintings; and 20th-century painting. A self-portrait by Taras Shevchenko is on display. A gallery devoted to the works of late-19th-century realist I. Repin, includes his famous work, *The Zaporizhski Kozaks Write a Letter to the Turkish Sultan.* The museum is open daily except Tuesday from 10 a.m. until 5 p.m. Phone (057) 706-33-94 (-95) (-96).

Affiliated with the fine arts museum is **The Museum of Folk Art of Slobozhanschyna** (Eastern and Northern Ukraine), next door at 9 Radnarkomivska Street, with the same hours. Phone (057) 706-33-94.

**Kharkiv Historical Museum** is in two buildings located at 5 and 10 Universytetska (Університетська) Street. Exhibits include items from archeological discoveries in eastern Ukraine and from the early history of

Kharkiv, as well as numismatic, ethnographic, and weaponry displays. Open every day but Monday from 10 a.m. to 5 p.m. Phone (057)712-73-48 or (057) 712-76-94.

**Museum of Nature of the Kharkiv University,** 8 Trynklera Street, displays animals and fossils from all over the world in 32 rooms. Hours are daily except Sunday from 8:30 until 4 p.m. Phone (057) 705-12-42.

Kharkiv has several unique museums: **Militia Museum,** 13 Radnarkomivska Street, details the history of Kharkiv police, and is open from 8:30 to 4 p.m. daily except Sunday; phone (057) 706-30-81.

The **Kharkiv Museum of the Holocaust,** is at 28 Petrovskoho Street, 2nd floor. Opened in 1996, the museum documents the fate of Kharkiv's Jewish population under the Nazi occupation. There are also materials about non-Jewish people who helped to save the Jews during that period. Phone (0572) 14-09-59.

For the performing arts, there's the **Lysenko Theater of Opera and Ballet.** Set in a massive modernistic auditorium at 25 Sumska (Сумська) Street, the theater contains small shops, cafés, and various exhibitions. The square in front is a lively scene of public gatherings and festivals.

**Ukrayina Concert Hall,** 35 Sumska Street, located inside Shevchenko City Garden, is used mostly for pop music concerts, while the **Kharkiv Philarmonic Society,** 21 Rymarska Street, presents classical music concerts.

The city's rich cultural life also includes: **T. Shevchenko Kharkiv Ukrainian Drama Theater,** 9 Sumska Street, **Pushkin Russian Drama Theater,** 11 Chernyshevsky Street; **Theater of Musical Comedy,** 32 Karl Marx Street; **Young Peoples' Theater** at 18 Poltavsky Shlakh Street; and **Puppet Theater** at 24 ploscha Konstitutsii.

The **Central Park of Culture and Recreation (Gorky Park),** a very popular city recreation site, is located on Sumska Street, north of Shevchenko Garden. It can be accessed by an aerial cable car that runs from Otakara Yarosha Street. The 340-acre park contains concert arenas, dance pavilions, tennis courts, a movie theater, library, and cafés. A children's diesel locomotive, built in 1940, transports passengers between Gorky Park and **Forest Park,** a large wooded area in the city.

**Hidropark,** a newly rebuilt recreation area, is northeast of the city where the Kharkiv river becomes wide and forms a basin. In Hidropark, Kharkivites enjoy watersports, sunbathing on a sandy beach, rental boats, and a restaurant *Melnitsa* (The Mill), which serves traditional food in a windmill-like building.

**"Day of Kharkiv":** The city's special day is celebrated on August 23. Kharkiv observed its 350th anniversary with extra festivities in 2004. For daily fun, Kharkiv has plenty of discos and nightclubs.

**Shopping.** Gifts, crafts, and souvenirs are abundant, with prices better than in Kyiv. *Salon Arka*, 48 Sumska Street, has lacquer boxes, stacking dolls, painted eggs, rings, and earrings. *Salon Kramnytsya*, 52 Pushkinska Street, features wood-carved boxes, paintings, traditional embroidery, and knitware. *Vernisazh*, 11 Sumska Street, sells lacquer boxes, miniature paintings, decorations, fancy earthenware, and paintings. *Ukrainskyy Suveniry*, 3 Moskovskyy Avenue, has a good selection of embroidery, wood carvings, and painted boxes.

For the biggest choice at best prices, the open-air *Art Market* at Constitution Square operates every day from early morning until 2 to 3 p.m.

Main department stores are *Central* (*TSUM*) at 1/3 Rosa Luxemburg Square; *Kharkiv*, at 137 Moskovsky Prospekt; *Dytyachyy Svit* (Children's World) at 9 Constitution Square; and *Pavlovsky* at 6 Rosa Luxemburg Square.

**Large supermarkets** are *BILLA* at 9-A Klochkivska Street and 33-A 23rd of August Street; *Target*, 120 vul. Akademika Pavlova; *Brig*, 3 vul. Tarasivska; *Class*, 259 Moskovsky Avenue; and *Rost*, 63 vul. Klochkivska

**Hotels.** The *Kharkiv* at 7 ploshcha Svobody , near the university, is the city's leading hotel with 16 stories and a wealth of amenities. Phone (0572) 19-46-15 or (0572) 45-61-25.

*Hotel Kyivska*, 4 Kultury Street, phone (0572) 14-31-00; *National* at 21 prospekt Lenina; and *Myr* at 27-A prospekt Lenina, are also good. The price of a standard double room ranges from US$36 in *Myr* to US$75 per night in the Kyivska.

**Restaurants and Cafés.** For local cuisine, *Metropol*, in an attractive setting at 50 Sumska Street, is considered Kharkiv's finest restaurant. Its extensive menu includes a large assortment of wines and cognacs. Entertainment is live 1950s music. Phone (0572) 19-40-40.

*Khatynka* (Peasant House), at 2 prospekt Gagarina, serves tasty Ukrainian cuisine.

*Sloboda* at 34a August 23 Street serves good Ukrainian and other European cuisines in a nice atmosphere.

*Stare Misto* (Old Town) at 12 Kvitky-Osnovyanenko Street and *Dykanka* at 7 Lermontovska Street serve tasty Ukrainian fare. *Konyky* at 21 Sumska Street serves Ukrainian fast food.

For American fast food, *McDonald's* are located at 6 Roza Luxemburg Square; at 9 Suzdalsky Ryady (at the Central Market); near the main railway station at the corner of Poltavsky Slyah and Krasnoarmiyska Streets; in Akademika Beketova Metro Station at the corner of Pushkinska and Skrypnyka Streets; and in Nauchna Metro Station at 96 prospekt Lenina.

**Transportation.** Kharkiv's metro system, operating since 1975, has some 28 stations on three lines. Buy tokens or plastic cards at metro cashier counters.

The **Railway Station**, *Pivdenny Vokzal,* is located at Pryvokzalna Square, over the Pivdenny Vokzal Metro Station. Trains go all over Ukraine and to neighboring countries. The Capital Express is a new state-of-the-art high-speed train that makes two daily runs between Kharkiv, the former capital, and Kyiv. A first-class ticket for the five-hour-and-45-minute ride costs about US$12. Tickets are sold in booking offices at the train stations and in some air booking offices.

**Kharkiv Airport** handles both domestic and international flights. Not entirely modernized, the airport lacks baggage carts, and staff speak primitive English, with the exception of Austrian Airlines employees, who are fluent in English. Trolleybus Route 5 runs between the city center and the airport; bus routes 115-T and 119-T connect the airport to Prospekt Gagarina Metro Station.

**Services.** In case of illness, contact **Central Clinical Hospital #5** at 5 pr. Balakireva, phone (0572) 33-07-11 or 33-06-44. The hospital is well run with excellent English-speaking doctors and a good staff. For emergencies, go to the **City Clinical Hospital of Urgent Medical Aid,** 3a pr. Bala-kireva, phone (0572) 32-05-04. For travel services or apartment rental in Kharkiv, email *UKRUS* at agency@ukrus.kharkov.ua or phone them at (057) 700-67-30.

The Donets Basin is an area about 60,000 square km (23,170 square mi) that contains one of the largest coal deposits in the world, estimated to last for another 300 years. Straddling the Ukraine-Russia border with two-thirds of it on the Ukrainian side, this vital fuel source and industrial region is composed of the **Donetska and Luhanska oblasts**.

**DONETSK** (Донецьк) has a population of 1,108,000. Founded in 1869, the city grew rapidly after Welshman John Hughes built factories and mining complexes based on the local coal supply. Today it's the largest center of coal mining and metallurgy in Ukraine with hundreds of industrial enterprises, primarily machine-building and chemicals. On its outskirts, the city doesn't seem very enticing, with the huge pyramids of coal that surround it, but Donetsk is surprisingly one of the greenest cities in Ukraine with many thousands of acres of park land and gardens, crisscrossed by wide tree-lined boulevards. Near the city center is a 280-hectare (692-acre) **Botanical Garden.**

A major center of learning and culture, Donetsk has five institutions of higher learning, and several dozen specialized secondary schools. The main street, **Artem Street** (вулиця Артема, *vulytsya Artema*), is five miles long and contains the city's main administrative and cultural buildings.

Performing arts in Donetsk include the **Opera and Ballet Theater**, 72 Artem Street; **Ukrainian Theater of Music and Drama**, 74-a Artem Street; **Puppet Theater**, 18 Illich Avenue (проспектІлліча, prospekt Illicha); **Philharmonic**, 117 Postyshev Street (вулиця Постишева, vulytsya Postysheva), and a circus.

The **Donetsk State Museum of Art** at 35 Pushkin Avenue exhibits 18th- to 19th-century landscapes and portraits by Russian and Western European artists. A surprising art venue is the *McDonald's* restaurant in the main square, ploshcha Lenina, on Artem Street in the very center of the city. In the central lobby is a spectacular 10-ton glass mosaic that McDonald's rescued from a Donetsk building destroyed during an urban renewal project. The mosaic, *Woman-Bird,* was the work of Alla Horska, a stained-glass artist and political activist, who was mysteriously murdered in Kyiv in 1970.

*Pragua* is a good small hotel half a mile from the center at 101 vul. Dubravna, phone (0623) 81-11-77. Directly in the center at 87 Artem Street is the large *Hotel Central*, phone (0623) 32-33-32.

**Svyatohirsky (Holy Mountains) Monastery** was built from the 17th to 19th centuries on the picturesque right bank of the Silversky Donets river, 160 k (100 mi) north of Donetsk. Sometimes referred to by its former

Soviet name, *Slovyanohirsk,* the magnificent monastery is in an area where Christian activity took place back in the 8th century.

The most spectacular sight is the 17th-century Ukrainian Baroque **St. Nicholas Church**, perched atop a 300-foot high chalk cliff overlooking the river valley below. Under the chalk base are 1,000 meters of passages dug by early monks for cells and burial places. Here they also defended themselves from Tartar raids and gave refuge to escapees from Tatar slavery.

After paying a small admission at the entrance gate, visitors may walk around on their own or pay a small extra fee for a guided tour. The tour starts at the base of the cliff, which is dominated by two 19th century churches, the gold-domed **Uspenskyy (Dormition) Cathedral** and the **Pokrovska Church**, with cobalt blue domes adorned with gold stars, and a bell tower. Guides take visitors through an archeological museum, where they view a video and visit a shop selling elegant tea sets and vases made from the milky white Donbas clay. A candlelit walk through the chalk caves culminates at St. Nicholas Church on the top of the cliff.

During Soviet times, the buildings were transformed into a sanatorium and theater. In 1992 the monastery became active again, and some 80 monks and Russian Orthodox followers are in residence, with the other half of the complex still devoted to cardiovascular patients.

Photography of monks and the cave interiors is not permitted, and women and girls must wear a head covering on the monastery grounds.

On a nearby hill is a gigantic statue of a miner's trade union leader, known affectionately as *Artyom*. A road winds around St. Nicholas Church to the base of the 90-foot statue and offers a photogenic view of the monastery and river valley below. A bus to Svyatohirsky leaves regularly from the Donetsk Krytyy Rynok bus station. The fare is less than the equivalent of US$4 one way for a two-and-a-half hour ride to the Slovyansk bus stop, where you can get a van or taxi for the short ride to the front gates of the monastery.

Also in the Donesk region, about 82 km (49 mi) north of Donetsk, is **ARTEMIVSK**, which dates back over 400 years. Site of the largest salt mine in the former Soviet Union, Artemivsk is also known for outstanding champagne. An abandoned salt mine keeps the temperatures of the thousands of aging bottles stable.

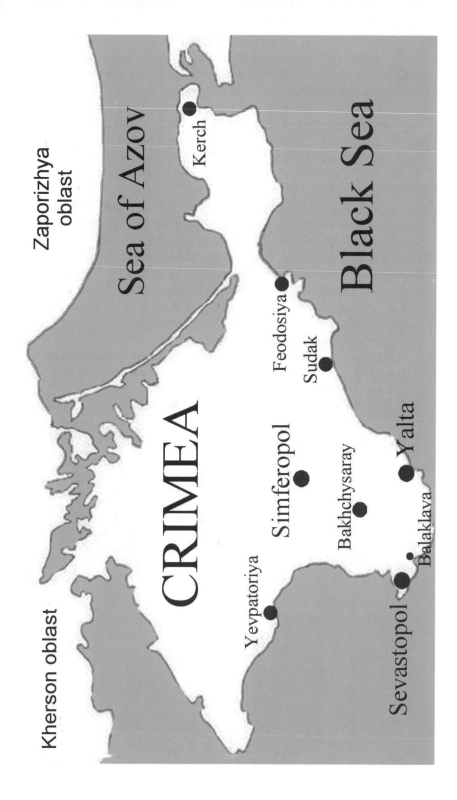

# CHAPTER 11.
# THE CRIMEA

КРИМ  krihm

The Crimean Autonomous Republic occupies a peninsula about the size of the state of Maryland. Geographically the land mass is an extension of Ukraine, while historically it has a greater association with Tatar peoples, and later with Russia. Crimea is diverse in terrain, climate, flora and fauna, and in history and culture. The northern three-quarters is semi-arid steppe cultivated with wheat, corn, and sunflowers. South of the capital city Simferopol, the plains rise to the high pastures and forests of the **Crimean Mountains**. The mountains reach a height of 1,500 m (5,000 ft) before dropping away to a narrow coastal strip of stony beaches. Most of the population of Crimea live in cities and towns that ring the Black Sea coast, considered the most unspoiled in Europe.

**Historical Highlights.** In the 15th century, Crimea, once dominated by the Golden Horde Mongols, came under the influence of the Ottoman Empire. They built mosques, Islamic schools, mausoleums, and public water systems. Russia annexed Crimea in 1783, resulting in suffering among the Tatar population. From 1854 to 1856 Crimea became a battleground of imperial Turkey and Russia, with the British and French siding with Turkey. In 1921, while populated largely by Tatars, Crimea became an autonomous republic under the Russian SSR even though it shared no border with Russia. During World War II the Nazis invaded, resulting in heavy fighting and destruction in several Crimean cities. Following three years of German occupation, Stalin falsely accused the Tatars of collaboration, deported them, and transferred the area to the Russian SSR.

In 1954 Nikita Khrushchev awarded Crimea to Ukraine in commemoration of the 300th anniversary of Russian-Ukrainian unity. The transfer seemed more ceremonial than consequential at the time, but after the breakup of the Soviet Union in 1991, Crimea became an independent state within the boundaries of Ukraine. In 1998 Crimean parliamentarians worked with representatives of the Ukrainian executive and legislative branches to draft a separate constitution. Adopted on December 23, 1998, the new Constitution allows Crimea to have its own government and legislature, to keep its own revenues, and to enter foreign trade agreements, so long as it does nothing to conflict with the laws of Ukraine.

**Population and Language.** Ethnic Russians constitute about 58 percent of the two million inhabitants of Crimea. Another 24 percent are Ukrainian. Following Ukrainian independence, the Tatar population started to return. They reclaimed old mosques, established new ones, and built schools. The Tatars, currently about 12 percent of the population, are increasing in number. Other significant groups are Byelorussians, Jews, Armenians, Greeks, Germans, Bulgarians, Poles, Czechs, and Italians. The new constitution theoretically puts all Crimean languages on par, but in reality Russian is the language seen and heard everywhere, while the Ukrainian and – to a much lesser extent – Tatar languages are taught in school.

**Tourism.** Crimea is a major tourist resort, famous for its perfect climate, scenic vistas, clear sea, and forested mountains. The bathing season extends from the third week of May until mid-October, and the peak tourist period is July though August. Long a Russian, then a Soviet vacation retreat, Crimea is too costly for many Ukrainians and other former Soviets, and a previously weak tourist infrastructure discouraged many Western tourists from discovering its charms.

The tourist amenities continue to improve though, and Westerners can find bargain rates for transportation, entertainment, and dining. Though European-level lodging is not inexpensive, for bargain hunters there are older "Soviet style" hotels as well as rental apartments offered by enterprising bus-stop *babushkas* to incoming tourists for the equivalent of US$10 to US$15 per night.

Tourist signs and markers are written in Russian and group tours conducted in Russian. For an English-speaking tour, you'll need to hire a private guide. For tourist services, contact *Black Sea-Crimea*, which is based in England: e-mail philbaker@Blacksea-crimea.com or phone (44) 208-200-6834, Web site www.blacksea-crimea.com; or *JSB Travel & Tours*, based in Texas: e-mail info@aroundcrimea.com, phone (210) 696-9962 or check out Web site www.aroundcrimea.com. For an English-speaking guide in Yalta, contact Vyacheslav at *rubel@yahoo.com*.

Crimean tours usually start and end with **SIMFEROPOL** (Сімферополь), the area's regional capital and crossroads. A city of 400,000, Simferopol is situated on the Salgyr (Салгир) River in the center of the Crimean peninsula, on the division between the plains and mountainous terrain of the peninsula. Many travelers fly in, and passport control can be a slow process. Train is a good way to reach Simferopol, since it's a major rail junction for larger cities in Ukraine and Russia. Across the parking lot of the train station is the bus station for any destination in Crimea, and the ticket office for the "world's longest trolley ride" to Yalta. For drivers, major highways lead to Simferopol.

Simferopol has a university and numerous colleges and institutes; several research institutes; an art museum; a chamber orchestra, and theaters of Russian drama, Ukrainian music, Tatar drama, and a children's puppet theater and a circus. Most of the shops, cafés, and tourist attractions are around Karl Marx and Pushkin streets and Kirov Avenue.

The **Crimea Ethnographic Museum** at 18 Pushkin Street displays housing and clothing styles of the various groups inhabiting Crimea, phone (0652) 25-52-23. Kirov Avenue crosses an attractive city park on the banks of the river. The most popular and largest city park is **Gargarin Park**. Inside the park is a large, good restaurant, *Christie Prudi*, with live music and dancing. Remnants of the city's old Tatar quarter with its narrow, winding streets and Oriental buildings lend an exotic ambience. Nevertheless, most tourists aren't reluctant to leave the traffic, noise, and concrete for Crimea's scenic wonders and recreation.

A mile southeast from the city center between Vorovsky and Krasnoarmeyskaya Streets is the 50-acre site of an important archeological excavation. Neapolis was a Scythian town from the 2nd century BCE to the 4th century CE, but was abandoned after attacks by the Goths and Huns. Excavations started in 1827 uncovered a thick-walled city containing stone buildings, some ornamented with tiles and frescoes. A royal mausoleum with burial chambers dug into the rock formations contained the graves of 72 Scythian noblemen with their gold ornaments and weapons. The treasures were placed in museums and there is nothing to see at the site.

Simferopol has several good hotels, but employees don't speak English. *Ukraina,* 7 Rosy Luxembourg Street, is a four-story hotel right in the center. Phone (0652) 51-01-65; *Moscow* is on Vernadskogo Street, phone (0652) 23-75-20, and *Tavria* is on Bespalova Street, phone (0652) 23-20-24. For help with accommodations, transportation, or personal escorting, contact Eugene, a representative of JSB Travel and Tours and Unipress BTD travel companies, at Yudjin@cris.net.

**BAKHCHYSARAY** (Бахчисарай), population approximately 30,000, is about a 50-minute taxi ride southwest of Simferopol. It served as the capital of the Crimean Khanate, the Tatar Moslem state, from the early 16th to the late 18th centuries. The **Khan's Palace** was originally constructed in 1519 by master builders from Iran, Italy, and Turkey along with Ukrainian and Russian captive slaves. Destroyed in1736 under a Russian army attack, it was rebuilt from the 16th to the 18th centuries – though not true to Islamic art and architecture – when Crimea was annexed to Russia.

Now the center of the **Bakhchisaray Historical and Archeological Museum**, the huge palace complex includes the original harem, mosque, gardens, cemetery, and tombs. In the inner courtyard is the city's landmark, the white marble **Fountain of Tears**, built in memory of the last Khan's lost love. Take the Stariy Gorod (Old Town) Marshrutka and get off when you approach the minarets. Several restaurants are near the museum.

Several miles southeast of Bakhchisaray, beyond the village of Staroselye, are the ruins of one of Crimea's largest cave settlements. **Chufut-Kale** was carved out of limestone bluffs, perhaps as early as the sixth century. Until the 19th century, it was inhabited by many different peoples. The name *Chufut-Kale*, Hebrew for "city," comes from its last regular inhabitants, a dissident Jewish sect called the Karaims. The ruins are administered by the Bakhchisaray Historical and Archeological Museum and include numerous cave dwellings, fortress walls, and cobblestone pathways. There's a Tatar mausoleum from 1437; an underground prison; the ruins of a mosque; and two temples, one with Hebrew inscriptions. In 2001, two historians from Simferopol University discovered a deep well at the bottom of Chufut-Kale. The well originally provided water for Chufut-Kale but was covered up in the 12th century. The climb to Chufut-Kale is fairly steep and requires adequate hiking shoes, but a marshrutni taxi from the Khan's Palace will get you to the base of the hill.

A 15-minute walk across the valley from Chufut-Kale is the **Uspensky Monastery**, founded in the 15th century in a spot where monastic activity had taken place since the 9th century. The reason a church and monks' cells were carved out of sheer limestone cliffs is the subject of several legends involving miraculous events. Illustrating the mysticism of Orthodox Christianity, it's said that some of the monks had themselves lowered into isolated caves to spend the rest of their days in silent prayer. The monastery was closed at the beginning of the Soviet era, but in the 1990s monks returned and the monastery was restored. Photography is not allowed.

South of Bakhchisaray, about 51 km (31 mi) down highway M-26, is **SEVASTOPOL**, a port city of 341,000 people. With its sparking limestone buildings set on broad tree-lined avenues, Sevastopol is a very attractive city with much to interest tourists.

About 420 BCE a Greek colony and city-state was founded near present-day Sevastopol. Known as Khersones, it became an important manufacturing and trading center, supplying wheat from southern Ukraine to Greece. In the first century CE the Romans ruled it and gave it a Latin name, Chersonesus Taurica. By the fourth century the area was part of the Byzantine Empire; in the tenth century it was captured by the Kyivan-Rus leader Volodymyr. Its influence waned in the 13th to the 14th centuries, and it was ruined by Tatar invasions that lasted until 1399. After Russia annexed Crimea in 1773, Catherine II ordered the fortress and naval port built as a base for the Russian Black Sea Fleet. The city endured heavy attacks during the Crimean and Second World Wars. A closed military city during the Soviet period, Sevastopol was the focus of a post-Soviet dispute between Russia and Ukraine over ownership of the naval fleet and control of the city. The issue was resolved by dividing the fleet and allowing Russia to share use of the port.

Sevastopol's naval connection is apparent from the warships in the harbor to sailors in ribboned caps. Navy Day is observed the last Sunday in July, with thrilling demonstrations of military prowess at the harbor.

Sevastopol is also a large fishing and fish processing center, with refrigerated ships and fish canneries. It's an important vegetable producer, and vineyards of high-quality grapes make Sevastopol a supplier of Ukraine's best wines and champagne.

The **Khersones National Historical Preserve**, east of Sebastopol at the tip of Quarantine Bay is a must-see. Covering 1,500 acres, the ruins of the 2,500-year-old Khersones settlement is an archeological site of world significance. Founded by the Greeks in the 5th century BCE, Khersones quickly developed into the main city of the Crimean peninsula with a flourishing economy based on trade. Over the centuries, it defended itself from numerous steppe people including Scythians, Sarmatians, Goths, Huns, and Polovtsians. It was absorbed by the Roman Empire and later by Byzantium. Weakened by numerous Tatar assaults in the 13th century, Khersones was sacked by one of the Khans at the end of the 14th century.

For the next 500 years, the ruins were buried. Excavations began in 1827 under the patronage of the Russian tsars. Today the preserve is regulated by Ukraine's Ministry of Culture, and international archeologists continue to unearth layers of civilizations. Acres of stone walls, pillars, portals, and columns stand against beautiful sea vistas by a beach where local residents sunbathe. Artifacts spanning two thousand years, uncovered during archeological digs, are on display in the **Khersones Historical-**

**Archeological Museum**, which is part of the preserve. Also at Khersones is the newly reconstructed all-stone St.Volodymyr's Church on the site where in about 987 CE, Kyivan Rus Grand Prince Volodymyr is believed to have accepted Christianity. Its Italian-made iconostasis is magnificent. Trolleybus No. 6 and 10 or Marshrutka No. 10 run from the central market to the excavation site.

Other museums worth seeing are the **Museum of the Black Sea Navy** at 11 Lenina Street, off of Suvorova Square (open 10 a.m. until 5 p.m. Wednesday through Sunday) and the **Art Gallery**, 9 Nakhimov Avenue, which has a good collection of paintings by Russian and Western artists. Phone (0692) 54-29-26. The **Panorama Museum** is the common name for the Museum of the Historic Defense and Liberation of Sevastopol, on Istorychesky Boulevard in the pretty central park. The centerpiece of the museum is the fantastic 14 by 115-meter circular panoramic oil painting, *Defense of Sevastopol 1854–1855* depicting one day in the Crimean War. There's also an oil diorama, *The Assault on Sapun-Mountain on the 7th of May, 1944*, depicting the struggle against Nazi invasion, as well as thousands of artifacts. Museum hours are 9:30 a.m. until 5:30 p.m. daily. Phone (0692) 54-40-31. Another attraction is the dolphin shows at the **Ukrainian Scientific Academy's Dolphinarium** at 2 Nakhimov Avenue.

Sixteen km (10 mi) southeast of Sevastopol is **BALAKLAVA** (Балаклава), a sleepy harbor town set on both sides of a narrow S-shaped inlet. The harbor area is reminiscent of a Mediterranean fishing village, with narrow streets dotted with stucco houses leading to the waterfront where boardwalk cafés, fishermen, and vendors hawk rental boats for about 50 hryvni per hour. Visible in the distance are the ruins of a Genoese fortress. During Soviet times, Balaklava was a submarine base and a closed city. It's best known as the site of an 1854 Crimean War battle immortalized by Alfred, Lord Tennyson in his poem, *Charge of the Light Brigade*. The ill-fated British charge at the Russian troops some 12 km outside of Balaklava near the base of the Sapun Mountain in the "Valley of Death" resulted in a devastating British loss. Although the Russians captured some ridges and enemy guns, the British and Turks managed to hold on to Balaklava thanks to the more successful charge of the heavy brigade. The former battlefield is now planted with vines and the area is known for production of high quality Riesling, Sauvignon, Chardonnay, and Champagne grapes.

In 2003 an unusual museum opened consisting of a former highly classified USSR underground nuclear submarine maintenance and repair facility. Located in a huge multilevel station which the Soviet military dug out of rock, the museum is accessed either by sailing a boat across the harbor and into a tunnel built inside a mountain, or driving around the bay to the entrance. Ukraine's single remaining submarine, no longer seaworthy, is visible as you approach. Inside the tunnel is old military equipment, but no submarines. The interior is lit and museum staff orient visitors.

## Greater Yalta

Crimea's main attraction is a 72-km (43-mi) stretch of Mediterranean-like coast along its southeast shore. This area, greater Yalta, has a population of 140,000. Here the Crimean Mountains culminate in their highest peaks and extend nearly to the clear, clean Black Sea. (Both the shore and bottom are rocky, so swimmers need good foot protection.) Separating the mountain peaks from the sea is a narrow strip – 1 to 7 miles wide – of cypress-dotted lowland with interesting rock formations jutting out over the sea. The coastal mountain slopes are covered with vineyards producing some superb wines. Muscat is the most important grape variety grown; others are Cabernet, Pinot Gris, and Riesling. Other major crops are tobacco and flowers for local perfumeries.

Charming resort cities and towns, all linked by a main highway, dot the scenic coast. The nucleus of the shoreline is **Yalta** (Ялта). To its east and west are pleasant little resort towns with parks and gardens, beaches, palaces, restaurants and hotels. A well-developed system of bus, trolleybus, minibuses, ferries, as well as numerous taxis, serves the greater Yalta area.
     The area also has scores of sanatoriums, full-service seaside resorts with swimming pools, saunas, and private beaches. Besides rest and recreation, the sanatoriums offer mud or mineral bath treatments. Their price range is from US$30 to US$600 daily for accommodations, meals, treatment, and excursions.

The coastal area is a vacationer's dream but, lacking an airport and train station, is off the beaten track. Many tourists arrive by cruise ships that dock at Yalta. The majority drive from Simferopol on a main highway that splits into scenic winding roads through the mountains to the popular coastal resorts. A popular route is the Simferopol-Yalta Road, which

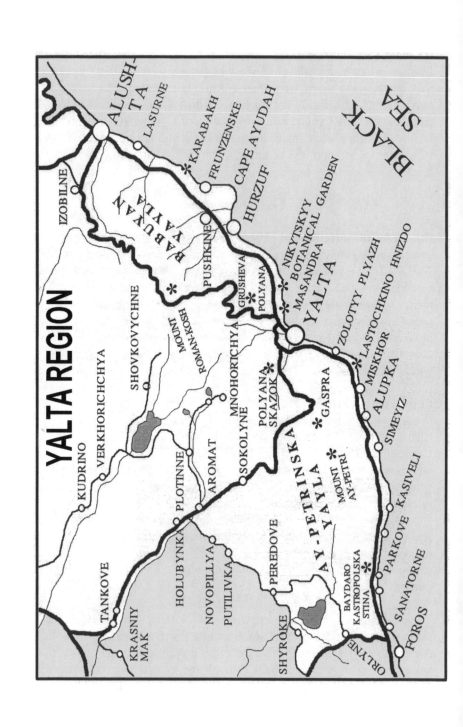

extends about 97 km (60 mi) through a scenic high pass in the Crimean Mountains, terminating at **ALUSHTA** (Алушта), the Crimea's second largest seaside resort. The drive takes about an hour, and taxis and *marshrutky* are waiting at the Simferopol airport or train station. A trolley, several cars long, runs frequently from Simferopol's railroad station to Alushta. The scenic ride takes two-and-a-half hours and costs several dollars. The route passes through the Yaila mountains and reaches a peak of 2,500 feet before dropping down to Alushta. There's also a bus from Simferopol, which is not as much fun, but quicker and even cheaper than the trolley.

Alushta is an ideal base for those who want to explore the mountains. Accessible are **Mount Demerdzhy**, which stands 1,239 m (4,065 ft) above sea level; the **Dzhur-Dzhur Waterfall**, the finest waterfall in the Crimean Mountains; and **Marble Cave,** widely regarded as one of the world's most beautiful caves. The cave is located at Chatyr-Dag plateau, a half-hour bus ride from Simferopol and 40 to 50 minutes from Alushta. Discovered in 1987, Marble Cave consists of 2,050 meters of picturesque caverns on three levels, the largest one as high as a ten-story building. Well-equipped for visitors, the caverns have 850 meters of illuminated concrete walks with handrails. Just 1000 meters from Marble Cave is **Emine-Bair-Hosar Cave**, which some tourists like even better than Marble Cave.

West of Alushta, extending toward the town of Massandra, is the 30,000-hectare (70,000-acre) **Nature Museum of the Crimean State Reserve**. Dedicated to protecting the forest and its native flora and fauna, the Reserve contains a variety of Crimean animals, such as mouflons, gazelles, and foxes. The reserve is closed to the public.

Greater Yalta's easternmost resort, **HURZUF** (Гурзуф), or Gurzuf in Russian, 18 km (11 mi) east of Yalta, offers particularly scenic views. Two headland rocks jut out of the curved bay. On the east side of the bay is **Mount Ayu-Dag** (Bear Mountain); to the west is a picturesque village of winding streets and old wooden houses, with stately parks, fountains, and gazebos. Hurzuf is a popular retreat for artists and writers and a summer camp site for young people.

A few miles east of Yalta on the Yalta-Alushta Highway is **MASSANDRA** (Массандра), where Crimean wine production started in 1785. Count Vorontsov, who had received the village as a gift from his mother-in-law, cultivated the land for vineyards and for a garden of exotic plants. In 1894 Tsar Nicholas II set out to build "the best winery in the world" in

Massandra, in order to supply guests at his summer palace. Production was based on the pool of grape varieties introduced by Vorontsov.

**Massandra Wine Factory** is on the east side of the town on the way to the palace. It specializes in heavy, sweet wines of various styles, with an abundance of port, sherry, Tokay, Madeira, and Muscat. Its Muscat is prize-winning, and among the best of its dry red wines is the rich and earthy-bouqueted *Oksamit Ukrainy*. The wine cellar holds a fantastic collection dating back to the 19th century; all the wine had been removed to secret hiding places during the Nazi assault on Crimea in 1941 and returned after the German army departed. Regular daily tours of the cellars including tastings are conducted for a small fee. There's no need to book in advance. The winery has a small café and a shop selling a wide price range of fine wines.

**Massandra Palace** was built by Tsar Alexander III from 1881 to 1902. The architect, M. Mesmakher, built it in the style of a French chalet, using yellow bricks. It was a summer home for Stalin, then was closed for 20 years until the Gorbachev administration converted it to a museum. Rooms have been meticulously restored with original furnishings, stucco reliefs, frescoes, and copper and tile stoves. Among the highlights is the large dining room table. On the table, elaborately set for ten, is a glass decanter with the insignia of the tsar. Take Trolley Bus No. 3 and get off at the sign that says "Массандра Дворец" (Massandra Dvorets). Phone (0654) 32-17-28.

The **Nikitsky Botanical Gardens** are about 6 km (4 mi) northeast of Yalta in **Botanicheskoe** (Ботаническое), a settlement on the outskirts of Massandra. The Gardens, divided into four parks, were established in 1812 on a square mile of terraced hillside extending to the sea. Nikitsky is a research garden for the study of Crimean flora. Of the 28,000 plant varieties, the arboreal plants are outstanding, with a huge number of coniferous and fruit trees. The view is most scenic from the Upper Park, containing perhaps the world's largest rose collection – approximately 2,000 cultivars. Gardens are open from 8 a.m. until 7 p.m. daily. There's a small admission fee, which does not cover the separate cactus garden. From Yalta take Trolleybus No. 2 or Marshrutka No. 38.

**YALTA** (Ялта), population 72,000, shows signs of settlements as far back as the Neolithic age. Bronze Age tools have been found in the vicinity, and in the first millennium BCE, the area was populated by indigenous Taurian tribes. According to ancient legend, its name comes from *yalos* or "coast," the cry of Greek sailors in a storm at sea who sighted the shoreline through the mist. In the first century BCE, the Greeks established a colony there named Yalita. Over the centuries Yalta passed through many hands, and in 1783 it was annexed by Russia. In 1823 Prince Mikhail Vorontsov decided to build up Yalta as the major settlement of the Crimean south shore. The prince's choice was ideal. Yalta is situated on a gently curving bay that shields it from the north winds. Summers are rarely uncomfortable; and roses bloom through December. The fragrance of magnolia and roses wafts among the palm trees and the slopes leading up to the mountains are ideal for vineyards and orchards.

The area's opulent summer estates and gardens were built by various noblemen from the mid-19th through the early 20th centuries. Yalta was a favorite vacation spot of Tsar Nicholas II as well as a popular resort for high government officials and bureaucrats during the Soviet era. Artists and writers, attracted by the peaceful beauty, found their inspiration in Yalta. Here Anton Chekhov wrote *The Cherry Orchard* and *Three Sisters*; Mark Twain called it "a beautiful spot" that reminded him of the Sierras; Maxim Gorky, Leo Tolstoy, and Sergei Rachmaninov visited; and noted Ukrainian poet Lesya Ukrayinka sought a cure for her tuberculosis.

In 1835, when Yalta was just a small fishing village near Polikurovsky Hill on St. John's Cape, a church named after St. John the Baptist was constructed. The church's bell tower still stands today and serves as an architectural landmark of the city and a navigational guide for ships. The main street of the business center is the **Central Embankment of Lenin** (Центральна набережна Леніна, *Tsentralna naberezhna Lenina*), an attractive seaside promenade along the pebbled beach lined with shops and cafés. Street vendors sell ice cream, postcards, flowers, and a variety of local arts and crafts, such as oil and watercolor landscapes and seascapes, and wooden jewelry fashioned from native trees. Evenings are especially lively, with an array of street performers, concerts, and even fireworks. The major vehicular thoroughfare through town is Kirov Street. The side streets are winding and increasingly steep as they lead up to the mountains.

**City Attractions**. A cable-car sky lift from the walkway behind the main post office on the Embankment provides a 10-minute ride over the rooftops to a pseudo-Greek temple mountain lookout on Darsan Hill. Northwest of the base of the lift on Sadovaya (Садовая) Street is the city's major functioning church, **Alexander Nevsky Cathedral**. Built in 1902 in a neo-

Byzantine style by architects N. Krasnov and L. Shapovalov, the church has functioned continuously.

The **Chekhov Museum**, at 112 Kirova (Кирова) Street, is the white two-story house which Chekhov built and in which he spent his final years before he died in 1904. Chekhov's devoted sister kept the house just as it was when he was alive and turned it into a museum. On display are the house, garden, editions of his works, and personal possessions. Open 10 a.m. until 5 p.m. Wednesday through Sunday. There's a small admission charge. Phone (0654) 32-50-42.

The **Armenian Church** on Zagorodnaya (Загородная) Street, built from 1909 to 1917, is noted for its medieval-style architecture.

The **Magarach Winery**, 31 Kirova Street, offers tours in Russian lasting an hour-and-a-half, including a visit to the Magarach museum and tasting wines and cognacs. Phone (0654) 32-55-91 or (0654) 32-94-69.

**Hotels.** Of Yalta's most established hotels, the most luxurious is the *Oreanda* at 35 Embankment Lenina, a half-mile from the city center and just half a block from the beach. In the heart of the resort area, its lobby can be very noisy. Phone (0654) 39-06-08. The *Hotel Yalta*, 50 Drazhinsky Street, is a lower-priced alternative. This vast 1,206-guest-room resort complex offers every sort of hotel service and leisure activity. It's located in Massandra Park, on its own beach, about a 20-minute walk east of the center. A pleasant sea view and breakfast come with the room. Phone (0654) 27-01-50 or fax (0654) 35-30-93. An inexpensive but comfortable choice is *Hotel Palas*, centrally located on the Embankment and just 75 yards from the beach. The hotel is a charming, renovated early-20th-century building with a New Orleans–style balcony on each room. There's always hot water, and breakfast is included with the room.

On the east end of the bay at 10 Roosevelt Street, opposite the boat passenger terminal, is *Hotel Yuzhnaya-Bristol*, a 26-room hotel that's been restored to its pre-Soviet glamour. Room rates are reasonable considering the European level of accommodation and service. The *Leto* has only 13 rooms and is more elegant and upscale than the Bristol. It is west of the center in Primorskiy Park and a five-minute walk to the nearest public beach. Rooms offer panoramic views of Yalta Bay.

**Restaurants** in hotels are good, but dining in town may be more interesting. The *Schooner Hispanola* (Шхуна Эспаньола) is a gourmet seafood restaurant on a ship from a movie-set. It's at the west end of the seaside, near the Oreanda Hotel.

Also near the hotel at 31a Lenina Embankment is the ornate *White Lion* (Белыйй лев).

*K. Valter* (К. Вальтер) at the corner of the Embankment and Morskaya Street, serves Japanese and Crimean food.

In *Aisha* (Айше), a Tatar restaurant at 9 Lenina Street at Nekrasova Square, you can recline Tatar-style on couches. Phone (39-49-93.

**The Palaces.** Tours of greater Yalta center on three grand palaces each in a different architectural style and beautiful in its own way. The palaces – Livadiya, Alupkinsky, and Massandra – have official hours, but when cruise ships are in the harbor, they'll open to accommodate the busloads of additional tourists. Visitors need to walk some distance from the parking area to the palaces. The longest walk is to Alupka Palace; it takes about 20 minutes on a peaceful, shady road lined with souvenir vendors. A small entrance fee to the palaces is charged and photography is permitted.

In 1860 the Russian royal family began to build a summer retreat 3 km (1.8 mi) west of Yalta at **Livadiya** (Лівадія). The centerpiece of the 60 structures is the **White** or **Great Palace,** an Early Italian Renaissance white limestone palace. Built for Nicholas II in 1911, the palace had 116 rooms. Under the direction of the architect, N. P. Krasnov, a palace park was laid out in a harmonious composition with the palace. Palm trees and expanses of fragrant bay leaf hedges set off the beautiful grounds that overlook a breathtaking view of the bay.

The palace was the location of the 1945 Yalta conference in which Stalin, Churchill, and Roosevelt planned the postwar order of Europe. The palace is sparsely furnished since not all of the original furnishings survived the political upheavals, but memorabilia and photos of the historic conference are on display. The adjacent chapel of the royal family is a lovely restoration in its original red, blue, and gold colors. The palace is open daily from 8 a.m. until 7:30 p.m. except on Wednesday in the summer months, with shorter hours from October through May. Signs are in Russian and English. A gift shop accepts credit cards. Phone (0654) 31-55-79.

In the center of Livadiya, daily organ recitals are held at 5 p.m. in **Organ Hall** on an organ that a Crimean master organ builder spent 12 years constructing. It's considered one of the best in Ukraine. To go to Livadia, take Bus No. 5 or 13 from the Yalta bus station or Marshrutka No. 15.

Ten km (6 mi) west of Yalta at **GASPRA** (Гаспра) is that quintessential image of Crimea, **Swallow's Nest** (Ласточкино гнездо, *Lastochkino gnezdo*). This scale model recreation of a medieval Danube castle was built by architect A. Sherwood in 1912 for a German baron. Sitting atop a 38 m-high (120-ft) rock pinnacle overlooking Ay-Todor Cape, Swallow's Nest was the location for the film of Agatha Christie's book, *Ten Little Indians*. The castle, which contains a museum and an Italian restaurant, is closed on Monday. Marshrutka No. 34 goes to Swallow's Nest, or you can hike to it on a trail that begins behind Livadia palace by the sundial. Originally made for Tsar Nicholas II, the Sun Trail (Солнечная тропа) takes an hour-and-a- half on foot, passing spectacular scenic views on the way down.

Boat taxis to Swallow's Nest and other points leave regularly from the Embankment in downtown Yalta behind the outdoor restaurant *Umbrellas*. Look for the ticket window (касса) underneath the restaurant. The ride to Swallow's Nest takes about 20 minutes, but passengers can get off at a number of stops including Livadia, Alupka, and several beaches, and catch a later boat for the return ride. Each way costs about the equivalent of US$2. The two-hour round trip on the 100-passenger boat costs about US$3 with guided narration in Russian over a loudspeaker.

In the Gaspra area are also several boarding houses that were former villas of the Romanovs, and a sanatorium, *Yasna Polyana,* that was once an elegant villa where Tolstoy stayed and received visitors, including the writers Gorky and Chekhov.

**ALUPKA** (Алупка), 17 km (10 mi) west of Yalta, has Crimea's most spectacular estate, the **Alupkinsky Palace and Park**.The palace was designed by noted British architect Edward Blore for the immensely wealthy English-educated count, Mikhail Vorontsov, who served as governor general of Crimea and Caucasus. It was completed in 1848 after some 20 years of construction. On the exterior, the palace is an odd conglomeration of styles – the northern entrance in Tudor style resembles a Scottish castle while the seaside facade is clearly Arabic. Of its150 rooms, the dozen or so on display contain 19th-century furniture, porcelain and crystal, rare books, and paintings by Western European, Russian, and Ukrainian masters. From the oak-paneled Tudor study the tour passes through several feminine-looking rooms decorated with chintz wallpaper, stucco moldings, marble fireplaces, and crystal chandeliers, before entering the winter garden. This sublime room, overlooking the sea, consists of a gray-and-white marble tile floor displaying an assortment of white marble statuary covered by the foliage of gigantic potted plants and climbing vines. Passing through the elegant dining room and the billiard room with a William Hogarth painting, you exit through the south Moorish facade. Surrounding the palace is a40-hectare (100-acre) hillside park with hundreds of exotic plants and trees, ponds, grottos, and waterfalls.

An art museum in the Shuvalovsky guest wing contains Russian and Western European painting of the 16th through the 19th centuries; applied art of England, France, and Russia; and collections of maps, engravings, and architectural drawings. A gift shop on the premises sells icons, and souvenir vendors lining the walk to the buses sell handcrafted items. The palace is open every day except Monday and the art museum is open from 10 a.m. to 5 p.m. Wednesday through Saturday. Take Marshrutka No.34. Phone (0654) 72-29-51.

Looming behind the northern facade of the palace is Crimea's highest peak, **Ay-Petri**, Greek for "sacred rock" because of the monastery that stood on a plateau until the Middle Ages. From the nearby village **MISKHOR** (Micxop), a cable car climbs 1,234 m (three-quarters of a mile) above the vineyards and the forest up the steep rocky side of the mountain to the top. The view of the coast is breathtaking, and on the plateau behind the summit is a Tatar village. There you can buy Tatar food, local wine, go horseback riding, and even see a camel or two. If you access Ay-Petri by car, you can visit the **Uchan-Su Waterfalls**, which are especially beautiful in the spring.

**FOROS** (Форос), the westernmost resort town of the greaterYalta coastline, is just a 15-minute drive from Yalta's center. Foros has some fine resort facilities and a beautifully designed 19th-century park. **Resurrection Church**, built in 1892 and restored in the1990s, looms high above the town on the 400-meter high Krasnaya Cliff. This functioning church gives the rugged coastline a fairytale look.

The last president of the USSR, Mikhail Gorbachev, was locked in his vacation home in Foros during the August 1991 coup d'état that preceded Ukraine's declaration of independence. The dacha is now the official vacation residence of the president of Ukraine. For others, the hotel *Foros* is a good choice; its restaurant serves Ukrainian cuisine and is open for breakfast and dinner.

## East of Greater Yalta

**SUDAK** (Судак), is a coastal town 107 km (60 mi) east of Yalta. Its population is under 15,000. In the 13th and 14th centuries, Italian traders from the city-states of Venice and Genoa were trading slaves they had captured in eastern Europe for spices, silk, and linen brought to Egypt by traders from the Far East. Sudak became an important trading city on the Great Silk Road, and in 1365 the Genoese seized it from the ruling Tatar Khans. Within a few years, Genoa controlled the entire coastline of the Black Sea, then known as Sudak Sea, and built a number of fortresses along the coast. The largest is the complicated fortress on the outskirts of Sudak, which has been substantially reconstructed, and is well worth a visit.

The **Genoese Fortress**, with its numerous towers, stands 150 m (500 ft) high above a steep cliff overlooking the sea. Within the battlements, a mosque that the Tatars had been constructing became a Catholic church. When the Turks seized control a century later, the church reverted to a mosque. In 1883 it became an Armenian Catholic chapel, but later the Russians turned it into an Orthodox church. Since the Russian Revolution, it's been functioning as a museum.

A pedestrian walk splits off from Lenina Street, the main road through town. All along the 30-minute walk to the sandy beach are souvenir venders and cafés serving Tatar food. The bus station is a short walk outside of town. Among the few buses options from Sudak, the best choice is to Alushta, an especially beautiful 67-km (40-mi) ride. *Hotel Horyzont*, 8 Tourist Road, is 600 m (660 yards) from the fortress. Phone (06566) 2-21-79.

Besides slave trading, the Genoese were engaged in wine production and planted vineyards in the area. In 1878 Prince Golitsin established a champagne winery a few miles west of Sudak, in the quieter and more secluded **NOVYY SVET** (Новый Свет), which has especially attractive rock outcroppings and scenic overlooks. The winery, *Noviy Svet* (New World), is known for its sweet champagne. Tours with tastings can be arranged through local tour agencies. Marshrutni taxis run between Sudak and Noviy Svet on the narrow, winding and beautiful road.

**KERCH** (Керч), is a coastal city near the eastern tip of Crimea. On a clear day the Russian coast is visible across the 4-km wide (2½-mi) waterway, Kerch Strait, which links the waters of the Black Sea to the waters of the

Azov Sea. Kerch is the most ancient settlement of Crimea and Ukraine. In the 6th century BCE the Greeks founded a colony called Pantikapeum on the site. A prosperous trading center, it later became the capital of the powerful Bosporan kingdom, which had become independent from the Greek homeland. With a strategic position between seas, Kerch was under siege, devastated, and changed hands many times throughout its long history. Following the Greeks, it was controlled by the Romans, Khazars, Huns and the other barbarian tribes, Tatars, Genoese, Turks, and Russians.

Remnants of several Greek towns, some dating back to the 6th century BCE, are visible in the city. Archeological excavations show evidence of the worship of ancient Greek gods, particularly Demeter, the Goddess of Agriculture and Fertility. Among the existing ancient wonders are 1,500 burial mounds (*kurhany*) and one of the largest collections in the world of ancient stone monuments. The area's geological wonders include 10 salt lakes with curative mud baths and even rarer cold mud volcanoes.

The main street, Lenina, is paved with red and white tiles. The center is pretty and clean, and well served by public transportation. It culminates in Lenina Square, which leads to the highest point in the city, **Mitridate Mountain**, which is actually just a hill. Stately **Mithridate Stairs** lead to the top where there's an ancient Greek acropolis, temples, and other remnants of Panticapaeum as well as a World War II memorial.

The hill affords a panoramic view of the city and bay, while the back side overlooks archeological sites, notably the **Yuz-Oba** (Tatar for "100 Hills") **Burial Mounds**, which occupy a chain of hills south of Mithridate Mountain.Right beneath the Mitridate Stairs is a re-creation of the 1st century CE **Demetra's Crypt**.Dedicated to the goddess of fertility, Demeter, the arched crypt was discovered in 1895 and contains splendid examples of ancient frescos. The original crypt is a bit of a distance away and undergoing restoration, but the replica is open daily except on Mondays from May through September from 10 a.m. until 5 p.m.

The **Melek-Chesmensky Kurhan**, about 4th century BCE, was the tomb for Bosporan nobility. Located on Gaydar Street near the bus station, the interior is open from 9 a.m. until 4 p.m. daily except on Mondays. Nineteenth-century excavations of the tombs uncovered a wealth of art, precious jewels, personal possessions and household objects of the occupants. Much of this was moved to distant museums, but you may see some of the treasures in the **Kerch Archeological Museum** at 22 Sverdlova Street. Hours are 9 a.m. until 4 p.m. daily except Mondays.

The **Picture Gallery**, at 36 Teatralnaya Street, displays local art, as well as antique glass, ceramics, sculpture, and theatrical masks. Open 9 a.m. until 4 p.m. daily except Wednesdays. The oldest Christian catacomb unearthed in Kerch dates to the 5th century CE. The earliest church still standing is **St. John the Baptist**, a functioning Russian Orthodox Church. First built in the Byzantine style between the 8th and 14th centuries, it underwent additions in the 19th century and restoration in 1980. The original frescoes were preserved.

The largest fortress in Crimea, **Enikale Fortress**, was built in 1703 by the Turks, who controlled Kerch from the end of the 15th to the end of the 18th century. Constructed with the help of French military engineers, Enikale guarded the entrance into the Kerch Strait. A city tour costs 25 hryvni and includes the fortress.

The city's beach, **Gorodsky**, is pebbly. A soft sandy beach, **Karantinsky**, is a 20-minute ride on Bus No.10 from the center to the Arshinsova region. There are also small beaches along the strait.

*Café Alyonka*, in Lenina Square in the business center, serves traditional Ukrainian cuisine. The better hotels are near the beach. *Hotel Zaliv,* 6a Kurortnaya Street, is a small hotel less than a block from the beach, phone (06561) 3-45-08. *Hotel Classic* is nearby at 9/2 Kurortnaya Street, phone (06561) 3-30-71 or e-mail tex@kerch.crimea.com.

A good time to visit Kerch is between the last week of June and the first week of July, when the city celebrates the *Bosporan Agons*, an eight-day-long international art and drama festival featuring drama, music, fine arts, and dance competitions. To plan a Kerch visit, contact *Bospor Tours,* 2 Naberezhnaya Street, #24, Kerch, Crimea. Phone (06561) 2-82-55 or 2-82-51 or e-mail bospor@kerch.krid.crimea.ua.

**ADZHIMUSHKAY**, a settlement northeast of Kerch, once supplied construction sandstone to the region. When German troops occupied Kerch from May 1942 to April 1944, the quarries became an underground fortress for Soviet soldiers and Kerch citizens, who heroically resisted the onslaught. Today the **Adzhimushkay Quarries** are an underground museum, where war relics are illuminated only by the flashlights of the guides. Also in Adzhimushkay is the **Tsar's Burial Mound**, the restored tomb of Bosporan nobles from the 4th century BCE. The structure is 56 feet high with an interior corridor and burial chamber. Hours for both the quarries and the burial mound are 9 a.m. until 4 p.m. daily except Monday. Adzhimushkay is a 40-minute ride on Bus No. 4 from the Kerch bus station.

# CHAPTER 12.
# CONVERSATION

Ukrainian Proverb:

Слово не горобець, вилетить не спіймаєш.
SLO-vo neh ho-ro-BEHTS' VIH-leh-tiht' neh
speeў-MAH-yehsh
*A word is not a sparrow, if it flies away, you won't catch it.*

Using just the right words helps to make a good first impression. In languages that have both polite and familiar forms of the word "*you*," it's essential to use the polite form in initial meetings. Use the familiar when conversing with a family member, a friend, a classmate, or anyone else with whom you're on close terms.

Many phrases that you'd use in interacting with people you meet during travel are given with only the formal *vy* (ви, *vih*) form of the word "you." If either the polite *vy* or the familiar *ty* (ти, *tih*) version of the phrase might be useful, the familiar (and singular) is given first, followed by the polite (plural) form.

To address a person directly by name, use the first name plus the middle name, or patronymic. The patronymic is formed by attaching a suffix to the first name of the father of the person you're addressing: For females add *-ivna* and for males add *-ovych*. For example, if Oksana's father is Mykhaylo, you address her as Oksana Mykhaylivna and if Ihor's father is Volodymyr, you call him Ihor Voldymyrovych. These forms are primarily for formal situations, such as a student addressing her teacher. They're not so widely used as they once were, and custom varies from city to city, with less use in western Ukraine.

The Ukrainian language uses forms of address equivalent to Mr., Mrs., and Miss. Mr. is *pan* (пан, pahn), Mrs. is *pani* (пані, PAH-nee), and Miss is *panna* (панна, PAHN-nah). Ordinarily, it's considered very impolite to address a person directly by their family name, so this form of address might be used at an initial meeting just to establish identity ("Are you Pan Melnyk?") or when referring to a person who is not present. A less official manner of address that conveys both friendliness and respect is the use of *pan, pani, panna* with the first name (″Hello, Pan Stepan and Panna Kateryna.″).

## Meetings

My name is . . .     Мене звати . . .     meh-NEH ZVAH-tih

What's your (first name) (patronymic) (last name)?

Як (ваше ім'я) (вас по-батькові) (ваше прізвище)?
yak (VAH-sheh eem'-YA) (vahs po-BAHT'-ko-vee)
(VAH-sheh PREEZ-vih-shcheh)

Pleased to meet you.
Приємно познайомитись.
prih-YEHM-no poz-nah-ў̆O-mih-tihs'

I'd like to present . . .
Я хочу представити вам . . .
ya kho-CHOO pred-STAH-vih-tih vahm

| | | |
|---|---|---|
| my colleague | мого колегу | MO-ho ko-LEH-hoo |
| my husband | мого чоловіка | MO-ho cho-lo-VEE-kah |
| my wife | мою дружину | MO-yu droo-Z͡HIH-noo |

This is my (acquaintance, *m.*) (boyfriend).
Це мій (знайомий) (друг).
tseh meeў̆ (znah-Y̆O-mihў̆) (drooh)

This is my (acquaintance, *f.*) (girlfriend).
Це моя (знайома) (подруга).
tseh mo-YA znah-Y̆O-mah/po-DROO-hah

As in English, the words "boyfriend" and "girlfriend" have a romantic connotation. Ukrainians seldom use these terms because − short of marriage − it's not customary to reveal the nature of a male-female relationship. Instead they will introduce someone of the opposite sex as an "acquaintance," regardless of how intimate they are.

These are my (acquaintances) (friends).
Це (мої знайомі) (мої друзі).
tseh mo-YEE znah-Y̆O-mee/mo-YEE DROO-zee

## Greetings

| | | |
|---|---|---|
| Hello, good day. | Добридень. | do-BRIH-dehn' |
| Good morning. | Доброго ранку. | DO-bro-ho RAHN-koo |
| Good afternoon. | Добрий день. | DO-brihў dehn' |
| Good evening. | Добрий вечір. | DO-brihў VEH-cheer |
| Good night. | Надобраніч. | nah-do-BRAH-neech |
| Good-bye. | До побачення. | do po-BAH-chehn-nya |
| Hi. (for close friends) | Привіт. | prih-VEET |
| How are you? | | |
| (familiar or sing.) | Як живеш? | yak z͡hih-VEHSH |
| (polite or plural) | Як ви живете? | yak vih Z͡HIH-veh-the |
| How do you do? | Здраствуй.(familiar) | ZDRAHST-vuў |
| | Здраствуйте.(polite) | ZDRAHST-vuў-teh |
| Very well, thanks, | Дуже добре, | DOO-z͡heh DO-breh |
| and you? | а (ти) (ви)? | ah (tih) (vih) |
| How's it going? | Як справи? | yak SPRAH-vih |
| Fine. | Добре. | DOB-reh |
| Not bad. | Непогано. | neh-po-HAH-no |
| So-so. | Так собі. | TAHK so-BEE |
| Bad. | Погано. | po-HAH-no |
| What's new? | Що нового? | shcho no-VO-ho |
| Nothing's new. | Нічого нового. | nee-CHO-ho NO-vo-ho |

**Do you speak …?** Чи ви говорите …?
chih vih ho-VO-rih-teh

| | | |
|---|---|---|
| English | англійською | ahn-HLEEЎ-s'ko-yu |
| Ukrainian | українською | oo-krah-YEEN-s'ko-yu |

I speak only English.
    Я говорю тільки англійською.
    ya ho-VOR-yu TEEL'-kih ahn-HLEEЎ-s'ko-yu
Does anyone here speak English?
    Чи хто-небудь тут говорить англійською?
    chih KHTO-neh-bood' toot ho-VO-riht' ahn-HLEEЎ-s'ko-yu
I can understand Ukrainian, but don't speak it well.
    Я розумію українську, але погано розмовляю нею.
    ya ro-zoo-MEE-yu oo-krah-YEENS'-koo ah-LEH
    po-HAH-no roz-mov-LYA-yu NEH-yu

Do you understand?
Чи ви розумієте?
chih vih ro-zoo-MEE-yeh-the

I'm sorry, but I don't understand you.
Пробачте, але я не розумію вас.
pro-BAHCH-teh a-leh ya neh ro-zoo-MEE-yu vahs

I don't understand everything.
Я розумію не все.
ya ro-zoo-MEE-yu neh vseh

Please repeat that.
Повторіт це, будь ласка.
pov-to-REET tseh bood' LAHS-kah

Please speak more slowly.
Прошу говорити повільніше.
PRO-shoo ho-vo-RIH-tih po-veel'-NEE-sheh

What do you call that in Ukrainian?
Як ви це називаєте по-українськи?
yak vih tseh nah-zih-VAH-yeh-teh po-oo-krah-YEEN-s'kih

Please spell it.
Прошу сказа побуквах.
PRO-shoo skah-ZAH-tih po-BOOK-vahkh

Please write it down.
Прошу записати мені це.
PRO-shoo zah-pih-SAH-tih meh-NEE tseh

## Saying Thanks

| | | |
|---|---|---|
| Yes, thank you. | Так, дуже дякую. | tahk DOO-zheh DYA-koo-yu |
| No, thanks. | Дякую, ні. | DYA-koo-yu nee |
| Thank you very much! | Дуже дякую! | DOO-zheh DYA-koo-yu |

Thank you for all your help.
Дякую за (твою, *s.*) (вашу. *pl.*) допомогу.
DYA-koo-yu zah (tvo-YU) (VAH-shoo) do-po-MO-hoo

Thank you for your trouble.
Дякую за (твої, *s.*) (ваші. *pl.*) зусилля.
DYA-koo-yu zah (tvo-YEE) (VAH-shee) zoo-SIHL-lya

I'm very grateful to you.
Я дуже (вдячний, *m.*) (вдячна, *f.*) (тобі, s.) (вам, pl.).
ya DOO-zheh (VDYACH-nihў) (VDYACH-nah) (to-BEE)
(vahm).

Not at all.               Нема за що.          neh-MAH ZAH shcho

**Pardon and Regrets**

Excuse me!               Вибачте!            vih-BAHCH-teh
  *in western Ukraine*:   Перепрошую!          peh-reh-PRO-shoo-yu

I'm extremely sorry. [*an apology*]
    Дуже перепрошую.
    DOO-zheh peh-reh-PRO-shoo-yu

I'm very sorry about that. [*expression of commiseration or regret*]
    Мені дуже жаль.
    meh-NEE DOO-zheh zhahl

That's too bad.          Шкода.              SHKO-dah

I apologize for being late.
    Пробачте за запізнення.
    pro-BAHCH-teh zah zah-PEEZ-nehn-nya

Please forgive me.
    Прошу вибачити мене.
    PRO-shoo VIH-bah-chih-tih meh-NEH

That's OK.               Нічого страшного.
                         nee-CHO-ho strash-NO-ho

**Best Wishes**

Congratulations.         Мої вітання.         mo-YEE vee-TAHN-nya

I wish you all the best.
    Я бажаю (тобі, *s.*) (вам, *pl.*) всього найкращого.
    ya bah-ZHAH-yu (to-BEE) (vahm) VS'O-ho
    nahў-KRAH-shcho-ho

I congratulate you on your . . .
  Я вітаю (тебе, *s.*) (вас, *pl.*) з . . .
  ya vee-TAH-yu (teh-BEH) (vahs) z

| birthday | днем | dnehm |
|---|---|---|
| | народження | nah-ROD-z͡hehn-nya |
| engagement | заручинами | zah-ROO-c͡hih-nah-mih |
| marriage | одруженням | od-ROO-z͡hehn-nyam |
| new baby | народженням | nah-ROD-z͡hehn-nyam |
| | дитини | dih-TIH-nih |
| success | успіхом | OOS-pee-khom |

Get well soon.
  (Виздоровлюй, *s.*) (Виздоровлюйте, *pl.*) швидше.
  (vihz-do-ROV-l'yuў) (vihz-do-ROV-l'yuў-teh) SHVIHD-sheh

My deepest sympathy.
  Мої співчуття.
  mo-YEE speev-choot-TYA

I wish you . . .    Я бажаю (тобі, *s.*) (вам, *pl.*)
          ya bah-Z͡HAH-yu (to-BEE) (vahm)
good luck        щастя        SHCHAHS-tya
a happy birthday    щасливого дня народження
          shchahs-LIH-vo-ho dnya nah-ROD-z͡hehn-nya
a happy holiday    веселих свят      veh-SEH-lihkh svyat
a happy new year    щасливого нового року
          shchahs-LIH-vo-ho NO-vo-ho RO-koo

Happy Easter!    Христос Воскрес!    KHRIHS-tos vos-KREH
*This greeting on Easter morning means "Christ is risen." The customary response is:*
Indeed, he's risen.    Воістину Воскрес.
          vo-EES-tih-noo vos-KREHS

Merry Christmas.    Христос Рождається.
          khrihs-TOS ROZH-dah-yeht'-sya
*This Christmas greeting means "Christ is born." The customary response is:*
Already he was born.    Вже вродився.    vz͡heh vro-DIHV-sya
*Another reply is:*
We glorify him.    Славімо його.    slah-VEE-mo ў o-HO

| Happy New Year! | З Новим Роком! | z NO-vihm RO-kom |
| Bon Voyage! | Щасливої Дороги! | |
| | | shchahs-LIH-vo-yee do-RO-hih |
| Long Life! | Сто Літ! | sto leet |
| Long Life! | Многая Літа! | MNO-hah-ya LEE-tah |

"Сто літ" means "100 years." Variations of it are expressed throughout Slavic countries on birthdays, anniversaries and other commemorative occasions. "Многая літа," an old Church Slavonic phrase meaning "many years," fell out of use during Soviet times but is popular again. It's often sung in lovely harmony to the honoree.

**Toasting.** At the dinner table, it's customary to wish your companions a good appetite and a pleasant dining experience. There are two ways to express this, depending on what part of the country you're in.

| *western Ukraine*: | Смачного. | smahch-NO-ho |
| *eastern Ukraine*: | Приємного апpetиту! | |
| | | prih-YEHM-no-ho ahp-peh-TIH-too |

*To toast an individual simply, just say*:

| To your health! | На здоров'я! | nah zdo-ROV'ya |

At a formal dinner, especially one in your honor, your host will rise, raise his glass and express at length his heartfelt appreciation of your mutual association. It's customary then for everyone at the table to swallow in a single gulp the drink in their glass – usually vodka or cognac. After a while, you reciprocate with a toast to your host. Subsequent toasts may follow during the meal, typically at the start of each course. The second set will be made by the second-ranked host, with response a bit later by the second-ranked guest. Men always rise when making a toast, but women may remain seated. Although it's not considered good form to just sip at the drink, Ukrainians understand that Westerners are not accustomed to downing the entire drink at once. And if you don't empty your glass, your host won't have a reason to refill it.

**Saying Good-bye**

| Good-bye. | До побачення. | do po-BAH-chehn-n'ya |
| See you later. | Побачимось пізніше. | |
| | | po-BAH-chih-mos' peez-NEE-sheh |

See you tomorrow.　　Побачимось завтра.
　　　　　　　　　　po-BAH-chih-mos' ZAHV-trah

*A more contemporary and casual good-bye is literally:*
Until meeting.　　До зустрічі.　　do ZU-stree-chee

I (we) had a wonderful time.
　　Мені (нам) було дуже приємно.
　　meh-NEE (nahm) BOO-lo DOO-zheh prih-YEHM-no

Thanks for everything.　　Дякую за все.　　DYA-koo-yu zah vseh

All the best.　　На все добре.　　nah vseh DOB-reh

When can we get together again?
　　Коли ми можемо зустрітись знову?
　　ko-LIH mih MO-zheh-mo zoos-TREE-tihs' ZNO-voo

Next time, come and visit (me) (us).
　　Наступного разу приходіть до (мене) (нас).
　　nahs-TOOP-no-ho RAH-zoo prih-kho-DEET' do ( MEHN-neh)
　　(nahs)

**Talking about the Weather.** Most of Ukraine has a moderate continental climate, that is, one characterized by four distinct seasons. There's an annual snowfall, summers that are wetter than winters, and a long, mild autumn. Spring and fall are especially pleasant; in summer your hosts may apologize for the discomfort if the temperature reaches the low 80s F.

Generally, annual average temperatures decrease as you travel from south to north and from west to east across Ukraine. Near the Russian border in Kharkiv, for example, temperatures may drop below freezing in the middle of October and the cold persists through the end of March. Crimea and the southern coast of the Black Sea have a subtropical climate, but winters can be chilly. In Odesa, the winter lasts only from the middle of December until the end of February.

Temperature in Ukraine is measured by the Celsius scale. The freezing point of water is 0°C = 32°F. For every 10° rise in Celsius there is an 18° rise in Fahrenheit, so 10°C = 50°F and 20°C = 68°F. Winter temperatures for the country as a whole average from -8° to +2°C (17.6° to 35.6°F) and summer temperatures average from +17° to 25°C (62.6° to 77°F).

There are rainy periods in Ukraine. Be sure to bring a raincoat, a folding umbrella, and shoes that won't be ruined if wet. To check weather in Ukraine go to http://weather.yahoo.com/regional/UPXX.html.

How's the weather today?
Яка погода сьогодні?
ya-KAH po-HO-dah s'o-HOD-nee
What will the weather be like tomorrow?
Яка буде погода завтра?
ya-KAH BOO-deh po-HO-dah ZAHV-trah
What a beautiful day!
Сьогодні чудова погода!
s'o-HOD-nee choo-DO-vah po-HO-dah
Is it cold outdoors?
Чи надворі холодно?
chih nahd-VO-ree KHO-lod-no
Am I dressed warmly enough?
Чи я (вдягнений, *m.*)(вдягнена, *f.*) достатньо тепло?
chih ya (VDYAH-neh-nihў) (VDYAH-neh-nah) dos-TAHT-n'o TEHP-lo
I'm freezing. Я замерзаю. ya zah-mehr-ZAH-yu
Is it going to (rain) (snow) (today) (tomorrow)?
Чи буде (дощ) (сніг) (сьогодні) (завтра)?
chih BOO-deh (doshch) (sneeh) (s'o-HOD-nee) (ZAHV-trah)
Do I need to carry an umbrella?
Чи буде мені потрібна парасоля?
chih BOO-deh MEH-nee pot-REEB-nah pah-rah-SO-lya
It looks like a storm.
Збирається на бурю.
zbih-RAH-yeht'-sya nah BOO-ryu
It's raining cats and dogs.
Лиє як із відра.
LIH-yeh yak eez veed-RAH
What terrible weather!
Яка погана погода!
ya-KAH po-HAH-nah po-HO-dah
How long will it stay like this?
Як довго буде така погода?
yak DOV-ho BOO-deh tah-KAH po-HO-dah

How are the road conditions between here and the (village) (farm)?
Який стан дороги звідси до (села) (ферми)?
ya-KIHЎ stahn do-RO-hih ZVEED-sih do (seh-LAH)
(FEHR-mih)

## Weather Vocabulary

| | | |
|---|---|---|
| Today is . . . | Сьогодн . . . і | s'o-HOD-nee |
| bright and sunny | сонячно | SON-yach-no |
| clear | ясно | YAS-no |
| hot and humid | гарячо і волого | hah-RYA-cho ee vo-LO-ho |
| warm | тепло | TEHP-lo |
| cool and cloudy | холодно і хмарно | KHO-lod-no ee KHMAHR-no |
| foggy | туманно | too-MAHN-no |
| frosty | морозно | mo-ROZ-no |
| windy | вітряно | VEET-rya-no |
| | | |
| It's raining. | Іде дощ. | ee-DEH doshch |
| It's snowing. | Іде сніг. | ee-DEH sneeh |
| | | |
| cloud | хмара | KHMAH-rah |
| fog | туман | too-MAHN |
| ice | лід | leed |
| lightning | блискавка | BLIHS-kahv-kah |
| moon | місяць | MEES-syats' |
| rain | дощ | doshch |
| sky | небо | NEH-bo |
| snow | сніг | sneeh |
| sun | сонце | SON-tseh |
| thunder | грім | hreem |
| thunderstorm | гроза | hro-ZAH |
| wind | вітер | VEE-tehr |

# CHAPTER 13.
# FAMILY AND FRIENDS

Ukrainian Proverb:
Яка хата, такий тин, який батько, такий син.
ya-KAH KHAH-tah, tah-KIHЎ tihn, ya-KIHЎ BAHT'-ko,
tah-KIHЎ sihn
*Like father, like son.*

Even with a high degree of urbanization, a high educational level, and a low birth rate, family life in Ukraine still follows a traditional, close-knit pattern. The extended family regards itself as a unit, with adults remaining close to their siblings as well as to their parents. They also form close relationships with in-laws. Family members enjoy each others' company, not only on holidays or important occasions, but even in their leisure hours.

The immediate family is small, averaging less than two children. While children are doted on, they are not spoiled. *Seen but not heard* is the rule for children when adults get together. When visitors come, if there's not enough room at the table, younger people will fade into the background so that guests and older family members can socialize.

Children receive a well-disciplined upbringing and are expected to contribute to the family by helping out. This sense of responsibility carries over to adulthood; Ukrainians feel obliged to help their parents however necessary, especially caring for them in their old age.

The attitude of sharing and responsibility serves Ukrainians well in view of the housing shortage that results in three or even four generations living together in the same apartment. Young people live with their parents longer than in Western countries, even years after marrying and having children. Ukrainian homes are characterized by a great deal of cooperation and delegation of responsibility. Someone is always available to care for children and aged grandparents, while another family member takes care of the necessary shopping.

Household responsibilities are largely delegated according to traditional, gender-related roles: Women provide the child care and kitchen work and men assume the heavier chores and maintenance jobs. A changing society requires flexibility and a sharing of tasks. Husbands and wives may take turns shopping, for example. The blurring of traditional roles is more noticeable among the younger generation in which women are as well-educated as men. Relationships between the sexes can be very interesting. Women are independent and do not consider themselves secondary to men; however, men are strong-willed and refuse to be subordinate to women.

| **Family** | родина | ro-DIH-nah |
| --- | --- | --- |
| aunt | тітка | TEET-kah |
| brother | брат | braht |
| brother-in-law | зять | zyaht' |
| 1. sister's husband | чоловік сестри | cho-lo-VEEK  sehs-TRIH |
| 2. wife's brother | брат жінки | braht Z͡HEEN-kih |
| 3. husband's brother | брат чоловіка | braht  cho-lo-VEE-kah |

cousin

The term for first cousin comes from prefixing the word for brother or sister with двоюрідн(-ий)(-на); it's common, however to simply call a first cousin "brother" or "sister." You might also hear an approximation of the English word "cousin" (*kyzen, m., kyzynka, f.*).

| male first cousin | двоюрідний брат | dvo-YU-reed-nihy̆  braht |
| --- | --- | --- |
| female first cousin | двоюрідна сестра | dvo-YU-reed-nah |
| | SEHS-trah | |

| daughter | донька | don'-KAH |
| --- | --- | --- |
| daughter-in-law | невістка | neh-VEEST-kah |
| father | батько | BAHT'-ko |
| father-in-law (wife's) | свекор | SVEH-kor |
|   (husband's) | тесть | tehst' |
| granddaughter | онучка | o-NOOCH-kah |
| grandfather | дід | deed |
| grandmother, grandma | бабуся, бабця | bah-BOO-sya,  BAB-tsya |
| grandson | онук | o-NOOK |
| husband | чоловік | cho-lo-VEEK |
| mother | мати | MAH-tih |
| mother-in-law (wife's) | свекруха | svehk-ROO-khah |
|   (husband's) | теща | TEH-shchah |
| nephew | племінник | pleh-MEEN-nihk |
| niece | племінниця | pleh-MEEN-nih-tsya |
| parents | батьки | baht'-KIH |
| sister | сестра | sehs-TRAH |

| sister-in-law | зовиця | zo-VIH-tsya |
|---|---|---|
| 1. brother's wife | братова | BRAH-to-vah͜ |
| 2. wife's sister | сестра жінки | sehs-TRAH Z͡HEEN-kih |
| 3. husband's sister | сестра чоловіка | |
| | sehs-TRAH cho-lo-VEE-kah | |
| son | син | sihn |
| son-in-law | зять | zyat' |
| uncle | дядько | DYAD'-ko |
| wife | жінка | Z͡HEEN-kah |

**Getting Acquainted.** As in other countries where both a familiar and a polite form of the word *you* is used, in Ukraine the familiar *ty* (ти, *tih*) form is becoming more common with the increasing informality of social relations. However, you should be aware that the    *vy* (ви, *vih*) form of address still characterizes the majority of relationships and interactions. *Vy* is the norm among business associates and casual acquaintances. In many families, particularly those with rural roots, children may address their mother with *vy*. *Note: In phrases in which the pronoun "you" is given or implied, the familiar, singular form is first, followed by the polite or plural form.*

Hello, my name is …
   Добрий день, мене звати …
   DO-brihy̆ den' meh-NEH ZVAH-tih
I'm so glad to meet you!
   Мені дуже приємно зустріти (тебе, *s.*) (вас, *pl.*)!
   meh-NEE DOO-z͡heh prih-YEHM-no zoo-STREE-tih (teh-BEH) (vahs).
I'm here for … days (weeks) (months).
   Я тут на … днів (тижднів) (місяців).
   ya toot nah … dneev (TIHZ͡HD-neehv) (MEE- sya-tseev)
Where do you live?
   Де (ти живеш, *s.*) (ви живете, *pl.*)?
   deh (tih z͡hih-VEHSH) (vih z͡hih-VEH-teh)
I'm staying at hotel …
   Я (зупинився, *m.*)(зупинилась, *f.*) в готелі …
   ya (zoo-pih-NIHV-sya) (zoo-pih-NIH-lahs') v ho-TEH-lee
Is your family well?
   Чи все добре в (твоїй, *s.*) (вашій, *pl.*) сім'ї?
   chih vseh DOB-reh v (TVO-yeey̆) (VAH-sheey̆) seem'YEE

We have all been well. У нас все добре. oo nahs vseh DOB-reh

My mother (my father) is (not) well.

Моя мати (мій батько) (не) почуває себе добре.

mo-YA MAH-tih (meeў BAHT'-ko) (neh) po-choo-VAH-yeh seh-BEH DOB-reh.

My parents are feeling their age.

Мої батьки відчувають вже вік.

mo-YEE baht'KIH veed-choo-VAH-yut' vzheh veek

I'm married.  Я (одружений, *m*.)(одружена, *f*.).

ya (od-ROO-zheh-nihў) (od-ROO-zheh-nah)

Are you married? (familiar, singular form of you)

Чи ти (одружений, *m*.)(одружена, *f*.)?

chih tih (od-ROO-zheh-nihў) (od-ROO-zheh-nah)

Are you married?  Чи ви одружені?

(polite or plural form of you)  chih vih od-ROO-zheh-nee

I'm single.  Я не (одружений, *m*.)(одружена, *f*.).

ya neh (od-roo-ЖHEN-nihў) (od-roo-ЖHEN-nah)

I'm (he's) divorced. [for men]  Я (він) розлучений.

ya (veen) roz-LOO-cheh-nihў

I'm (she's) divorced. [for women]  Я (вона) розлучена.

ya (vo-NAH) roz-LOO-cheh-nah

Have you any children?

Чи (ти маєш, *s*.) (ви маєте, *pl*.) дітей?

chih (tih MAH-yehsh) (vih MAH-yeh-teh) dee-TEHЎ

How old are your children?

Скільки років (твоїм, *s*.) (вашим, *pl*.) дітям?

SKEEL'-kih RO-keev (TVO-yeem) (VAH-shihm) DEE-tyam

| I have | Я маю | ya MAH-yu |
|---|---|---|
| a son (two sons) | сина (два сина) | SIH-nah (dvah SIH-nah) |
| a daughter | доньку | DON'-koo |
| two daughters | дві доньки | dvee DON'-kih |
| two children | двоє дітей | DVO-yeh dee-TEHЎ |
| three children | троє дітей | TRO-yeh dee-TEHЎ |
| I'm (she's) pregnant. | Я (вона) вагітна. | ya (vo-NAH) vah-HEET-nah |

**At home**  Вдома  VDO-mah

**In the apartment**  На квартирі  nah kvahr-TIH-ree

Ukraine's population is more than two-thirds urban, and in cities and towns virtually all families live in apartments. Older apartments are usually more substantial and have larger rooms with higher ceilings than the newer apartments. Although many Soviet era apartment buildings look shabby and disreputable, the individual apartments are clean, tidy, and well-kept. There is no air conditioning, but homes are rarely uncomfortable because of the solid construction and temperate climate. Private ownership of apartments is increasing; in addition, more than ten percent of city apartment dwellers own a very simple lodging or *dacha* (дача, DAH-chah) in the country where they go for rest and recreation and to raise vegetables. Families with the financial means are likely to renovate the *dachas*.

Rural Ukrainian homes are noted for their tidy and attractive appearance. They are often colorfully painted and accented with patches of flowers. Because the houses may lack indoor plumbing, the property might include a well, a small pool for rinsing clothes, and an outhouse. Rural homes might also include a number of outbuildings such as a woodshed, a greenhouse, and a summer kitchen. Heating is by means of ceramic wood-burning stoves, which usually provide adequate heat in the winter.

When you're invited to a home, it's customary to bring a gift, such as a box of candy, a cake, or bouquet of flowers. If there's a child in the house, bring him or her a small gift also. Casual dress is expected. Your hosts may prefer that you remove your shoes at the door and may have slippers handy, but if you fail to notice this practice, they won't call your attention to it.

This is an attractive (home) (apartment).
Це (гарий дім) (гарна квартира).
tseh (HAHR-nihў deem) (HARH-nah kvahr-TIH-rah).

How long have you lived here?
Як довго ви живете тут?
yak DOV-ho vih zhih-VEH-teh toot

| | | |
|---|---|---|
| Do you mind if I …? | Чи можна мені … ? | |
| | chih MOZH-nah meh-NEE | |
| take a shower | прийняти душ | prihў-NYA-tih doosh |
| take a bath | прийняти ванну | prihў-NYA-tih VAHN-noo |
| turn on the radio | включити радіо | vklyu-CHIH-tih RAH-dee-o |
| watch TV | подивитись телевізор | po-dih-VIH-tihs' teh-leh-VEE-zor |
| open the window | відкрити вікно | veed-KRIH-tih veek-NO |
| close the window | закрити вікно | zah-KRIH-tih veek-NO |

I'd like to take a short nap.

Я би (хотів, *m.*) (хотіла, *f.*) подрімати трошки.

yah bih (kho-TEEV) (kho-TEE-lah) pod-rih-MAH-tih TROSH-kih

When Ukrainians want to smoke at home, they usually go out for a walk or step outside on the balcony deck. In some homes, smoking is permitted in the kitchen only. If you must smoke, it's best to first ask:

Where may I smoke?     Де я можу покурити?

deh ya MO-zhoo po-koo-RIH-tih

**Living Room**        вітальна          vee-TAHL'-nah

Compact living conditions – by our standards – result in rooms that are multipurpose. The living room is often someone's bedroom and may also serve as the library or study.

| | | |
|---|---|---|
| armchair | крісло | KREES-lo |
| bookcase | книжкова шафа | |
| | knihzh-KO-vah  SHAH-fah | |
| sofa | софа, диван | so-FAH, dih-VAHN |
| TV set | телевізор | teh-leh-VEE-zor |

How does the        Як працює телевізор?
 television work?    yak prah-TSYU-yeh  teh-leh-VEE-zor

**Bedroom**          спальня          SPAHL--nya

| | | |
|---|---|---|
| bed | ліжко | LEEZH-ko |
| blanket | ковдра | KOVD-rah |
| pillow | подушка | po-DOOSH-kah |
| sheet | простирало | pros-tih-RAH-lo |
| wardrobe | шафа для одягу | SHAH-fah  dlya OD-ya-hoo |

Good night.        Надобраніч.        nah-do-BRAH-neech
(*Say* Надобраніч *only immediately before retiring.*)

Good morning.        Добрий ранок.        DO-brihў RAH-nok
I slept very well.    Я (спав, *m.*) (спала, *f.*) дуже добре.
                     ya (spahv) (SPAH-lah) DOO-zheh  DO-breh
The bed is very      Ліжко дуже зручне.
 comfortable.        LEEZH-ko DOO-zheh ZROOCH-neh

**Bath.** In Ukrainian homes, bathroom facilities are usually separated into two different rooms, the toilet in one and the bathtub in another.

Where's the toilet (bath), please?
Перепрошую, де туалет (ванна)?
peh-reh-PRO-shoo-yu deh too-ah-LEHT (VAHN-nah)

| | | |
|---|---|---|
| soap | мило | MIH-lo |
| toilet paper | туалетний папір | too-ah-LEHT-nihў pah-PEER |
| towel | рушник | roosh-NIHK |
| water | вода | vo-DAH |

How does the shower work?
Як працює душ?
yak prah-TSYU-yeh doosh
I need to wash out a few things.
Мені треба випрати декілька речей.
meh-NEE TREH-bah VIH-prah-tih DEH-keel'-kah reh-CHEHЎ

| | | |
|---|---|---|
| **Dining Room** | столова | sto-LO-vah |

At meals in Ukrainian homes, an array of dishes are placed on the table within reach and the diners help themselves. Don't expect your hostess to pass the dishes to you, but she might put some food from a serving dish directly onto your plate. Ukrainians enjoy feeding guests and you should do your best not to disappoint your hosts.

That tasted delicious. Це було дуже смачно.
tseh BOO-lo DOO-zheh SMAHCH-no
Won't you give me the recipe for this dish?
Чи ви би не могли дати мені рецепт цієї страви?
chih vih bih neh moh-LIH DAH-tih meh-NEE reh-TSEHPT tsee-YEH-yee STRAH-vih

| | | |
|---|---|---|
| **Kitchen** | кухня | KOOKH-nya |
| cold tap | холодний кран | kho-LOD-nihў krahn |
| hot tap | гарячий кран | hahr-YA-chihў krahn |
| garbage can | смітник | smeet-NIHK |
| kitchen sink | раковина | RAH-ko-vih-nah |

| stove | плита | plih-TAH |
|---|---|---|
| refrigerator | холодильник | kho-lod-DIHL'-nihk |
| washing machine | пральна машина | PRAHL'-nah mah-SHIH-nah |

**Gifts.** It's customary to give your hostess a small gift, especially after an overnight stay. Gift giving can be an art in Ukraine. If you're a guest for several days or more, smaller gifts given periodically are more gracious and pleasing than a single larger one at the end of your visit.

Thank you for your hospitality.
Дякую за (твою, *s.*) (вашу, *pl.*) гостинність.
DYA-koo-yu zah (TVO-yu) (VAH-shoo) hos-TIHN-neest'

Please accept this gift. Прошу взяти цей подарунок.
PRO-shoo VZYA-tih tsehў po-dah-ROO-nok

**Invitations and Going Out.** Ukrainians are extremely hospitable and generous to guests and will not only offer visitors help with travel arrangements, but may want to host you in their home or out on the town where they may insist on picking up the check. Although casual clothes may be worn in the home, when Ukrainian women go out for an evening, they like to dress up. It's polite for a man to extend an arm for a lady to take hold, particularly when they're on streets that are difficult to walk in high heels, but he should never grab the woman's arm.

Give me your address and telephone number.
(Дай, *s.*) (Дайте, *pl.*) мені (твою, *s.*) (вашу, *pl.*) адресу і телефон.
(dahў) (DAHЎ-teh) meh-NEE (TVO-yu) (VA-shoo) AHD-rehs-oo ee teh-leh-FON

Drop in to see (me) (us). Заходьте до (мене) (нас).
zah-KHOD'-teh doh (MEH-neh) (nahs)

Do you want to go out somewhere with (me) (us) tonight?
(Хочеш, *s.*) (Хочете, *pl.*) піти (зі мною) (з нами) кудись сьогодні ввечері?
(KHO-chehsh) (KHO-cheh-teh) pee-TIH (zee MNO-yu) (z NAH-mih) koo-DIHS' s'o-HOD-nee VVEH-cheh-ree

With great pleasure! О, з радістю! o, z RAH-dees-tyu

I'm sorry, I have other plans.
Д'якую, але я маю інші плани.
D'YA-koo-yu ah-LEH ya MAH-yu EEN-shee PLAH-nih

Can we do it another time?

Чи ми можемо зробити це другим разом?

chih mih MO-zheh-mo zro-BIH-tih tseh DROO-hihm RAH-zom

Where (when) shall we meet?

Де (коли) нам зустрітись?

deh (ko-LIH) nahm zoo-STREE-tihs'

I'll pick you up.

Я зайду за (тобою, *s.*) (ваму, *pl.*). [*on foot*]

ya zahў-DOO zah (to-BO-yu) (VAH-mih)

Я заїду за (тобою, *s.*) (ваму, *pl.*). [*by vehicle*]

ya zah-YEE-doo zah (to-BO-yu) (VAH-mih)

See you later.

Побачимося пізніше.

po-BAH-chih-mo-s'ya peez-NEE-sheh

Please, let me pay for this.

Я заплачу за це.

ya zah-plah-CHOO zah tseh

May I escort you home?

Можна (тебе, *s.*) (вас, *pl.*) провести додому?

MOZH-nah (teh-BEH) (vahs) pro-VEHS-tih doh-DOH-moo

May I give you a ride home?

Можна підвезти (тебе, *s.*) (вас, *pl.*) додому?

MOZH-nah peed-VEHZ-tih (teh-BEH) (VAHS) doh-DOH-moo

I had a wonderful time.

Мені було дуже приємо.

meh-NEE BOO-lo DOO-zheh prih-YEHM-no.

When can I see you again?

Коли я можу побачити (тебе, *s.*) (вас, *pl.*) знову?

ko-LIH ya MO-zhoo po-BAH-chih-tih (teh-BEH) (vahs)
ZNO-voo

*For a growing friendship, you might want to say*:

I like you very much.     Ви мені дуже подобаєтесь.

vih meh-NEE DOO-zheh po-DO-bah-yeh-tehs'

Literally, this phrase means "You appeal to me." Don't use it in a casual manner, but save it for a rather personal situation in which increasing intimacy is the goal. If the sentiment is reciprocated, you will need to switch from "*vy*" (ви, *vih*) to "*ty*" (ти, *tih*) in all subsequent conversations. And occasionally, no phrase is more useful than:

| I love you. | Я люблю (тебе, *s.*) (вас, *pl.*). |
|---|---|
| | ya lyu-BLYU (TEH-beh) (vahs). |

The meaning of "I love you" and the occasions for saying it are exactly the same as in the English language. It's used primarily for lovers and family members. *Tebe*, the familiar form of "you," is usually appropriate when saying "I love you", but a child might use the polite form *Vas* when speaking to an adult.

**Proposing Marriage.** Pen pal and dating services are bringing many Western men to Ukraine to meet women with whom they've long been corresponding. The brevity of the visit forces the couples to make a quick decision on whether to marry. Most do. Engagements in Ukraine are not sealed with a ring or other symbolic token, and are generally low key; a Western man should understand that his new fiancée may be reluctant to publicize the relationship to family and friends or to show public displays of affection.

When proposing marriage, use a phrase that makes your intentions absolutely clear. Asking the lady "would you marry me?" may put her in the awkward position of having to reveal her feelings when she's not clear about your intentions. It's better to ask:

| Will you marry me? | Вийдеш за мене заміж? |
|---|---|
| | VIHẎ-dehsh zah MEH-neh ZAH-meezh |
| *Or, more poetically:* | |
| I offer you my hand and heart. | Я пропоную тобі руку і серце. |
| | ya pro-po-NOO-yu to-BEE ROO-koo ee SEHR-tseh |

While asking parental permission is not a modern custom in Ukraine, it's certainly a thoughtful gesture that will make a good impression.

I want to marry your daughter.
Я хочу одружитись з вашою донькою.
ya KHO-choo od-roo-ZHIH-tihs' z VAHSH-o-yu don'-KO-yu

May I ask your blessing?
Можна просити вашого благословення?
MOZH-nah pro-SIH-tih VASH-o-ho blah-hos-lo-VEHN-nya

# CHAPTER 14.
# AT THE HOTEL

Ukrainian Proverb:
Добре їсти, гарно спати, Бог здоров'я мусить дати.
DOB-reh YEES-tih HAHR-no SPAH-tih, boh zdo-ROV'-ya
MOO-siht' DAH-tih
*Eat well, sleep well, God has to give health.*

In Ukraine, a hotel (готель, ho-TEHL) is more than a place to spend the night. It's a travel agency, a bank, a restaurant, a bar, a beauty parlor, a souvenir shop, and a ticket window. During the Soviet era, hotels were run by Intourist for the convenience of foreign tour groups, and attempted to provide what travelers might need so they would not have to wander around the city. Now accustomed to business persons and other affluent travelers, hotels no longer focus on tour groups, but still provide an array of convenient services.

With privatization, the hospitality industry in Ukraine is rapidly improving. Luxury hotels have opened up in major cities and tourist destinations and almost all towns have at least one nice hotel that's comparable to mid-range Western hotels. Service has improved everywhere. Older hotels have renovated their lobbies and restaurants and are refurbishing their rooms, floor by floor. Rates for remodeled rooms have gone up substantially, and because of the high taxes hotels pay, rates often seem high for what is offered. Unimproved hotels are still a bargain, but may lack hot water when you want it.

In Kyiv and Crimea, rooms are more available in the off-season. In smaller or more remote towns, lodging is almost always available without reservations, but the staff isn't likely to understand English. Hotels in larger cities accept credit cards, while payment in smaller cities and towns where the rooms are cheaper may be in cash only. You may book a number of leading hotels in cities across Ukraine online at the Web site www.hotelsukraine.com.

Hotel room categories are "single room" (одноособовий номер, od-no-os-o-BO-vihў NO-mehr), suitable for one person; "double двоособовий номер, dvo-o-so-BO-vihÿ NO-mehr), for two persons, which may come in "standard" or "superior;" and (люкс, lyuks) "deluxe," for either one or two occupants. Prices vary with size and quality. "Standard" double rooms are the most typical.

Remember that the lobby is on the "ground floor" and the floor above is the "first floor." Expect your room to have a TV set and a small refrigerator. The bathroom may have a scant supply of toilet paper and — according to European custom — towels, but no wash cloths. In unimproved hotels, the water rarely runs hot, but leading hotels and those in larger cities have their own water heating system.

With normal precautions, you and your possessions should be perfectly safe in a Ukrainian hotel.

**Checking In.** Upon checking in, you'll be asked to turn over your passport to the desk clerk, who will return it in a day or two. You'll be issued a "hotel card" which is your identification for entry into the hotel, picking up your keys, and being served breakfast. Be sure to ask the desk for the phone number of your room; if there's no hotel switchboard your room phone may be on a direct city line. When you go out, leave your keys at the front desk or with the floor monitor.

| | | |
|---|---|---|
| My name is . . . | мене звати . . . | meh-NEH ZVAH-tih |
| I reserved a room . . . | Я (замовляв, *m.*) (замовляла, *f.*) номер . . . ya (zah-mov-LYAV) (zah-mov-LYA-lah) NO-mehr | |
| two days ago | два дні назад | dvah dnee nah-ZAHD |
| a week ago | тиждень назад | TIHZH-dehn' nah-ZAHD |
| a month ago | місяць назад | MEE-tsyats' nah-ZAHD |
| two months ago | два місяця назад | dvah MEE-sya-tsya nah-ZAHD |
| We've reserved two rooms. | Ми замовляли дві кімнати. | mih zah-mo-BLYA-lih dvee keem-NAH-tih |
| Here's the confirmation. | Ось підтвердження. | os' peed-TVEHRD-zhehn-nya |
| *"Fill out this form."* | Заповніть цю форму. | zah-POV-neet' tsyu FOR-moo |

| *"Your passport, please."* | Прошу, ваш паспорт.<br>PRO-shoo vash PAHS-port |

In case you haven't got a reservation, these phrases may come in handy:

I'd like to reserve a room.
Я хочу замовити номер.
ya KHO-choo zah-MO-vih-tih NO-mehr

Do you have a room available?
Чи ви маєте вільний номер?
chih vih MAH-yeh-teh VEEL'-nihў NO-mehr

I need a room for one.
Мені треба номер на одного.
meh-NEE TREH-bah NO-nehr nah od-NO-ho

We need a double room . . .
Нам треба номер на двох . . .
nahm TREH-bah NO-mehr nah dvokh

| with a bath | з ванною | z VHN-no-yu |
| with a shower | з душем | z DOO-shehm |
| with a balcony | з балконом | z bahl-KO-nom |
| facing the street | з вікнами на вулицю<br>z VEEK-nah-mih nah VOO-lih-tsyu | |
| facing the back | з вікнами на задній двір<br>z VEEK-nah-mih nah ZAHD-neeў dveer | |

I want a quiet room.   Я хочу тихий номер.
ya KHO-choo TIH-khihў NO-mehr

Do you have a deluxe room?    Чи є вас люкс?
chih yeh vahs lyuks

| We'll be here . . . | Ми пробудемо . . . | mih pro-BOO-deh-mo |
| one night | одну ніч | od-NOO neech |
| two days | два дні | dvah dnee |
| one week | один тиждень | o-DIHN TIHZH-dehn' |
| half a month | пів місяця | peev MEE-sya-tsya |

Is a room ready?    Чи номер готовий?
chih NO-mehr ho-TO-vihў

| | | |
|---|---|---|
| What does the room cost . . . ? | Скільки коштує номер . . . ? | SKEEL'-kih kosh-TOO-yeh NO-mehr |
| per night | за ніч | zah neech |
| per week | за тиждень | zah TIHZH-dehn' |
| with breakfast | зі сніданком | zee snee-DAHN-kom |
| with full board | із повним харчуванням | eez POV-nihm khahr-choo-VAHN-nyam |
| This is too expensive. | Це задорого. | tseh zah-DO-ro-ho |

Do you have something less expensive?
Чи ви маєте щось дешевше?
chih vih MAH-yeh-teh shchos' deh-SHEHV-sheh

| | | |
|---|---|---|
| Does the room have . . . ? | Чи є в номері . . . ? | chih yeh v NO-meh-ree |
| a private bathroom | туалет | too-ah-LEHT |
| hot water | гаряча вода | hah-RYA-chah vo-DAH |
| heat | отоплення | o-TOP-lehn-nya |
| radio | радіо | RAH-dee-o |
| a TV set | телевізор | teh-leh-VEE-zorair |
| air conditioning | кондиціонер | kon-dih-tsee-o-NEHR |

May I see a room?
Чи можна мені подивитись номер?
chih MOZH-nah meh-NEE po-dih-VIH-tihs' NO-mehr

| | |
|---|---|
| I'll take this room. | Я візьму цей номер. ya veez'-MOO tsehў NO-mehr |
| I (don't) like the room. | Мені (не) подобається номер. meh-NEE (neh) po-DO-bah-yeht'-sya NO-mehr |
| Do you have something else? | Чи ви маєте інший номер? chih vih MAH-yeh-teh EEN-shihў NO-mehr |

What's the phone number for my room?
Який телефон в моєму номері?
ya-KIHЎ teh-leh-FON v mo-YEH-moo NO-meh-ree

Where can I park my car?
Де я можу поставити машину?
deh ya MO-zhoo pos-TAH-vih-tih mah-SHIH-noo

| Do you have a safe? | Чи ви маєти сейф? |
| | chih vih mah-YEH-teh sehўf |

| May I have . . . ? | Чи можу я мати в номер . . . ? |
| | chih MO-zhoo ya mah-tih v NO-mehr |
| another blanket | другу ковдру | DROO-hoo KOV-droo |
| another key | другий ключ | DROO-hihў klyuch |
| a few hangers | декілька вішаків |
| | DEH-keel'-kah VEE-shah-keev |
| an iron | праску | PRAHS-koo |
| a sewing kit | набір для зашивання |
| | nah-BEER dlya zah-shih-VAHN-nya |
| another towel | другий рушник | DROO-hihў roosh-NIHK |
| a TV set | телевізор | teh-leh-VEE-sor |

| Is there . . . | |
| in the hotel? | Чи є в готелі . . . ? | chih yeh v ho-TEH-lee |
| an elevator | ліфт | leeft |
| laundry service | пральня | PRAHL'-nya |
| a restaurant | ресторан | rehs-to-RAHN |
| a bar | бар | bahr |
| a post office | пошта | POSH-tah |
| a service bureau | сервісне бюро | SEHR-vees-neh byu-RO |
| a snack bar | буфет | boo-FEHT |

Is room service available?
Чи можна замовити їжу в номер?
chih MOZH-nah zah-MO-vih-tih YEE-zhoo v NO-mehr

May I have (breakfast) (dinner) in my room?
Чи я можу замовити (сніданок) (обід) у мій номер?
chih ya MO-zhoo zah-MO-vih-tih (snee-DAH-nok) (o-BEED)
oo meeў NO-mehr

May I eat in the restaurant without a reservation?
Чи можу я поїсти в ресторані без попереднього замовлення?
chih MO-zhoo ya po-YEES-tih v rehs-to-RAH-nee behz po-peh-REHD-n'o-ho zah-MOV-lehn-nya

Can I change money in the hotel?
Чи я можу обміняти валюту в готелі?
chih ya MO-zhoo ob-mee-NYA-tih vah-LYU-too v ho-TEH-lee

Where is the currency exchange office?
Де можна обміняти валюту?
deh MOZH-nah ob-mee-NYA-tih vah-LYU-too

Please wake me at . . . o'clock.
Прошу розбудити мене в . . . годині.
PRO-shoo roz-boo-DIH-tih meh-NEH v ... ho-DIH-nee

**Problems and Complaints**  Проблеми та Скарги
pro-BLEH-mih tah SKAHR-hih

I don't have my hotel card.
Я не маю з собою перепустки.
ya neh MAH-yu z so-BO-yu peh-reh-POOST-kih

My room isn't clean.  Мій номер не прибранний.
meeў NO-mehr neh PRIHB-rahn-nihў

There is/are no . . . in the room.  В номері нема . . .
v NO-meh-ree neh-MAH

| | | |
|---|---|---|
| hot water | гарячої води | hah-RYA-cho-yee vo-DIH |
| light | світла | SVEET-lah |
| towels | рушникив | roosh-NIH-kihv |
| blanket | ковдри | KOVD-rih |
| pillows | подушок | po-DOO-shok |
| soap | мила | MIH-lah |
| toilet paper | туалетного паперу | too-ah-LEHT-no-ho pah-PEH-roo |
| drinking glass | склянки | SKLYAN-kih |

The . . . in my room isn't working.

В моєму номері не працює . . .

v mo-YEH-moo NO-meh-ree neh prah-TSYU-yeh

| | | |
|---|---|---|
| air conditioning | кондиціонер | kon-dih-tsee-o-NEHR |
| electrical outlet | електрична розетка | eh-lehk-TRIHCH-nah ro-ZEHT-kah |
| fan | вентилятор | vehn-tih-LYA-tor |
| heat | опалення | o-PAH-lehn-nya |
| light | світло | SVEET-lo |
| lock | замок | zah-MOK |
| shower | душ | doosh |
| toilet | туалет | too-ah-LEHT |
| TV set | телевізор | teh-leh-VEE-zor |
| radio | радіо | RAH-dee-o |

The washbasin is clogged.

Раковина забита.

RAH-ko-vih-nah zah-BIH-tah

The bathtub won't drain.

Вода з ванни не випускається.

vo-DAH z BAHN-nih neh vih-poo-SKAH-yeht'-sya

The curtains are stuck.

Занавіски не затуляються.

zah-nah-VEES-kih neh zah-too-LYA-yut'-sya

The door (window) won't (open) (close).

Двері (вікно) не (відчиняється) (зачиняється).

DVEH-ree (veek-NO) neh (veed-chih-NYA-yeht'-sya) (zah-chih-NYA-yeht'-sya)

Can you repair it?

Чи ви можете це відремонтувати?

chih vih MO-zheh-teh tseh veed-reh-MON-too-VAH-tih

**Laundry and Cleaning**

Прання та Чистка

prahn-NYA tah CHIHST-kah

Large hotels may still have a female attendant on each floor. She will help with your special needs, from bringing up dishes and glasses for a snack to doing your laundry for you.

| These clothes need to be . . . | Ці речі потрібно . . .<br>tsee REH-chee po-TREEB-no | |
|---|---|---|
| dry-cleaned | почистити в хімчистці<br>po-CHIHS-tih-tih v kheem-CHIHST-tsee | |
| ironed | попрасувати | po-prah-soo-VAH-tih |
| washed | випрати | VIHP-rah-tih |

Can you get this stain out?
Чи ви можете вивести цю пляму?
chih vih MO-zheh-teh VIH-veh-stih tsyu PLYA-too

Can you mend this rip?
Чи ви можете залатати цю дірку?
chih vih MO-zheh-teh zah-lah-TAH-tih tsyu DIHR-koo

| I need it . . . | Мені треба це . . . | meh-NEE TREH-bah tseh |
|---|---|---|
| today | сьогодні | s'o-HOD-nee |
| tonight | сьогодні ввечері<br>s'o-HOD-nee VVEH-cheh-ree | |
| tomorrow morning | завтра вранці | ZAHV-trah VRAHN-tsee |

| Is my laundry ready? | Чи мої речі попрані?<br>chih mo-YEE REH-chee PO-prah-nee | |
|---|---|---|

| This isn't mine. | Ця річ не моя. | tsya reech neh mo-YA |
|---|---|---|

| I'm missing something. | Тут не вистарчає деяких речей.<br>toot neh vihs-tahr-CHAH-yeh DEH-ya-kihkh<br>reh-CHEHY̆ | |
|---|---|---|

| Nice job. | Гарна робота. | HAHR-nah ro-BO-tah |
|---|---|---|

How much do I owe you?
Скільки я повинен заплатити?
SKEEL'-kih ya po-VIH-nehn zah-plah-TIH-tih

## Tipping          Чаєві          chah-yeh-VEE

The term for "tip" in Ukrainian comes from the word for tea, perhaps because when the custom originated a gratuity was supposed to buy the recipient no more than a cup of tea. Under the Soviet system, the practice of giving a monetary tip was not encouraged, and travelers would reward

Intourist employees with small gifts. Tipping is still more optional in Ukraine than in North America, and a traveler need not feel obligated to reward service, particularly if it's less than satisfactory. Lipstick or a pair of panty hose are still a nice parting gift for the maid. Giving a small monetary tip to a maid, porter, taxi driver, guide, or interpreter for a job well done is entirely appropriate, however, and is expected more and more.

| Where's the . . . ? | Де . . . ? | deh |
|---|---|---|
| hall/floor monitor | коридорний | ko-rih-DOR-nihÿ |
| doorman, porter | портьєр | por-T'YEHR |
| maid | горнічна (*E Ukr.*) | HOR-neech-nah |
| | покоївква(*W Ukr.*) | po-ko-YEEV-kah |
| bellboy | носильник | no-SIHL'-nihk |
| manager | менеджер | MEH-nehd-zhehr |
| receptionist | адміністратор | ahd-mee-nees-TRAH-tor |
| waitperson | офіціант | o-fee-tsee-AHNT |

Thank you. Keep that for yourself.
Дякую, лишіть це собі.
DYA-koo-yu lih-SHEET' tseh so-BEE

**Checking Out.** Be sure to pick up your passport and any valuables you may have deposited in the safe.

When is check-out time?    Коли час розрахунку?
                       o-LIH chas roz-rah-KHOON-koo

I'm leaving tomorrow . . .    Я від'їзжаю завтра . . . .
                       ya veed'-yeez-ZHAH-yu ZAHVT-rah

| morning | вранці | VRAHN-tsee |
|---|---|---|
| noon | в обід | v o-BEED |
| afternoon | після обіду | PEES-lya o-BEE-doo |

I need an itemized bill. (item by item)
Мені треба деталний рахунок. (окремо за кожен предмет)
meh-NEE TREH-bah deht-TAHL-nihÿ rah-KHOO-nok
(ok-REH-mo zah KO-zhehn prehd-MEHT)

Do you charge for local phone calls?

Чи треба платити додатково за місцеві телефонні розмови?

chih TREH-bah plah-TIH-tih do-daht-KO-vo zah mees-TSEH-vee teh-leh-FON-nee roz-MO-vih

What additional charges are included in the bill?

Які додаткові плати включені в рахунок?

ya-KEE do-daht-KO-vee PLAH-tih BKLYU-cheh-nee v rah-KHOO-nok

Do you accept this credit card?

Чи ви приймаєте цю кредитну картку? [showing card]

chih vih prihў-MAH-yeh-teh tsyu kreh-DIHT-noo KAHRT-koo

Can I pay with traveler's checks?

Чи я можу заплатити дорожніми чеками?

chih ya MO-zhoo zah-plah-TIH-tih do-ROZH-nee-mih CHEH-kah-mih

I'd like my passport back, please.

Поверніть мій паспорт, будь ласка.

po-vehr-NEET' meeў PAHS-port bood' LAHS-kah

I think you made a mistake.

Я думаю, що ви зробили помилку.

ya DOO-mah-yu shcho vih zro-BIH-lih-lih po-MIHL-koo

Can you order a taxi for (me) (us)?

Чи ви можете замовити таксі для (мене) (нас)?

chih vih MO-zheh-teh zah-MO-vih-tih tahk-SEE dlya (MEH-neh) (nahs)

Would you have that luggage taken to the taxi?

Чи ви можете попросити принести цей багаж до таксі?

chih vih MO-zheh-teh po-pro-SIH-tih prih-NEHS-tih tsehў bah-HAHZH do tahk-SEE

Please forward my mail to this address.

Прошу перешліть мою пошту на цю адресу.

PRO-shoo peh-rehsh-LEET' mo-YU POSH-too nah tsyu ahd-REH-soo

Thank you, everything was fine.

Дякую, все було добре.

DYA-koo-yu vseh BOO-lo DOB-reh

## Bed and Breakfasts and Home Stays

For a cozy and personal alternative to the hotels, two kinds of home lodging are available. In a bed and breakfast arrangement, a private family provides your lodging and breakfast and possibly dinner. During the day you go your own way. Many travel agencies that specialize in Ukraine can arrange this type of accommodation.

In a home-stay arrangement, you stay with a private family for a week or more and the host family takes an active role in providing your touring and entertainment. You're expected to spend time with them. Home-stays are sometimes sponsored by organizations devoted to fostering people-to-people contact with residents of the former Soviet Union. A green tourism movement is opening up homes in scenic rural areas.

When staying in a home, you'll be sharing a bath, and those in rural areas may lack accustomed amenities. Rates vary according to the amenities and additional services provided, but will be a bargain compared to hotels. Your host family will usually provide airport transfer and one or two meals, but may also arrange guided sightseeing, tickets for cultural events, and inter-city transportation. Agencies may be able to match you with families according to professional and personal interests or habits, such as smoking preference. Families may or may not speak English, but you may request a home where you are comfortable with the language spoken. It's customary to bring small gifts for your hosts.

## Apartment Rental

A furnished apartment is more spacious, comfortable, and less expensive than a hotel. The cost should be in the range of US$30 to US$80 per day, depending on the size of the city you're visiting and the location and amenities of the apartment. Apartments are usually cheaper by the week and may be leased on a long-term basis.

You can locate an apartment by contacting a travel agency in the city you'll visit or by searching on the Internet for apartment listings in Ukraine. One Web site, www.uaapartments.com for example, lists apartments in Kyiv, Odesa, Kharkiv, and Vinnytsya; you can book online. Be sure to check how close the apartment is to the center of the city or to the place you'll be working and to public transportation and shopping. Check also what floor it's on, whether or not there's an elevator, and ask about security provisions for the building. For most cities you need to check whether the apartment has a continuous water supply or if the water is shut off during the night, and if and how the water is heated. Find out what comes with the apartment. A phone is an absolute necessity and a lease might even include daily room service and optional laundry and cooking services.

# CHAPTER 15.
# PUBLIC TRANSPORTATION

Ukrainian Proverb:     В тісноті, та не в обіді.
                       v tees-no-TEE tah neh v o-BEE-dee
                       *There's no offense in crowding.*

Public transportation is adequate, cheap, and reliable in Ukrainian cities. Generally, all cities and villages are served by bus; the larger cities have streetcars, trolleys, and new minibuses; and the three largest, Kyiv, Kharkiv, and Dnipropetrovsk, have subway systems. Despite sardine-like conditions, a general attitude of good humor and friendliness pervades the public transportation in Ukraine. It's customary for riders to give up their seats to the elderly, the infirm, and pregnant women.

**Taxis**              Таксі                   tahk-SEE

Book a taxi by phoning 058 or ask the service bureau or doorman of your hotel to help you. There may be a small charge for this service, and taxis from hotel taxi stands will charge top fare. When going to the theater, airport, or train station, it's best to reserve a taxi in advance, but the simplest way to hail a taxi is to stand at the roadside and hold out a hand, palm down. When one stops, state your destination or show a note with the destination written in Ukrainian, and ask the price:

How much?              Скільки?                SKEEL'kih

If you end up with a private car that's acting as a taxi, the fare will probably be much lower than charged by an official taxi. The driver may be reluctant to set a price in advance, especially when transporting several Westerners, hoping for generous voluntary contributions. The condition of volunteer vehicles varies from acceptable to dilapidated, and driving styles similarly range from tolerable to "take a deep breath." Be sure not to get into a car containing two or more people. A quirky Ukrainian custom: If you sit in the front next to the driver, he may forbid you to wear the seatbelt, since they're not required in cities. Do it anyway.

Where can I find a taxi?   Де я можу знайти таксі?
                           deh yah MO-zhoo znahў-TIH tahk-SEE

| | |
|---|---|
| Where is the taxi stop? | Де зупинка таксі?<br>deh  zoo-PIHN-kah  tahk-SEE |
| I need to go to . . . | Мені треба їхати . . .<br>meh-NEE  TREH-bah  YEE-khah-tih |
| Hotel — | до готелю —     do  ho-TEH-lyu |
| the airport | до аеропорту   do  ah-eh-ro-POR-too |
| the train station | на вокзал        nah  vok-ZAHL |
| downtown | до центру       do  TSEHN-troo |
| this address | по цій адресі   po  tseeў  AHD-reh-see |

How long will the ride take?
Як довго треба їхати?
yak  DOV-ho  TREH-bah  YEE-khah-tih

| | |
|---|---|
| I'm in a hurry. | Я поспішаю.     ya  po-spee-SHAH-yu |

Turn (left) (right) at the next corner.
Прошу повернути (наліво) (направо) на наступному повороті.
PRO-shoo  po-vehr-NOO-tih  (nah-LEE-vo)  (nah-PRAH-vo)  nah
nah-STOOP-no-moo  po-vo-RO-tee

| | |
|---|---|
| Go straight ahead. | Прямо.          PRYA-mo |
| Please stop here. | Прошу зупинитись тут.<br>PRO-shoo  zoo-pih-NIH-tihs'  toot |
| Please wait for me. | Прошу зачекати мене.<br>PRO-shoo  zah-cheh-KAH-tih  meh-NEH |

I'll be back in . . . minutes.
Я повернусь через . . . хвилин.
yah  po-vehr-NOOS'  CHEH-rehz ... khvih-LIHN

**Payment.** Be sure to have a prior agreement on the fare. Some drivers may accept American dollars if you have no hryvni. Tipping is optional. If you'd like to leave a tip, 10 to 15 percent is appropriate.

What is the fare to . . . ?
Скільки буде коштувати до . . . ?
SKEEL'-kih  BOO-deh  kosh-too-VAH-tih  do

Thank you. Keep the change.
Дякую.  Візьміть здачу собі.
DYA-koo-yu  veez'-MEET'  ZDAH-choo  so-BEE

## City Transportation

Posted signs give the name of the stop and the type of vehicles that serve it. Stops are marked "A" for bus, "Тр" for tram, "Т" for trolley, and "М" for metro or subway. Signs also tell the route number, the name of the terminal stop, and departure times..

The difference between a tram (streetcar) and a trolley is that a tram runs on rails and is attached to an overhead electric wire, while a trolley has wheels like a bus and is attached to two overhead wires. Usually these operate from 6 a.m. until 12 p.m.

| bus | автобус "А" | ahv-TO-boos |
| tram | трамвай "Тр" | trahm-VAHY̆ |
| trolley | тролейбус "Т" | tro-LEHY̆-boos |
| subway | метро "М" | meh-TRO |

Where's the nearest stop for the (bus) (streetcar) (trolley) (metro)?
Де найближча зупинка (автобуса) (трамваю) (тролейбуса) (метро)?
deh nahy̆-BLIHZ͡H-chah zoo-PIHN-kah (ahv-TO-boo-sah) (tro-LEHY̆-boo-sah) (trahm-VAH-yu) (meh-TRO)

**Buses, Trams, Trolleys.** Tickets for city buses, trams, and trolleys are interchangeable. They're sold at kiosks, or you may buy as many as you need from the *konduktor* when you get on. On the trams, the rider tears a ticket off and cancels it by running it through a mechanized box on the vehicle that punches it. Those not within reach of the validation box can pass their tickets along to the person nearest the machine, who punches it and passes it back. The honor system is backed up by a fine for those caught with unpunched tickets. On trolleys and city buses – and sometimes on trams – the box is no longer used, and a conductor validates your ticket. Vehicles in service carry a tremendous number of passengers, especially during the rush hour. Those at the end of the queue may not be able to board; once on board it may be impossible to get near the validation box or even pass your ticket down. The crush of people may also make it impossible for the conductor to spot check for punched tickets. Hence, despite good intentions, you may wind up riding for free. Be alert when your stop is approaching – you'll have to push aggressively to get off.

Please, I want a book of ten tickets.
Прошу дати мені десять талонів.
PRO-shoo DAH-tih meh-NEE DEHS-yaht' tah-LO-neev

When's the next (bus) (streetcar) (trolley)?
Коли прийде наступний (автобус) (трамвай) (тролейбус)?
ko-LIH prihў-DEH nahs-TOOP-nihў (avh-TO-boos)
(trahm-VAHЎ) (tro-LEHЎ-boos)

Does this bus go to . . . ?
Чи цей автобус їде до . . . ?
chih tsehў ahv-TO-boos yee-DEH do

I want to go to . . .    Мені треба до . . .
                         meh-NEE TREH-bah do

Please tell me when to get off.
Скажіть будь ласка, коли мені виходити.
skah-ZHEET' bood' laska ko-LIH meh-NEE vih-KHO-dih-tih

What is this stop?    Яка це зупинка?
                      ya-KAH tseh zoo-PIHN-kah

I need to get off at the next stop.
Мені треба вийти на наступній зупинці.
meh-NEE TREH-bah VIHЎ-tih nah nahs-TOOP-neeў
zoo-PIHN-tsee

Excuse me, I'm getting off.
Перепрошую, я виходжу.
peh-reh-PRO-shoo-yu ya vih-KHOD-zhoo

May I get through, please?
Чи можна мені пройти?
chih MOZH-nah meh-NEE proў-TIH

I missed my stop.
Я (пропустив, *m*.) (пропустила, *f*.) мою зупинку.
ya (pro-poos-TIHV) (pro-poos-TIH-lah) mo-YU zoo-PIHN-koo

Wait!          Почекайте!          po-cheh-KAHЎ-teh
Ouch!          Ой!                 oy

Cities have introduced a more convenient form of transportation, privately
run *marshrutni taksi*, minibuses for 14 or 16 people. A *marshrutka*

(маршрутка, mahrsh-ROOT-kah) costs a bit more, but is more comfortable and runs more frequently than the larger vehicles, especially during rush hour. A marshrutka stop can be identified by a circular sign with a checkered symbol and a route number printed on it. Generally they run along the same set routes as the larger vehicles, picking up excess passengers, but they stop upon passenger request rather than at fixed stops. If you can't get to the front of the marshrutka to pay the driver directly, pass the money along and the driver will pass back a receipt to you. During rush hour (*chas pik* is the Russian term used) you'll need exact change; however, it's best to avoid public transportation during rush hour. When you approach where you want to get off, say loudly:

Stop here please!     Зупиніть тут будь ласка.
               zoo-pih-NEET' toot bood' LAH-ska


**Subway**     Метро     MEH-tro "M"

Kyiv's subway, one of the deepest in the world, consists of three lines that intersect near the city center and cover most of the city. The subway runs from 6 a.m. until 1 a.m. It's efficient, clean, and safe. Travelers are impressed with the friendly atmosphere on the subway cars in which passengers are likely to engage in polite and friendly chit-chat. Tokens are sold at all metro stations. The current price of a token is 50 kopiyky and allows you to transfer from line to line. Monthly metro passes are also available. Enter by dropping a token in the turnstile slot. Kharkiv and Dnipropetrovsk also have metro systems, and like Kyiv, they are in a process of building new stops.

How much does a subway token cost?
      Скільки коштує жетон на метро?
      SKEEL'-kih kosh-TOO-yeh zheh-TON nah meht-RO

I'd like two subway tokens.
      Мені треба два жетони на метро.
      meh-NEE TREH-bah dvah zheh-TO-nih nah meht-RO

Here are some signs you may see in the metro station:

ВИХІД ДО МІСТА            EXIT TO CITY
ПЕРЕХІД НА СТАНЦІЮ        TRANSFER TO STATION
ПЕРЕХІД НА ЛІНІЮ          TRANSFER TO LINE

**Long-Distance Travel.** A network of trains and buses link cities and villages. If the trains are full, buses are an adventuresome way to get from place to place. These are crowded; you may end up standing in the aisle, sharing a seat with someone who also holds a ticket for it, or carrying a child on your lap. Luggage that won't fit under the bus may be stacked in the stairwell. Nevertheless, the ride is cheap, reliable, and friendly.

Where can I get a schedule for the (bus) (train) (plane)?
    Де можна знайти розклад на (автобуси) (потяги) (літаки)?
    deh MOZH-nah znahỹ-TIH ROZ-klahd nah (ahv-TO-boo-sih) (po-TYA-hih) (lee-tah-KIH)

Where is the nearest (train) (air) ticket office?
    Де найближчі квиткові каси на (поїзди) (літаки)?
    deh nahỹ-BLIHZH-chee kviht-KO-vee KAH-sih nah (PO-yeezd) (lee-tah-KEE)

I need to go to the . . .
    Мені потрібно їхати . . .
    meh-NEE po-TREE-no YEE-khah-tih

| | | |
|---|---|---|
| airport . . . | в аеропорт . . . | v ah-eh-ro-PORT |
| bus station . . . | на автовокзал . . . | nah AHV-to-vok-ZAHL |
| train station . . . | на вокзал . . . | nah vok-ZAHL |
| right now | тепер | teh-PEHR |
| today at noon | сьогодні в обід | s'o-HOD-nee v O-beed |
| this evening | сьогодні ввечері | s'o-HOD-nee VVEH-cheh-ree |
| tomorrow at [*time*] | завтра в | ZAHV-trah v |
| tomorrow morning | завтра зранку | ZAHVT-rah ZRAHN-koo |

**Going by Rail.** Train travel is the major means of transportation, with efficient and inexpensive service to virtually all towns. Ukrainian trains run on time. The most primitive are local trains serving the villages. Electric commuter trains, *elektropotyahy,* used by weekend and summer travelers, have hard wooden benches and no amenities.

The long-distance routes usually involve overnight travel, which will save you the cost of lodging. Long-distance trains are clean and generally comfortable, though slow with numerous stops. A popular choice is the *Grand Tour* car on trains between Lviv and Kyiv. Managed by the Grand

Hotel in Lviv, the car's well-maintained and comfortable two-bed compartments are equipped with lavatories with running water and provide attentive porter service. Book a *Grand Tour* compartment at the Grand Hotel on prospekt Svobody.

Ukraine has some excellent new fast trains. These run smoothly and are practically nonstop, greatly reducing the travel time. Their comfort level is on par with any European train. The first to go into service makes two daily trips between Kyiv and Kharkiv. The second links Kyiv to Odesa, stopping in Dnipropetrovsk. Others are planned for Lviv and Simferopol. The *vokzals,* or depots, are also being upgraded throughout the country.

Train tickets must be purchased within Ukraine. Availability of tickets isn't a problem, you may even buy your ticket from the conductor. For a long trip, particularly on the most popular routes and summer vacation spots, it's advisable to get a ticket in advance of your travel date, but reservations are not taken more than 45 days prior to your travel. For advance tickets, go to the special first class advance window at the train station. The ticket must be bought in your name to avoid suspicion that it's for black market, but a travel service or friend in Ukraine may do this for you and give you the tickets when you arrive. For train schedules, check at www.poezda.net. The site lists every stop along your route, but you must plug in the strange spellings of city names, e.g., for Kharkiv, type Harkov, and Lviv is spelled by its Russian name, Lvov.

Railroad stations are full of women with shopping bags bulging with produce or other items to sell in towns along the route. Some just come during mealtime to sell food to passengers during train stops. Depots may also attract shady characters, so carefully watch your personal items.

How can I get to the railroad station?
Як можна добратись до вокзалу?
yak MOZH-nah do-BRAH-tihs' do vok-ZAH-loo

Where is the ticket window?
Де квиткова каса?
deh kviht-KO-vah KAH-sah

Where is the advance reservation window?
Де каса попереднього продажу?
deh KAH-sah po-peh-REHD-n'o-ho PRO-dah-zhoo

I want to buy a ticket for . . . [date].
Я хочу купити квиток на . . .
ya KHO-choo koo-PIH-tih kvih-TOK nah

I need a ticket to ...
Мені треба квиток до ...
meh-NEE TREH-bah kvih-TOK do

I want to go on Friday at ... o'clock.
Я хочу їхати в п'ятницю в ... годині.
ya KHO-choo YEE-khah-tih v P'YAT-nih-tsyu v ...
ho-DIH-nee

I need a return ticket on Saturday ...
Мені потрібен зворотній квиток на суботу ...
meh-NEE po-TREE-behn zvo-ROT-neeў kvih-TOK nah
soo-BO-too

| | | |
|---|---|---|
| at ... o'clock. | на ... годину. | nah ... ho-DIH-noo |
| anytime during the day | в любий час напротязі дня. | |
| | v lyu-BIHЎ chahs nah-PRO-tya-zee dnya | |
| in the morning | на ранок | nah RAH-nok |
| in the afternoon | на після обіду | nah PEES-lya o-BEE-doo |
| in the evening | на вечір | nah VEH-cheer |
| What does it cost? | Скільки це коштує? | |
| | SKEEL'-kih tseh kosh-TOO-yeh | |

The station will have a booth giving information about scheduled trains. Most stations have a large board that lists trains by number and destination, giving the arrival and departure time, track number, and whether the train is on schedule or running late.

Where is the information booth?
Де довідкове бюро?
deh do-veed-KO-veh byu-RO

Where is the information board?
Де розклад?
deh ROZ-klahd

The following terms may be on the information board:

| НОМЕР | NUMBER |
|---|---|
| ПРИБУТТЯ | ARRIVAL |
| ВІДПРАВЛЕННЯ | DEPARTURE |
| ПЕРОН | TRACK |
| ПЛАТФОРМА PLATFORM | |
| ПО РОЗКЛАДУ | ON SCHEDULE |
| ЗАПІЗНЮЄТЬСЯ НА ... | RUNNING LATE BY |
| | (amount of time) |

When does train number — ... ?
Коли поїзд (потяг in W. Ukraine) номер ...
ko-LIH  PO-yeezd (PO-tyah)  NO-mehr

| leave | відправляється | veed-prah-VLYA-yeht'-sya |
|---|---|---|
| arrive | прибуває | prih-boo-VAH-yeh |

Is train number ... on schedule?
Чи поїзд (потяг in W. Ukraine) номер ... їде по-розкладу?
chih  PO-yeezd (PO-tyah)  no-MEHR ... yee-DEH  po
ROZ-klah-doo

From which platform does train number ... leave?
З якої платформи відправляється поїзд номер ...?
z ya-KO-yee plaht-FOR-mih veed-prah-VLYA-yeht'-sya PO-yeezd
NO-mehr

From which end of the train does the numbering start?
З якого кінця поїзду починається нумерація вагонів?
z ya-KO-ho keen-TSYA PO-yeez-doo po-chih-NAH-yeht'-sya
noo-meh-RAH-tsee-ya vah-HO-neev

**On the Train**  На Потяг  nah PO-tyahh

Many travelers find Ukrainian trains an especially enjoyable experience, but it's good to be prepared. Dress comfortably; layered clothing is preferable, since the comfort level varies with the season. Windows don't open on air-conditioned trains, and the beginning of the ride may be stifling. Dining cars may not have a wide selection or may be a long distance from your seat, so it's a good idea to bring enough food and bottled water to last the journey. On overnight trips, you can expect to have tea served in your sleeping cars for a small fee. To guard against a bad reaction to inadequately washed tea glasses, carry your own cups. A samovar at the end of the car dispenses boiling water, so with your own cup and tea bags or instant coffee, you're all set.

When you buy a ticket, you're assigned a seat, or on overnight trains, sleeping accommodations. Sleeping compartments are in the "soft car" (м'ягкий вагон, m'yah-KIHЎ vah-HON). First-class compartments contain two berths and are usually air-conditioned and fairly nice. Second class compartments have four berths or four seats that convert into berths. For privacy and comfort, purchase all four tickets for your compartment. Shortly after leaving the depot, an attendant will bring bedding to your compartment. You pay him or her for their rental (the cost has gone up a bit to compensate for the cheap fares) and make your own bed. The attendant will also collect your ticket and return it to you in the morning before you arrive at your station. First- and second-class compartments should have doors that lock from within.

Where's (my seat) (my compartment) (my berth)?
    Де (моє місце) (моє купе) (моя полиця)?
    deh  mo-YEH  MEES-tseh (mo-YEH koo-PEH)
    (mo-YA po-LIH-tsya)

Permit me to pass, please.
    Дозвольте пройти буд ласка.
    doz-VOL'-teh  proў-TIH  bood LAHS-kah

Is this seat taken?
    Чи це місце зайняте?
    chih  tseh  MEES-tseh  ZAHЎ-nya-teh

What is (this) (the next) station?
    Яка (це) (наступна) станція?
    ya-KAH (tseh)  (nahs-TOOP-nah) STAHN-tsee-ya

How long does the train stop here?
    Як довго стоїть тут поїзд?
    yak  DOV-ho  sto-YEET'  toot  PO-yeez

When does the train arrive in …?
    Коли поїзд прибуває до …?
    KO-lih  PO-yeezd  prih-boo-VAH-yeh  do

How long does it take to get to …?
Як довго до …?
yak DOV-ho do

Does this train have a dining car?
Чи є в цьому поїзді вагон-ресторан?
chih yeh v TSO-moo PO-yeez-dee vah-HON rehs-to-RAHN

I need bedding for (two) (three) persons.
Мені потрібна постілъ для (двох) (трьох) чоловік.
meh-NEE po-TREEB-nah PO-steel' dlya (dvokh) (tr'okh)
cho-lo-VEEK

I need an extra blanket.
Мені потрібна ще одна ковдра.
meh-NEE po-TREEB-nah shcheh od-NAH KOVD-rah

| I don't have … | Я не маю … | ya neh MAH-yu |
|---|---|---|
| a mattress | матрацу | mah-TRAH-tsoo |
| a pillow | подушки | po-DOOSH-kih |
| a blanket | ковдри | KOVD-rih |
| bed linens | постелі | pos-TEH-lih |

When do you serve tea?
Коли буде чай?
ko-LIH BOO-deh chahy̆

What do you serve with tea?
Що ви маєте до чаю?
shcho vih MAH-yeh-teh do CHAH-yu

**Domestic Flights.** The comfort and safety level of domestic flights has improved with the use of modern aircraft, and should not cause anxiety. Though prices seem low by Western standards, most Ukrainians can't afford to fly, so planes are rarely full and smaller airports sometimes seem deserted. Flights to popular destinations are increased during the tourist season, and it's a good idea to inquire from a sales representative before booking more than a month in advance. Scheduled flights that are only half full may be cancelled, so it's wise to plan departure from the larger cities and to reconfirm your flight. Two private airlines offer good service: *Ukraine International Airlines* (UIA) flies from Borispil Airport in Kyiv to major Ukrainian cities including Lviv, Chernivtsi, Uzhhorod,

Odesa, Donetsk, Dnipropetrovsk, Zapporizhya, and Simferopol. There are more than 170 UIA ticket outlets throughout the country. Tickets may be reserved on line at www.ukraine-international.com and paid for at one of the numerous ticket outlets throughout the country, preferably more than three days prior to departure. The head UIA office is at 63a B. Khmelnitskoho Street, Kyiv, phone (044) 461-50-50. Ticket sales and reservations offices are also at 4 Lysenko Street, phone (044) 224-45-28, and at Boryspil Airport, phone (044) 296-74-55. For information on other locations, phone (044)-461-56-56.

*Aerosvit* runs daily flights from Kyiv's Boryspil Airport to Kharkiv and also serves other major cities in Ukraine with a fleet of Boeings 737s. The main office is at 9/2 V.Vasylkovska Street, Kyiv, phone (044) 490-34-90 with ticket offices in the cities where it operates. For information and online reservations check www.aerosvit.com.

The baggage allowance for domestic flights ranges from 20 to 28 kg. There's a charge amounting to about US$1 for each kg overweight. When transferring to and from an international flight, you're permitted the international baggage allowance. When connecting to an international flight, be sure to have your passport ready at the initial point, because airline personnel will check your passport and visas to make sure there will be no problem in making connections.

How can I get to the airport?
Як можна добратись в аеропорт?
yak MOZH-nah do-BRAH-tihs' v ah-eh-ro-PORT

Where can I buy a plane ticket?
Де я можу купити квиток на літак?
deh ya MO-zhoo koo-PIH-tih kvih-TOK nah lee-TAHK

Round-trip tickets are not sold in Ukraine.You may be able to purchase at a single window a ticket to your destination plus a return ticket, but for the most part, tickets are sold only in the city where the flight originates.

I need a ticket to … on …
Мені потрібен квиток до … на …
meh-NEE po-TREE-behn kvih-TOK do … nah …

I need a return ticket for …
Мені треба зворотній квиток на …
meh-NEE TREH-bah zvo-ROT-neeў kvih-TOK nah …

Can you help me schedule a flight to ...?

Чи можете ви допомогти мені вибрати рейс до ...?

chih MO-zheh-teh vih do-po-mo-HTIH meh-NEE VIH-brah-tih rehўs do

I need a ticket to Kyiv on ..., then a ticket from Kyiv to Odesa on ... and then a return ticket to Lviv on ...

Мені треба квиток до Києва на ..., потім квиток від Києва до Одеси на ..., а потім зворотній квиток до Львова на ...

meh-NEE TREH-bah kvih-TOK do KIH-yeh-vah nah ..., po-TEEM kvih-TOK veed KIH-yeh-vah do o-DEH-sih nah ..., ah po-TEEM zvo-ROT-neeў kvih-TOK do L'VO-vah nah ...

How long before the flight should I check in?

Як задовго до відльоту мені треба зареєструватися?

yak zah-DOV-ho do veed-L'O-too meh-NEE TREH-bah zah-reh-heest-roo-VAH-tih-sya

When (Where) should I confirm a ticket?

Де (Коли) мені треба підтвердити квиток?

deh (ko-LIH) meh-NEE TREH-bah peed-tvehr-DIH-tih kvih-TO

When is the next flight with an available seat?

Коли наступний рейс, на який є місце?

ko-LIH nas-TOOP-nihў rehўs nah ya-KIHЎ yeh mees-TSEH

I want to return a ticket.

Я хочу здати квиток.

ya KHO-choo ZDAH-tih kvih-TOK

Where can I change a ticket?

Де я можу поміняти квиток?

deh ya MO-zhoo po-mee-NYA-tih kvih-TOK

Where is flight number ...?

Де знаходиться рейс ...?

deh znah-KHO-diht'-sya rehўs

From what gate does the plane leave?

З якого сектора відлітає літак?

z ya-KO-ho SEHK-to-rah veed-lee-TAH-yeh lee-TAHK

Where can I find a (porter) (luggage cart)?

Де я можу знайти (носильника) (візок для багажу)?

deh ya MO-z͡hoo znahy̆-TIH (no-SIHL'-nih-kah)
(vee-ZOK dlya bah-hah-Z͡HOO)

What time do we (leave) (arrive)?

Коли ми (відлітаємо) (прилітаємо)?

ko-LIH mih (veed-lee-TAH-yeh-mo) (prih-lee-TAH-yeh-mo)

How long will our flight be delayed?

Як на довго затримується наш рейс?

yak nah DOV-ho zah-TRIH-moo-yeht-sya nahsh rehy̆s

There are two information boards at the airport, one for arrivals and
another for departures:

| ПРИЛІТ | ARRIVAL |
|--------|---------|
| ВІДЛІТ | DEPARTURE |

| boarding gate | сектор | SEHK-tor |
|---------------|--------|----------|
| boarding pass | посадочний талон | po-SAH-doch-nihy̆ tah-LON |
| pilot | пілот | pee-LOT |
| stewardess | стюардеса | styu-ahr-DEH-sah |

| Fasten the seat belt. | Застебніть прив'язні ремені |
|-----------------------|------------------------------|
| | zahs-tehb-NEET' prih-V'YAZ-nee REH-meh-nee |

# CHAPTER 16.
# COMMUNICATIONS

*Ukrainian Proverb*:
Моя хата скраю, нічого не знаю.
mo-YA KHA-tah SKRAH-yu, nee-CHO-ho neh ZNAH-yu
*My house is on the edge, I don't know anything.*

Modern technology has made the villager's lament about lack of communication seem quaint indeed. Thanks to UTEL, the Ukrainian Telecommunications system privatized in 2000, Ukraine's antiquated electromechanical telephone system has been replaced by a state-of-the-art digital system. Visitors to Ukraine can now dial home directly or through an operator rather than ordering a long-distance call from an operator and waiting hours for it to go through. Cellular phones, called *mobilniy telefon,* are increasingly popular. A half dozen or so companies provide cellular connections in Ukraine. Sim cards, prepaid time chips that plug into the phone, can be purchased at shops identified with the orange and blue Sim card logo.

**TELEPHONING.** Information kiosks prominently located throughout the larger cities or at railroad stations in smaller cities can provide you with telephone numbers and addresses of local businesses, cultural facilities, and public offices. For local telephone numbers to private homes, there are no telephone books, but you can dial 09 for directory assistance. You'll need to know the person's full name, including patronymic, and the address. There is no information service for long distance numbers.

What is the phone number for ...?
Який номер телефону для ...?
ya-KIHŬ no-MEHR teh-leh-FO-noo dlya

**Local Calls**. Phone booths for local calls in Ukraine are not standardized, but come in various colors. In smaller cities, the phones require tokens or *zhetony*, available at kiosks or in the post office, but in bigger cities, all the token phone booths have been replaced by those that require phone cards. Besides the phone card shops, the cards may be purchased at every post office. With local calls, a busy signal is common.

Where is the nearest phone?
Де найближчий телефон?
deh nahў-BLIHẐH-chihў the-leh-FON

| Where can I get …? | Де я можу придбати …? |
| | deh ya MO-ẑhoo prihd-BAH-tih |
| telephone tokens | жетони для телефону |
| | ẑheh-TO-nih dlya teh-leh-FON-noo |
| a phone card | телефонну карту |
| | teh-leh-FON-noo KAHR-too |

**Intercity Phones.** To make a long-distance call to other cities in Ukraine or to one of the newly independent countries, use an intercity phone. These phones are usually referred to by the Ukrainian word for intercity, "міжміський" (meeẑh-mees'-KIHY), but in some places the Russian word "міжгородній" (meeẑh-go-ROD-neeў) will be more useful.

Generally, a post office is the best place to find an intercity phone and to buy a phone card. At each phone, there's a list of city codes and instructions for use. There should also be a clerk nearby to help.

After you hear the dial tone, dial 8. After the second dial tone, dial the city code followed by the local telephone number. When dialing to a 6-digit number, use the full city code; if dialing to a 7-digit number, omit the last digit of the city code, so the digits always total 10. If you're calling within the same oblast, however, omit the zero preceding the city code.

I need to call another city.
Мені треба подзвонити в інше місто.
meh-NEE TREH-bah pod-zvo-NIH-tih v EEN-sheh MEES-to

Where's an intercity phone?
Де міжміський (міжгородній) телефон?
deh meeẑh-mees'-KIHY (meeẑh-go-ROD-neeў) teh-leh-FON

How can I call to …?
Як можна подзвонити до …?
yak MOẐH-nah podz-vo-NIH-tih do

Please help me use this phone.
Прошу допомогти мені подзвонити з цього телефону.
PRO-shoo do-po-moh-TIH meh-NEE pod-zvo-NIH-tih z ts'o-ho teh-leh-FO-noo

**International Calls.** For 24-hour English-speaking operator assistance, dial 8-192. Remember that except for Crimea, Ukraine is on Kyiv Standard Time, which is 7 hours ahead of New York and Toronto, and 10 hours ahead of California. International rates for calls originating from Ukraine will be higher than rates for calls from home to Ukraine.

I need the international operator.

Мені потрібно міжнародного оператора.

meh-NEE  po-TREEB-no meezh-nah-ROD-no-ho  o-peh-RAH-to-rah

I have to make an international call to … now.

Мені треба подзвоннити закордон до … тепер.

meh-NEE  TREH-bah  pod-zvon-NIH-tih  zah-kor-DON  do …
teh-PEHR

**Direct Dialing.** To make an international call from your hotel, inquire at the reception desk. Hotels may be reluctant to put them through because they're afraid a guest may slip out without paying the phone bill.

To direct dial an international call, listen for the dial tone; dial 8 and wait for a second dial tone; dial 10, the international access code; dial the country code (1 for the USA and Canada), followed by the area code and your party's 7-digit number. Calls to the U.S. cost approximately US$2 per minute but may be much higher if the hotel service bureau is involved. Collect international calls are not permitted.

Is it possible to direct dial to … ?

Чи можна набрати прямо з автомату до …?

chih  MOZH-nah  nahb-RAH-tih  PRYAH-mo  z
ahv-to-MAH-too  do …

**Phone Cards.** In Kyiv you can charge your calls to your calling card number through your regular phone company, or buy a UTEL card, which allows you to make international or domestic long-distance calls from special blue and yellow phone booths in the major hotels or at the airport. UTEL cards in denominations of US$5, US$10, and US$20 are available at the post office, airports, major hotels, newsstands, and some businesses.

Inexpensive Ukrtelecom phone cards for local and intercity calls are more widely available and may be used in any phone booth.

| I'd like to buy a phone card. | Я б (хотів, *m.*) (хотіла, *f.*) купити телефонну карту.<br>ya b (kho-TEEV, *m.*), (kho-TEE-lah, *f.*) koo-PIH-tih teh-leh-FON-noo KAHR-too |

## Making a Call

May I use your phone?
Чи я можу подзвонити з вашого телефону?
chih ya MO-zhoo pod-zvo-NIH-tih z VAH-sho-ho
teh-leh-FO-noo

Hello. Is this number ... ?
Ало. Чи це номер ...?
ah-LO chih tseh NO-mehr

I'd like extension ... please.
Прошу додатковий ...
PRO-shoo do-daht-KO-vihў

May I speak with ...    Чи можу я говорити з ...
                        chih MO-zhoo ya ho-vo-RIH-tih z
I'll call again later.  Я буду дзвонити пізніше.
                        ya BOO-doo dzvo-NIH-tih peez-NEE-sheh
at ... o'clock.         в ... годині.
                        v ... ho-DIH-nee

Please ask (him) (her) to call me back.
Прошу попросити (його) (її) передзвонити мені.
PRO-shoo po-pro-SIH-tih (ўo-HO) (yee-YEE)
peh-rehd-zvo-NIH-tih meh-NEE

My number is ...        Мій номер є ...
                        meeў NO-mehr yeh
I don't understand you. Я не розумію вас.
                        ya neh ro-zoo-MEE-yu vahs

I don't understand Ukrainian (Russian).
Я не розумію української (російської).
ya neh ro-zoo-MEE-yu oo-krah-YEEN-s'ko-yee (ro-SEEЎ-s'ko-yee)

Do you speak English?
Чи ви говорите англійською?
chih vih ho-VO-rih-teh ahn-HLEEЎ-s'ko-yu

I can't hear you.       Я не чую вас.
                        ya neh CHOO-yu vahs

Please talk louder.     Прошу говорити голосніше.
                        PRO-shoo ho-vo-RIH-tih ho-los-NEE-sheh

| Please speak more slowly. | Прошу говорити повільніше. |
|---|---|
| | PRO-shoo ho-vo-RIH-tih po-veel'-NEE-sheh |

Sorry, I must have the wrong number.
Пробачте, я (помилився, *m.*) (помилилась, *f.*) номером.
pro-BAHCH-teh ya (po-mih-LIHV-sya, *m.*) (po-mih-LIH-lahs', *f.*)
NO-meh-rom

| I can't get through. | Я не можу додзвонитись. |
|---|---|
| | ya neh MO-zhoo dod-zvo-NIH-tihs' |
| We were interrupted. | Нас перервали. |
| | nahs peh-rehr-VAH-lih |

**TELEGRAMS.** A telegram is a quicker way to send an international message than express mail and a lot cheaper than phoning. Most post offices and hotels can help you send a telegram within the country. To send one abroad, go to the window with the sign "Телеграми" in the main post office or the central telegraph office. Incoming telegrams, addressed to you at your hotel with your date of arrival, work very well.

In Kyiv, you can send a telegram on credit to all points in Ukraine and the newly independent states simply by dialing 066 from a residential phone. This service is available 24 hours, seven days a week including holidays.

May I send a telegram from here?
Чи я можу звідси відіслати телеграму ?
chih ya MO-zhoo ZVEED-sih vee-dee-SLAH-tih
teh-leh-HRA-moo

| I want to send … | Мені потрібно відіслати … |
|---|---|
| | meh-NEE po-TREEB-no vee-dee-SLAH-tih |
| a domestic telegram | телеграму  teh-leh-HRAH-moo |
| an international telegram | міжнародну телеграму  meezh-nah-ROD-noo teh-leh-HRAH-moo |

Do you have an international telegram form?
Чи ви маєте бланк міжнародної телеграми?
chih vih MAH-yeh-teh blahnk meezh-nah-ROD-no-yee
teh-leh-HRAH-mih

| What is the cost per word …? | Яка ціна за слово …? |
|---|---|
| | ya-KAH tsee-NAH zah SLO-vo |

| | |
|---|---|
| to Canada | до Канади |
| | do kah-NAH-dih |
| to the United States | до Сполучених Штатів |
| | do spo-LOO-cheh-nihkh  SHTA-teev |
| for a domestic | по країні |
| telegram | po  krah-YEE-nee |

**TELEX (телекс), FAX (факс), and E-MAIL (електронна пошта)**

Electronic communications technology is making telegramming obsolete except for contact with the smallest towns and villages. Telex is a common means of communication in Ukraine, and many businesses use fax machines. To send an international telex or fax, go to the main post office or telegraphic office or check at your hotel. Privately run communications companies or travel services also provide telex, fax, and e-mail services. Internet cafés in many cities provide e-mail connections at a reasonable hourly fee, but connection speed may be slow, depending on the quality of the telephone line. For your laptop computer, prepaid time cards for internet connections can be purchased at computer shops and newsstands.

I need a fax machine.   Мені треба факс машина.

meh-NEE  TREH-bah  fahks  mah-SHIH-nah

Do you have access to the Internet or another e-mail system?

Чи ви маєте вихід на Інтернет або на іншу систему?

chih  vih  MAH-yeh-teh  VIH-kheed  nah  EEN-tehr-neht  AH-bo
nah  EEN-shoo  sihs-TEH-moo

*Note: The English term "e-mail" is commonly used in Ukraine.*

**POSTAL SERVICES.** Ukrposhta (Укрпошта), the state-run postal service operates more than 16,000 offices throughout the country. These provide a number of services at reasonable rates. Besides mailing, you can make international and intercity calls, and send a fax or a telegram. Hours for post offices vary according to their size, but main post offices in large cities are open as long as 10 hours on weekdays with shorter hours on weekends and holidays. The communications centers of large tourist hotels also provide some postal services, selling postcards, stamps, and envelopes, and offering express mail.

For sending a package to North American, Ukrposhta charges a flat rate per package (about the equivalent of US$12) plus a rate for the weight (equivalent to about US$3 per pound). The maximum weight for airmail is 10 kilograms or 22 pounds. Shipping by sea is not available through post offices. If you want to mail a package out of Ukraine, bring it to a post office unwrapped with your wrapping paper and tape. It will be weighed, wrapped, and stamped for you. Private delivery services exist that are faster and more efficient, but far more costly.

When sending a letter home, you may write the address as you usually do, using English, but be sure to write the name of the country of destination prominently at the top of the address. Postal employees can usually read English, but are in the habit of looking first to the top of the envelope for the country, since Ukrainians write envelope addresses in reverse order from the way we address them.

If sending a letter within Ukraine or to one of the other newly independent states, write the country name and the 5-digit postal index number on the top line, the oblast on the second line, followed by the city. Under the city write the street name and number and apartment number, and, on the bottom line, the name of the recipient. Mail boxes on the street are typically a dark blue color, but may be blue and yellow as well.

According to Ukrposhta, travel time for a letter is 11 days to the U.S., 9 to 14 to Canada, and from 2 to 12 days to Western European countries. However, mail has been known to take longer. For more efficient service at a higher cost, several international delivery services have branches in Ukraine. DHL is the leading international courier.

Where is the nearest (mail box) (post office)?
Де найближча (поштова скринька) (пошта)?
deh nahÿ-BLIHZH-chah (posh-TO-vah SKRIHN'-kah) (POSH-tah)

Is the post office open now?
Чи пошта відкрита тепер?
chih POSH-tah veed-KRIH-tah teh-PEHR

| What are the hours for the post office? | Коли працює пошта? ko-LIH prah-TSYU-yeh POSH-tah | |
|---|---|---|
| Can I buy ... here? | Чи можу я купити ... тут? chih MO-zhoo yah toot koo-PIH-tih | |
| an envelope | конверт | kon-VEHRT |
| stamps | марки | MAHR-kih |
| a postcard | поштову картку | posh-TO-voo KAHRT-kooa |
| telephone tokens | жетони для телефону zheh-TO-nih dlya teh-leh-FON-noo | |

| I want to send ... | Я хочу відіслати ... | |
| | ya KHO-choo vee-dees-LAH-tih | |
| a letter | лист | lihst |
| a postcard | поштову картку | posh-TO-voo KAHRT-koo |
| money to ... | гроші до | hro-SHEE do |
| a parcel | пакунок | pah-KOO-nok |
| a registered letter | рекомендований лист | |
| | reh-ko-mehn-DO-vah-nihў lihst | |
| a letter by certified | лист з повідомленням про доставку | |
| mail | lihst z po-vee-DOM-lehn-nyam pro | |
| | dos-TAHV-koo | |

I want to send this by express mail.
Я хочу відіслати це поштою-експрес.
ya KHO-choo vee-dee-SLAH-tih tseh POSH-to-yu ehk-SPREHS

| How long will it | Як довго це буде іти? |
| take to get there? | yak DOV-ho tseh BOO-deh ee-TIH |

How many stamps do I need to mail this?
Скільки марок треба тут наклеїти?
SKEEL'-kih MAH-rok TREH-bah toot nah-KLEH-yee-tih

Can you help me ...?
Чи ви можете допомогти мені ...?
chih vih MO-zheh-teh do-po-mo-HTIH meh-NEE

| write this address | написати адресу |
| | nah-pih-SAH-tih ahd-REH-soo |
| wrap this | загорнути це |
| | zah-hor-NOO-tih tseh |

Can you wrap it so it won't break?
Чи ви можете це загорнути так, щоб воно не розбилось?
chih vih MO-zheh-teh tseh zah-hor-NOO-tih tahk shchob
vo-NO neh roz-BIH-los'

How much do I owe you?
Скільки я повинен заплатити?
SKEEL'-kih ya po-VIH-nehn zah-plah-TIH-tih

# CHAPTER 17.
# AROUND TOWN

Ukrainian Proverb:

Краще один раз побачити ніж сто раз почути.
KRAH-shch o-DIHN rahz po-BAH-chi-tih neezh sto rahz
po-CHOO-tih
*It's better to see something once than hear about it a hundred times.*

**Reading Street Names.** When expressed in writing, the type of thoroughfare — "street," "avenue," "lane," etc. — precedes the proper name and is not capitalized. Taras Shevchenko Boulevard, for example, is бульвар Тараса Шевченка (boulevard of Taras Shevchenko) and Freedom Avenue is проспект Свободи (avenue of Freedom). Note that street names in the Ukrainian language are in the possessive case, thus accounting for the many names on street signs that end in the letters -а, -и, -ого, or -их. Here are some words you're likely to see on signposts.

| | | |
|---|---|---|
| алея (а.) | ah-LEH-ya | alley |
| бульвар (бул.) | bool'-VAHR | boulevard |
| вулиця (вул.) | VOO-lih-tsya | street |
| дорога (д.) | do-RO-HAH | road |
| набережна (наб.) | NAH-beh-rehzh-nah | embankment |
| площа (пл.) | PLO-shchah | square |
| провулок (пр.) | pro-VOO-lok | lane, alley |
| проїзд (п.) | pro-YEEZD | passage |
| проспект (просп.) | pros-PEHKT | prospect, avenue |
| спуск (сп.) | spoosk | descent |
| узвіз (уз.) | ooz-VEEZ | ascent |
| шосе (ш.) | sho-SEH | highway |

**Arranging a Tour.** Your hotel service bureau (Бюро послуг, byu-RO POH-slooh) or a tourist agency in town can arrange for an English-speaking guide. Expect to pay about $20 per hour, depending on the size of the city, the experience of the guide, and the professional credentials of the agency, and an additional $15 if you need a car and driver. Special excursions such as a river cruise, mountain sports, or a festival or craft fair, may be available.

Where is ... the service bureau?    Де ... бюро послуг?
                                         deh  byu-RO  po-SLOOH

... the nearest travel agency?
    ... найближче транспортне аґентсво?
    nahў-BLIHZH-cheh  TRAHNS-port-neh  ah-HEHNS-vo

May I have a map of the city?
    Можна я взяти  карту міста?
    MOZ͡H-nah  yah  VZYA-tih  KAHR-too  MEES-tah

What do you recommend I see?
    Що ви порадите мені подивитись?
    shcho  vih  po-RAH-dih-teh  meh-NEE  po-dih-VIH-tihs'

Can you ...?              Чи ви можете...?    chih  vih  MO-z͡heh-teh

| | |
|---|---|
| recommend a good restaurant | порадити добрий ресторан<br>po-RAH-dih-tih  DOB-rihў  rehs-to-RAHN |
| order theater tickets for me | замовити квитки в театр для мене<br>zah-MO-vih-tih  kviht-KIH  v  teh-AHTR  dlya  MEH-neh |
| call a taxi for me | викликати мені таксі<br>BIH-klih-kah-tih  meh-NEE  tahk-SEE |
| arrange a city tour for me | влаштувати для мене екскурсію по місту<br>vlahsh-too-VAH-tih  dlya  MEH-neh  ehks-KOOR-see-yu  po  MEES-too |

Where can I rent a car?
    Де можна найняти машину?
    deh  MOZ͡H-nah  nahў-NYA-tih  mah-SHIH-noo

I need a car with a (driver) (guide) for (a day) (several days).
    Мені потрібна машина з (водієм) (ґідом) на (один день)
    (декілька днів).
    meh-NEE  po-TREEB-nah  MAH-shih-nah  z  (vo-dee-YEHM)
    (GEE*-dom)  nah  (o-DIHN  dehn')  (DEH-keel'-kah  dneev)
    [* GEE as in *geek*, not as in *gee-whiz*]

Where can I find a guide-translator?
    Де я можу знайти ґіда-перекладача?
    deh  ya  MO-z͡hoo  znahў-TIH  *GEE-dah-peh-reh-klah-dah-CHAH

How much do you charge per (day) (week)?
Скільки це буде коштувати за (день) (тиждень)?
SKEEL'-kih tseh BOO-deh kosh-too-VAH-tih zah (dehn')
(TIHZH-den')?

Do you have any special excursions?
Чи ви маєте планові екскурсії?
chih vih MAH-yeh-teh PLAH-no-vee ehks-KOOR-see-yee

How much does the tour cost?
Скільки коштує екскурсія?
SKEEL'-kih kosh-TOO-yeh ehks-KOOR-see-ya

Does the cost include lunch?
Чи обід входить в плату?
chih o-BEED VKHO-diht' v PLAH-too

When (where) does the tour start?
Коли (Де) починається екскурсія?
ko-LIH (deh) po-chih-NAH-yeht'-sya ehks-KOOR-see-ya

What time will we return?
Коли ми повернемось назад?
ko-LIH mih po-vehr-NEH-mos' nah-ZAHD

Will we have to walk much?
Чи ми будемо багато ходити?
chih mih BOO-deh-mo bah-HAH-to kho-DIH-tih

**City Highlights**

What important historical sites are here?
Які історично-важливі місця знаходяться тут?
ya-KEE ees-to-RIHCH-no vazh-LIH-vee mees-TSYA
znah-KHO-dyat'-sya toot

How can I get to …?
Як можна добратись до …?
yak MOZH-nah do-BRAH-tihs' do

| the downtown area | центру | TSEHNT-roo |
| the opera theater | оперного театру | O-peh-no-ho teh-AHT-roo |
| the nearest park | найближчого | nahў-BLIHZH-cho-ho |
| | парку | PAHR-koo |

| the river | річки | REECH-kih |
| … Church | церкви … | TSEHRK-vih |
| … Street | вулиці … | VOO-lih-tsee |
| … Square | площі … | PLOSH-chee |

What's that (building) (monument)?
Що це за (будинок) (пам'ятник)?
shcho tseh zah (boo-DIH-nok) (PAH-m'yat-nihk)

Can we take a look inside?
Чи можна зайти і подивитись всередину?
chih MOZH-nah zahў-TIH ee po-dih-VIH-tihs'
vseh-reh-DIH-noo

Who was the architect?   Хто архітектор?
khto ar-khee-TEHK-tor

Which monuments are worth seeing?
Які пам'ятники варто подивитись?
ya-KEE PAH-m'yat-nih-kih VAHR-to po-dih-VIH-tihs'

| How old is it? | Скільки йому років? |
| | SKEEL'-kih ўo-MOO RO-keev |

| Has it been restored? | Чи він був реставрований? |
| | chih veen boov rehs-tahv-RO-vah-nihў |

| Can we go to the park? | Чи ми можемо піти в парк? |
| | chih mih MO-zheh-mo pee-TIH v pahrk |

I want to go to the open market.
Я хочу піти на базар.
ya KHO-choo pee-TIH nah bah-ZAHR

Where's the nearest folk craft market?
Де найближчий ярмарок?
deh nahў-BLIHZH-chihў YAHR-mah-rok

| How much does this cost? | Скільки це коштує? |
| | SKEEL'-kih tseh kosh-TOO-yeh |

**Taking Photos.** Museums and churches may forbid the use of flashbulbs
or ban cameras entirely, and museums that allow photography usually
charge an additional fee. When photographing vistas that include people,
it's a good idea to exercise common courtesy. To some, being photographed

without consent is an invasion of privacy. Unless you can be entirely unobtrusive, ask permission first.

You may, however, encounter people who would appreciate a nice photo of their children, since many Ukrainians don't own cameras. If photography as a means of making friends is a priority, a Polaroid camera is a great ice-breaker and solves the problem of having to send prints over when you return home. For Ukrainians with access to Internet, digital photos are ideal.

May I photograph (you) (it)?
Чи можна (вас) (це) фотографувати?
chih MOZH-nah (vahs) (tseh) fo-to-hrah-foo-VAH-tih

Would you take a photo of us, please?
Чи можна вас попросити сфотографувати нас?
chih MOZH-nah vahs po-pro-SIH-tih sfo-to-hrah-foo-VAH-tih nahs

Where's the nearest camera shop?
Де найближчий фотомагазин?
deh nahy̆-BLIHZH-chihy̆ fo-to-mah-ha-ZIHN

**Museums.** The condition of museums in Ukraine ranges from splendid to decrepit and overcrowded. Though they usually contain a wealth of well-organized creative exhibits, you'll find no high-tech, interactive displays. Only the most popular big-city museums use English-language labels along with the Ukrainian.

Buy the admission ticket at the cashier booth (каса). You'll pay the same fee charged Ukrainian citizens. There's usually a room near the entrance for checking your coat and bags. Attendants will turn the lights on and off as you pass through the galleries.

Of special interest are the "local lore" or "regional studies" museums. Located in the main city of each oblast, they feature the region's archeological, historical, cultural, and natural attractions.

It pays to check in advance whether the museum you want to see is going to be open during its stated hour; sometimes museums close for special reasons, such as cleaning or hosting receptions.

Is the museum open (today) (tomorrow)?
Чи музей відкритий (сьогодні) (завтра)?
chih moo-ZEHЎ VEED-krih-tihў (s'o-HOD-nee) (ZAHV-trah)

When does this (open) (close)?
Коли це (відкривається) (закривається)?
ko-LIH tseh (veed-krih-VAH-yeht'-sya) (zah-krih-VAH-yeht'sya)

What's the admission fee?
Яка вхідна плата?
ya-KAH vkheed-NAH PLAH-tah

Two adults, please.
Два дорослих, будь ласка.
dvah do-ROS-lihkh bood' LAHS-kah

Is there an English-speaking guide?
Чи там є гід, який говорить англійською?
chih tahm yeh geed yah-KIHЎ ho-VO-riht' ahnh-LEEЎS'-ko-yu

Where is the (cloakroom) (restroom)?
Де (гардероб) (туалет)?
deh (hahr-deh-ROB) (too-ah-LEHT)

May I take a photo?
Чи можна тут фотографувати?
chih MOZH-nah toot fo-to-hrah-foo-VAH-tih

What's the highlight of this museum?
Що видатного в цьому музеї?
shcho vih-daht-NO-ho v TS'O-moo moo-ZEH-yee

Who's the (artist) (sculptor)?
Хто є (художник) (скульптор)?
kho yeh (khoo-DOZH-nihk) (SKOOLP'-tor)

From what (region) (period) are these crafts?
З якого (району) (періоду) ці вироби?
z ya-KO-ho (rah-ЎO-noo) (peh-REE-o-doo) tsee VIH-ro-bih

**Performing Arts.** Independence has been a mixed blessing for Ukraine's strong tradition of performing arts. Greater freedom has meant greater experimentation and increased exploration of Ukrainian topics, use of the Ukrainian language, and inclusion of religious music and themes. The number of artistic groups and of new festivals has increased, and the level of artistry is impressive. Unfortunately, however, the state cannot afford to subsidize the arts to the extent to which they were accustomed, and have curtailed funding of the more expensive Ukrainian arts, such as film making. However, private funding and foreign partners are on the rise.

**Buying Tickets.** Theater tickets are quite inexpensive. Ask for them at the service bureaus in hotels or go to special ticket kiosks. For a cheaper price, purchase your tickets directly at the box office. Look for the ticket window, the *kasa* (каса).

Where are concert tickets sold?
Де продаються квитки на концерти?
deh pro-dah-YUT-sya kviht-KIH nah kon-TSEHR-tih
(The word *kontsert* (концерт) is a very general term that includes all sorts of entertainment from plays to musical performances.)

Are there any tickets for (today's) (tonight's) ...
Чи є квитки на (сьогодні) (вечір) ...
chih yeh kviht-KIH nah (s'o-HOD-nee) (VEH-cheer)

| | | |
|---|---|---|
| ballet | на балет | nah bah-LEHT |
| circus | до цирку | do TSIHR-koo |
| concert | на концерт | nah kohn-SEHRT |
| folk dance | на концерт народних танців | nah KOHN-tsert nah-ROD-nihkh TAHN-tseev |
| opera | на оперу | nah O-peh-roo |
| play | на виставу | nah vihs-TAH-voo |
| symphony | на симфонічний концерт | nah sihm-fo-NEECH-nihy̆ kohn-SEHRT |

For which day do you have tickets?
На який день ви маєте квитки?
nah ya-KIHY̆ dehn' vih MAH-yeh-teh kviht-KIH

I'd like to reserve two tickets ...
Я хочу зарезервувати два квитки ...
ya KHO-choo zah-reh-zehr-voo-VAH-tih dvah kviht-KIH
for the Wednesday matinee
на денну виставу на середу
nah DEHN-noo vihs-TAH-voo nah SEH-reh-doo

for Friday evening
   на п'ятницю вечір
   nah P'YAT-nih-tsyu VEH-cheer

| I want to sit … | Я хочу сидіти … | ya KHO-choo sih-DEE-tih |
|---|---|---|
| in the orchestra stalls | в партері | v pahr-TEH-ree |
| in the center | в центрі | v TSEHT-ree |
| on the right side | праворуч | prah-VO-rooch |
| on the left side | ліворуч | lee-VO-rooch |
| in the balcony | на балконі | nah bahl-KO-nee |
| in a box | в ложі | v LO-zhee |

If you can't find a ticket at an official outlet, go down to the theater early and see if tickets are still available. If no tickets are left, it's a common practice to try to buy a spare ticket from someone outside the theater. Simply ask:

Excuse me, do you have any spare tickets?
   Перепрошую, чи ви не маєте зайвого квитка?
   peh-reh-PRO-shoo-yu chih vih neh MAH-yeh-teh ZAHY-vo-ho KVIHT-kah

**Opera and Ballet Theaters.** In Ukraine's largest cities, opera and ballet companies share a single theater. These theaters are not only architectural gems, they also have superior acoustics for the orchestral accompaniment of the works.

Ballet repertoires in Ukraine include both classical Western and Russian ballet, as well as Ukrainian ballet which developed largely in the last 40 years from a synthesis of classical ballet and national folk dance.

Which company is performing?
   Яка трупа виступає?
   ya-KAH TROO-pah vihs-too-PAH-yeh

Who's performing the lead?
   Хто виконує головну партію?
   khto vih-ko-noo-yeh ho-lov-NOO PAHR-tee-yu

Operas are performed in the original language of the composer or translated into Ukrainian. In addition to Italian and occasional German operas, companies usually include some Ukrainian opera in their repertoire. A few of the best-known are the comic opera *The Kozak Beyond the Danube,* by Semen Hulak-Artemovsky; *Taras Bulba,* by Mykola Lysenko, who was the founder of Ukrainian classical music; and *Kupalo,* by Western Ukrainian composer Anatol Vakhnianyn.

What's the name of the opera?
Як називається опера?
yak nah-zih-VAH-yeht'-sya O-peh-rah

Who's singing the lead?
Хто співає головну партію?
khto vih-ko-noo-yeh ho-lov-NOO PAHR-tee-yu

**In the Theater**　　В Театрі　　v teh-AH-tree

Evening performances of most plays and concerts usually begin at 7 p.m. (Your ticket will say 19.00).

Where can I get a program?
Де я можу взяти програму?
deh ya MO-zhoo VZYA-tih pro-HRAH-moo

Allow me to pass, please.
Дозвольте пройти.
doz-VOL'-teh proy̆-TIH

That's my seat, please.
Перепрошую, це моє місце.
peh-reh-PRO-shoo-yu tseh mo-YEH MEES-tseh

How long will the intermission last?
Як довго буде перерва?
yak DOV-ho BOO-deh peh-REHR-vah

What a wonderful performance!
Яка чудова вистава!
ya-KAH choo-DO-vah vihs-TAH-vah

Where is the …?
Де знаходиться …?
deh znah-KHO-diht'-sya

cloakroom　　роздягальня　　roz-dyah-AL'-nya

| designated smoking | місце для куріння | |
|---|---|---|
| area | MEES-tseh dlya KOO-reen-nya | |
| entrance to the | | |
| auditorium | вхід до залу | vkheed do ZAH-loo |
| exit | вихід | VIH-kheed |
| phone | телефон | teh-leh-FON |
| restroom | туалет | too-a-LEHT |
| snack bar | буфет | boo-FEHT |

**Stage and Screen.** Ukraine has many drama companies as well as a strong tradition of musical comedy. The development of drama has suffered, however, because of historical restrictions on the Ukrainian language.

Starting back in the days of silent film, studios in Kyiv, Kharkiv, and Odesa produced movies with Ukrainian themes. Despite a history of government suppression of "nationalistic" elements, the Ukrainian film industry has managed to flourish with many artistic successes. The major motion-picture studio in Ukraine is the Kyiv Film Studio, which produced the internationally honored film *Shadows of Forgotten Ancestors* (Тіні Забутих Предків, TEE-nee zah-BOO-tihk PREHD-keev), by lauded director Serhiy Paradzhanov.

Ukrainians are avid movie-goers. You'll find many cinemas and a wide choice of international films, including many of questionable merit. Dubbing rather than subtitles is the preferred method of presenting foreign films. Films acquired from Western countries are dubbed into the Ukrainian language, while those coming by way of Russia have been dubbed into Russian. Foreign film festivals are popular in Ukraine; for festivals of newly released, yet-undubbed films, an interpreter stands at a microphone in front of the theater and translates the dialogue, as it's spoken, from the original language into Ukrainian. Theaters in larger cities have started to show Western movies in their original language, usually English, for the growing segment of the Ukrainian population interested in polishing their foreign language skills.

Buy your movie ticket directly from the box office. You will have an assigned seat. In taking your seat, it's polite to enter your row with your face, rather than your back, to those already seated. And it's not considered polite to enter a movie theater once the film has started. Refreshments are not allowed in the theater, and chattering to your companion during the screening is definitely a no-no.

To check what's playing in town, look for a printed circular showing a listing of the current movies. Check *What's On* and the *Kyiv Post* as well.

What's playing at the movies tonight?
Яке кіно демонструється сьогодні ввечері?
yah-KEH kee-NO deh-mon-STROO-yeht'-sya s'o-HOD-nee
v-VEH-cheh-ree
What language is it in?
На якій мові це кіно?
nah yah-KEEĬ MO-vee tseh kee-NO
Who's the director? Хто режисер?
khto reh-z͡hih-SEHR

| I like … | Я люблю … | ya lyub-LYU |
|---|---|---|
| an action film | бойовик | vo-ў̆o-VIHK |
| a comedy | комедію | ko-MEH-dee-yu |
| documentary film | документальний фільм | |
| | do-koo-mehn-TAHL'-niĥў feel'm | |
| drama | драму | DRAH-moo |

There are separate theaters for documentary films. Children's films, which also have their own theaters, consist mostly of cartoon features.

documentary film theater
кінотеатр документального фільму
kee-no-teh-AHTR do-koo-mehn-TAHL'-no-ho FEEL'-moo

children's theater
кінотеатер для дітей
kee-no-teh-AHTR dlya dee-TEHĬ

**Circus.** The Ukrainian love for the circus (цирк, tsihrk) is reflected in the many professional troupes throughout the country. A circus performer might spend years at the Kyiv Circus School perfecting an acrobatic routine and then join a circus company. Each city with a population greater than 500,000 has a resident circus housed in a handsome permanent building. Every year the circus presents an all-new program with a new theme. Popular acts involve bareback riding, gymnastic feats, juggling, clowns, and lots of animals, all accompanied by live music. During the summer, the resident circus may be closed, but you might be able to catch a troupe on tour in one of the smaller towns.

Where is the circus?
Де знаходиться цирк?
deh znah-KHO-diht'-sya tsihrk

Is the circus in town now?
Чи цирк тепер в місті?
chih tsihrk teh-PEHR v MEES-tee

What's the program called?
Як називається програма?
yak nah-zih-VAH-yehts'-sya pro-HRAH-mah

| | | |
|---|---|---|
| acrobats | акробати | ahk-ro-BAH-tih |
| animal trainer | дресирувальник | dreh-sih-roo-VAHL'-nihk |
| clowns | клоуни | KLO-oo-nih |
| jugglers | жонглери | ZHONH-leh-rih |
| strongmen | атлети | aht-LEH-tih |

**Puppet Theaters.** Puppetry ( ляльковий театр, lyal'-KO-vih ў teh-AH-tehr) is a popular art throughout Europe. In Ukraine every sizable city has a puppet theater whose actors use hand puppets — and occasionally marionettes — to act out classic fairy tales, such as *Pinocchio*. Ukrainian folklore is also a source of themes. The best companies participate in international festivals, which are sometimes held in Ukraine. Ukrainian puppet companies differ from those in Western Europe by employing a much larger staff — typically two dozen professional actors — and relying less on mechanical equipment.

**Sports Events**. The most popular spectator sport in Ukraine is soccer. The team Dynamo in Kyiv is a repeat national champion. Other popular sports with organized competitions are ice and field hockey, volleyball, tennis, table tennis, wrestling, and motorcycle racing. Most team sports, from basketball to water polo, have both men's and women's teams. Inter-city competitions draw avid crowds, and outstanding individual athletes enjoy national and international fame. The brothers Vitalii and Volodymyr Klitschko in boxing, Tetyana Hutsul and Hryhory Misyutin in gymnastics, Serhiy Bubka in track and field, and Oksana Baiul and Viktor Petrenko in figure skating are known to sports fans around the world.

Which sporting events are going on now in the city?
Які спортивні міроприємства проходять тепер в місті?
ya-KEE spor-TIHV-nee mee-ro-prih-YEHM-strah pro-KHO-dyat'
teh-PEHR v MEES-tee

Is it an international competition?
Чи це міжнародні змагання?
chih tseh meezh-nah-ROD-nee zmah-HAHN-nya

Who's playing?     Хто грає?
                   kho HRAH-yeh

Where can I get a ticket?
Де я можу придбати квиток?
deh ya MO-zhoo prihd-BAH-tih kvih-TOK

How can I get to the stadium?
Як добратись до стадіону?
yak do-BRAH-tihs' do stah-dee-O-noo

Who's winning?     Хто виграє?
                   kho vih-hrah-YEH
What's the score?  Який рахунок?
                   ya-IHY̆ rah-KHOO-nok

That was a good game.
Це була добра гра.
tseh boo-LAH DO-brah hrah

**Nightlife.** The older Ukrainian nightclubs and discos, usually found in
tourist hotels, are pretty much the same everywhere  − crowded, noisy,
smokey, and lacking atmosphere other than that of a bar. New
establishments, with names like Casino Rio, Opium Dance Club, Club
Flamingo, and Hollywood Night Club, cater to Kyiv's youthful movers and
shakers. The clubs attempt to have an American ambience, with lots of
neon lights and exotic drinks. Besides gaming tables, dance floors, and
Western-style floor shows, some of these clubs feature fine European-style
dining. They're open until 4 or 6 a.m.

Where can we go dancing?
Куди ми можемо піти на танці?
koo-DIH mih MO-zheh-mo pee-TIH nah TAHN-tsee

Can you recommend a good (nightclub) (disco)?
Чи ви можете порадити гарний (нічний клуб) (диско)?
chih vih MO-zheh-teh po-RAH-dih-tih HAHR-nihў
(neech-NIHЎ kloob) (DIHS-ko)

We have (haven't) a reservation.
Ми (не) замовляли попередньо.
mih (neh) zah-MO-vlya-lih po-peh-REHD'no

Ukrainians are fond of dancing, and it's not uncommon for a man to ask a stranger to be his partner. If someone who wants to try out the latest Western dance craze approaches you, he may ask:

*"May I have this dance?"*
Чи можна вас запросити?
chih MOZH-nah vahs zah-pro-SIH-tih

That was fun!　　　　Було дуже гарно!
　　　　　　　　　　BOO-lo DOO-zheh HAHR-no

If you don't care to dance, simply say:

No, thank you.　　　Ні, дякую.　　　　nee DYA-koo-yu

or you may feel that:

This dance is too fast for me.
Ця музика зашвидка для мене.
tsya MOO-zih-kah zah-SHVIHD-kah dlya MEH-neh

# CHAPTER 18.
# DINING OUT

Ukrainian Proverb:
Апетит приходить під час їди.
ah-peh-TIHT prih-KHO-diht' peed chahs yee-DIH
*The appetite comes during the meal.*

**Types of Dining Establishments.** Delicious meals can be found everywhere, and except for upscale and international restaurants in the largest cities, are very reasonably priced.

Whether you're looking for a quick meal in an informal setting or a multicourse meal with music and dancing, you'll be able to find something to suit your taste. The old Soviet anecdote that the only answer to the waiter's question, *What do you want?* is *What do you have?* is no longer true.

Look for the word **Ресторан** (rehs-tor-AHN) over the door for a multi-course meal and table service. The ambience may range from an elegant, white-tablecloth setting to casual, but attractive decor is important in new restaurants. Ukrainians don't regularly patronize restaurants, but wait until they're celebrating special occasions or looking for an evening's entertainment along with dining. Dinner may be followed by cognac and champagne with a round of toasts, followed by singing or dancing.

There are also limited-menu cafés which are named after a specific featured dish. Perhaps the most common is the *pyrizhkova* (пиріжкова), which specializes in ready-made *pyrizhky*, pastries filled with either fruit, vegetables, or meat. The *varenychna* (варенична) specializes in dumplings and the *shashlychna* (шашлична) serves shish kebab. These cafés also have tea, coffee, milk, and juice. You pay at the cashier and may stand at a counter rather than sit down.

A cafeteria (їдальня, yee-DAHL'-nya) is a self-service dining room where you can get anything from a snack to a whole meal in an informal setting. Also called *stolova* (столова), cafeterias are found primarily in public institutions. A *kulinariya* (кулінарія) is a shop that sells ready-cooked dishes for take-out or to eat in.

A *bufet* (буфет) is a snack bar serving light meals in a place not specializing in food, such as a theater. Street food is not a Ukrainian tradition, but ready-to-eat dishes may be sold at open markets or festivals.

Ukrainian fast food restaurants, such as **Shvidko** (*Quickly*) in Kyiv, have arrived. Modeled after the McDonald's chain, which has numerous franchises in big cities throughout Ukraine, these serve the quintessential national dishes.

**Reservations.** Most restaurants don't have a rapid turnover, so it's a good idea to make reservations for popular ones, either through a service bureau or by stopping in the restaurant earlier in the day.

Can you recommend a good restaurant nearby?
Чи ви можете порекомендувати гарний ресторан поблизу?
chih vih MO-zheh-teh po-reh-ko-mehn-doo-VAH-tih HAHR-nihў rehs-to-RAHN po-BLIH-zoo

I'd like to reserve a table for four people ...
Я хочу замовити столик на чотирьох персон ...
ya KHO-choo zah-MO-vih-tih STO-lik nah cho-tih-R'OKH pehr-SON

|  |  |  |
|---|---|---|
| for 6 o'clock | на шосту годину | nah SHOS-too ho-DIH-noo |
| for 6:30 | на пів сьомої | nah peev S'O-mo-yee |
| for 7 o'clock | на сьому годину. | nah S'O-moo ho-DIH-noo |

**In the Restaurant**     В Ресторані          v rehs-to-RAH-nee

Restaurants which begin serving at 11 a.m. or noon are generally open until 11 p.m. Some may close for several hours during the day, typically between 4 and 7 p.m. Restaurants are usually smoke-free, with the exception of those that feature evening entertainment. These nightclub-type restaurants aren't likely to provide a special section for nonsmokers. Some restaurants display their menus outside, but posting menus is not universal. It's okay to go inside and check the menu and prices. Opposite the prices are a series of numbers that tell the amount of grams per serving of meat, starch, and vegetables, respectively, in a given dish.

When you arrive at the restaurant, wait to be seated.

We've reserved a table for [name of party]
Ми замовляли столик на прізвище ...
mih zah-MO-vlya-lih STO-lihk nah PREEZ-vih-shcheh

May we sit over there?
Чи можемо ми сісти ось там?
chih MO-zheh-mo mih SEES-tih os' tahm

Is this table available?
Цей столик вільний?
tsehў STO-lihk VEEL'-nihў

Would you set another place?
Ви можете зробити ще одне місце?
vih MO-zheh-teh zro-BIH-tih shcheh od-NEH MEES-tseh

Please bring a menu.
Прошу принести меню.
PRO-shoo prih-NEHS-tih meh-NYU

[*To summon the waiter*] Waiter! Waitress!
Офіціант! Офіціантка!
o-fee-tsee-AHNT, o-fee-tsee-AHNT-kah

What do you recommend?
Що ви порадите?
shcho vih po-RAH-dih-teh

Which local specialties do you serve?
Які місцеві делікатеси ви пропонуєте?
ya-KEE mees-TSEH-vee deh-lee-kah-TEH-see vih
pro-po-NOO-yeh-teh

Do you have …?  Чи ви маєте …?
chih vih MAH-yeh-teh

Would you first bring …?
Чи ви можете принести спочатку …?
chih vih MO-zheh-teh prih-NEHS-tih spo-CHANT-koo

Then I'd like …  Потім я хочу …
PO-teem ya KHO-choo

I'd like to order this.  Я хочу замовити це.
[*pointing*]  ya KHO-choo zah-MO-vih-tih tseh

Would you please bring more (bread) (water)?
Прошу принести більше (хліба) (води)?
PRO-shoo prih-NEHS-tih beel'-sheh (KHLEE-bah) (vo-DIH)

Please bring an extra plate.
Прошу принести додаткову тарілку.
PRO-shoo prih-NEHS-tih do-daht-KO-voo tah-REEL-ko

Please pass the salt.
Передайте мені, будь ласка, сіль.
peh-reh-DAHY̆-teh meh-NEE bood' LAHS-kah seel'

Nothing more, thanks.
Ні, дякую.
nee DYA-koo-yu

Thank you, everything (tasted good) (was fine).
Дякую, все було (смачно) (добре).
DYA-koo-yu vseh boo-LO (SMAHCH-no) (DOB-reh)

Where's the restroom?
Де туалет?
deh too-ah-LEHT

**Breakfast**      Сніданок      snee-DAH-nok

Since city restaurants generally open at lunchtime, cafés or hotel dining rooms are a good place to find breakfast. Hotels generally, but not always, include breakfast in the cost of the room. Inexpensive hotels will provide a simple breakfast, while an expensive one will serve a lavish buffet. Have your hotel card handy to show the waiter.

*Kasha* (каша) or cooked cereal may be available, with a choice of buckwheat or other grain. Cheese, ham, and eggs may also be on the menu, and there will be excellent rolls, butter, jam and a pot of steaming tea.

When is breakfast served?
Коли сніданок?
ko-LIH snee-DAH-nok

| I'd like ... | Я би (хотів, *m.*) (хотіла, *f.*) | |
|---|---|---|
| | ya bih (kho-TEEV) (kho-TEE-lah) | |
| fruit juice | фруктовий сік | frook-TO-vihy̆ seek |
| boiled egg | варене яйце | vah-REH-neh yay̆-TSEH |
| fried egg | яєшню | ya-YEHSH-nyu |
| bacon | бекон | beh-KON |

| ham | шинку | SHIHN-koo |
|---|---|---|
| jam | повидло | po-VIHD-lo |
| sausage | ковбасу | kov-bah-SOO |
| toast | грінки | HREEN-kih |
| some bread | хліб | khleeb |
| some butter | масло | MAHS-loh |
| sour cream | сметану | smeh-TAH-noo |
| hard cheese | твердий сир | tvehr-DIHĬ sihr |
| cottage cheese | сир | sihr |
| yogurt | йогурт | ĬO-hoort |
| buckwheat cereal | гречану кашу | hreh-CHAH-noo KAH-shoo |
| millet cereal | пшоняну кашу | pshon-YA-noo KAH-shoo |
| rice cereal | рисову кашу | RIH-so-voo KAH-shoo |
| oatmeal | вівсяну кашу | veev-SYA-noo KAH-shoo |
| a cup of tea | чашку чаю | CHASH-koo CHAH-yu |
| coffee | каву | KAH-voo |
| milk | молоко | mo-lo-KO |
| hot chocolate | гарячий шокол | hah-RYAH-chih ĭ sho-ko-LAHD |
| sugar | цукор | TSOO-kor |

**Dinner.** A restaurant dinner (Обід, o-BEED) consists of several courses. Since eating plays an important role in Ukrainian social life, you can expect to spend hours at the table and eat and drink more than you had anticipated.

**Appetizers**    Закуски    zah-KOOS-kih

An appetizer is called *zakuska* (закуска), which means "little bite." However, the appetizer course can be a meal in itself. Most *zakusky* are served cold — smoked or jellied meats, jellied or pickled fish, pickled vegetables, and aged cheese. For hot appetizers, try *pyrizhky* with savory fillings.

For starters I want …
    На початок я би (хотів, *m.*) (хотіла, *f.*) …
    nah po-CHA-tok ya bih (kho-TEEV) (kho-TEE-lah)

| mixed appetizers | ассорті | as-sor-TEE |
|---|---|---|
| black caviar | чорну ікру | CHOR-noo eek-ROO |
| red caviar | червону ікру | cher-VO-noo eek-ROO |

| cheese | сир | sihr |
|---|---|---|
| eggs under mayonnaise | яйце під майонезом | YAЎ-tseh peed mah-ўo-NEH-zom |
| fish in aspic | заливна риба | zah-lihv-NAH RIH-bah |
| pate | паштет | pash-TEHT |
| pickled … | мариновані … | mah-rih-NO-vah-nee |
| cucumber | огірки | o-heer-KIH |
| mushrooms | гриби | hrih-BIH |
| tomatoes | помідори | po-mee-DO-rih |
| sausage | ковбасу | kov-bah-SOO |
| smoked cured pork | копчену шинку | KOP-cheh-noo SHIHN-koo |
| smoked salt pork | копчене сало | KOP-cheh-neh SAH-lo |

## Soup                Суп                soop

No Ukrainian meal is complete without soup, often served with a dollop of sour cream. Soups aren't considered strictly cold weather food; you'll find them at eating establishments all year round. *Borshch* (борщ),the quintessential Ukrainian soup, is the most common. Some other favorites:

I'd like …
 Я би (хотів, *m.*) (хотіла, *f.*) …
 ya bih (kho-TEEV) (kho-TEE-lah)

| barley soup | крупник | KROOP-nihk |
|---|---|---|
| bouillon | бульйон | bool'-ЎON |
| chicken noodle soup | курячий росіл KOOR-yah-chiЎ ro-SEEL | |
| pickled cucumber soup | розсільнік | roz-SEEL'-nihk |
| fish soup | юшку | YUSH-koo |
| fruit soup | фруктовий суп | frook-TO-vihў soop |
| green borshch (from nettles, sorrel or other wild greens) | | |
| | борщ зелений | borshch zeh-LEH-nihў |
| mushroom soup | грибний суп | hrihb-NIHЎ soop |
| pea soup | гороховий суп | ho-RO-kho-vihў soop |
| potato soup | картопляний суп | kahr-top-LYA-nihў soop |
| rice soup | рисовий суп | rih-SO-vihў soop |
| sauerkraut soup | капусняк | kah-poos-NYAK |
| vegetable soup (cold) | открошку | ot-KROSH-koo |

**The Main Course**     Друге          DROO-heh

For the entree I'd like this. [*pointing*]
  На друге я хочу це.
  nah DROO-heh ya KHO-choo tseh

What kind of meat do you have?
  Яке м'ясо ви маєте?
  ya-keh M'YA-so vih MAH-yeh-teh

I'd like fish, please.
  Я би (хотів, *m.*) (хотіла, *f.*) рибу.
  ya bih (kho-TEEV) (kho-TEE-lah) RIH-boo

May I have it …?
  Чи я можу мати це …?
  chih ya MO-zhoo MAH-tih tseh

| | | |
|---|---|---|
| baked | печене | PEH-cheh-neh |
| boiled | варене | VAH-reh-neh |
| fried | смажене | SMAH-zheh-neh |
| grilled | на грилі | nah HRIH-lee |
| marinated | мариноване | mah-rih-NO-vah-neh |
| smoked | копчене | KOP-cheh-neh |
| steamed | парене | PAH-reh-neh |

**Popular Meat Dishes.** Chicken Kiev (котлети по-київськи, kot-LEH-tih po KIH-yeev-s'kih) is boneless, skinless chicken breasts, pounded flat, stuffed with butter, rolled in seasoned flour, and deep fried. Menus will offer an extensive list of main dishes. Here are a few you may find:

| | | |
|---|---|---|
| goulash | гуляш | hoo-LYASH |
| hare in sour cream | заєць в сметані | |
| | ZAH-yets' v smeh-TAH-nee | |
| jellied pigs' feet | | |
| *in western Ukraine:* | холодець | kho-lo-DEHTS' |
| *in eastern Ukraine:* | студенець | stoo-deh-NEHTS' |
| shish kebab | шашлик | shash-LIHK |
| Siberian dumplings (filled with beef, pork and onions) | | |
| | пельмені | pehl'-MEH-nee |
| roasted meat pieces in sauce | | |
| | піджарка | peed-ZHAHR-kah |

| veal cutlet | теляча котлета | teh-LYA-chya kot-LEH-tah |
|---|---|---|

I'd like a vegetarian meal.
Я хочу вегетеріанську їжу.
ya KHO-choo veh-heh-teh-ree-AHNS'-koo YEE-z͡hoo

Which vegetables do you have?
Які овочі ви маєте?
a-KEE O-vo-chee vih MAH-yeh-teh

Do you have … potatoes?
ви маєте … картоплю?
vih MAH-yeh-teh … kahr-TOP-lyu

| baked | печену | PEH-cheh-noo |
|---|---|---|
| boiled | варену | VAH-reh-noo |
| fried | смажену | SMAH-z͡heh-noo |
| mashed | пюре | pyu-REH |

**Dessert**    Десерт    deh-SEHRT

What do you have for dessert?
Що ви маєте на десерт?
shcho vih MAH-yeh-teh nah deh-SEHRT

Something light please.
Щось легке будь ласка.
shchos' LEH-keh bood' LAHS-kah

Please bring me …
Будь ласка, принесіть мені …
bood' LAHS-kah prih-neh-SEET' meh-NEE

| baked cheese | сирник | SIHR-nihk |
|---|---|---|
| chocolate ice cream | шоколадне морозиво | |
| | | sho-ko-LAHD-neh mo-RO-zih-vo |
| vanilla ice cream | ванільне морозиво | |
| | | vah-NEEL'-neh mo-RO-zih-vo |
| ice cream with fruit | морозиво з варенням | |
| | | mo-RO-zih-vo z vah-REHN-nyam |
| a piece of cake | кусок торту | koo-SOK TOR-too |
| a slice of … pie | кусок пирога … | koo-SOK pih-ro-HAH |
| apple | з яблуками | z YAB-loo-kah-mih |
| cherry | з вишнями | z VIHSH-nya-mih |

| plum | зі сливами | zee SLIH-vah-mih |
| a small pastry | тістечко | TEES-tehch-ko |

Nothing more, thank you.
Дякую, нічого більше.
DYA-koo-yu nee-CHO-ho BEEL'-sheh

**Drinks** Напої nah-PO-yee

The most popular alcoholic beverages in Ukraine are beer, vodka, cognac, champagne and wine. Mixed drinks are not popular. Vodka (*horilka*, горілка) is always drunk very cold; the bartender may ask if you want your beer cold or warm ('холодне або тепле," kho-LO-neh AH-bo TEHP-leh).

I'd like ...
Я би (хотів, *m*.) (хотіла, *f*.) ...
ya bih (kho-TEEV) (kho-TEE-lah)

| a bottle of beer | пляшку пива | PLYAHSH-koo PIH-vah |
| a cold beer, on tap | холодне бочкове пиво | |
| | kho-LOD-neh boch-KO-veh PIH-vo | |
| cognac | коньяк | kon'-YAK |
| cherry liqueur | вишневий лікер | vihsh-NEH-vihў lee-KEHR |
| chocolate liqueur | шоколадний лікер | |
| | sho-ko-LAHD-nihў lee-KEHR | |
| citrus liqueur | цитрусовий лікер | |
| | TSIHT-roo-so-vihў lee-KEHR | |
| coffee liqueur | кавовий лікер | kah-VO-vihў lee-KEHR |
| vodka | горілку | ho-REEL-koo |

Vodka comes in various flavors, from black currant to the berries of the *kalyna*, the viburnum tree. By far, the most popular is the pungent hot pepper vodka.

I want a shot of ...
Чи можу я мати келішок ...
chih MO-zhoo ya MAH-tih KEH-lee-shok

Ukrainian pepper vodka
Української з перцем
oo-krah-YEENS'-koo z PEHR-tsehm

lemon vodka
лимонної горілки
lih-MOHN-no-yee ho-REEL-kih

honey brandy        медовуха        meh-do-VOO-kha

Please bring a (glass) (bottle) …
Прошу принести (склянку) (пляшку) …
PRO-shoo prih-NEHS-tih (SKLYAN-koo) (PLYASH-koo)

| | | |
|---|---|---|
| of white wine | білого вина | BEE-lo-ho vih-NAH |
| of red wine | червоного вина | chehr-VO-no-ho vih-NAH |
| of dry wine | сухого вина | soo-KHO-ho vih-NAH |
| of sweet wine | солодкого вина | so-LOD-ko-ho vih-NAH |
| of fruit wine | фруктового вина | frook-TO-vo-ho vih-nah |

I want a bottle of your best champagne.
Я хочу пляшку вашого найкращого шампанського.
ya KHO-choo PLYASH-koo VAH-sho-ho nahŷ-KRAH-shcho-ho
shahm-PAHNS'-ko-ho

I want … champagne. Я хочу … шампанське.
                     ya KHO-choo … shahm-PAHNS'-keh

| | | |
|---|---|---|
| sweet | солодке | so-LOD-keh |
| half sweet | напівсолодке | nah-PEEV-so-lod-keh |
| dry | сухе | soo-KHEH |
| half dry | напівсухе | nah-PEEV-soo-kheh |
| very dry | брют | bryut |

| | | |
|---|---|---|
| Please bring | Прошу принести ще … | |
| another … | PRO-shoo prih-NEHS-tih shcheh | |

| | | |
|---|---|---|
| beer | пива | PIH-vah |
| vodka | горілку | ho-REEL-koo |
| wine | вина | vih-NAH |

**Problems**        Проблеми        pro-BLEH-mih

Can you seat us at a different table?
Чи можна нам сісти за інший столик?
chih MOZ͡H-nah nahm SEES-tih zah EEN-shihŷ STO-lihk

Over there.        Ось там.        os'-tahm

I'm sorry, we're in a hurry.
Перепрошую, ми поспішаємо.
peh-reh-PRO-shoo-yu mih po-spee-SHAH-yeh-mo

| I don't have a … | Я не маю … | ya neh MAH-yu |
|---|---|---|
| fork | виделки | vih-DEHL-kih |
| knife | ножа | no-ZHAH |
| spoon | ложки | LOZH-kih |
| glass | келиха | KEH-lih-khah |
| plate | тарілки | tah-REEL-kih |
| napkin | серветки | sehr-VEHT-kih |
| ashtray | попільнички | po-peel'-NIHCH-kih |

This isn't clean. Це не чисте. tseh neh CHIHS-teh

I (we) didn't order that.
Я (ми) це не (замовляв, *m.*) (замовляла, *f.*) (замовляли, *pl.*).
ya (mih) tseh neh (zah-mov-LYAV) (zah-mov-LYA-lah)
(zah-mov-LYA-lih)

I (we) asked for …
Я (ми) (просив, *m.*) (просила, *f.*) (просили, *pl.*)
ya (mih) (pro-SIHV) (pro-SIH-lah) (pro-SIH-lih)

I'd like to change that.
Я хочу поміняти це.
ya KHO-choo po-mee-NYA-tih tseh

| I don't care for it. | Мені це не подобається. | |
| | meh-NEE tseh neh po-DO-bah-yeht'-sya | |
| It isn't fresh. | Це не свіже. | tseh neh SVEE-zheh |
| This is too salty. | Це засолене. | tseh zah-so-LEH-neh |
| It's bitter. | Це гірке. | tseh heer-KEH |

**Paying.** A wealth of international restaurants, cafés and bars have opened in Ukraine, especially in Kyiv. These, and hotel restaurants, usually accept credit cards as well as hryvni. Restaurants in smaller cities expect payment in Ukrainian currency. They're not allowed to accept foreign currency, but in settling the bill they may change your currency, though not at the most favorable rate.

The check may include a charge for items such as bread, butter, and cream that you assumed were complimentary. Look for a service charge of five to ten percent at the bottom of the bill. You may choose to round up the sum to the next whole figure. If the gratuity is not included, a five to ten percent tip is appropriate. Don't put the tip on your credit card because the waiter is not likely to receive it.

[*To summon the waiter*] Waiter! Waitress!

Офіціант! Офіціантка!

o-fee-tsee-AHNT, o-fee-tsee-AHNT-kah

Please give the check (to me) (to us).

Прошу розрахуватись (зі мною) (з нами).

PRO-shoo roz-rah-khoo-VAH-tihs' (zee MNO-yu) (z NAH-mih)

We'd like a single check please.

Прошу один рахунок на всіх.

PRO-shoo o-DIHN rah-KHOO-nok nah vseekh

We'd like separate checks please.

Прошу рахунок для кожного окремо.

PRO-shoo rah-KHOO-nok dlya KOZH-no-ho o-KREH-mo

Is a service charge included?

Обслуговування входить в рахунок?

ob-sloo-ho-voo-VAHN-nyah VKHO-diht' v rah-KHOO-nok

Do you accept this credit card? [*showing card*]

Чи ви приймаєте цю кредитну картку?

chih vih prihў-MAH-yeh-teh tsyu creh-DIHT-noo KAHRT-koo

I think you made a mistake.

Я думаю, що ви помились.

ya DOO-mah-yu shcho vih po-MIH-lihs'

Thank you. Keep that for yourself.

Дякую, залиште це собі.

DYA-koo-yu zah-LIHSH-teh tseh so-BEE

# CHAPTER 19.
# SHOPPING

*Ukrainian Proverb:*
Скупий два рази платить.
skoo-PIHỸ dvah RAH-zih PLAH-tiht'
*The miser pays twice.*

The term for "shopping" is ***robyty pokupky*** (робити покупки, ro-BIH-tih po-KOOP-kih), which literally means to make purchases. For Ukrainians, who can't afford to waste a single kopek and never buy on impulse, shopping is more work and less fun than for the carefree tourist.

## The Kiosk   Кіоск   kee-OSK

Kiosks are little booths on busy thoroughfares or near metro or bus stations that function much like our convenience stores. They're the place to go for every necessity: newspapers and magazines, cigarettes, drinks, snacks, local bus tickets, and phone tokens or cards, stamps and stationery. Kiosks may specialize in a single item, such as newspapers or souvenirs, or stock all sorts of Western items such as Snickers bars and Christian Dior perfumes.

Where is the nearest cigarette kiosk (newstand)?
Де найближчий сигаретний кіоск (газетний кіоск)?
deh nahỹ-BLIHZH-chihỹ sih-hah-REHT-nihỹ kee-OSK
(hah-ZEHT-nihỹ  kee-OSK )
Do you have American (newspapers) (magazines)?
Чи ви маєте американські (газети) (журнали)?
chih vih MAH-yeh-teh  ah-meh-rih-KAHNS'-kee  (hah-ZEH-tih)
(zhoor-NAH-lih)

| Do you have …? | Чи є у вас …? | chih yeh oo vahs |
|---|---|---|
| a city map | карта міста | KAHR-tah MEES-tah |
| postage stamps (for | поштові марки (закордон) | |
|  overseas mail) | posh-TO-vee MAHR-kih  (zah-kor-DON) | |
| souvenirs | сувеніри | soo-veh-NEE-rih |
| tokens … | жетони … | zheh-TO-nih |
|  for the telephone | для телефону | dlya teh-leh-FON-noo |
|  for the subway | на метро | zheh-TO-nih  nah  meht-RO |

| tickets for … | талони на … | tah-LO-nih nah |
| the city bus | автобус | ahv-TO-boos |
| the minibus | маршрутку | mahrsh-ROOT-koo |
| the trolley | тролейбус | tro-LEHY̆-boos |
| the streetcar | трамвай | trahm-VAHY̆ |

Soft drinks and mineral water in half-liter bottles are sold at kiosks. Noncarbonated water is often difficult to find. Ask for ne-hah-zo-BAH-nah vodah (негазобана вода) or vo-dah bez hah-zu ( вода без газу). For slightly carbonated water, look for слабогазобана (slah-bo-hah-zo-BAH-nah). You can also purchase small cartons of fruit juice (фруктовий сік, FROOK-to-vihy̆ seek) in many different flavors, sometimes labeled with the Russian word for juice, сок.

**Open Market**   Базар (*west Ukraine*)   bah-ZAHR
            Ринок (*east Ukraine*)   RIH-nok

In most cities, a huge area in the center of town is reserved for bazaar stalls rented by the month. Most private vendors have a specialty, so you'll find a booth stocked with children's clothes next to one that sells woolen sweaters or leather jackets or purses. Items come from Ukraine and other former Soviet countries, as well as from an array of eastern European and Middle eastern countries. Quality of the goods varies, but you'll be certain to find some wonderful items at bargain prices. Bargaining is acceptable, but because prices are not greatly inflated, you can expect only a small reduction off the asking price. Outdoor markets open earlier and close later than shops. They're usually closed one day a week, but stay open on Sunday when the shops are closed.

A farmers' market may be part of a bazaar  or − more likely − found at separate locations. At open food markets (which may actually be in a covered building), you'll find cheeses, meats, produce, baked goods, as well as prepared foods and even flowers. The individual stalls are run by independent merchants who set prices according to supply and demand.

**Stores**      Магазини      mah-hah-ZIH-nih

Large department stores are typically open from 8 a.m. until 9:30 p.m. Grocery stores open at 9 a.m. and close at 8 p.m. or 9 p.m. Smaller shops, such as those selling books or souvenirs, may open later in the morning. Stores are usually closed on Sunday except for those selling food. Tax on store-bought goods is 20 percent, but in most stores the tax is included on the sticker price. Be sure to bring a shopping bag.

While *mahazyn* (магазин, mah-hah-ZIHN) is the general name for store, the word *kramnytsya (*крамиця, krahm-NIH-tsya*)*, meaning "shop," is found on many small stores in Ukraine.

| Where is the nearest …? | Де найближчий (-ча)? deh nahӳ-BLIHZH-chihӳ (chah) | |
|---|---|---|
| antique shop | антикварний магазин | ahn-tihk-VAHR-nihӳ mah-hah-ZIHN |
| art gallery | художній салон | khoo-DOZH-neeӳ sah-LON |
| bookstore | книгарня | knih-HAR-nyah |
| camera shop | фототовари | fo-to-to-VAH-rih |
| children's clothing store | дитячий одяг | dih-TYA-chihӳ OD-yahh |
| clothing store | магазин одягу | mah-hah-ZIHN O-dya-hoo |
| department store | універмаг | oo-nee-vehr-MAHH |
| fabric store | магазин тканин | mah-hah-ZIHN tkah-NIHN |
| florist | магазин квітів | mah-hah-ZIHN KVEE-teev |
| furniture store | мебельний магазин | MEH-behl-nihӳ mah-hah-ZIHN |
| gift shop | подарунки | po-dah-ROON-kih |
| grocery | продуктови or продукти | pro-dook-TO-vih, pro-DOOK-tih |
| housewares store | господарьскі товари | hos-po-DAHR-skee to-VAH-rih |
| jewelry shop | ювелірний магазин | yu-veh-LEER-nihӳ mah-hah-ZIHN |
| shoe store | магазин взуття | mah-hah-ZIHN vzoot-TYA |
| souvenir shop | сувенірний | soo-veh-NEER-nihӳ |
| toy store | іграшки | EEH-rahsh-kih |

**Grocery Stores.** A *universam* (універсам, oo-nee-vehr-SAHM) is a large Western-style supermarket which carries household items as well as food. A *hastronom* (гастроном, hahs-tro-NOM) or *produkty* (продукти, pro-DOOK-tih) is a grocery store with counter service that carries meats, cheeses, fish, produce, and canned items. The English word *supermarket* (супермаркет) is increasingly used. There are also a number of food specialty shops, often just identified by the generic name of the product:

| bakery булочна | BOOL-och-nah | |
|---|---|---|
| candies | цукерки | tsu-KHER-kih |

*(often just the brand name is on the shop, for example "Svitoch")*

| cheeses | сири | SIH-rih |
|---|---|---|
| confectionery | кондитерська | kon-DIHT-tehrs'-kah |
| dairy products | молочні продукти | |
| | mo-LOCH-nee pro-DUK-tih | |
| deli | кулінарія | koo-lee-nah-REE-ya |
| fish | рибний | RIHB-nihў |
| ice cream | морозиво | mo-RO-zih-vo |
| liquor store | алкогольні напої | |
| | ahl-KO-hol-nee nah-PO-yee | |
| meat market | м'ясо | MYAH-co |
| milk | молоко | mo-lo-KO |
| pastry shop | тістечка | tis-TECH-kah |
| produce market | овочі | O-vo-chee |
| sausage shop | ковбаси | kov-BAH-sih |

**Metric Measures.** Food is commonly sold by the metric system. Dry ingredients are measured by kilograms, and liquid ingredients by liters.

Here are a few equivalents:

◻ There are approximately 28 grams (грами, HRAH-mih) in an ounce.
◻ 1 kilogram (кілограм, kee-lo-HRAHM) equals 2.2 pounds.
◻ 1 liter (літр, LEE-tr) is slightly more than 1 quart.
◻ There are 3.8 liters (літри, LEE-trih) in a gallon.

When making a selection, Ukrainians ask for a specific weight rather than a number. If you want to buy something by the piece, ask for so many *shtuky* (штуки, SHTOO-kih). The concept "dozen" is unfamiliar in countries using the metric system; Ukrainians are more likely to ask for a quantity of ten: *desyatok* (десяток, deh-SYA-tok).

| I want … | Я хочу … | ya KHO-choo |
|---|---|---|
| some of these | трошки цих | TROSH-kih tsihkh |
| that one on the shelf | ось те на полиці | os' teh nah po-LIH-tsee |
| a loaf of bread | буханку хліба | boo-KHAHN-koo |
| | | KHLEE-bah |
| a roll | булку | BOOL-koo |
| a cake | торт | tort |
| a chocolate bar | шоколадку | sho-ko-LAHD-koo |

| a small box of tea | пачку чаю | PAHCH-koo CHAH-yu |
| 200 grams of sausage | двісті грам ковбаси | |
| | | DVEES-teehrahm kov-bah-SIH |
| a (bottle) (carton) of | (пляшку) (пакет) молока | |
| milk | (PLYASH-koo) (pah-KEHT) mo-lo-KAH | |
| hard cheese | твердий сир | tvehr-DIHЎ sihr |
| ice cream | морозиво | mo-RO-zih-vo |
| kefir (a yogurt drink) | кефір | KEH-feer |
| some apples | декілька яблук | DEH-keel'-kah YAB-look |
| some oranges | декілька апельсин | |
| | | DEH-keel'-kah ah-pehl'-SIH |
| Is it fresh? | Це свіже? | tseh SVEE-z͡heh |

## In the Drugstore          В Аптеці          v ahp-TEH-tsee

The *apteka* (аптека, ahp-TEH-kah) carries prescription drugs and other medicines (including some antibiotics) that can be purchased without a prescription. The word for medicine is *liky* (ліки, LEE-kih). In the apteka you'll also notice a *hemiopatychnyy* (геміопатичний, heh-mee-o-pah-TIHCH-nihҙ) department, which stocks a fascinating array of herbal remedies and homeopathic cures. Because Ukrainians are reluctant to take drugs and prefer more natural methods of healing, traditional homeopathy is popular among all segments of the population including well-educated urban people.

Where's the nearest pharmacy?          Де найближча аптека?

          deh naj͡hBLIHZ͡H-chah ahp-TEH-kah

I want something for …
          Я хочу щось від …
          ya KHO-choo shchos' veed

| allergy | аллергії | ahl-LEHR-hee-yee |
| bee sting | укусу бджоли | oo-KOO-soo BDZ͡HO-lih |
| a cold | простуди | pros-TOO-dih |
| a cough | кашлю | KAHSH-lyu |
| a headache | головної болі | ho-lov-NO-yee BO-lee |
| insect bite | укусів комах | oo-KOO-seev ko-MAHKH |
| nausea | тошноти | tosh-no-TIH |
| sunburn | сонячного опіку | SO-nyach-no-ho O-pee-koo |
| travel sickness | морської хвороби | mors'-KO-yee kho-RO-bih |

Can I get it without a prescription?
Чи можна це отримати без рецепту?
chih MOZH-nah tseh ot-RIH-mah-tih behz reh-TSEHP-too

Can you prepare this prescription for me?
Чи ви можете виписати цей рецепт для мене?
chih vih MO-zheh-teh VIH-pih-sah-tih tsehў reh-TSEHPT
dlya MEH-neh

May I wait?
Можна мені зачекати?
MOZH-nah meh-NEE zah-cheh-KAH-tih

When do I need to come back?
Коли мені треба прийти знову?
ko-LIH meh-NEE TREH-bah prihў-TIH ZNO-voo

| Do you have ...? | Чи є у вас ...? | chih yeh oo vahs |
|---|---|---|
| adhesive bandages | пластер | PLAHS-tehr |
| antibiotics | антибіотики | ahn-tih-bee-O-tih-kih |
| antiseptic cream | антисептичний крем | |
| | | ahn-tih-sehp-TIHCH-nihў krehm |
| aspirin | аспірин | ahs-pee-RIHN |
| bandage | бинт | bihnt |
| calcium supplement | кальцій глюканат | |
| | | KAHL'-tseeў hlyu-kah-NAHT |
| contraceptives | контрасептиви | kon-trah-sehp-TIH-vih |
| ear drops | вушні каплі | voosh-NIH KAHP-lee |
| eye drops | очні каплі | och-NEE KAHP-lee |
| iodine | йод | ўod |
| iron supplement | гематоген | heh-mah-to-HEHN |
| sanitary napkins | марлеві серветки | |
| | | mahr-LEH-vee sehr-VEHT-kih |
| throat lozenges | таблетки для горла | |
| | | tah-BLEHT-kih dlya HOR-lah |
| vitamins | вітаміни | vee-tah-MEE-nih |

## Toiletries and Cosmetics
Туалетні та Косметичні Аксесуари
too-ah-LEHT-nee tah kos-meh-TICH-nee ahk-seh-soo-AH-rih

For toiletries and cosmetics, look for a *parfyumeriya* (парфюмерія, pahr-fyu-MEH-ree-ya) or *kosmetyka* (косметика, kos-MEH-tih-kah).

| Do you have ...? | Чи є у вас ...? | chih yeh oo vahs |
|---|---|---|
| bath salts | екстракт для ванни | |
| | EHKS-trahkt dlya VAHN-nih | |
| blush | рум'яна | room'-YA-nah |
| comb | гребінець | hreh-bee-NEHTS' |
| deodorant | дезодорант | deh-zo-do-RAHNT |
| eyeliner | олівець для вік | o-lee-VEHTS' dlya veek |
| eyeshadow | тіні для вік | TEE-nee dlya veek |
| face cream | крем для лиця | krehm dlya LIH-tsya |
| face powder | пудра | POOD-rah |
| hairbrush | щітка для волосся | |
| | SHCHEET-kah dlya vo-LOS-sya | |
| hair coloring | фарба для волосся | |
| | FAHR-bah dlya vo-LOS-sya | |
| hairspray | лак для волосся | lahk dlya vo-LOS-sya |
| hand cream | крем для рук | krehm dlya rook |
| lip balm | гігієнічна помада | |
| | hee-hee-yeh-NEECH-nah po-MAH-dah | |
| lipstick | губна помада | hoob-NAH po-MAH-dah |
| makeup | косметика | kos-MEH-tih-kah |
| makeup remover | лосьон для зняття косметики | |
| | los'-ON dlya znyat-TYA kos-MEH-tih-kih | |
| manicure scissors | манікюрні ножиці | |
| | mah-nee-KYUR-nee NO-zhih-tsee | |
| mascara | туш для вій | toosh dlya veey̆ |
| nailbrush | щітка для нігтів | |
| | SHCHEET-kah dlya NIH-teev | |
| nail file | пилка для нігтів | PIHL-kah dlya nih-TEEV |
| nail polish | лак для нігтів | lahk dlya nih-TEEV |
| nail polish remover | рідина для змиваиня лаку | |
| | ree-dih-NAH dlya zmih-VAHN-nya LAH-koo | |
| perfume | парфуми | pahr-FOO-mih |
| razor | бритва | BRIHT-vah |

| | | |
|---|---|---|
| razor blades | леза для бритви | |
| | LEH-zah dlya BRIHT-vih | |
| shampoo | шампунь | shahm-POON' |
| shaving cream | крем для гоління | |
| | krehm dlya ho-LEEN-nya | |
| soap | мило | MIH-lo |
| sponge | губка | HOOB-kah |
| sunblock | закгисний крем від сонція | |
| | zahk-HIHS-nihỹ krehm veed SON-tsee-yah | |
| suntan cream | крем для загару | krehm dlya zah-HAH-roo |
| talcum powder | тальк | tahl'k |
| toilet paper | туалетний папір | |
| | too-ah-LEHT-nihỹ pah-PEER | |
| toothbrush | зубна щітка | |
| | zoob-NAH SHCHEET-kah | |
| toothpaste | зубна паста | zoob-NAH PAHS-tah |
| tweezers | пінцет | peen-TSEHT |

**Camera Supply Shop**     фототовари          fo-to-to-VAH-rih

Western and Japanese film franchises are found on virtually every corner of any big city and may even have outlets in larger stores or in the big tourist hotels, but the price of film is no bargain in Ukraine. If you're buying from a kiosk or another newly private entrepreneur, check the expiration date since it's possible that outdated film is being sold.

I want film for this camera. [*showing the camera*]
     Я хочу плівку для цього фотоапарату.
     ya KHO-choo PLEEV-koo dlya TS'O-ho fo-to-ahp-ah-RAH-too

**Photo Developing Shop**     Фотопроявка     fo-to-pro-YAV-kah

It's not difficult to locate a *fotoproyavka,* and if you'll be in Ukraine long enough to pick up the prints, you shouldn't be disappointed with the results.

(Where can I) (Can you) develop this film?
     (Де я можу) (Чи ви можете) проявити цю плівку?
     (deh ya MO-zhoo) (chih vih MO-zheh-teh) pro-yah-VIH-tih
     tsyu PLEEV-koo

How much do you charge for processing?
Скільки коштує проявка?
SKEEL'-kih kosh-TOO-yeh pro-YAV-kah

When will the film be ready?
Коли буде готова плівка?
ko-LIH BOO-deh ho-TO-vah PLEEV-kah

Can you mail them to this address?
Чи ви можете надіслати їх на цю адресу?
chih vih MO-zheh-teh nah-dees-LAH-tih yeekh nah tsyu
ahd-REH-soo

| **Clothing** | Одяг | od-YAH |
|---|---|---|
| I need a … | Мені треба … | meh-NEE TREH-bah |
| swim suit (women's) | купальник | koo-PAHL'-nihk |
| swim trunks (men's) | плавки | PLAHV-kih |
| bathrobe | халат | khah-LAHT |
| blouse | блузка | BLOOZ-kah |
| bra | бюстгальтер | byust-HAHL'-tehr |
| coat (summer) | плащ | plashch |
| coat (winter) | пальто | pahl'-TO |
| dress | сукня | SOOK-nya |
| fur coat | шуба | SHOO-bah |
| fur hat | хутрова шапка | |
| | khoot-RO-vah SHAHP-kah | |
| gloves | рукавиці | roo-kah-VIHT-see |
| jacket | куртка | KOORT-kah |
| jeans | джінси | DZHEEN-sih |
| nylons | панчохи | pahn-CHO-khih |
| pajamas | піжама | pee-ZHAH-mah |
| panty hose | колготи | kol-HO-tih |
| raincoat | плащ від дощу | |
| | plahshch veed do-SHCHOO | |
| shirt | сорочка | so-ROCH-kah |
| skirt | спідниця | speed-NIH-tsya |
| socks | шкарпетки | skhahr-PEHT-kih |
| suit | костюм | kos-TYUM |
| sweater | светер | SVEH-tehr |
| sweatshirt | футболка | foot-BOL-kah |

| | | |
|---|---|---|
| T-shirt | футболка | foot-BOL-kah |
| underwear | нижня білизна | |
| | NIHZH-nya bee-LIHZ-nah | |
| for women | для жінок | dlya ZHEE-nok |
| for men | для чоловіків | dlya cho-lo-vee-KEEV |
| for girls | для дівчат | dlya deev-CHAHT |
| for boys | для хлопців | dlya KHLOP-tseev |
| for children | для дитини | dlya dih-TIH-nih |

May I try this on?
    Чи можу я це приміряти?
    chih MO-zhoo ya tseh prih-MEER-ya-tih
Do you have a mirror?
    У вас дзеркало?
    oo vahs DZEHR-kah-lo
It (fits) (doesn't fit) me.
    Це (підходить) (не підходить) мені.
    tseh (peed-KHO-diht') (neh peed-KHO-diht') meh-NEE
Do you have this in another color?
    Чи ви маєте інший колір?
    chih vih MAH-yeh-teh EEN-shihy ko-LEER

| | | |
|---|---|---|
| Is it washable? | Чи це можна прати? | |
| | chih tseh MOZH-nah PRAH-tih | |
| I'll take this one. | Я візьму це. | ya veez'-MOO tseh |

| | | |
|---|---|---|
| **Footwear** | Взуття | vzoot-TYA |
| I'd like … | Я би (хотів, *m.*) (хотіла, *f.*) … | |
| | ya bih (kho-TEEV) (kho-TEE-lah) | |

| | | |
|---|---|---|
| boots | чоботи | CHO-bo-tih |
| sandals | сандалі | sahn-DAH-lee |
| flat shoes | туфлі | TOOF-lee |
| high-heeled shoes | черевики | cheh-reh-VIH-kih |
| slippers | домашнє взуття | |
| | do-MAHSH-nyeh vzoot-TYA | |
| tennis shoes | кросовки | kro-SOV-kih |

Is this genuine leather?
    Чи це натуральна шкіра?
    chih tseh nah-too-RAHL'-nah SHKEE-rah

| These are too … | Вони є … | vo-NIH yeh |
|---|---|---|
| narrow/wide | завузькі / заширокі | |
| | zah-vooz'-KEE / zah-shih-RO-kee | |
| small/large | замалі / завеликі | |
| | zah-mah-LEE / zah-veh-LIH-kee | |

**Conversion Chart for Clothing**

*Women's Sizes*    *Жіночні розміри*
Clothes (dresses, suits, coats)

| | | | | | | |
|---|---|---|---|---|---|---|
| Ukrainian | 44 | 46 | 48 | 50 | 52 | 54 |
| American | 6 | 8 | 10 | 12 | 14 | 16 |
| Shoes | | | | | | |
| Ukrainian | 35 | 36 | 36½ | 37 | 38 | 39 |
| American | 5½ | 6½ | 7 | 7½ | 8½ | 9½ |

*Men's Sizes*    *Чоловічі розміри*
Suits and Coats

| | | | | | | |
|---|---|---|---|---|---|---|
| Ukrainian | 46 | 48 | 50 | 52 | 54 | 56 |
| American | 36 | 38 | 40 | 42 | 44 | 46 |
| Shirts | | | | | | |
| Ukrainian | 39 | 40 | 41 | 42 | 43 | 44 |
| American | 15 | 15½ | 16 | 16½ | 17 | 17½ |
| Shoes | | | | | | |
| Ukrainian | 40 | 41 | 42 | 43 | 43 | 44 |
| American | 7½ | 8½ | 9½ | 10 | 10½ | 11½ |

**Sizes**    Розміри    ROZ-mee-rih

Clothing is sized according to the metric system, and all clothing – whether women's, men's, or children' – is based on a single scale. Like American clothing, standardization of sizing in ready-made garments is not perfect. The chart above is a guide when buying for others, for yourself; it's best to try it on.

I don't know my size.
  Я не знаю мій розмір.
  ya neh ZNAH-yu meeў ROZ-meer

It's too (big) (small).
  Це (завелике) (замале).
  tseh (zah-veh-LIH-keh) (zah-mah-LEH)

It's too (long) (short).
Це (задовге) (закоротке).
tseh (zah-DOV-heh) (zah-ko-ROT-keh)

Do you have a (larger) (smaller) size?
Чи ви маєте (більший) (менший) розмір?
chih vih MAH-yeh-teh (BEEL'-shihў) (MEN-shihў) ROZ-meer

**Selecting and Paying for Merchandise.** In small stores, Western-style stores, and in open markets, you simply pay the salesperson. In larger stores, purchasing may be a little more complicated. After deciding on an item, note the price, then go to the cash desk and pay for it. You'll receive a receipt (чек, chehk), which you take to another counter to pick up your purchase.

Would you please show me …? [*pointing*]
Чи ви можете мені показати ...?
chih vih MO-zheh-teh meh-NEE po-kah-ZAH-tih

| this one | це | tseh |
|---|---|---|
| something like that | щось таке як це | |
| | shchos' tah-KEH yak tseh | |
| that one in the window | то на вітрині | to nah vee-TRIH-nee |

This isn't quite what I want.
Це не зовсім, що я хочу.
tseh neh ZOV-seem shcho ya KHO-choo

I would like better quality.
Я би (хотів, *m.*) (хотіла, *f.*) крашої якості.
ya bih (kho-TEEV) (kho-TEE-lah) KRAH-sho-yee YA-kos-tee

I'll take this one.          Я візьму це.
                             ya veez'-MOO tseh

What does it cost?          Скільки це коштує?
                             SKEEL'-kih tseh kosh-TOO-yeh

Where do I pay?            Де мені заплатити?
                             deh meh-NEE zahp-lah-TIH-tih

Do you accept this credit card? [*showing card*]
Чи ви приймаєте цю кредитну картку?
chih vih prihў-MAH-yeh-teh tsyu kreh-DIHT-noo KAHRT-koo

I need a receipt.
Мені потрібен чек.
meh-NEE po-TREE-behn chehk

## BUYING SOUVENIRS AND GIFTS

*Ukrainian Proverb*:
Очі бачили що руки брали.
O-chee BAH-chih-lih shcho ROO-kih BRAH-lih
*The eyes see what the hands are taking.*

A customary no-exchanges or returns policy made Ukrainians cautious shoppers, with a keen eye for quality and value. Now, some private shops do accept returns, but a tourist on the move needs to make irrevocable decisions when choosing souvenirs. The conventional wisdom of resisting impulse buying may not apply when traveling because you may not find a cheaper or better item later.

### Ukrainian Traditional Crafts

Ukraine has very well-developed, sophisticated folk art, some of which dates back to antiquity. During prehistoric times, religious beliefs and natural events determined symbols, motifs, and colors. Over time, designs were influenced by contacts with foreign cultures and civilizations. Byzantium and the Far East as well as Western styles such as Gothic, Renaissance, and Baroque, left their mark on indigenous art forms

There is a similarity of basic patterns among the different media, whether *pysanky* or tapestry. Intricate geometric patterns developed earliest and are still the most common today. Plant and animal motifs developed later out of the geometric forms. Colors and patterns vary according to region. For example, in eastern Ukraine black and red are the predominant colors, but blue and white are also common. Green is favored in certain western areas. Each village has its own designs.

Folk art traditions are cherished throughout Ukraine. In each region ethnological museums display beautiful collections of sophisticated design and superb craftsmanship. For crafts makers there are *tekhnikum* of folk handicrafts, while designers attend schools of applied art. Handcrafted items are widely sold — in art salons, gift and souvenir shops, department stores, museum shops, kiosks, and on city sidewalks. You'll also find plenty of the usual touristy plastic knickknacks and T- shirts for sale.

These major types of folk arts are crafted throughout the country, with variations in motifs, design, color and pattern:

**Weaving** (ткацтво, TKAHTS-tvo) had developed into a cottage industry by the 14th century. Weavers produced various articles of folk dress, bed and table coverings, *kylyms*, and *rushnyky*, from flax, hemp, or woolen thread. Especially important is the *kylym* (килим), an ornamental woven floor or wall covering. Folk carpet-making dates back to antiquity, but the opening of large mills in the 18th century made kylym production widespread. The basic designs of geometric and plant motifs show some oriental and southern European influence; over time individual weavers developed their own styles, composition, and harmonized coloration. In homes throughout Ukraine, walls are frequently covered with kylyms, but they are rarely used as floor coverings.

*Rushnyky* (Рушники), literally meaning "towels," are about 3 to 8 inches wide and 3 to 12 feet long, with geometric or floral patterns primarily near the ends. Traditionally, the *rushnyk* was used in various folk rituals and religious celebrations. It played a role in every milestone of human life, from birth to death. You can find rushnyky hanging on walls in many homes, particularly in rural areas, where they're draped over icons or favorite paintings. Intricately embroidered ones are used in wedding ceremonies. Factories throughout Ukraine produce both kylyms and rushnyky.

**Embroidery** (вишивка, VIH-shiv-kah), the most popular Ukrainian folk art, reveals a variety and complexity of stitches, wealth of colors, and intricacy of designs. In traditional culture, all household linens and items of folk dress, both female and male, were elaborately embroidered. There were special patterns for special occasions. Today virtually every family has an expert embroiderer. The most common embroidered items are towels, blouses, and shirts. The towels are used for accenting furniture or — stitched with religious motifs — as the cover for the ritual basket of food taken to church for the Easter blessing. The sign of skilled embroidery is a reverse side as neat and finished as the front.

**Pottery** (кераміка, keh-RAHM-ee-kah) production is widespread in Ukraine because of the large deposits of various clays, particularly kaolin (china clay). Ceramic arts date back to prehistoric times. The elegant forms and polychrome designs of the clay artifacts of the Trypillian culture (5000 to 4000 BCE) indicate a high level of sophistication in the process of clay preparation, firing, and decoration. Later ceramics showed complicated geometric designs and were formed in the figures of birds and animals. The introduction of the potter's wheel after the Mongol period changed the craft. With the development of the stove in the 18th century, all ceramic-producing centers in Ukraine began to produce enameled tiles. Today ceramic centers turn out much functional ceramic ware – pitchers, plates, candle holders, and tiles, and also some ornamental sculpture and toys.

**Pysanky** (писанки, PIH-sahn-kih), Easter eggs colored with intricate traditional symbolic designs, are perhaps the most widely known items of Ukrainian culture. The name *pysanky* comes from the verb *pysaty,* meaning "to write," because the designs are written on the shell of a whole raw egg with melted beeswax. A batik technique is used: The egg is dipped in a series of dye baths, ranging from the lightest color to the darkest, with wax designs applied by means of a fine-pointed stylus following each bath. After hours of work, the wax is removed from the completed egg.

Pysanky have been traced back to prehistoric times, when eggs had a ritual significance. The yolk represented the sun, a pagan god, and eggs were believed to possess magic power to protect against evil, thunder, or fire. Under Christianity, the eggs also became objects of good fortune that could bring luck, wealth, health, fertility, good harvest, and protection from harm. As soon as the cock crowed on Ash Wednesday, women and girls rushed to the barns to collect the eggs. They then spent the 40 days of Lent creating the designs. On Easter morning they brought the pysanky along with ritual food to church to blessed, but these special eggs were not for eating. The best were given to potential suitors as a not-so-subtle invitation to courtship.

Authentic pysanky incorporate traditional symbols that have evolved over millennia. The earliest designs were sun motifs; the meander, or endless line that represents eternity, comes from the Neolithic era. With Christianity came crosses and miniature churches combined with decorative geometrical designs. Animal motifs originated much later. Colors also have meaning. Each region, even each village, has its own designs and pigments.

The symbols, designs, and colors used in pysanky are repeated in other forms of Ukrainian art.In gift shops you'll find a variety of wood-crafted pysanky – lacquered, carved, or inlaid – and with luck you should come across some real ones.

**Woodcarving** (художне різьблення, khoo-DOZH-neh RIHZ-blehn-nya). Ukrainian wood sculpture developed along with church architecture, resulting in elaborate icon stands, lecterns, and columns. At the same time, the common people began decorating the interior and exterior of their homes with carved and ornamented details. The Hutsul region in western Ukraine, with its forest resources, is the major woodcarving center in Ukraine. Hutsul work is characterized by geometric designs ornamented with inlays of colored wood, bone, mother-of-pearl, beads, and metal work. Carved boxes — both rectangular and round — and plates are the most popular examples. Candle-holders, spoon racks, pipes, and the *bulava,* or hetman's mace, are also typical Hutsul woodcrafts. When pricing inlaid woodcrafts, notice how much of the ornamentation is actually inlaid compared to what is merely painted on the wood. Lemkos, an ethnic group along the Polish border, are noted for their woodcarvings of animal figures. North of Kyiv, in the Chernihiv area, wooden folk music instruments such as the *bandura,* are produced.

In addition to traditional crafts, signed artwork is widely available. Landscape and still life paintings and pottery and ceramic works are the most common. When buying directly from the artisan, bargaining is possible, but don't expect greater than a twenty percent reduction of the original asking price.

Would you please show me ...?
    Прошу мені показати ...?
    PRO-shoo meh-NEE po-kah-ZAH-tih

| this [*pointing*] | це | tseh |
|---|---|---|
| that bandura | ту бандуру | too bahn-DOO-roo |
| that blouse | ту блузку | too BLOOZ-koo |
| that embroidery | ту вишивку | too VIH-shihv-koo |
| that picture | ту картину | too kahr-TIH-noo |
| that plate | ту тарілку | too tah-REEL-koo |
| that scarf | той шаль | toў shahl' |
| that sculpture | ту скульптуру | too skool'p-TOO-roo |
| that shirt | ту сорочку | too so-ROCH-koo |

Can you show me those ...?
    Прошу мені показати ті ...?
    PRO-shoo meh-NEE po-kah-ZAH-tih tee

| painted eggs | писанки | PIH-sahn-kih |
|---|---|---|
| dolls | ляльки | LYAL'-kih |
| glassware | шкляні вироби | shklya-NEE VIH-ro-bih |

| jewelry | ювелірні вироби |
|---------|----------------|
|         | yu-veh-LEER-nee VIH-ro-bih |

Do you have …? Чи є у вас …? chih yeh oo vahs

| amber | яантар | yahn-TAHR |
|-------|--------|-----------|
| chess sets | шахи | SHAH-khih |
| icons | ікони | ee-KO-nih |
| musical | музичні інструменти | |
| instruments | moo-ZIHCH-nee eens-stroo-MEHN-tih | |
| pottery | кераміка | keh-RAH-mee-kah |
| wooden boxes | дерев'яні скриньки | |
|  | deh-reh-V'YA-nee SKRIHN'-kih | |
| wood crafts | різьба по дереву | |
|  | REEZ'-bah po DEH-reh-voo | |

Can I take this out of the country?
Чи можна це вивозити закордон?
chih MOZH-nah tseh vih-VO-zih-tih zah-kor-DOHN

Would you please wrap it for me?
Чи ви це можете загорнути?
chih vih tseh MO-zheh-teh zah-hor-NOO-tih

**Books and Stationery**     Книжки та Канцелярія
                             KNIHZH-kih tah kahn-tseh-LYA-ree-ya

Among the best tourist buys are the wonderfully inexpensive books, postcards, and posters of Ukrainian history, art, and culture.

I want a book about …
Я хочу книжку про …
ya KHO-choo KNIHZH-koo pro

| Kyiv | Київ | KIH-yeev |
|------|------|----------|
| this city | це місто | tseh MEES-to |
| Ukrainian art | українське мистецтво | |
|  | oo-krah-YEENS'-keh mihs-TEHTST-vo | |
| Ukrainian folklore | Український фолькльор | |
|  | oo-krah-YEENS'-kihў fol'k-L'OR | |
| Ukrainian history | Історію України | |
|  | ees-TO-ree-yu oo-krah-YEE-nih | |

| I want … | Я хочу … | ya KHO-choo |
|---|---|---|
| a calendar | календар | kah-lehn-DAHR |
| a city map | план міста | plahn MEES-tah |
| that poster | той плакат | toỹ plah-KAHT |

| Where are the …? | Де …? | deh |
|---|---|---|
| dictionaries | словники | slov-NIH-kih |
| maps | географічні карти | he-ho-hrah-FEECH-nee KAHR-tih |
| colored postcards | поштові листівки | posh-TO-vee lihs-TEEV-kih |

**Recorded Music** Музичний Записи
  moo-ZIHCH-nihỹ

If you don't know what kind of Ukrainian music you like, you'll usually be allowed to listen to sample cassettes and CDs before you make a purchase.

| I'm looking for … | Я шукаю … | ya shoo-KAH-yu |
|---|---|---|
| records … | пластинки … | plahs-TIHN-kih |
| cassettes … | записи … | ZAH-pih-sih |
| CDs … | компакт диски … | KOM-pahkt DIHS-kih |
| of classical music | класичної музики | klah-SIHCH-no-yee MOO-zih-kih |
| of folk music | народної музики | nah-ROD-no-yee MOO-zih-kih |
| of jazz | джазу | DZHAH-zoo |
| of pop music | поп-музики | pop MOO-zih-kih |

May I listen to this record?
  Чи я можу прослухати цей запис?
  chih ya MO-zhoo pro-SLOO-kha-tih tsehỹ ZAH-pihs

Do you have any videos about …
  Чи у вас відео про …
  chih oo vahs VEE-deh-o pro

# CHAPTER 20.
# WORK AND STUDY

Ukrainian Proverb:
Робота не вовк, в ліс не втече.
ro-BO-tah neh vovk v lees neh vteh-CHEH
*Work isn't a wolf; it won't run away into the forest.*

Even though Ukrainians joke about having to go to work, they have a reputation of being among the most industrious and diligent people of Europe. The labor force consists of about 22.8 million workers, less than half of the population. About 32 percent are employed in industry and construction; 24 percent in agriculture and forestry; and 44 percent in services, including health, education, trade. An eight-hour shift, Monday through Friday, is the standard work day with a lunch break between 1 and 2 p.m. The official retirement age is 56 for women and 60 for men. Economic restructuring following independence has led to deteriorating labor conditions, a decline in production, and a high incidence of unemployment.

*Note: In phrases containing the pronoun "you", the familiar, singular form is first, followed by the polite or plural form.*

Where do you work?
Де (ти працюєш, *s.*) (ви працюєте, *pl.*)?
deh (tih prah-TSYU-yehsh) (vih prah-TSYU-yeh-teh)

Do you like your job?
(Ти любиш, *s.*) (ви любите, *pl.*) свою роботу?
(tih LYU-bihsh) (vih LYU-bih-teh) svo-YU ro-BO-too

How much do you earn per month?
Скільки (ти заробляєш, *s.*) (ви заробляєте, *pl.*) в місяць?
SKEEL'-kih (tih zah-ro-BLYA-yehsh) (vih zah-ro-BLYA-yeh-teh) v MEE-syats'

**Occupations**

What is your occupation?
Яка (твоя, *s.*) (ваша, *pl.*) професія?
ya-KA (tvo-YA) (VAH-shah) pro-FE-see-ya

| I'm (a) an … | Я … | ya |
|---|---|---|
| actor | актор | ahk-TOR |
| agronomist | агроном | ah-hro-NOM |
| artist | митець | mih-TEHTS' |
| auto mechanic | автомеханік | AHV-to-meh-KHA-neek |
| baker | пекар | PEH-kahr |
| bank teller | банківський працівник | |
| | BAHN-keev-s'kihў prah-tseev-NIHK | |
| beekeeper | бджільник | bdzheel'-NIHK |
| bookkeeper | бухгалтер | bookh-HAHL-tehr |
| bricklayer | муляр | MOO-lyar |
| bus driver | водій автобуса | vo-DEEЎ av-TO-boo-sah |
| businessman | бізнесмен (*m.* or *f.*) | beez-nehs-MEHN |
| carpenter | тесля | TEHS-lya |
| childcare worker | вихователь | vih-kho-VAH-tehl' |
| computer operator | оператор комп'ютера | |
| | o-peh-RAH-tor kom-P'YU-teh-rah | |
| construction worker | робітник-будівельник | |
| | ro-beet-NIHK-boo-dee-VEHL'-nihk | |
| cook | кухар | KOO-khahr |
| dentist | зубний лікар | zoob-NIHЎ LEE-kahr |
| doctor | лікар | LEE-kahr |
| economist | економіст | eh-ko-no-MEEST |
| electrician | електрик | eh-LEHKT-rihk |
| engineer | інженер | een-zheh-NEHR |
| factory worker | робітник на заводі | |
| | ro-beet-NIHK nah zah-VO-dee | |
| farmer | фермер | FEHR-mehr |
| firefighter | пожежник | po-ZHEHZH-nihk |
| journalist | журналіст | zhoor-nah-LEEST |
| lawyer | адвокат | ahd-vo-KAHT |
| librarian | бібліотекер | beeb-lee-o-TEH-kahr |
| mailman | поштар | posh-TAHR |
| manager | менеджер | MEH-neh-zhehr |
| mechanic | механік | meh-KHAH-neek |
| merchant | продавець | pro-dah-VEHTS' |
| miner | шахтар | shahkh-TAHR |
| musician | музикант | moo-zih-KAHNT |
| nurse | медсестра | med-sehst-RAH |
| office worker | служабовець | sloo-zhah-BO-vehts' |

| | | |
|---|---|---|
| pharmacist | фармацевт | fahr-mah-TSEHVT |
| plumber | сантехнік | sahn-TEHKH-neek |
| police officer | міліціонер | mee-lee-tsee-o-NEHR |
| postal worker | поштар | posh-TAHR |
| professor | професор | pro-FEH-sor |
| programmer | програміст | pro-hrah-MEEST |
| retiree | пенсіонер | pehn-see-oh-NEHR |
| salesclerk | продавець | pro-dah-VEHTS' |
| scientist | вчений | VCHEH-nihỹ |
| stonecutter | каменяр | kah-meh-NYAR |
| student | студент | stoo-DEHNT |
| tailor | кравець | krah-VEHTS' |
| teacher | вчитель | VCHIH-tehl' |
| technician | технік | TEHKH-neek |
| truck driver | шофер | sho-FEHR |
| waitperson | офіціант | o-fee-tsee-AHNT |
| writer | письменник | pihs'-MEHN-nihk |

**Doing Business in Ukraine.** In a country where until recently capitalism was synonymous with evil, Ukrainians are still learning the ethics of doing business. Aspects of a free market economy that we might take for granted – the need to risk money, to commit time and talent on long-term projects that may bring little return, to enter associations requiring trust and cooperation with virtual strangers – are relatively new ideas to a labor force that's not accustomed to a climate of free enterprise.

Western firms are attracted by the low cost of production, a skilled and highly education labor market, and new markets for their product. A market exists in Ukraine, for example, for such consumer goods as soaps and cleansers, footwear, processed foods, furniture, and household appliances. In the first ten years following independence, foreign investments have totaled US$1.6 billion, mostly in the food industry, machine building, and the financial sector. Ukraine would like to attract US$1 billion annually.

Investment experts, however, point to the obstacles of setting up a business in Ukraine: an economy still not entirely privatized with a government that shows little enthusiasm for a market economy or reforms; constantly changing tax laws and government decrees; government corruption and organized crime. Experts advise investors to be prepared to risk capital, be flexible in their way of doing things, and not to expect to make a quick profit but to regard a venture as a long-term enterprise and give it at least five years.

Be careful with whom you get involved. Those who may want to be your associates may lack the experience or know-how to provide meaningful help. Especially avoid government bureaucrats in your dealings: at best they are ignorant of the requirements of a successful enterprise; but more likely, they're out to get a piece of the profits. On the other hand, it's difficult to set up a business without an insider who's thoroughly familiar with the bureaucratic maze.

There are, of course, many competent and reliable potential business partners in Ukraine. Don't make the mistake of underestimating Ukrainian business acumen. Ukrainians are sharp traders and can sense a good opportunity. Expect to solidify the business relationship over a lavish dinner with ceremonial undertones, during which many toasts are made to a successful partnership.

| My name is … | Моє ім'я … | mo-YEH EEM'-ya |
| I'm here on business. | Я тут по справах. | ya toot po SPRAH-vahkh |
| I represent … company. | Я представляю компанію … | ya prehd-stahv-LYA-yu kom-PAH-nee-yu |
| I have my own business. | Я маю свій бізнес. | ya MAH-yu sveeў BEES-nehs |
| Here's my card. | Ось моя візитка. | os' mo-YA vee-ZIHT-kah |
| May I introduce … | Я хочу представити … | ya KHO-choo prehd-STAH-vih-tih |

We are looking for partners in Ukraine.
Ми шукаємо партнерів на Україні.
mih shoo-KAH-yeh-mo pahrt-NEH-reev nah oo-krah-YEE-nee

What's the current rate of inflation?
Яка тепер інфляція?
ya-KAH teh-PEHR een-FLYA-tsee-ya

Can you estimate the cost?
Чи ви можете оцінити вартість?
chih vih MO-zheh-teh o-tsee-NIH-tih VAHR-teest'

I look forward to doing business together.
Я сподіваюсь, що ми можемо співпрацювати.
ya spo-dee-VAH-yus' shcho mih MO-zheh-mo speev-prah-tsyu-VAH-tih

## Business Vocabulary

| | | |
|---|---|---|
| account | рахунок | rah-KHOO-nok |
| accountant | бухгалтер | bookh-HAHL-tehr |
| to advertise | рекламувати | rehk-lah-moo-VAH-tih |
| advertisement | реклама | rehk-LAH-mah |
| agribusiness | агробізнес | ah-hro-BEEZ-nehs |
| agriculture | сільське господарство | |
| | seel'-S'KEH hos-po-DAHRST-vo | |
| bankruptcy | банкрутство | bahnk-ROOTST-vo |
| to bargain | торгу-ватись | tor-hoo-VAH-tihs' |
| to bid | виступати з пропозицією | |
| | vihs-too-PAH-tih z pro-po-ZIH-tsee-yeh-yu | |
| bill | рахунок | rah-KHOO-nok |
| black market | чорний ринок | CHOR-nihў RIH-nok |
| board of directors | рада директорів | |
| | RAH-dah dih-rehk-to-REEV | |
| broker | брокер | BRO-kehr |
| businessman | бізнесмен | beez-nehs-MEHN |
| buyer | покупець | po-koo-PEHTS' |
| capital | капітал | kah-pee-TAHL' |
| cash | наявні гроші | nah-YAV-nee HRO-shee |
| cash payment | плата готівкою | PLAH-tah ho-TEEV-ko-yu |
| collective farm | колективне господарство | |
| | ko-lehk-TIHV-neh hos-po-DAHRST-vo | |
| commission | комісійні | ko-mee-SEEЎ-nee |
| commodity market | товарна біржа | to-VAHR-nah BEER-zhah |
| consumer | споживач | spo-zhih-VAHCH |
| contract | контракт | kon-TRAHKT |
| to accept a contract | прийняти контракт | |
| | prihў-NYA-tih kon-TRAHKT | |
| to break a contract | перервати контракт | |
| | pehr-ehr-VAH-tih kon-TRAHKT | |
| cooperative enterprise | кооперативне підприємцтво | |
| | ko-o-peh-rah-TIHV-neh peed-prih-YEHMST-vo | |
| cost | вартість | VAHR-teest' |
| credit | кредит | kreh-DIHT |
| customer | клієнт | klee-YEHNT |
| debt | борг | borh |
| deposit | внесок | VNEH-sok |

| | | |
|---|---|---|
| discount | скидка | SKIHD-kah |
| down payment | аванс | ah-VAHNS |
| economy | економіка | eh-ko-NO-mee-kah |
| employer | наймач | nahў-MAHCH |
| employees | працівники | prah-tseev-nih-KIH |
| enterprise | підприємство | peed-prih-YEHMST-vo |
| expenses | витрати | VIHT-rah-tih |
| exports | експорт | EHKS-port |
| import | імпорт | EEM-port |
| income | дохід | do-KHEED |
| insurance | страхування | strah-khoo-VAHN-nya |
| insurance company | страхова компанія | |
| | strah-kho-VAH kom-PAH-nee-ya | |
| interest | проценти | pro-TSEHN-tih |
| investment | інвестування | een-vehs-too-VAHN-nya |
| joint venture | сумісне підприємство | |
| | soo-MEES-neh peed-prih-YEHMST-vo | |
| loss | втрати | VTRAH-tih |
| management | управління oop-rahv-LEEN-nya | |
| manager | менеджер | MEH-nehd-zhehr |
| market | ринок | RIH-nok |
| domestic market | внутрішній ринок | |
| | vnoot-REESH-neeў RIH-nok | |
| market economy | риночна економіка | |
| | RIH-noch-nah eh-ko-NO-mee-kah | |
| free market | вільний ринок | VEEL'-nihў RIH-nok |
| ownership | власність | VLAHS-neest' |
| land ownership | земляна власність | |
| | zehm-lya-NAH VLAHS-neest' | |
| payment | оплата | o-PLAH-tah |
| price | ціна | tsee-NAH |
| private ownership | приватна власність | |
| | prih-VAHT-nah VLAHS-neest' | |
| privatization | приватизація | prih-vah-tih-ZAH-tsee-ya |
| production | виробництво | vih-rob-NIHTST-vo |
| profits | прибутки | prih-BOOT-kih |
| rent | оренда | o-REHN-dah |
| revenue | дохід | do-KHEED |
| risk | ризик | RIH-zihk |
| salary | зарплата | zahr-PLAH-tah |

| stock market | біржа | BEER-z͡hah |
| tax | податок | po-DAH-tok |
| income tax | від прибутку | veed prih-BOOT-koo |
| property tax | податок на нерухомість | |
| | po-DAH-tok nah neh-roo-KHO-meest' | |

## At the Office     В Офісі     v O-fee-see

I have an appointment with ... at ... o'clock.
У мене ділова зустріч з ... в ... годині.
oo MEH-neh dee-lo-VAH ZOOST-reech z ... v ... ho-DIH-ee.

| Where can I ... | Де я можу ... | deh ya MO-z͡hoo |
| send a fax | відіслати факс | vee-dee-SLAH-tih fahks |
| make a photocopy | зробити копію | ZROBIH-tih KO-pee-yu |

Can I receive a fax here?
Чи я можу тут отримати факс?
chih ya MO-z͡hoo toot ot-RIH-MAH-tih fahks

Can you help me e-mail a message?
Чи ви можете мені допомогти послати електронну пошту?
chih vih MO-z͡heh-teh MEH-nee do-po-moh-TIH po-SLAH-tih
eh-lehk-TRON-noo POSH-too

Do you have access to the Internet?
Чи ви маєте вихід на Інтернет?
chih vih MAH-yeh-teh VIH-kheed nah een-tehr-NEHT

| agenda | розпорядок | roz-po-RYA-dok |
| answering machine | автовідповідач машина | |
| | ahv-to-veed-po-vee-DAHCH mah-SHIH-nah | |
| conference | конференція | kon-feh-REHN-tsee-ya |
| calculator | калькулятор | kahl'-koo-LYA-tor |
| computer | комп'ютер kom-P'YU-tehr | |
| computer software | програмне забезпечення | |
| | pro-HRAHM-neh zah-behz-PEH-chehn-nya | |
| copy machine | копіювальна машина | |
| | ko-pee-yu-VAHL'-nah mah-SHIH-nah. | |

(*The word* ксерокс *(khseroks), from Xerox, is commonly used for "copy machine."*)

| e-mail | електронна пошта | |
| | eh-lehk-TRON-nah POSH-tah | |

| computer mail | комп'ютерна пошта |
| | kom-P'YU-tehr-nah POSH-tah |

*(It's customary just to use the English term "e-mail.")*

| fax machine | факс машина | fahks mah-SHIH-nah |
| message | повідомлення | po-vee-DOM-lehn-nya |
| meeting | збори | ZBO-rih |
| office supplies | канцелярія | kahn-tseh-LYA-ree-ya |
| print (*noun*) | друк | drook |
| telephone | телефон | teh-leh-FON |
| typewriter | друкарська машинка | |
| | droo-KAHRS'-kah mah-SHIHN-kah | |

**Education.** Education in Ukraine is compulsory for ages 7 through 16. The first four grades are called elementary school (початкові класи, po-chah-KO-vee KLAH-sih). After eighth grade, a student chooses to either complete three more academic grades or to enter a two-year vocational school. Those completing 11th grade have several options for higher education. They can enter a technical college (технікум, TEKH-nee-koom) which is lower level than a university, or they can enroll in a special institute, on the same level as a university, but providing specialized training for a particular profession:

**Institutes of Higher Learning**

| agricultural institute | сільсько-господарський інститут |
| | SEEL'-s'-ko hos-po-DAHRS'-kihў eens-tih-TOOT |
| conservatory | консерваторія |
| | kon-sehr-vah-TO-ree-ya |
| construction | інженерно-будівельний інститут |
| engineering | een-zheh-NEHR-no boo-deev-VEHL'-nihў |
| institute | eens-tih-TOOT |
| fine arts institute | інститут прикладного мистецтва |
| | eens-tih-TOOT prih-klahd-NO-ho |
| | mihs-TEHTS-tvah |
| forestry institute | лісо-технічний інститут |
| | lee-so-tehkh-NEECH-nihў eens-tih-TOOT |
| medical institute | медичний інститут |
| | meh-DIHCH-nihў eens-tih-TOOT |
| pedagogical institute | педагогічний інститут |
| | peh-dah-ho-HEECH-nihў eens-tih-TOOT |

polygraphic (printing) поліграфічний інститут
   institute            po-lee-hrah-FEECH-nihy̆ eens-tih-TOOT
polytechnical institute політехнічний інститут
                        po-lee-tehk-NEECH-nihy̆ eens-tih-TOOT
(*Many are now called "university," but haven't changed their programs.*)
veterinary institute      зоо-ветеринарний інститут
                        ZO-O-veh-teh-rih-NAHR-nihy̆ eens-tih-TOOT

**University Study.** A third option for higher education is to pass an admissions test for a university (університет, oo-nee-vehr-sih-TEHT). Though the university system is becoming similar to the Western pattern, the bulk of Ukrainian university study follows the pattern dating back to Soviet times in which the five-to-six-year period of study has no formally defined gradation between the undergraduate and graduate level, and there's no equivalent to the BA. The university contains departments or *fakultety* (Факультети, fah-kool'-TEH-tih) ranging from a few hundred to a few thousand students. Each *fakultet* is divided into several divisions or branches called *kafedry* (кафедри, kah-FEHD-rih), headed by research professors and containing labs. The head of a fakultet is a *dekan* (декан, deh-KAHN) and his office is called the *dekanat* (деканат, deh-kah-NAHT). Each fakultet has a set curriculum, with no elective course choices. After three years of study, a student is assigned to a certain *kafedra* which defines his or her specialty. After completion of the standardized courses, a student undertakes an individual project and writes and defends his or her "diploma work" (дипломна робота, dih-PLOM-nah ro-BO-tah) to receive a degree that is comparable to a Master's degree. At this stage, the student earns an occupational title, such as engineer or medical doctor, and enjoys full status in his or her chosen profession.

    A student who wants to go on to perform scientific research, becomes an *aspirant* (аспірант, ahs-pee-RAHNT), that is, an applicant to a rigorous competition for admission to a 3-year period of study and research that leads to a PhD. Upon successful completion of this program, the student receives the equivalent of a PhD degree and is called a candidate of science (кандидат наук, kahn-dih-DAHT nah-OOK). Candidates may apply for the position of *docent* (доцент, do-TSEHNT), which allows them to teach at the university level. There is a much higher degree, Doctor of Science, which requires a PhD plus an additional dissertation of much higher scientific value. A Doctor of Science who teaches at a university is called a Professor.

Universities perform both teaching and research although approximately 70 to 80 percent of research is concentrated in special research institutes which are under the academies of science. There are three academies of science: Academy of Science, Academy of Medical Science, and Academy of Pedagogical Science. Here are some of the major departments or fakultety in Ukrainian educational institutions. Because the educational system is highly specialized, these concentrations are offered only at their specific institutions.

| | | |
|---|---|---|
| applied math | прикладної математики | |
| | prih-klahd-NO-yee | mah-teh-MAH-tih-kih |
| architecture | архітектурний | ahr-khee-teh-TOOR-nihў |
| biology | біологічний | bee-o-lo-HEECH-nihў |
| building construction | будівельний | boo-dee-VEHL'-nihў |
| chemistry | хімічний | khee-MEECH-nihў |
| dentistry | стоматологічний | sto-mah-to-lo-HEECH-nihў |
| electronics | електроніки | eh-lehk-TRON-nee-kih |
| folk art | народного мистецтва | |
| | nah-ROD-no-ho | mihs-TEHTST-vah |
| foreign language | іноземних мов | ee-no-ZEHM-nikh  mov |
| geophysics | геофізичний | heh-o-fee-ZIHCH-nihў |
| history | історичний | ees-to-RIHCH-nihў |
| instrumental music | інструментальної музики | |
| | eens-troo-mehn-TAHL'-no-yee | MOO-zih-kih |
| literature | літературний | lee-tehr-rah-TOOR-nihў |
| machinery | машинобудування | |
|   construction | mah-shih-no-boo-doo-VAHN-nya | |
| mathematics | математичний | mah-teh-mah-TIHCH-nihў |
| painting | живопису | zhih-VO-pih-soo |
| pediatrics | педіатричний | peh-dee-ah-TRIHCH-nihў |
| physics | фізичний | fee-ZIHCH-nihў |
| sculpture | скульптури | skool'p-TOO-rih |
| surgery | хірургічний | khee-roor-HEECH-nihў |
| technology | технологічний | tekh-no-lo-HEECH-nihў |
| vocal music | вокальний | vo-KAHL'-nihў |

The student-faculty relationship in Ukraine follows the European pattern in which the student does not question the authority of the professor. Private colleges, however, are adapting western educational practices that were formerly appalling to Ukrainians, such as filling out evaluation forms rating professors. In western Ukraine, the proper way to address a teacher is by the equivalent of Mr. or Mrs. followed by the first name, for example, "Good Morning, Pani Iryna. In central and eastern parts of the country, the teacher is addressed by her title and surname, "Good Morning, Professor Melnyk."

Where are you studying?    Де ви вчитесь?
deh vih vchih-TEHS'

I'm a student of ... University.
Я є (студент, *m*.) (студентка, *f*.) ... університету.
ya yeh (stoo-DEHNT) (stoo-DEHNT-kah) ...
oo-nee-vehr-sih-TEH-too

In which department are you?    На якому ви факультеті?
nah ya-KO-moo vih fah-kool'-TEH-tee

I'm in the physics department.
Я на фізичному факультеті.
ya nah fee-ZIHCH-no-moo fah-kool'-TEH-tee

In which division are you?    На якій ви кафедрі?
nah ya-KEEY vih KAH-fehd-ree

I'm in ... division.    Я на кафедрі ...
ya nah KAH-fehd-ree

My field is ...    Моя галузь ...
mo-YA GAH-looz' ...

What will your major be?
Яка буде ваша спеціальність?
ya-KAH BOO-deh VAH-shah speh-tsee-AHL'-neest'

I'm majoring in ...    Я спеціалізуюсь в області ...
ya speh-tsee-ah-lee-ZOO-yus' v O-blahs-tee

What year are you?    На якому ви курсі?
nah ya-KO-moo vih KOOR-see

I'm a [*use ordinal number, see p.380*] year student.
Я (студент, *m*.) (студентка, *f*.) третього ... курсу.
ya (stoo-DEHNT) (stoo-DEHNT-kah) TREHT'-o-ho ... KOOR-soo

I'm here on an exchange program.
Я тут по-обміну.
ya toot po-OB-mee-noo

The program is between [*name institutes*].
Ця програма між …
tsya pro-HRAH-mah meezh
I'll be here … (weeks) (months) (years).
Я буду тут … (тижднів) (місяців) (років).
ya BOO-doo toot …(TIHZHD-neev) (MEES-ya-tseev)
(RO-keev).

| I'll be teaching … | Я буду викладати … |  |
|---|---|---|
|  | ya BOO-doo vih-klah-DAH-tih |  |
| agribusiness | агробізнес | ah-hro-BEEZ-nehs |
| business | бізнес | BEEZ-nehs |
| economics | економіку | eh-ko-NO-mee-koo |
| English | англійську мову | ahn-HLEEЎS'-koo MO-voo |
| I live in the dorm. | Я живу в гуртожитку. |  |
|  | ya zhih-VOO v hoor-TO-zhiht-koo |  |

**New Models of Education.** Under the Soviet system, higher education was free for qualified students. While scientific and technological education was among the finest in the world, the social sciences suffered from lack of the method of free inquiry, and dependence on rote memorization stifled the development of critical thinking. Since independence, several private liberal arts institutions, not under the control of the Ministry of Education, have opened. These attempt to offer a well-rounded education, rather than a narrow specialization, and to produce independent thinkers. Also, these newer schools do not tolerate academic misconduct, such as cheating, plagiarism, and bribes. The first private liberal arts university in Ukraine was the National University of Kyiv-Mohyla Academy (NaUKMA), which opened in 1992 in Kyiv's historic Podil section. Located on the site of a prestigious 17th century liberal arts university which was closed more than 175 years ago by Tsar Alexander III who found its humanistic teachings threatening, NaUKMA is modeled after Western-style universities. It offers a four-year bachelor's and a two-year master's program, as well as doctoral programs. Concentrations are in liberal arts, economics, sociology, social work, law, business, information technologies, and natural science. Official languages of instruction are Ukrainian and English. The university has exchanges with more than 50 universities worldwide.

The Kyiv-Mohyla Academy uses an anonymous testing system to ensure that students are selected on merit. The school is growing rapidly, with 4,000 applicants each year and a student body of more than 2,200. The

National University of Ostroh Academy in the Rivne oblast, a former affiliate of Kyiv-Mohyla Academy, is an independent semiprivate university that offers degrees in law, linguistics, history, and cultural studies. Also recently established is the first Jewish institution of higher learning in the entire thousand-year history of Jewry in Ukraine. The International Solomon University in Kyiv attempts to revive Jewish culture and education in Ukraine. Among its departments are history and philosophy, biology, economics and sociology. Admission is open to all faiths. The Ukrainian Catholic University in Lviv (www.lta.lviv.ua), originally founded in 1929, was closed by the Soviets in 1946, and reopened in 1994. As the major educational institution of the Ukrainian Greek Catholic Church, it offers a strong concentration in theology, with philosophy, history, arts, and classic and modern languages. Catholic University emphasizes scholarly research, professional preparation, the formation of spiritual and social values, and personal responsibility. It has more than 900 students and 105 faculty members. While these private institutions are far more expensive than the public universities, like Western universities, they award scholarships and financial aid.

### Education Vocabulary

| | | |
|---|---|---|
| courses of study | предмети | prehd-MEH-tih |
| exams | екзамени | ehk-ZAH-meh-nih |
| higher education | вища освіта | VIH-shcha os-VEE-tah |
| humanities | гуманітарні науки | |
| | hoo-mah-nee-TAHR-nee nah-OO-kih | |
| Ph.D. thesis | кандидатська диссертація | |
| | kahn-dih-DAHTS'-kah dihs-sehr-TAH-tsee-ya | |
| preliminary exams | кандидатський мінімум | |
| | kahn-dih-DAHTS'-kihў MEE-nee-moom | |
| professor | професор | pro-FEHS-sor |
| semester | семестр | seh-MEHSTR |
| state-paid education | державне навчання | |
| | dehr-ZHAHV-neh nahv-CHAHN-nya | |
| student-paid education | платне навчання | |
| | PLAHT-neh nahv-CHAHN-nya | |
| student | студент | stoo-DEHNT |
| university head | ректор | REHK-tor |

*Under the traditional system of education*:

| undergraduate student | студент початкових курсів | stoo-DEHNT po-chaht-KO-vihkh KOOR-seev |
| graduate student | аспірант | ahs-pee-RAHNT |

*Under the newer educational system*:

| bachelor's degree student | студент бакалавр | stoo-DEHNT bah- `kah-LAHVR |
| specialist | спеціаліст | speh-tsee-ah-LEEST |

(intermediate degree between bachelor's and master's)

| master's student | студент магістр | stoo-DEHNT mah-GEESTR |
| PhD student | докторант | dok-to-RAHNT |

**The Campus.** The main campus is likely to be in the city center, with newer additions, such as sports facilities, on the outskirts of the city. Dormitories offer less comfort and fewer amenities than American students are accustomed to. Typically only special category students, such as athletes and those on special diets, choose to use the cafeteria. The majority of students can't afford the cafeteria and cook their own meals in the kitchens on each floor. Foreign exchange students are usually housed in the more comfortable married student dorms, with cooking facilities in individual rooms. They often buy provisions at open markets. Smoking is not permitted anywhere on university property − inside the buildings or on campus.

| Where is the …? | Де …? | deh |
| administration building | головний корпус | ho-lov-NIHЎ KOR-poos |
| cafeteria | їдальня, кафе | yee-DAHL'-nya, kah-FEH |
| gymnasium | спортивний корпус | por-TIHV-nihyў KOR-poos |
| lecture hall | аудиторія | ahoo-DIH-to-ree-ya |
| married students dorm | гуртожиток для сімейних | hoor-TO-zhih-tok dlya see-MEЎ-nihkh |

# CHAPTER 21.
# RELIGION IN UKRAINE

Ukrainian Proverb:  Як тривога, то до Бога.
yak trih-VO-hah to do BO-hah
*When in trouble, then you'll turn to God.*

## Religious Life

In 1988 Ukraine commemorated the millennium of the conversion of ancient Kyiv to Byzantium Christianity under its ruler Volodymyr the Great. No less noteworthy was the return – following Ukrainian independence – of the churches to their historic Ukrainian hierarchies, which had been outlawed under communism and replaced by the Russian Orthodox Church. The reemergence of traditional religions saw the construction of new churches, refurbishing of decrepit ones, and the reopening of monasteries and seminaries. Other forms of religious expression, such as catechism classes for children and adults, were revived.

Three-quarters of Ukrainians profess the Orthodox faith, but they're split among three churches. Two of the Orthodox churches, the Kyiv Patriarchate and the Autocephalous Ukrainian church are indigenous to Ukraine, while the Moscow Patriarchate is under the Russian Orthodox Church. Because of the unsettled religious climate, the ecumenical patriarch of Constantinople, the "first among equals" of Orthodox hierarchs, recognizes the Moscow Patriarchate. The two other Ukrainian Orthodox churches regard it as an extension of Russian interests in Ukraine. Many of the faithful are not aware of the procedural differences or are unconcerned with the politics and distrust among the various churches, while the leaders dream of the eventual resolution of these differences and a union of all Ukrainian Orthodox.

The Ukrainian Greek-Catholic Church (UGCC) emerged from the underground where it had survived since it was outlawed in 1946. Sometimes called the Ukrainian Catholic Church, this church gives allegiance to the Vatican but uses the Byzantine style of worship. An uninformed Westerner probably can't distinguish – either architecturally or liturgically – a Greek-Catholic from an Orthodox church. UGCC faithful constitute about 13 percent of the population and live primarily in the western oblasts of Ternopilska, Ivano-Frankivska, and Lvivska, The seat of the UGCC has been in Lviv for several hundred years, but is moving to Kyiv.

About a million Roman Catholics worship in 200 parishes, primarily in west Ukraine, where many Poles and Hungarians live. Other significant Christian denominations include Baptists, Pentecostals, Seventh Day Adventists, Lutherans, Reformed, and Jehovah's Witnesses. With an estimated Jewish population of 400,000 to 600,000, there's a resurgence of Jewish life and culture throughout the country. Ukraine has more than 250 Jewish organizations and many operating schools and synagogues. Muslim mosques and Islamic schools are active in Crimea. There are even Buddhists and animists in Ukraine, although they have no organized expression. In fact, there's an estimated 80 different faiths and over 22,000 religious communities in Ukraine.

The number of existing churches is not adequate to satisfy the claims for them. Sadly, there have been struggles – some physical – among the traditional denominations for the possession of church property. Evangelical Christians, who function without elaborate church buildings, are making great inroads. Many who find the rituals of the traditional churches incomprehensible are flocking to these churches that preach the Bible and emphasize a more personal relationship with God. The Ukrainian government has not discouraged proselytizing, and has allowed all religious groups to operate openly and freely.

## Church Architecture

As early as the 9th century, Christian churches existed in the Kyivan-Rus territories. Constructed of wood, often covered with shingles, these first churches were small in size and built according to a tripartite plan, with the nave (нава, NAH-vah), or the central part or assembly, flanked on the west by a vestibule (притвор, PRIHT-vor) and to the east by the sanctuary (святилище, svya-tih-LIH-shcheh). Often the central nave area stood taller than the adjoining sections. The segments were capped with domed cupolas.

As church architecture became more sophisticated, five-frame, seven-frame, and even nine-frame churches were built. The layout was always in the form of a cross, with the central nave surrounded by side chapels. There are many wooden churches in Ukraine; the oldest preserved churches, dating from the 16th and 17th centuries, are in the Carpathians. Stone churches date back to the beginning of the 11th century, especially in Kyiv and Chernihiv to the north. Their style also followed the Byzantine cross structure. The practice of building freestanding bell towers carried over from wooden church construction.

Eventually, a national style of church architecture developed in Ukraine. Churches built or rebuilt between approximately 1650 and 1750 were designed in the style known as Ukrainian Baroque, a fusion of the Byzantine-cross church with the Western European baroque basilica. According to the Ukrainian Baroque style, the cupola evolved from a bud to a pear shape and the inner space expanded upward from the floor to the cupola. The facades were embellished with colorful glazed ceramic rosettes and inserts, while the window and door lintels were embellished with fanciful stucco moldings incorporating vegetable and floral motifs.

Ukrainian church interiors are splendidly decorated with mosaics, murals, and icons. The highlight of the interior design is the icon stand or iconostasis (іконостас, ee-ko-no-STAHS), a large screen or partition that separates the sanctuary from the body or nave of the church. It contains several doors that serve as the entrance and exit for the priest.The iconostasis may be composed of as many as six tiers of icons whose purpose is to instruct the faithful in the tenets of their faith by depicting Christ, the Virgin, John the Baptist, and other saints and prophets.

Where is the cathedral?   Де собор?
                          deh so-BOR

What's the name of this church?
   Як називається ця церква?
   yak nah-zih-VAH-yeht'-sya tsya TSEHRK-vah

What denomination is it?
   До якої церкви він належить?
   do ya-KO-yee TSEHRK-vih veen nah-LEH-zhiht'

When was it built?   Коли він був побудований?
                     ko-LIH veen boov po-boo-DO-vah-nIHЙ

Is it all right to look inside?
   Чи можна зайти в середину?
   chih MOZH-nah zahй-TIH v seh-reh-DIH-noo

Is it all right to take a picture?
   Чи можна тут фотографувати?
   chih MOZH-nah toot fo-to-hrah-foo-VAH-tih

**The Monastery**   монастир   mo-nahs-TIHR

A monastery is a community of monks or nuns that includes an ensemble of buildings – churches, a seminary, dormitories and a refectory. Historically monasteries were important centers of religious, educational, scholarly, cultural, and artistic life. A *lavra* (лавра, LAHV-rah) is a large and important monastery under the direct jurisdiction of the patriarch. Two Orthodox monasteries in Ukraine have *lavra* status, the Pecherska Lavra in Kyiv and the Pochayivska Lavra in the Ternopil region, both under the Russian Orthodox Church.

May I see the (monastery) (lavra)?
Чи я можу подивитись (монастир) (лавру)?
chih ya MO-zhoo po-dih-VIH-tihs' (mo-nahs-TIHR) (LAHV-roo)

How old is this monastery?
Скільки років цьому монастирю?
SKEEL'-kih RO-keev TS'O-moo mo-nahs-tih-RYU

| | | |
|---|---|---|
| monks | монахи | mo-NAH-khih |
| nuns | монашки | mo-NAHSH-kih |

**Attending a Service.** Visitors are not only welcome at church services, it's common for the worshipers to step aside and urge a foreigner to the front, no matter how crowded the church. Orthodox and Greek-Catholic liturgies can be of marathon length by Western standards, so you needn't feel uncomfortable arriving late or leaving before the conclusion so long as you aren't disruptive.

Participants stand throughout the service as there are no pews or kneelers. Chairs provided for the elderly or infirm may ring the sides of the church. The lack of seating allows the worshipers mobility. Rather than appearing to follow the actions of the priest, many move about to visit icons during the service. Don't be fooled by this apparently casual behavior: worshipers are attentive and deeply respectful, even those who may have to stand outside and listen to the service over the loudspeakers.

Instrumental music is never used in traditional churches. There is, however, a rich tradition of choral liturgical music in Ukraine. The choirs are magnificent and you shouldn't hesitate if given the chance to attend a choir service. Ukrainian is the language of the service and the choir in the Ukrainian Orthodox and Ukrainian Catholic churches, while the Moscow branch Orthodox church uses the Russian language. It's customary for women to wear skirts and cover their heads during a church service; however only in the *lavra* churches are dresses mandatory, and shorts on men are forbidden. While discreetly taking photographs during a service is acceptable, it would be bad manners to distract the priest or worshipers with a flash.

Where's the nearest ...?
Де найближча ...?
deh nahў-BLIHZH-chah

Ukrainian Orthodox church
Українська Православна церква
oo-krah-YEENS'-kah  prah-vo-SLAHV-nah  TSEHRK-vah
Russian Orthodox church
Російська Православна церква
ro-SEEЎS'-kah  prah-vo-SLAHV-nah  TSERHK-vah
Ukrainian Greek-Catholic church
Українська Греко-Католицька церква
oo-krah-YEENS'-kah  HREH-ko  kah-to-LIHTS'-kah  TSERHK-vah
Roman Catholic church
Римо-Католицька церва
RIH-mo  kah-to-LIHTS'-kah  TSEHRK-vah
(*In western Ukraine,* Костьол (kos-T'OL) *is the term for a Roman Catholic church.*)

| Protestant church | Протестантська церква | |
|---|---|---|
| | pro-tehs-TAHNTS'-kah  TSEHRK-vah | |
| synagogue | синагога | sih-nah-HO-hah |
| mosque | мечеть | meh-CHEHT' |

When is the next service?
Коли наступна служба?
ko-LIH  nahs-TOOP-nah  SLOOZH-bah

Will the choir be singing?
Чи буде співати хор?
chih  BOO-deh  spee-VAH-tih  khor

How long will the service last?
Як довго буде служба?
yak  DOV-ho  BOO-deh  SLOOZH-bah

I'd like to meet the (priest) (rabbi).
Я би (хотів, *m.*) (хотіла, *f.*) побачити (священника) (равина).
ya  bih  (kho-TEEV)  (kho-TEE-lah)  po-BAH-chi-tih
(svya-SHCHEHN-nih-kah)  (rah-VIH-nah)

| baptism | хрещення | KREH-shchehn-nya |
| Bible | Біблія | BEEB-lee-ya |
| Buddhist | будист | boo-DIHST |

| Christian (*noun*) | християнин | khrihs-tih-YA-nihn |
|---|---|---|
| Christian (*adj.*) | християнський, (-а) | |
| | | khrihs-tih-YANS'-(kihў̑)(-kah) |
| convent | жіночий монастир | |
| | | z͡heen-NO-chihў̑ mo-nahs-TIHR |
| to convert | залучити | zah-loo-CHIH-tih |
| cross | хрест | khrehst |
| Divine Liturgy | Служба Божа | SLOOZH-bah BO-z͡hah |
| (*term for the Orthodox and Greek-Catholic worship service*) | | |
| funeral (burial) | похорон | PO-kho-ron |
| funeral service | відспівування | veed-SPEE-voo-vahn-nya |
| God | Бог | boh |
| hymn | гімн | heemn |
| holy | святий, свята | svya-TIHЎ̑, svya-TAH |
| holy day | свято | SVYA-to |
| icons | ікони | ee-KO-nih |
| Jesus | Ісус | ee-SOOS |
| Jew | єврей, *m.* | yehv-REHЎ̑ |
| | єврейка, *f.* | yehv-REHЎ̑-kah |
| Jewish | єврейський, *m.* | yehv-REHЎ̑-s'kihў̑ |
| | єврейська, *f.* | yehv-REHЎ̑-s'kah |
| Mass (RC) | месса | MEHS-sah |
| missionary | місіонер | mees-see-o-NEHR |
| Moslem | мусульманин | moo-sool'- MAH-nihn |
| Mother of God | Мати Божа | MAH-tih BO-z͡hah |
| offering | підносіння | peed-nos-SEEN-nya |
| panakhyda | панахида | pah-nah-KHIH-dah |
| (*a memorial service celebrated on the 40th day after a death and on every anniversary*) | | |
| prayer book | молитвенник | mo-LIHT-vehn-nihk |
| prayers | молитви | mo-LIHT-vih |
| preacher | проповідник | pro-po-VEED-nihk |
| relics, saints' bones | мощі | MO-shchee |
| saint | святий, *m.* свята, *f.* | |
| | | svya-TIHЎ̑, svya-TAH |
| wedding | весілля | veh-SEEL-lya |

# CHAPTER 22.
# RECREATION

Ukrainian Proverb:
Зробив діло, гуляй сміло.
zro-BIHV DEE-lo hoo-LYAЎ SMEE-lo
*When the work is done, have some fun.*

Ukraine offers plenty of recreational opportunities, with numerous facilities for swimming, bathing, tennis, skiing, hunting and a wealth of other outdoor and indoor activities for fun and fitness. Larger cities have fitness centers and health clubs, and in the mountains extreme sports such as hanggliding and river rafting are popular. Rental equipment in recreation areas is still in short supply, but you'll find sporting equipment stores in the cities.

| **Summer Sports** | Літні Види Спорту |
|---|---|
| | LEET-nee VIH-dih SPOR-too |

| I'd like to play ... | Я хочу пограти в ... |
|---|---|---|
| | ya KHO-choo po-hrah-tih v | |
| badminton | бадмінтон | bahd-meen-TON |
| basketball | баскетбол | bahs-keht-BOL |
| soccer | футбол | foot-BOL |
| tennis | теніс | TEH-nees |
| volleyball | волейбол | vo-lehў-BOL |

| I'd like to ... | Я хочу ... | ya KHO-choo |
|---|---|---|
| go bicycling | покататись на велосипеді | |
| | po-kah-TAH-tihs' nah veh-lo-sih-PEH-dee | |
| go hiking | піти в похід | pee-TIH v po-KHEED |
| go mountain climbing | піднятись в гори | peed-NYA-tihs' v HO-rih |
| go rock climbing | піти на скали | pee-TIH nah SKAH-lih |
| go rowing | піти повеслувати | |
| | pee-TIH po-vehs-LOO-vah-tih | |
| go swimming | піти поплавати | pee-TIH po-PLAH-vah-tih |

| go water skiing | кататись на водних лижах |
| | kah-TAH-tihs' nah VOD-nihkh LIH-z͡hahkh |

That was good exercise.
Було дуже добре позайматись.
BOO-lo DOO-z͡heh DOB-reh po-zahy̆-MAH-tihs'

## Winter Sports

| **Winter Sports** | Зимові Види Спорту |
| | zih-MO-vee VIH-dih SPOR-too |
| I want to go … | Я хочу …               ya KHO-choo |
| cross country skiing | кататись на бігових лижах |
| | kah-TAH-tihs' nah bee-ho-VIHKH LIH-z͡hahkh |
| downhill skiing | покататись на гірський лижах |
| | po-kah-TAH-tihs' nah HIR-s'kihy̆ LIH-z͡hahkh |
| skating | покататись на ковзанах |
| | po-kah-TAH-tihs' nah kov-zah-NAHKH |
| sledding | покататись на санах |
| | po-kah-TAH-tihs' nah SAH-nahkh |
| I'd like to rent … | Я хочу взяти на прокат … |
| | ya KHO-choo VZYA-tih nah pro-KAHT |
| skates | ковзани                kov-zah-NIH |
| skis | лижі                LIH-z͡hee |
| a sled | сани                SAH-nih |

## Sports Vocabulary

| ball | м'яч | m'yach |
| basketball | баскетбол | bahs-keht-BOL |
| basketball court | баскетбольна площадка | |
| | bahs-keht-BOL'-nah plo-SHCHAHD-kah | |
| bicycle racing | гонки на велосипедах | |
| | HON-kih nah veh-lo-sih-PEH-dahkh | |
| boxing | бокс | bohks |
| figure skating | фігурне катання | |
| | fee-HOOR-neh kah-TAHN-nya | |
| gymnastics | гімнастика | heem-NAHS-tih-kah |
| handball | гандбол | hahnd-BOL |
| horse racing | скачки | SKAHCH-kih |
| kickboxing | кікбоксінг | keek-BOK-sihnh |

| net | сітка | SEET-kah |
|---|---|---|
| pole vaulting | стрибки з шестом | strihb-KIH z shes-TOM |
| skates | ковзани | kov-zah-NIH |
| skis | лижі | LIH-zhee |
| sled | санки | SAHN-kih |
| soccer | футбол | foot-BOL |
| soccer field | футбольне поле | foot-BOL'-neh PO-leh |
| speed skating | біг на ковзанах | |
| | | beeh nah kov-zah-NAHKH |
| racquet | ракетка | rah-KEHT-kah |
| swimming | плавання | PLAH-vahn-nya |
| swimming pool | басейн | bah-SEHỸN |
| table tennis | настільний теніс (пінг-понг) | |
| (ping-pong) | | nahs-TEEL'-nihỹ TEH-nees (peenh-ponh) |
| tennis | теніс | TEH-nees |
| tennis court | тенісні корти | TEH-nees-nee KOR-tih |
| volleyball | волейбол | vo-lehỹ-BOL |
| volleyball court | волейбольна площадка | |
| | | vo-lehỹ-BOL'-nah plo-SHCHAHD-kah |
| water polo | водне поло | VOD-neh PO-lo |
| weightlifting | важка атлетика | |
| | | vahzh-KAH aht-LEH-tih-kah |
| wrestling | боротьба | bo-rot'-BAH |

**The Sauna**   Сауна   SAH-oo-nah

*Ukrainian Proverb*:
В здоровому тілі, здоровий дух.
v zdo-RO-vo-moo TEE-lee zdo-RO-vihỹ dookh
*In a healthy body, a healthy mind.*

In ancient Kyivan Rus, each home had a log cabin that the whole family used for bathing. Rural homes may still have their own bathhouses, but the practice has been institutionalized in public saunas that are found in resorts and in cities of every size. In a sauna, you lounge around in a steam-filled room, flog your naked body with a bundle of oak or birch branches, then plunge into cold water, all in the pursuit of invigoration, relaxation, and good health. If this isn't your idea of fun or you don't think the health benefits are worth the bodily punishment, you'd best not try a sauna, and it's definitely not for those with high blood pressure or a heart condition.

Ukrainians have two kinds of saunas. In the Finnish sauna (сауна, SAH-oo-nah), the participant sits in a room of dry steam, that is, one in which the temperature remains so hot (hovering above 212°F) that the water vapor does not condense. In the Russian wet bath or *banya* (баня, BAHN-ya), the temperature is kept just below boiling so that the steam that fills the room condenses on the bather. In either one, the session in the wood-lined steam room is capped off by jumping into a pool of cold water. Large hotels or fitness centers often have swimming pools with sauna rooms. In rural settings the sauna pool may be outdoors with a hole cut through the ice in the winter.

I'd like to go to the baths.
Я би (хотів, *m.*) (хотіла, *f.*) піти в баню.
ya bih (kho-TEEV) (kho-TEE-lah) pee-TIH v BAH-nyu

| Where's the entrance... | Де вхід ... | deh vkheed |
| for men? | для чоловіків? | dlya cho-lo-vee-KEEV |
| for women? | для жінок? | dlya zhee-NOK |

Where's the pool? Де басейн? deh bah-SEHY̌N

Where are the lockers? Де роздягальня? deh roz-dyah-AHL'-nyh

## At the Beach На Пляжі nah PLYA-zhee

Along Ukraine's coastlines, beaches may be either sandy or rocky. In urbanized areas, such as Odesa or greater Yalta, some beaches are public while others are reserved for use by health resorts or hotels. Unsupervised stretches of coastline are common in less populated areas, and you can still find secluded beaches that are rarely visited. Along the Dnipro, island beaches are a great attraction, with amusements and snacks.

Is the beach sandy or stony?
На пляжі пісок чи каміння?
nah PLYA-zhee pee-SOK chih kah-MEEN-nya

Is the water cold? Чи вода холодна?
chih vo-DAH kho-LOD-nah
Is it deep here? Чи тут глибоко?
chih toot hlih-BO-ko

Is it safe to swim here?
Чи безпечно тут плавати?
chih behz-PEHCH-no toot PLAH-vah-tih

Is there a lifeguard on duty?
Чи тут є рятувальна служба?
chih toot yeh rya-too-VAHL'-nah SLOOZ͡H-bah

I prefer a swimming pool.
Я надаю перевагу басейнові.
ya nah-dah-YU peh-reh-VAH-hoo bah-SEHY̆-no-vee

**In the Forest and Mountains**
В Лісі та в Горах     v LEES-see tah v ho-RAHKH

Ukraine has two beautiful mountainous regions. The Carpathians, a relatively low eastward continuation of the Alps, are in the southwestern corner of the country. The tallest mountain is Mt. Hoverla at 6,679 feet. Coniferous forests, alpine meadows, and charming villages nestled among the rolling hills make this part of the country worth a visit. The Crimean Mountains are along the southern part of the Crimean peninsula. These are a chain of low, rocky mountains whose narrow foothills taper into a coastline along the Black Sea.

Let's go hiking in a forest.
Давайти підем до лісу.
dah-VAHY̆-teh PEE-dehm do LEE-soo

I'd like to go mushroom hunting.
Я хочу піти за грибами.
ya KHO-choo pee-TIH zah hrih-BAH-mih

Can we hike over there?
Чи можемо ми піти туди?
chih MO-z͡heh-mo mih pee-TIH too-DIH

May we rest for a while?
Чи можемо ми трохи відпочити?
chih MO-z͡heh-mo mih TRO-khih veed-po-CHIH-tih

If you please, I don't want to go any farther.
Перепрошую, я не хочу іти далі.
peh-reh-PRO-shoo-yu ya neh KHO-choo ee-TIH DAH-lee

What's the name of that (plant) (tree)?

Як називається (ця рослина) (це дерево)?

yak nah-zih-VAH-yeht'-sya (tsya ros-LIH-nah) (tseh DEH-reh-vo)

Can we go to the mountains?

Чи ми можете піти в гори?

chih mih MO-zheh-teh pee-TIH v HO-rih

I'm a mountain climber.

Я альпініст.

ya ahl'-pee-NEEST.

I want to climb that mountain.

Я хочу піднятись на ту гору.

ya KHO-choo peed-NYA-tihs' nah too HO-roo

How difficult is it to climb there?

Як важко піднятись туди?

yak VAZH-ko peed-NYA-tihs too-DIH

**Hunting and Fishing**  Полювання та Рибалка

po-lyu-VAHN-nya tah rih-BAHL-kah

Ukraine is blessed with a diversity of wild game in picturesque regions of the country. There's a designated hunting season for each kind of game – for example, deer season is from May 1 though January 31. You'll need a license for fishing or hunting in Ukraine; the licensing of hunting is especially strictly enforced because of strict gun control laws. You'll also need a permit to bring a hunting rifle into Ukraine and additional paperwork for bringing your trophy out. For information, or to find the nearest hunting ground or fishing hole, ask at a fishing-hunting club (клуб риболова-мисливця, kloob rih-bo-LO-vah mihs-LIHV-tsya). A tourist service agency can arrange a hunting or fishing excursion and provide transportation and guides to the hunting area and lodging at nearby cottages or hotels.

Where is the nearest fishing-hunting club?

Де найближчий клуб риболова-мисливця?

deh nahỹ-BLIHZH-chihỹ kloob rih-bo-LO-vah mihs-LIHV-tsya

I want to go (fishing) (hunting).

Я хочу піти на (рибалку) (полювання).

ya KHO-choo pee-TIH nah (rih-BAHL-koo) (po-lyu-VAHN-nya)

Is the fishing good here?
Чи тут добра рибалка?
chih toot DOB-rah  rih-BAL-kah

| | | |
|---|---|---|
| Is the hunting good here? | Чи тут добре полювання? | |
| | chih toot DOB-reh pol-yu-VAHN-nya | |
| bait | наживка | nah-ZHIHV-kah |
| fish | риба, *s*., риби, *pl.* | RIH-bah, RIH-bih |
| to fish | рибачити | rih-BAH-chih-tih |
| fisherman | рибалка, риболов | rih-BAHL-kah, rih-bo-LOV |
| fishing pole | вудка | VOOD-kah |
| fishing pole, small | вудочка | VOO-doch-kah |
| hook | гачок | ha-CHOK |
| line | жилка | ZHIHL-kah |
| hunter | мисливець | mihs-LIH-vehts' |
| game | дичина | dih-chih-NAH |
| rifle | рушниця | roosh-NIH-tsya |

**Camping**          Кемпінг          KEHM-peenh

Developed campsites are rare in Ukraine. Outside of some major cities are camping facilities that offer an alternative to hotels. The best might have cabins with private toilets.

Where is the nearest campground?
Де найближчий кемпінг?
deh nahў-BLIHZH-chihў KEHM-peenh?

| | | |
|---|---|---|
| Does this campground have ...? | Чи є на кемпінгу...? | |
| | chih yeh nah KEHM-peen-hoo | |
| electricity | електроенергія | |
| | eh-LEHK-tro-eh-NEHR-hee-ya | |
| hot water | гаряча вода | hah-RYA-chah vo-DAH |
| a grocery | продуктовий магазин | |
| | pro-dook-TO-vihў mah-hah-ZIHN | |
| a shower | душ | doosh |
| a swimming pool | басейн | bah-SEHЎN |
| a restaurant | ресторан | rehs-to-RAHN |
| Where can I...? | Де можна ...? | deh MOZH-nah |

| | | |
|---|---|---|
| park a car | поставити машину | |
| | pos-TAH-vih-tih mah-SHIH-noo | |
| light a fire | палити вогнище | |
| | pah-LIH-tih VOH-nih-shcheh | |
| pitch a tent | поставити намет | |
| | pos-TAH-vih-tih nah-MEHT | |

Where can I buy camping equipment?

Де я можу придбати обладнання для туризму?

deh ya MO-zhoo prihd-BAH-tih ob-lahd-NAHN-nya dlya too-RIHZ-moo

| I need ... | Мені треба ... | meh-NEE TREH-bah |
|---|---|---|
| a backpack | рюкзак | RYUK-zahk |
| a small portable camping stove | примус | PRIH-moos |
| a can opener | консервний ніж | kon-SEHRV-nihў neezh |
| a compass | компас | KOM-pahs |
| dishes | посуда | po-SOO-dah |
| first-aid kit | аптечка | ahp-TEHCH-kah |
| a flashlight | ліхтар | leekh-TAHR |
| a lighter | запальничка | zah-pahl'-NIHCH-kah |
| matches | сірники | sihr-nih-KIH |
| a mattress | матрас | maht-RAHS |
| a sleeping bag | спальний мішок | SPAHL'-nihў mee-SHOK |
| a tent | намет | nah-MEHT |

May we camp here?

Чи тут можна влаштувати стоянку?

chih toot MOZH-nah vlahsh-too-VAH-tih sto-YAHN-ko

May we pitch a tent here?

Чи тут можна поставити намет?

chih toot MOZH-nah pos-TAH-vih-tih nah-MEHT

May we build a fire here?

Чи тут можна палити вогнище?

chih toot MOZH-nah pah-LIH-tih VOH-nih-shcheh

We'll be using a gas stove.

Ми будемо користуватись примусом.

mih BOO-deh-mo ko-rihs-too-VAH-tihs' PRIH-moo-som

**River Cruises.** Ukraine's largest river, the Dnipro (Дніпро), bisects the country from west to east, flowing past scenic vistas and historic sites. From May through mid-September or October, pleasure cruises originate either in Kyiv, the northern port, or Odesa, the southern port, on a number of comfortable, modern river-sea vessels. Most of the ships were built in Germany in the 1980s and '90s and renovated in the 2000s to meet the highest international standards. The cruise ships typically have four decks of air-conditioned cabins with large picture windows. Primarily serving Western tourists, English is the most common language on-board. Amenities include several restaurants, bars, beauty salon, sauna, massage room, meeting and recreation halls, on-duty doctor, and souvenir shop.

Cruise ships include the *General Lavrinenko, Taras Shevchenko, Marshal Koshovyy, Dnipro Princess, General Vatutin,* and *Marshal Ribalko.* The ships are owned by a private company, Ukrainian River Fleet (Укррічфлот, *Ukrrichflot*), which handles many aspects of river transportation in Ukraine, from shipbuilding to moving cargo to cruises.

Cruises last 11 to 15 days, with stops at a variety of port cities: Cherkasy, Kremenchuk, Dnipropetrovsk, Zaporozhya, Nova Kakhovka, Kherson, and Sebastopol, on the Black Sea. A few cruises dock in foreign ports as well, for example, in Romania, Bulgaria, and Russia. Luxury cruises are never cheap, but a Dnipro cruise is less costly than river cruising in other European countries.

***London Sky River Shipping Company***, based in Odesa, is a sales agent for Ukrrichflot. Contact them at lstravel@te.net.ua. ***Chervona Ruta***, based in Kyiv, handles cruises for several of the ships. Contact them at office@ruta-cruise.com.

Besides the luxury cruise ships, other types of vessels ply the river and Black Sea. The hydrofoil is the speediest boat from one port to another, but the view from its airplane-like cabin is somewhat restricted.An especially popular hydrofoil excursion goes from Kyiv to the Taras Shevchenko grave site and museum at Kaniv.Purchase tickets one to five days in advance at the ticket office at the ferry station at Poshtova Square (ploshcha Poshtova, площа Поштова) near the metro station "Dnipro."

Ferry boats sail the Black Sea from Odesa to Sebastopol, and also to Istanbul. Cruise ships, ferries, or hydrofoils from Odesa leave from the Sea Passenger Terminal at the bottom of the Potomkin Stairs.

Where is the river (sea) transport station?

Де знаходиться річковий (морський) вокзал?

deh znah-KHO-diht'-sya reech-ko-VIHЎ (MORS-kihў) vok-ZAHL

I want to go on the excursion to Kaniv.
Я хочу поїхати на екскурсію до Канева.
ya KHO-choo po-YEE-khah-tih nah ehks-KOOR-see-yu do KAH-neh-vah

| When is the tour | Коли екскурсія до ...? |
| to ...? | ko-LIH ehks-KOOR-see-ya do |

I'd like a ticket for tomorrow's cruise to ...
Мені треба квиток на завтрішній круїз до ...
meh-NEE TREH-bah kvih-TOK nah ZAHV-treesh-neeў kroo-YEEZ do

What time does the boat leave?
Коли відпливає пароплавь?
ko-LIH veed-plih-VAH-yeh pah-ro-PLAHV'

What stops does the (ship) (boat) make?
Де зупиняється (корабель) (пароплав)?
deh zoo-pih-NYA-yeht'-SYA (ko-rah-BEHL') (pah-ro-PLAHV)

How long will we have in ... [*name city*]?
Як довго ми будемо в ...?
yak DOV-ho mih BOO-deh-mo v

| boat (small, either motorized or with oars) | | |
| --- | --- | --- |
| | човен | CHO-vehn |
| boat (medium-sized) | катер | KAH-tehr |
| boat (larger, steamer) | пароплав | pah-ro-PLAHV |
| boat (large ship or ocean liner) | корабель | ko-rah-BEHL' |
| Black Sea | Чорне Море | CHOR-neh MO-reh |
| dock | причал | prih-CHAHL |
| Dnipro River | Дніпро | dneep-RO |
| Dnister River | Дністер | DNEES-tehr |
| ferry | пором | po-ROM |
| hydrofoil | човен на підводних крилах | CHO-vehn nah peed-VOD nihkh KRIH-lahkh |
| life boat | рятувальний човен | rya-too-VAHL'-nihў CHO-vehn |
| port | порт | port |

Life jacket under seat.
Рятувальний жилет під сидінням
rya-too-VAHL'-nihў zhih-LEHT peed sih-DEEN-nyam

# CHAPTER 23.
# MOTORING

Ukrainian Proverb:
Хто має висіти, той не утоне.
khto MAH-yeh vih-SEE-tih toў neh oo-TO-neh
*If you're going to be hanged, you won't drown.*

On every journey, there's a low point. For those who go to Ukraine and have anything to do with a car, the worst moment is likely to involve that car. The number of vehicles on the road and inexperienced new drivers are increasing. Traffic is less regulated than in North America, drivers take more chances, road signs are less common and usually written entirely in Cyrillic, and road service is limited. A car can also be more of a liability than an advantage because of the risk of theft or – more likely – some of its parts being stolen. If you choose to travel by car, the following information may be helpful.

**Traffic Police Inspectors** are called DAI (ДАІ, dah-EE). They wear dark grey or blue uniforms and carry black and white batons. During rush hours they may regulate traffic at city intersections. Mostly you'll notice them when you drive outside the cities. Stationed at checkpoints, they may stop your car, check your license, and inspect the car if they suspect you of criminal activity.

The DAI used to be empowered to collect fines for driving infractions, but their overzealousness was legendary. Now they're required to give you a ticket and a court date when you can pay the judge. For intercity travel, it's usually inconvenient for the driver to report to a city court, and often the driver ends up paying off the traffic policeman for not ticketing him. Your best bet is to be careful, drive above reproach, and hope not to attract attention.

**Speed limits** in Ukraine are 110 kph (70 mph) on highways; 90 kph (56 mph) on minor roads in unpopulated areas outside of towns; and 60 kph (37 mph) in cities and villages. Limits are usually not posted, so be sure to slow down when approaching a village. Wearing seat belts is required on highways but not inside of cities.

**Car Rental.** Most visitors who want the convenience of a car and driver when going off the beaten track rely on their Ukrainian connections. For the adventurous, several major international car rental companies have offices in the largest cities, and you might also check the service bureaus of some larger tourist hotels for self-drive rental cars.

To drive in Ukraine, you'll need a valid license from your home state and an International Driving Permit (IDP), which basically is a translation of your license. The IDP can be obtained from the American Automobile Association (AAA). You'll also need a passport with the date for entering Ukraine recorded by the customs inspection. By law, auto insurance is required for all vehicles in Ukraine. Generally, rental cars include insurance.

Where can I rent a car?
Де я можу взяти машину напрокат?
deh ya MO-zhoo VZYA-tih mah-SHIH-noo nah-pro-KAHT

I need a car for ... days.
Мені треба машина на ... днів.
meh-NEE TREH-bah mah-SHIH-nah nah ... dneev

Can I leave the car ...?
Чи можу я лишити машину ...?
chih MO-zhoo ya lih-SHIH-tih mah-SHIH-noo

| at the airport | в аеропорту | v ah-ehro-por-TOO |
| in the hotel | в готелі | v ho-TEH-lee |
| somewhere in | десь в ... | dehs' v |
| [*name of city*] | | |

What is the charge per (day) (week)?
Скільки це коштує за (день) (тиждень)?
SKEEL'-kih tseh kosh-TOO-yeh zah (dehn') (TIHZH-den')

Do you charge by the day or by mileage?
Ви берете плату за дні чи за кілометри?
vih beh-REH-teh PLAH-too zah dnee chih zah
kee-lo-MEHT-rih

**Parking.** Finding parking in the center of big cities can be difficult. Be sure to park in designated areas only, although you'll notice some creative solutions to the lack of street parking. Better hotels often provide parking, and there are also a few parking lots around Kyiv, with cost varying according to location.

Where can I leave my car?

Де я можу поставити мою машину?

deh ya MO-zhoo pos-TAH-vih-tih mo-YU mah-SHIH-noo

May I leave my car here?

Чи я можу тут поставити машину?

chih ya MO-zhoo toot po-STAH-vih-tih mah-SHIH-noo

For how long?　　　　Як довго?　　　　yak DOV-ho

How much will it cost …?

Скільки це коштує …?

SKEEL'-kih tseh kosh-TOO-yeh

| | | |
|---|---|---|
| per hour | за годину | zah ho-DIH-noo |
| per day | за день | zah dehn' |

Is it safe to leave a car here?

Чи безпечно лишити тут машину?

chih behz-PEHCH-no lih-SHIH-tih toot mah-SHIH-noo

Is this parking lot guarded?

Чи ця стоянка охороняється?

chih tsya sto-YAN-kah o-kho-ro-NYA-yeht'-sya

**Road Service**　　　Дорожній Сервіс　　　do-ROZH-nihў SEHR-vees

The network of roads and highways in Ukraine is not dense. Two-lane highways link the major cities, single-lane roads link intermediate cities, and travel in rural areas is on unpaved roads.

　　Road names are numbered (M-17 is the main east-west route, for example) but they're informally identified by the direction in which one is heading, for example, the Poltava-Hadyach road. Because of new road construction, you may by hindered by a detour sign: Об´ЇЗД.

　　Service areas (автосервіс, ahv-to-SEHR-vees) are scattered throughout the country on main roads. Usually they're located on roads leading out of the cities. *Avtoservis* consists of a filling station and a repair station, and increasingly shops are attached that sell not only car accessories, but food as well. Customer service is not customary, and usually you'll have to prepay for the gas. You may indicate you want a full tank by placing a hand over your head.

Where can I find some gasoline?

Де я можу знайти бензин?

deh ya MO-zhoo znahў-TIH behn-ZIHN

Where is the nearest gas station?

Де найближча бензозаправочна станція?

deh nahў-BLIHZH-chah behn-zo-zahp-RAH-voch-nah STAHN-tsee-ya

Can you sell me some gas?

Чи ви можете продати мені бензин?

chih vih MO-zheh-teh pro-DAH-tih meh-NEE behn-ZIHN

I need 20 liters of 91 octane gas. [One liter is a little over 1/4 gallon.]

Мені треба двадцять літрів дев'яносто першого бензину.

meh-NEE TREH-bah DVAHD-tsyat' lee-TREEV deh-VYA-NOS-to PEHR-sho-ho behn-ZIHN-noo

Do you have diesel?

Чи ви маєте дизельне паливо?

chih vih MAH-yeh-teh DIH-zehl'-neh PAHL-lih-vo

| | | |
|---|---|---|
| Full tank, please. | Прошу, повний бак. | |
| | PRO-shoo POV-nihў bahk | |
| Please check the ... | Прочу перевірити ... | |
| | PRO-shoo peh-reh-VEE-riht-tih | |
| oil | масло | MAHS-lo |
| water | воду | VO-doo |
| brake fluid | гальмівну рідину | |
| | hahl'-meev-NOO ree-dih-NOO | |
| battery | аккумулятор | ahk-koo-moo-LYA-tor |
| tire pressure | тиск в шинах | tihsk v SHIH-nahkh |

Would you wash the car windows?

Чи ви можете помити вікна в машині?

chih vih MO-zheh-teh po-MIH-tih veek-NAH v mah-SHIH-nee

Can you fix this flat tire?

Чи ви можете залатати дірку в колесі?

chih vih MO-zheh-teh zah-lah-TAH-tih DEER-koo v ko-leh-SEE

Please pump up the spare tire.

Прошу накачати запасну шину.

PRO-shoo nah-kah-CHAH-tih zah-pahs-NOO SHIH-noo

| | | |
|---|---|---|
| I need to change the ... | Мені треба замінити ... | |
| | meh-NEE TREH-bah zah-mih-NIH-tih ... | |
| tire | шину | SHIH-noo |

| spark plugs | свічки | SVEECH-kih |
| wipers | щітки | SHCHEET-kih |
| fan belt | ремінь | reh-MEEN' |

I need a windshield wiper.
Мені треба двірники.
meh-NEE TREH-bah dveer-nih-KIH

How much do I owe you?
Скільки я повинен заплатити?
SKEEL'-kih ya po-VIH-nehn zah-PLAH-tih-tih

**Car Breakdown**
Поломка Машини
po-LOM-kah mah-SHIH-nih

Where is the nearest service station?
Де найближчий автосервіс?
deh nahȳ-BLIHZ͡H-chihȳ ahv-to-SEHR-vees

My car has broken down.
Моя машина зламалась.
mo-YA mah-SHIH-nah zlah-MAH-lahs'

I can't start my car.
Я не можу завезти машину.
ya neh MO-z͡hoo zah-VEHZ-tih mah-SHIH-noo

I ran out of gasoline.
У мене закінчився бензин.
oo MEH-neh zah-KEEN-chihv-sya behn-ZIHN

The battery is dead. Аккуммулятор сів.
ahk-koom-moo-LYA-tor seev

My brakes won't work.
У мене не працюють гальма.
oo MEH-neh neh prah-TSYU-yut' HAHL'-mah

My lights won't work. Не працюють фари.
neh prah-TSYU-yut' FAH-rih

I have a flat tire.
У мене проколота шина.
oo MEH-neh pro-KO-lo-tah SHIH-nah

I can't shift gears.
Я не можу переключити швидкість.
ya neh MO-z͡hoo peh-reh-klyu-CHIH-tih SHVIHD-keest'

My steering wheel doesn't work.
У мене не працює кермо.
oo MEH-neh neh prah-TSYU-yeh kehr-MO

I don't have oil.
Я не маю масла в двигуні.
ya neh MAH-yu MAHS-lah v dvih-hoo-NEE

| I don't have any coolant. | Я не маю води в радіаторі. |
| | ya neh MAH-yu VO-dih v rah-dee-AH-to-ree |
| I need gasoline. | Мені треба бензин. |
| | meh-NEE TREH-bah behn-ZIHN |

**Road Emergency**    Допомога на Дорозі
do-po-MO-hah nah do-RO-zee

If you're traveling at night, you may find roadblocks at the outskirts of the bigger cities with the DAI recording license plate numbers and drivers' registrations. Presumably this is for your safety. Otherwise, you're not likely to find much official help on the road. If you're involved in an accident, summon the traffic police inspectors by dialing 02. Be prepared to leave information about yourself, show your insurance certificate, and inform your insurance company of the accident within two working days. If you need an ambulance, call 03.

| Please help me! | Прошу помогти мені! |
| | PRO-shoo po-moh-TIH meh-NEE |
| Please call the police! | Прошу, подзвонити в міліцію! |
| | PRO-shoo podz-VO-nih-tih v mee-LEE-tsee-yu |
| Where can I call …? | Де я можу подзвонити …? |
| | deh ya MO-zhoo podz-VO-nih-tih |
| the police | в міліцію        v mee-LEE-tsee-yu |
| an ambulance | в швидку допомогу |
| | v shvihd-KOO do-po-MO-hoo |
| *What happened?* | Що трапилось?    shcho TRAH-pih-los' |
| An accident. | Аварія.          ah-VAH-ree-ya |
| A breakdown. | Поломка.         po-LOM-kah |

A person in the car is (sick) (injured) and needs help.
Людина в машині (хвора) (поранена) і потребує допомоги.
lyu-DIH-nah v mah-SHIH-nee (KHVO-rah) (po-RAH-neh-nah)
ee po-treh-BOO-yeh do-po-MOH-hih

Please take (her) (him) (them) to the hospital.
Прошу, завезти (її) (його) (їх) до лікарні.
PRO-shoo ZAH-vehz-tih (yee-YEE) (ЎHO-ho) (yeekh) do
LEE-kahr-nee

| Nobody is injured. | Ніхто не постраждав. |
| | nee-KHTO neh pos-trahzh-DAHV |

# CHAPTER 24.
# GETTING HELP

Ukrainian Proverb:
Лякана ворона і куща боїться.
LYA-kah-nah  VO-ro-nah  ee  koo-SHCHAH  bo-YEET'-sya
*A scared crow is even afraid of the bushes.*

Problems that might seem trivial at home can be overwhelming when one is away. In troubling circumstances, it's natural to long for the comfort of a familiar setting and the accustomed ways of doing things. Receiving help in strange surroundings delivered in a strange language does not always put one at ease, and when that help is different from the way it's done at home, we tend to question its value all the more.

**Various Problems**  Різні Проблеми  REEZ-nee pro-BLEH-mih

I'm lost.  Я заблудився.  ya zah-bloo-DIHV-sya

I missed my (plane) (train) (bus).
Я (пропустив, *m.*) (пропустила, *f.*) мій (літак) (потяг) (автобус).
yah (pro-poos-TIHV) (pro-poos-TIH-lah) meeў (LEE-tahk) (PO-tyah) (ahv-TO-boos)

I forgot my (money) (keys).
Я (забув, *m.*) (забула, *f.*) (гроші) (ключі).
ya (zah-BOOV) (zah-BOO-lah) (HRO-shee) (klyu-CHEE)

I've been robbed.  Мене пограбували.
MEH-neh poh-rah-boo-VAH-lih

They stole my...  У мене вкрали ...
oo MEH-neh VKRAH-lih

I lost my ...  Я (загубив, *m.*) (загубила, *f.*) ...
ya (zah-hoo-BIHV) (zah-hoo-BIH-lah)

camera  фотоапарат  fo-to-ah-pah-RAHT
car  машину  mah-SHIH-noo
documents  документи  do-koo-MEHN-tih
keys  ключі  kloo-CHEE

| luggage | багаж | bah-HAHZ̑H |
| money | гроші | HRO-shee |
| passport | паспорт | PAHS-port |
| purse/suitcase | сумку | SOOM-koo |
| wallet | гаманець | hah-mah-NEHTS' |

(He's) (they're) bothering me.
(Він переслідує) (вони переслідують) мене.
(veen peh-reh-SLEE-doo-yeh) (vo-NIH peh-reh-SLEE-doo-yut')
meh-NEH

| Go away. | Відійдіть від мене. |
| | vee-deeў-DEET' veed MEH-neh |
| Get help quickly. | Покличте допомогу. |
| | po-KLIHCH-teh do-po-MO-hoo |

**Lost Objects.** In Ukraine, there's a "finders-keepers" attitude toward found personal objects. Nevertheless, railroads, bus stations, and airports do have a place called the "room of forgotten things" for storage of lost and found items.

| Where's the lost and | Де камера забутих речей? |
| found room? | deh KAH-meh-rah zah-BOO-tihkh reh-CHEHЎ |

**Lost Passport or Visa.** If you lose your passport, you'll need a police report and two identical passport photos in order to be issued a new one, so go first to the local police station, then to a portrait studio. Once you have the proper documentation, go to your embassy's consular section. The Consular Division of the American Embassy is a 10-minute walk northwest of the Embassy to 6 Mykoly Pimonenka (Миколи Пионенка) Street in Kyiv. Hours are Monday through Friday from 8:30 a.m. until 12:30 p.m. Phone (044) 490-44-22. The Canadian Embassy is at 31Yaroslaviv Val (Ярославів Вал) Street; phone (044) 464-11-44, and the British Embassy is at 4 Hlybochitska (Глибочіцька) Street, phone (044) 494-34-00.

The replacement process will be easier if you've packed a photocopy of the identification page of your passport, your visa number, and two passport-sized photos.

Your country's consulate is also there for an emergency situation such as severe illness. The office is open anytime for an emergency.

**Asking Directions.** If you are lost, these phrases might be helpful:

Excuse me, would you please help me?
Прошу, допомогти мені.
PRO-shoo do-po-MOH-tih meh-NEE

I can't find my hotel.    Я не можу знайти мій готель.
                         ya neh MO-zhoo znahў-TIH meeў HO-tel'

Can you show me on the map where I am?
Прошу, показати мені на карті де я зараз є?
PRO-shoo po-kah-ZAH-tih meh-NEE nah KAHR-tee deh ya
ZAH-rahz yeh

Is this the road to the airport?
Чи це дорога в аеропорт?
chih tseh do-RO-hah v ah-eh-ro-PORT

How far is it from here to the center?
Як далеко звідси до центру?
yak DAH-leh-ko ZVEED-sih do tsehn-TROO

Is it too far by foot?
Це далеко пішки?
tseh dah-leh-ko PISH-kih

Please tell me where is …
Прошу сказати мені де …
PRO-shoo skah-ZAH-tih meh-NEE deh

| …Street | вулиця … | VOO-lih-tsya |
|---|---|---|
| Hotel … | Готель … | ho-TEHL' |
| this address | ця адреса | tsya ahd-REH-sah |
| a hospital | лікарня | lee-KAHR-nya |
| a pharmacy | аптека | ahp-TEH-kah |
| the police | міліція | mee-LEE-tsee-ya |

the (American) (Canadian) Embassy
(Американське) (Канадське) Посольство
(ah-meh-rih-KAHNS'-keh) (kah-NAHD-s'keh) po-SOL'ST-vo
the (American) (Canadian) Consulate
(Американське) (Канадське) Консульство
(ah-meh-rih-KAHNS'-keh) (kah-NAHD-s'keh) KON-sool'st-vo

| north | північ | PEEV-neech |
|---|---|---|
| to the north | на північ | nah PEEV-neech |

| south | південь | PEEV-dehn' |
| to the south | на південь | nah PEEV-dehn' |
| west | захід | ZAH-kheed |
| to the west | на захід | nah ZAH-kheed |
| east | схід | skheed |
| to the east | на схід | nah skheed |

**Emergency Phone Numbers.** Three phone numbers for specific emergencies are engraved in every public phone booth and displayed on phones in private homes. They are universal throughout Ukraine:

01   Fire Department   Пожежної Служби
po-Z͡HEHZ͡H-no-yee  SLOOZ͡H-bih

02   Police   Міліція
meel-ee-TSEE-ya

03   Ambulance   Швидкої Допомоги
shvihd-KO-yee  do-po-MO-hih

In addition, the universal phone number for a natural gas emergency is 04.

**Police.** There are two types of police in Ukraine. Under the jurisdiction of the local governments is the traffic police inspection, Державна Авто Інспекція,(dehr-Z͡HAHV-nah  AVH-to eens-PEHK-tsee-ya). Commonly called DAI, (ДАІ, dah-EE), the traffic police are responsible for traffic control and violations. They may stop a driver and ask to see the driver's license, as well as inspect the car upon suspicion of criminal activity. The regular police force, under the jurisdiction of the Minister of Internal Affairs, investigates all crime that does not involve motor vehicles. Citizens are not required to show their driver's license to them.

If you are involved in a traffic accident or a crime that occurs on the highways, notify the state traffic inspection. Call the regular police for all other needs.

| Call the police. | Викличте міліцію. |
| | VIH-klihch-teh  mee-LEE-tsee-yu |

If stopped or detained, cooperate with the law enforcement officers, but make it known that you're an American citizen.If arrested, insist on notifying the Consulate at (044) 490-4422 or (044) 490-4000 after hours.

I want to contact the American Consulate.
Я хочу звіязатись з Американським консульством.
ya KHO-choo zvee-ya-ZAH-tihs' z ah-meh-rih-KAHNS'-kihm KON-sool'st-vom

**I Need a Doctor**   Мені Потрібен Лікар
meh-NEE po-TREE-behn LEE-kahr

Ukraine's health care is undergoing rapid modernization, with a great deal of Western money, resources, and expertise flowing in. The availability of basic medical supplies, including disposable needles and gloves, antibiotics, and anesthetics, has improved. Though medical facilities are still inadequate for diagnosis and treatment of complicated problems, medical personnel will do their best to help you with what they have.

Treatment is dispensed on a walk-in basis at a polyclinic (поліклініка, po-lee-KLEE-nee-kah) or in a hospital (лікарня, lee-KAHR-nya). Once free, public clinics and hospitals now charge a small fee, payable on the spot. If you need a doctor, look for a Railway Hospital (formerly only for railroad employees and their families).Military and customs services hospitals are also good, and open to paying foreigners. The wait is shorter in private clinics. They cost more than public clinics, but some foreign insurance policies are valid in Ukraine. Other options are foreign-owned private clinics that accept American medical insurance, and a few employee clinics set up by foreign businesses for their factory workers.

Where can I get medical care?
Де я можу отримати медичну допомогу?
deh ya MO-zhoo o-TRIH-mah-tih meh-DIHCH-noo do-po-MO-hoo

I want a private clinic.
Я хочу приватну клініку.
ya KHO-choo prih-VAHT-noo KLEE-nee-koo

Where's the nearest hospital?
Де знаходиться найближча лікарня?
deh znah-KHO-diht'-sya nahỹ-BLIHZH-chah lee-KAHR-nya

I want to see ...   Я хочу бачити ...
ya KHO-choo BAH-chih-tih

| a cardiologist | кардіолога | kahr-dee-O-lo-hah |
| a general practitioner | терапевта | teh-rah-PEHV-tah |
| a gynecologist | гінеколога | hee-neh-KO-loh-hah |
| an ophthalmologist | окуліста | o-koo-LEES-tah |
| a pediatrician | педіатора | peh-dee-AH-to-rah |
| a neurologist | неврапатолога | neh-vrah-pah-TO-lo-hah |
| a surgeon | хірурга | khee-ROOR-hah |

How long must I wait for the doctor?
Як довго чекати на лікаря?
yak DOV-ho cheh-KAH-tih nah LEE-kahr-ya

I feel sick.
Я почуваю себе (хворим, *m.*) (хворою, *f.*).
ya po-choo-VAH-yu seh-BEH (KHVO-rihm) (KHVO-ro-yu)

| I feel nauseous. | Мене нудить. | meh-NEH NOO-diht' |
| I've been vomiting. | Мене рве. | MEH-neh rveh |

I feel dizzy.     У мене крутиться голова.
oo MEH-neh KROO-tiht'-sya ho-lo-VAH

I feel weak.     Я відчуваю слабість.
ya veed-choo-VAH-yu slah-BEEST'

I ache all over.     У мене все болить.
oo MEH-neh vseh bo-LIHT'

I have an earache.     У мене болить вухо.
oo MEH-neh bo-LIHT' VOO-kho

I have a headache.     У мене болить голова.
oo MEH-neh bo-LIHT' ho-lo-VAH

I have a sore throat.     У мене болить горло.
oo MEH-neh bo-LIHT' HOR-lo

It hurts here. [*point*]     У мене болить тут.
oo MEH-neh bo-LIHT' toot

I have a fever.     У мене гарячка.
oo MEH-neh hah-RYACH-kah

According to the Celsius thermometer used in Ukraine, anything over 37°C (98.6°F) is considered an elevated temperature. 38°C is equal to 100.4°F and 39°C is equal to 102.2°F.

| I have a runny nose. | У мене нежить. | oo MEH-neh NEH-zhiht' |
|---|---|---|
| I have a bloody nose. | У мене тече кров з носа. | |
| | | oo MEH-neh teh-CHEH krov z NO-sah |
| I have a cough. | Я кашляю. | ya KAHSH-lya-yu |
| I'm taking this medication | Я приймаю ці ліки. | |
| | | ya-prihў-MAH-yu tsee LEE-kih |
| I'm ... | Я є ... | ya yeh |
| allergic | аллергик | ahl-LEHR-hihk |
| asthmatic | астматик | ahst-MAH-tihk |
| diabetic | діабетик | dee-ah-BEH-tihk |
| pregnant | вагітна | vah-HEET-nah |
| I'm constipated. | У мене запор. | oo MEH-neh zah-POR |
| I've got diarrhea. | У мене пронос. | oo MEH-neh pro-NOS |

I have a pain in my chest.
Я відчуваю біль в грудах.
ya veed-choo-VAH-yu beel' v HROO-dahkh

I have a heart condition.
У мене слабе сердце.
oo MEH-neh slah-BEH SEHRD-tseh

I have (high) (low) blood pressure.
У мене (високий) (низький) кров'яний тиск.
oo MEH-neh (vih-SO-kihў) (nihz'-KIHЎ) krov'-ya-NIHЎ tihsk

Please check my blood pressure.
Прошу поміряти мій тиск.
PRO-shoo po-MEE-rya-tih meeў tihsk

| What's wrong with me? | Що зі мною? | shcho zee MNO-yu |
|---|---|---|
| Is it a virus? | Чи це вірус? | chih tseh VEE-roos |
| Is it ...? | Чи це ...? | chih tseh |
| serious | серйозно | sehr-ЎOZ-no |
| contagious | заразне | zah-RAHZ-neh |

| bleeding | кровотеча | kro-vo-TEH-chah |
| infected | інфекція | een-FEHK-tsee-ya |
| healing | загоюється | zah-HO-yu-yeht'-sya |

Is there a
complication?

Чи є ускаднення?

chih yeh oos-KLAHD-nehn-nya

When will I feel better?

Коли я поправлюсь?

ko-LIH ya po-PRAHV-lyus'

Do I need medicine?

Чи треба мені приймати ліки?

chih TREH-bah meh-NEE prihў-MAH-tih LEE-kih

I'm allergic to penicillin.

У мене алергія до пеніциліну.

oo MEH-neh ahl-LEHR-hee-ya do peh-nee-tsih-LEE-noo

Does this medication have side effects?

Це лікарство має повічну дію?

tseh lee-KAHRST-vo MAH-yeh po-VICH-noo DEE-yu

| **Afflictions/Diseases** | Хвороби | **khvo-RO-bih** |
| --- | --- | --- |
| AIDS | СНІД | sneed |
| appendicitis | апендицит | ah-pehn-dih-TSIHT |
| bronchitis | бронхіт | bron-KHEET |
| cancer | рак | rahk |
| chicken pox | вітряна віспа | veet-rya-NAH VEES-pah |
| cholera | холера | kho-LEH-rah |
| cold | простуда | pros-TOO-dah |
| coronary | тромбофлібіт | trom-bo-flee-BEET |
| diphtheria | дифтерит | dihf-teh-RIHT |
| flu | грип | hrihp |
| heart condition | слабе сердце | slah-BEH SEHRD-tseh |
| hemorrhage | крововилив | kro-vo-VIH-lihv |
| hepatitis | гепатит | heh-pah-TIHT |
| infection | інфекція | een-FEHK-tsee-ya |

| jaundice | жовтуха | z͡hov-TOO-khah |
|---|---|---|
| measles | кір | keer |
| migraine | мігрень | mee-HREHN' |
| mumps | свинка | SVIHN-kah |
| pneumonia | запалення легень | zah-PAH-lehn-nya leh-HEHN' |
| smallpox | віспа | VEES-pah |
| stroke | інсульт | een-SOOL'T |
| tetanus | стовбняк | stovb-NYAK |
| tuberculosis | туберкульоз | too-behr-koo-L'OZ |
| ulcer | виразка | VIH-rahz-kah |

**A Visit to the Dentist**   Візит до Зубного Лікаря
vee-ZIHT do zoob-NO-ho LEE-kah-rya

Western dental clinics are open in Kyiv; in other cities you should be able to find skilled dentists who charge substantially less than you'd pay at home, but who aren't likely to understand English.

Please recommend a good dentist.
Прошу порекомендувати доброго зубного лікаря.
pro-SHOO po-reh-ko-mehn-doo-VAH-tih DO-bro-ho zoob-NO-ho LEE-kah-rya

I'd like to make an appointment.
Я хочу записатись на прийом.
ya KHO-choo zah-pih-SAH-tihs' nah prih-Y͡OM.

It's urgent!   Це терміново!   tseh tehr-mee-NO-vo

How long will I have to wait?
Скільки мені треба чекати?
SKEEL'kih meh-NEE TREH-bah cheh-KAH-tih

My gums are very sore.
Мої десна дуже чутливі.
mo-YEE DEHS-nah DOO-z͡heh choot-LIH-vee

My gums are bleeding.   Мої десна кровоточать.
mo-YEE DEHS-nah kro-vo-TO-chat'

| | |
|---|---|
| I have a toothache. | У мене болить зуб. |
| | oo MEH-neh bo-LIHT' zoob |
| I've lost a filling. | У мене випала пломба. |
| | oo MEH-neh VIH-pah-lah PLOM-bah |
| I have a broken tooth. | У мене зламався зуб. |
| | oo MEH-neh zlah-MAHV-sya zoob |
| Can you repair it? | Прошу полікувати це? |
| | pro-SHOO PO-lee-koo-vah-tih tseh |
| I don't want it pulled. | Я не хочу його рвати. |
| | ya neh KHO-choo ўo-HO RVAH-tih |

What kind of anethestic do you use?

Яку анестезію ви застосовуєте?

ya-KOO ah-nehs-teh-ZEE-yu vih zah-sto-SO-voo-yeh-teh

# CHAPTER 25.
# MISCELLANEOUS INFORMATION

## Public Holidays

Following independence, Ukrainians showed an obsession for holidays. They started to commemorate Ukrainian self-rule and made traditional religious observances public holidays. They even continued to observe holidays dating back to Soviet rule, but put a new face on them.

On public holidays, school is out and the post office, government offices, and shops are closed. Only essential services such as medical and transportation services operate. When holidays fall on a weekend, they are generally observed on the following Monday.

| | |
|---|---|
| January 1 | New Year's Day |
| January 7 | Christmas |
| March 8 | Women's Day |
| May 1 and 2 | Labor Days |
| variable date | Easter Monday |
| May 9 | Victory in Europe Day |
| variable date | Holy Trinity Monday |
| June 28 | Constitution Day |
| August 24 | Independence Day |

Note that the religious holidays are observed according to the Old Style or Julian Calendar, although in everyday life the Gregorian calendar is used. Other special days that are not official national holidays are the church New Year on January 14, Defenders of the Fatherland Day on February 28, and Revolution Day on November 7, which is dear to the hearts of a increasing minority. In addition, each city observes its own special day in a party atmosphere that usually includes a parade, food and craft vendors, and a pop music concert or other public entertainment. The *Day of Kyiv,* for example, is the last weekend in May and Odesa's *Humorina Day* takes place on April 1.

## Ukrainian Surnames

While a last name does not conclusively reveal ethnic identity, and though there's some overlap between Ukrainian names and those of other Slavic groups, there are certain signs that a name may be of Ukrainian origin. Ukrainian family names are often short and some have only one syllable. Names ending in -ko tend to be Ukrainian; in eastern Ukraine, many end in -enko. In western Ukraine, many names end in -chuk or -iak or -iuk.

Like English names, Ukrainian names have their origin in occupations, in common objects, and in common concepts such as colors. Melnyk (Мельник), for example, means "miller"; Chumak (Чумак) means "carter"; Bily (Білий) means "white"; and Svoboda (Свобода) is "freedom". Animal names are also common surnames: Vovk (Вовк) – sometimes spelled Wowk in English – is wolf. Generally, Ukrainian names are more fanciful than English surnames: Skovoroda (Сковорода), the name of the 18th-century Ukrainian philosopher, means "frying pan"; Smetana (Сметана) – a name Ukrainians share with the Czech composer – means "sour cream;" Mak (Мак) is "poppy;" and we've even known a Neyizhsalo (Неїжсало) or "don't eat lard."

## Signs, Abbreviations, and Acronyms

### Names on Buildings

| | | |
|---|---|---|
| Аптека | Pharmacy | ahp-TEH-ka |
| Банк | Bank | bahnk |
| Гастроном | Grocery | hahs-tro-NOM |
| Кафе | Café | KAH-feh |
| Лікарня | Hospital | lee-KAHR-nya |
| Медпункт | Nurse's Station | mehd-POONKT |
| Міліція | Police Station | mee-LEE-tsee-ya |
| Поліклініка | Clinic | po-lee-KLEE-nee-kah |
| Пошта | Post Office | POSH-tah |
| Продукти | Grocery | pro-DOOK-tih |
| Ресторан | Restaurant | rehs-tor-AHN |
| Телеграф | Telegraph | teh-leh-HRAHF |
| Телефон | Telephone | teh-leh-FON |
| Школа | School | SHKO-lah |

### Signs Posted Inside or On Buildings

| | |
|---|---|
| Вихід | Exit |
| Відкрито | Open |
| Від Себе | Push |
| Вільно | Unoccupied |

| | |
|---|---|
| Вхід | Entrance |
| Вхід через Другі Двері | Entrance Other Door |
| До Себе | Pull |
| Ескалатор | Escalator |
| Години Роботи | Working Hours |
| Зайнято | Occupied |
| Закривайте Двері | Keep Door Closed |
| Закрито | Closed |
| Закрито на Обід | Closed for Lunch |
| Закрито на Переоблік | Closed for Inventory |
| Закрито на Перерву | Closed for A Break |
| Ліфт | Elevator |
| Ласкаво Просимо | Welcome (″We kindly ask you in″ |

*is seen over the entrance to many businesses and schools.*)

| | |
|---|---|
| Не Входити | Don't Enter |
| Не Курити | No Smoking |
| Не Торкатись | Don't Touch |
| Не Фотографувати | No Photography |
| Не Шуміти | Don't Make Noise |
| Нема Виходу | No Exit |
| Нема Входу | No Entrance |
| Обережно Пофарбовано | Caution − Wet Paint |
| Пожежний Вихід | Fire Exit |
| Прошу Входити | Please Enter |
| Ремонт | Renovations |
| Ремонтні Роботи | Maintenance |
| Руками не Торкатись | Don't Touch (Hands Off) |
| Службовий Вхід | Employees' (Service) Entrance |
| Сходи | Stairs |
| Тихо | Quiet |
| Туалет | Toilet |

**Outdoor, Street, and Traffic Signs**

| | |
|---|---|
| Висока Напруга | High Voltage |
| Идіть | Go |
| Небезпечно | Danger |
| Небезпечно для Життя | Life in Danger |
| Нема Ходу | Not a Thoroughfare |
| Нема Переходу | No Crossing |
| Нема Проходу | No Trespassing |

| Обережно | Caution |
|---|---|
| Обережно Газ | Caution Gas |
| Об´їзд | Vehicle Detour |
| Обхід | Foot Detour |
| Перехід | Crossing |
| Повільно | Go Slow |
| Прохід | Throughway |
| Стійте | Wait |
| Стоп | Stop |

## Abbreviated Signs

| А | [автобус, автобусна зупинка] | bus, bus stop |
|---|---|---|
| Ж | [жіночий] | women's rest room |
| М | [метро] | subway |
| Т(м) | [трамвай, трамвайна зупинка] | streetcar, streetcar stop |
| Т(р) | [тролейбус, тролейбусна зупинка] | trolley, trolley stop |
| Ч | [чоловічий] | men's restroom |

## Other Abbreviations

| авт | автобус | bus |
|---|---|---|
| а/с | абонемета скріпка | post office box |
| д., буд. | дім, будинок | building |
| г., год. | година | hour |
| г. | гора | mountain |
| гр-н. | громадянин | Mr. or Mrs. |
| гр. | гривня | hryvnya |
| кв. | квартира | apartment |
| корп. | корпус | corpus |
| | *(part of a structure, for example, a particular building at a university)* | |
| ім. | імені | named after … |
| м. | місто | city |
| п., пн. | пан, пані | Mr., Mrs. |
| обл. | область | *oblast* (region) |
| оз. | озеро | lake |
| р. | ріка | river |
| р-н. | район | *rayon* (county) |

| c. | село | village |
| сел. | селище | settlement |
| хв. | хвилина | minute |

## About Time

Except for Crimea, Ukraine is in a single time zone, which is seven hours ahead of Eastern Standard Time in New York and Toronto, and two hours ahead of Universal Time. Crimea is an hour ahead of the rest of the country. Daylight savings time starts the last Sunday of March, and ends the last Sunday of October.

**The 24-Hour Clock.** Timetables, official notices, and tickets for events and travel in Ukraine use the European or military system of numbering the hours of the day from 0 to 24. Figuring 0 for midnight, noon is 12.00, 1:00 p.m. is 13.00, 2:00 p.m. is 14.00, etc. To convert the 24-hour system to the a.m.-p.m. system, subtract 12 if the time is 13 or more. For example, a theater ticket that says 19.00 is for 7 p.m.

In common usage, Ukrainians divide the 24-hour day into four periods: morning, afternoon, evening, and night. The division between the periods is not absolute, and there may be a bit of overlap. Morning or ранку (RAHN-koo) starts at 3:00 or 4:00 a.m. and continues until 11:00 a.m. or noon. Afternoon or дня (dnya) is from 12:00 p.m. until 4:00 p.m. Evening or вечора (VEH-cho-rah) is from 5:00 p.m. until 11:00 p.m., and night or ночі (NO-chee) is from 12 or 1:00 a.m. until 3:00 or 4:00 a.m.

### Expressing Time in Writing
Note that a period is used rather than a colon to separate the minutes from the hours: 17.00, 17.12, 17.40, for example. Sometimes the minutes are written as a superscript and underlined: $17\underline{^{40}}$.

### Phrases Involving Time

| What time is it? | Котра година? |
| | kot-RAH   ho-DIH-nah |

| It's (late) (early). | Це (пізно) (рано). |
| | tseh  PEEZ-no  (RAH-no) |

| This clock/watch is fast. | Цей годинник відстає. |
| | tsehў  ho-DIHN-nihk  veed-stah-YEH |

| | |
|---|---|
| My clock/watch is slow. | мій годинник спішить.<br>meeў ho-DIHN-nihk spee-SHIHT' |
| My clock/watch stopped. | У мене зупинився годинник.<br>oo MEH-neh zoo-pih-NIHV-sya ho-DIH-nihk |
| I'm sorry I'm late. | Пробачте, я (запізнився, *m*.)<br>(запізнилась, *f* ).<br>pro-BAHCH-teh ya (zah-peez-NIHV-sya)<br>(zah-peez-NIH-lahs') |
| What day is it today? | Який сьогодні день?<br>ya-KIHУ s'o-HOD-nee dehn' |
| What's today's date? | Яке сьогодні число?<br>ya-KEH s'o-HOD-nee chihs-LO |

**Hours and Minutes**

| | |
|---|---|
| hourly | кожну годину<br>KOZH-noo ho-DIH-noo |
| in ten minutes | через десять хвилин<br>CHEH-rehz DEH-syat' khvih-LIHN |
| in a quarter of<br>an hour | через п'ятнадцять хвилин<br>CHEH-rehz p'yat-NAHD-tsyat' khvih-LIHN |
| in half an hour | через пів години<br>CHEH-rehz peev ho-DIH-nih |
| in three quarters of<br>an hour | через сорок п'ять хвилин<br>CHEH-rehz SO-rok p'yat' khvih-LIHN |
| in an hour | через годину<br>CHEH-rehz ho-DIH-noo |
| in two hours | через дві години<br>CHEH-rehz dvee ho-DIH-noo |
| until what time? | до котрої години<br>do ko-TRO-yee ho-DIH-nih |

**Days and Weeks**

The names of the days are not capitalized in Ukrainian.

| Today is … | Сьогодні … | s'o-HOD-nee … |
|---|---|---|
| Monday | понеділок | po-neh-DEE-lok |
| Tuesday | вівторок | veev-TO-rok |
| Wednesday | середа | seh-reh-DAH |
| Thursday | четвер | cheht-VEHR |
| Friday | п'ятниця | P'YAHT-nih-tsya |

| | | |
|---|---|---|
| Saturday | субота | soo-BO-tah |
| Sunday | неділя | neh-DEE-lya |
| | | |
| I'll be going... | Я їду ... | ya yee-DOO ... |
| We'll be going ... | Ми їдемо ... | mih YEE-deh-mo ... |
| | | |
| on Monday | в понеділок | v po-neh-DEE-lok |
| on Tuesday | в вівторок | v veev-TO-rok |
| on Wednesday | в середу | v SEH-reh-doo |
| on Thursday | в четвер | v cheht-VEHR |
| on Friday | в п'ятницю | v P'YAT-nih-tsyu |
| on Saturday | в суботу | v soo-BO-too |
| on Sunday | в неділю | v neh-DEE-lyu |
| | | |
| weekday | день тижня | dehn' TIHZH-nya |
| weekend | вихідні | vih-kheed-NEE |
| in the morning | вранці | VRAHN-tsee |
| this morning | сьогодні вранці | s'o-HOD-nee VRAHN-tsee |
| at noon | о полудні | o po-LOOD-nee |
| in the afternoon | після обіду | PEES-lya o-BEE-doo |
| this afternoon | сьогодні після обіду | s'o-HOD-nee PEES-lya o-BEE-doo |
| this evening, tonight | сьогодні ввечері | s'o-HOD-nee v-VEH-cheh-ree |
| at midnight | о півночі | o PEEV-no-chee |
| daily | кожний день | KOŽH-nihў dehn' |
| yesterday evening | минулого вечора | mih-NOO-lo-ho VEH-cho-rah |
| last night | минулої ночі | mih-NOO-lo-yee NO-chee |
| yesterday | учора | oo-CHO-rah |
| day before yesterday | позавчора | po-zahv-CHO-rah |
| three days ago | три дні тому | trih dnee to-MOO |
| last week | минулого тижня | mih-NOO-lo-ho TIHŽHD-nya |
| tomorrow | завтра | ZAHV-trah |
| tomorrow morning | завтра вранці | ZAHV-trah VRAHN-tsee |

| tomorrow afternoon | завтра після обіду | ZAHV-trah PEES-lya o-BEE-doo |
| tomorrow evening | завтра ввечері | ZAHV-trah v-VEH-cheh-ree |
| day after tomorrow | післязавтра | pees-lya-ZAHV-trah |
| next week | наступного тиждня | nahs-TOOP-no-ho TIH͡ZHD-nya |
| in two weeks | через два тиждні | CHEH-rehz dvah TIH͡ZHD-nee |
| every week | кожний тиждень | KO͡ZH-nihў TIH͡ZH-dehn' |

## Months and Years

The names of the months are not capitalized in Ukrainian.

| January | січень | SEE-chehn' |
| in January | в січні | v SEECH-nee |
| February | лютий | LYU-tih |
| in February | в лютому | v LYU-to-moo |
| March | березень | BEH-reh-zehn' |
| in March | в березні | v BEH-rehz-nee |
| April | квітень | KVEE-tehn' |
| in April | в квітні | v KVEET-nee |
| May | травень | TRAH-vehn' |
| in May | в травні | v TRAHV-nee |
| June | червень | CHEHR-vehn |
| in June | в червні | v CHEHRV-nee' |
| July | липень | LIH-pehn' |
| in July | в липні | v LIHP-nee |
| August | серпень | SEHR-pehn' |
| in August | в серпні | v SEHRP-nee |
| September | вересень | VEH-reh-sehn' |
| in September | в вересні | v VEH-rehs-nee |
| October | жовтень | Z͡HOV-tehn' |
| in October | в жовтні | v Z͡HOVT-nee |
| November, | листопад | lihs-to-PAHD |
| in November | в листопаді | v lihs-to-PAH-dee |
| December | грудень | HROO-dehn' |
| in December | в грудні | v HROOD-nee |
| this month | цього місяця | TS'O-ho MEE-sya-tsya |

| | | |
|---|---|---|
| last month | минулого місяця<br>mih-NOO-lo-ho MEE-sya-tsya | |
| six months ago | пів року назад<br>peev RO-koo nah-ZAHD | |
| next month | наступного місяця<br>nahs-TOOP-no-ho MEE-sya-tsya | |
| year | рік | reek |
| last year | минулого року<br>mih-NOO-lo-ho RO-koo | |
| next year | наступного року<br>nahs-TOOP-no-ho RO-koo | |
| decade | декада | deh-KAH-dah |
| century | вік, століття | veek, sto-LEET-tya |
| the year 2000 | двохтисячний рік<br>dvokh-TIH-syach-nihў reek | |
| the year 2005 | двохтисяча п'ятий рік<br>dvokh-TIH-sya-cha P'YA-tihў reek | |
| the year 2010 | двохтисяча десятий рік<br>dvokh-TIH-sya-cha deh-SYA-tihў reek | |

## Seasons and Special Days

| | | |
|---|---|---|
| spring | весна | vehs-NAH |
| in spring | весною | vehs-NO-yu |
| summer | літо | LEE-to |
| in summer | літом | LEE-tom |
| fall/autumn | осінь | O-seen' |
| in fall/autumn | восени | vo-seh-NIH |
| winter | зима | zih-MAH |
| in winter | зимою | zih-MO-yu |
| last winter | минулої зими<br>mih-NOO-lo-yee zih-MIH | |
| next spring | наступної весни<br>nahs-TOOP-no-yee vehs-NIH | |
| every summer | кожного літа<br>KOZH-no-ho LEE-tah | |
| during the fall | цілу осінь | TSEE-loo O-seen' |
| work day | робочий день | ro-BO-chihў dehn' |

| day off | відгул | veed-HOOL |
|---|---|---|
| holiday/feast day | св'ятковий день<br>sv'yat-KO-vihў dehn' | |
| vacation | відпустка | veed-POOST-kah |
| school holiday | канікули | kah-NEE-koo-lih |
| birthday | день народження<br>dehn' nah-ROD-z͡hehn-nya | |

## General References to Time

| a long time ago | давно | DAHV-no |
|---|---|---|
| after | після | PEES-lya |
| always | завжди | ZAHVZ͡H-dih |
| any time | в будь-який | v bood' YA-kihў |
| before | перед | PEH-rehd |
| earlier | раніше | rah-NEE-sheh |
| for a long time | дуже довго | DOO-z͡heh DOV-ho |
| immediately | зараз | ZAH-rahz |
| later | пізніше | peez-NEE-sheh |
| never | ніколи | nee-KO-lih |
| now | тепер | teh-PEHR |
| often | часто | CHAHS-to |
| rarely | рідко | REED-ko |
| recently | скоро | SKO-ro |
| soon | незабаром | neh-zah-BAH-rom |
| sometimes | інколи | EEN-ko-lih |
| suddenly | відразу | veed-RAH-zoo |

## Numbers
### Cardinal Numbers

| 0 | нуль | nool' |
|---|---|---|
| 1 | один (m.), одна (f.), одно (n.) | o-DIHN, od-NAH, od-NO |
| 2 | два (m., n.), дві (f.) | dvah, dvee |
| 3 | три | trih |
| 4 | чотири | cho-TIH-rih |
| 5 | п'ять | p'yat' |
| 6 | шість | sheest' |
| 7 | сім | seem |
| 8 | вісім | VEE-seem |

| | | |
|---|---|---|
| 9 | дев'ять | DEHV'-yat' |
| 10 | десять | deh-SYAT' |
| 11 | одинадцять | o-dih-NAHD-tsyat' |
| 12 | дванадцять | dvah-NAHD-tsyat' |
| 13 | тринадцять | trih-NAHD-tsyat' |
| 14 | чотирнадцять | cho-tihr-NAHD-tsyat' |
| 15 | п'ятнадцять | p'yat-NAHD-tsyat' |
| 16 | шістнадцять | sheest-NAHD-tsyat' |
| 17 | сімнадцять | seem-NAHD-tsyat' |
| 18 | вісімнадцять | vee-seem-NAHD-tsyat' |
| 19 | дев'ятнадцять | dehv'-yat-NAHD-tsyat' |
| 20 | двадцять | DVAHD-tsyat' |
| 21 | двадцять один | DVAHD-tsyat' o-DIHN |
| 22 | двадцять два | DVAHD-tsyat' dvah |
| 23 | двадцять три | DVAHD-tsyat' trih |
| 24 | двадцять чотири | DVAHD-tsyat' cho-TIH-rih |
| 25 | двадцять п'ять | DVAHD-tsaht' p'yat' |
| 26 | двадцять шість | DVAHD-tsyat' sheest' |
| 27 | двадцять сім | DVAHD-tsyat' seem |
| 28 | двадцять вісім | DVAHD-tsyat' VEE-seem |
| 29 | двадцять дев'ять | DVAHD-tsyat' DEHV'-yat' |
| 30 | тридцять | TRIHD-tsyat' |
| 31 | тридцять один | TRIHD-tsyat' o-DIHN |
| 32 | тридцять два | TRIHD-tsyat' dvah |
| 33 | тридцять три | TRIHD-tsyat' trih |
| 40 | сорок | SO-rok |
| 50 | п'ятдесять | p'yat-deh-SYAT' |
| 60 | шістдесять | sheest-deh-SYAT' |
| 70 | сімдесять | seem-deh-SYAT' |
| 80 | вісімдесять | vee-seem-deh-SYAT' |
| 90 | дев'ятносто | dehv-ya-NOS-to |
| 100 | сто | sto |
| 150 | сто п'ятдесять | sto p'yat-deh-SYAT' |
| 175 | сто сімдесять п'ять | sto seem-DEH-syat' p'yat' |
| 200 | двісті | DVEES-tee |
| 300 | триста | TRIHS-tah |
| 400 | чотириста | cho-TIH-rihs-tah |
| 500 | п'ятсот | p'yat-SOT |
| 600 | шістсот | sheest-SOT |
| 700 | сімсот | seem-SOT |

| 800 | вісімсот | vee-see-SOT |
|---|---|---|
| 900 | дев'ятсот | dehv'yat-SOT |
| 1,000 | тисяча | TIH-sya-chah |
| 1,100 | тисяча сто | TIH-sya-chah sto |
| 1,500 | тисяча п'ятсот | TIH-sya-chah p'yat-SOT |
| 2,000 | дві тисячі | dvee TIH-sya-chee |
| 5,000 | п'ять тисяч | p'yat' TIH-syach |
| 10,000 | десять тисяч | DEH-syat' TIH-syach |
| 100,000 | сто тисяч | sto TIH-syach |
| 1,000,000 | мільйон | meel'-ỸON |

## Ordinal Numbers

Ordinal numbers are adjectives which change their endings according to gender, number, and case. Here are the forms for the nominative singular, for masculine, feminine, and neuter, respectively.

| first | перший, перша, перше | PEHR-shihỹ, PEHR-shah, PEHR-sheh |
|---|---|---|
| second | другий, друга, друге | DROO-hihỹ, DROO-hah, DROO-heh |
| third | третій, третя, третє | TREH-teeỹ, TREH-tya, TREH-tyeh |
| fourth | четверт(ий)(-а)(-е) | cheht-VEHR-(tihỹ), (-tah), (-teh) |
| fifth | п'ят(ий) (-а) (-е) | P'YA-(tihỹ), (-tah), (-teh) |
| sixth | шост(ий) (-а) (-е) | SHOS-(tihỹ), (-tah), (-teh) |
| seventh | сьом(ий) (-а) (-е) | S'O-(mihỹ), (-mah), (-meh) |
| eighth | восьм(ий) (-а) (-е) | VOS'-(mihỹ), (-mah), (-meh) |
| ninth | дев'ят(ий) (-а) (-е) | deh-V'YA-(tihỹ), (-tah), (-teh) |
| tenth | десят(ий) (-а) (-е) | deh-SYA-(tihỹ), (-tah), (-teh) |
| twelfth | дванадцят(ий) (-а) (-е) | dvah-NAHD-tsya-(tihỹ), (-tah), (-teh) |
| fifteenth | п'ятнадцят(ий) (-а) (-е) | p'yat-NAHD-tsya-(tihỹ), (-tah), (-teh) |
| twentieth | двадцят(ий)(-а)(-е) | dvahd-TSYA-(tihỹ), (-tah), (-teh) |
| fortieth | сороков(ий) (-а) (-е) | so-ro-KO-(vihỹ), (-vah), (-veh) |
| hundredth | сот(ий) (-а) (-е) | SO-(tihỹ), (-tah), (-teh) |

## Agriculture

**What is that plant?**      Яка це рослина?

                        ya-KAH   tseh   ros-LIH-nah

Plants and their cultivation are very important in Ukraine, not only because agriculture is an important part of the economy but because Ukrainians love nature and love to grow things. They enjoy plants for their beauty as well as value them for their usefulness.

Some agricultural concepts associated with Ukraine:

The *steppe* (степ) is the broad band of grassland covering almost the entire southern part of Ukraine up to the foothills of the Crimean Mountains. Like the American prairie, almost all of the steppe's wild grass vegetation has given way to cultivation.

*Chornozem* (чорнозем) is the rich fertile soil that covers almost half of Ukraine, primarily the steppe belt. *Chornozem* is a deep layer of dark grey soil with a granular-lumpy structure and a high percentage of decomposed matter. The *chornozem* layer is soft and absorbs water and air well, promoting bacterial development and plant nourishment. Deep plowing increases the fertility resulting in the highest possible yields of all types of agricultural crops.

Twentieth-century Ukrainian agriculture was based on collectivization, which was forcibly introduced in the late 1920s and early 1930s as a means of providing the state with maximum cost-free capital for developing heavy industry, supporting the military, and maintaining the bureaucracy. A typical collective farm, a *kolhosp* (колгосп), had about 1,000 hectares of land. The state farm or *radhosp* (радгосп), more common in southern and central than in western Ukraine, was a more socialist form of agricultural organization than the collective farm, with the state owning not only the land but the means of production as well. After reelection in 1999, President Kuchma called for the reorganization of collective farms into private enterprises and agricultural cooperatives.

A hectare (гектар, hehk-TAHR) or 10,000 square meters is approximately 2.5 acres.

With Ukraine's reputation as the "breadbasket of Europe," it's not surprising that grains are the most important crops. Millet, spring wheat, and barley cultivation date back to the Trypillian period (4,000–3,000 BCE), rye appeared a couple of thousand years later, buckwheat in the first century CE, followed by oats. Corn cultivation dates to the eighteenth century and rice didn't come into use until after World War II. The mainstay of Ukrainian grain agriculture is wheat, especially winter wheat. The black soil (*chornozem*) and the warm, moderately rainy summers, primarily in southern and eastern regions of the country, provide ideal conditions for its cultivation.

Grain harvest declined radically after independence due to antiquated and deteriorating machinery, lack of adequate storage and distribution, and lagging land and marketing reforms. Weather problems also contributed greatly. By 2000 the harvest was less than half the Soviet yield, which had typically been 50 million tons of grain annually. The harvest occasionally rallies although reforms are still lagging.

**Beekeeping**     Бджільництво     bdzheel'-NIHTST-vo

Plants such as wildflowers, buckwheat, clover, and linden are important because their blossoms provide nectar for bees. Each honey has a distinct color and flavor, ranging from light and delicately flavored wildflower honey to the dark, strong-tasting buckwheat.

Beekeeping or apiculture has been widespread in Ukraine since ancient times. The practice declined in the 17th and 18th centuries with deforestation; the cultivation of the steppes; and the prominence of sugar. In the first half of the 19th century, apiculture was revived and entered a modern period with the invention of the first frame hive by Peter Prokopovych, a landowner in the Chernihiv area. By the eve of World War I, beekeeping was highly developed in Ukraine with about 2 million hives. With collectivization, nearly all large farms began to keep bees. While beekeeping remained a popular individual enterprise, the collectives became the primary source of honey production in Ukraine. Apiculture is most developed in the forest-steppe and steppe regions.

Ukrainians value honey not only for its sweetening ability but also for its medicinal properties. Several books have been published in Ukraine about the use of honey as treatment for many diseases, especially those of the lungs, throat, and skin. The *propolis* (прополіс), a sticky substance bees collect from tree buds and bark, is a powerful antibiotic against bacteria.

| apiary | пасіка | PAH-see-kah |
| bees | бджоли | BDZHO-lih |
| beehive | вулик | VOO-lihk |
| honey | мед | mehd |

# INDEX